Foundations of Human Memory

Foundations of Human Memory

Michael Jacob Kahana

OXFORD
UNIVERSITY PRESS

OXFORD
UNIVERSITY PRESS

Published in the United States of America by Oxford University Press, Inc.,
198 Madison Avenue, New York, NY, 10016
United States of America

Oxford University Press, Inc. publishes works that further Oxford University's
objective of excellence in research, scholarship, and education

Oxford is a registered trademark of Oxford University Press in the UK and in certain
other countries

Library of Congress Cataloging-in-Publication Data

Kahana, Michael J.
  Foundations of human memory / Michael J. Kahana.
    p. cm.
  Includes bibliographical references and index.
  ISBN 978-0-19-533324-4 (hardback : alk. paper) 1. Memory. I. Title.
  BF371.K14 2012
  153.1'2–dc23   2012007685

3 5 7 9 10 8 6 4 2

Typeset in ArnoPro
Printed on acid-free paper
Printed in the United States of America

To Jessica

PREFACE

This book aims to provide a theoretically oriented introduction to the scientific study of human episodic memory—memory for events experienced in a specific context. As is often the case, this work emerged out of a set of readings that I developed for my undergraduate course on human memory. Although there are several excellent surveys of human memory research that are appropriate for the intermediate and advanced undergraduate student, the present text seeks to provide a more theoretically based treatment of the subject in a manner that is accessible to the scientifically oriented undergraduate student. This reflects my view that the modern study of human memory cannot be divorced from a theoretical, model-oriented approach.

Research on human memory is incredibly broad in its scope, intersecting with research in many areas of psychology, neuroscience, neurology, cognitive science, computer science, education, and probably numerous other areas. At this point in the history of science, it would be foolhardy to attempt a summary of the entire field. As such, the present treatment omits many important and interesting topics or relegates them to brief side comments. My choice of topics is strongly influenced by the organization of memory research presented in Ben Murdock's classic monograph *Human Memory: Theory and Data*, published more than 30 years ago. Because theories of memory necessarily rely on some level of mathematical formalism, the reader is assumed to be comfortable with high-school–level mathematics including precalculus. When discussion of a topic requires additional mathematical background, an asterisk is placed at the start of the heading. Those sections can be omitted without losing the thread of the text.

I want to begin by thanking Professor Ben Murdock for providing thoughtful feedback on the entire manuscript. Ben has been a continued source of inspiration to me. I also want to thank several former students and current colleagues who have helped to shape much of my thinking on human memory.

My first doctoral student, Professor Marc Howard of Boston University, has helped to clarify my views on many central issues described in this text, especially in the areas of item recognition and free recall. My thinking about issues of associative and serial-order memory have also been strongly influenced by Professor Jeremy Caplan of the University of Alberta and Professor Arne Ekstrom of the University of California at Davis. Professors Per Sederberg (Ohio State University) and Sean Polyn (Vanderbilt University) have helped shape my views on the interactions between episodic and semantic memory and the dynamics of memory search.

I owe a special thanks to Pauline Johnsen, Emily Rosenberg, Julia Barnathan, Matt Mollison, Jonathan Miller, Neal Morton, John Burke, Lynne Gauthier, Lev Gottlieb, Jeremy Manning, Lynn Lohnas, Dov Kogen, Joel Kuhn, Kylie Hower, Patrick Crutchley and professors Marieke van Vugt and Christoph Weidemann for proofreading the entire draft and suggesting many improvements. For comments on specific chapters I am grateful to Professors Saul Sternberg, Marc Howard, Per Sederberg, and Sean Polyn. Finally, I owe a special debt of gratitude to the brave students who took my Human Memory course during the years of 2005–2010. These students provided invaluable feedback on the clarity of the material, or the lack thereof.

Attempting to explain the great puzzles of human memory has provided me with a continuous source of amusement, frustration, and bewilderment over the last two decades. I hope that this book stimulates at least some readers to help us fill in the many missing pieces of this amazing puzzle.

Michael Jacob Kahana
Philadelphia, PA
December 2010

The central problem of the mind, if you will, or the nervous system, is this: when an animal learns something, it can do something different than it could do before, and its brain must have changed too, if it is made out of atoms. In what way is it different? We do not know where to look, or what to look for, when something is memorized. We do not know what it means, or what change there is in the nervous system, when a fact is learned. This is a very important problem which has not been solved at all. Assuming, however, that there is some kind of memory thing, the brain is such an enormous mass of interconnecting wires and nerves that it probably cannot be analyzed in a straightforward manner.

— Richard Feynman, 1963

As I see it, a human being is a person who remembers... We are the last witnesses who remember. After we die, the memory will be in documents, court verdicts, in cinema, in video, in the various kinds of literature and no longer by means of the living voice. All cultures prefer the living voice, as a witness over the above mentioned substitutes and reservoirs... Each day that passes intensifies our need to prove that our memory is sincere and honest. But every day that passes covers more and more the surface of the memory.

— Jona Laks, 2001

CONTENTS

Foundations of Human Memory

1

Introduction

The foregoing sketch of our knowledge concerning memory makes no claim to completeness. To it might be added such a series of propositions known to psychology as the following: "He who learns quickly also forgets quickly," "Old people forget most quickly the things they learned last," and the like. Psychology is wont to make the picture rich with anecdote and illustration. But even if we particularize our knowledge by a most extended use of illustrative material, everything that we can say retains the indefinite, general, and comparative character of the propositions quoted above. . . . But if our curiosity carries us further and we crave more specific and detailed information concerning these dependencies and interdependencies, both those already mentioned and others—if we put questions, so to speak, concerning their inner structure—our answer is silence.

HERMANN EBBINGHAUS, *On Memory* (1885) p. 4

It is hard to imagine a life without memory. Our memories define who we are, and our ability to learn and make new memories largely determines who we become. Our ability to perform even the simplest and most important acts of life rely on our ability to remember what we have just done and what we plan to do next. Our ability to communicate relies on our acquisition of large stores of information about the meanings of words and the way sequences of words combine to convey complex ideas. A brief reflection on one's recent activities (assuming you can remember them) provides testimony to the power of memory and to its importance in our daily lives. It is thus of great value to society to understand how memory works. Going beyond an intellectual exercise, an understanding of memory can lead us to improve educational practices, to design better interfaces for computers and machines, to understand the strengths and limitations of our own memories, and to understand, and ultimately to help cure, diseases of memory that afflict millions of people every year.

1.1 HISTORICAL BACKGROUND

The study of human memory has a long and rich history spanning the wisdom literatures of ancient civilizations and continuing through the philosophical tradition of the British empiricist and associationist movements.[1] But the scientific history of human memory began with the publication in 1885 of Hermann Ebbinghaus' treatise titled *On Memory*. Although much has been written about the history of memory before Ebbinghaus, we will begin our discussion with Ebbinghaus' work and refer the interested reader to Gorfein and Hoffman (1987) and Yates (1966) for a discussion of the earlier period.

1.1.1 The Work of Hermann Ebbinghaus

Ebbinghaus (1850–1909), a philosopher at the University of Berlin, argued for the need to bring memory under experimental scrutiny and devised experimental methods aimed at doing so. Rather than trying to explain the complex manifestations of memory in our daily lives, Ebbinghaus sought to develop a simple method for studying memory under highly controlled conditions. He designed special learning materials for this purpose—lists of randomly arranged syllables, where each syllable was formed by linking a consonant, a vowel, and a second consonant. For example, one of Ebbinghaus' study lists might include the syllables: *DEF, FOL, GUD, RIN, MUS, NAS*. The crucial feature of these lists was that the series was ordered randomly.

---

1. According to the empiricists, knowledge derives largely from sensory experience. Closely related to this view was the idea that associations, and the laws governing their formation and subsequent retrieval, play a central role in determining human thought and behavior.

Figure 1.1 The humble beginnings of a science. Cartoon of Hermann Ebbinghaus learning a list of syllables (Courtesy of S. Polyn, illustrator).

Ebbinghaus realized that his syllables could have meaning individually.[2] Yet, he believed that there would be little meaning in a randomly ordered sequence of these syllables. Using these materials, Ebbinghaus conducted a series of carefully controlled experiments for which he served as the sole participant (Figure 1.1).

In studying random series of syllables, Ebbinghaus sought to define a measurable correlate of the Aristotelian notion of association. Aristotle proposed, based on his own self-reflection (or introspection), that if two events A and B have some relation, they will tend to co-occur consistently in our thoughts. If thinking of A can help you recall B, then it is said that A and B are associated. Aristotle proposed that A will tend to evoke B if A and B possess similar or opposite meanings (e.g., the concepts of *sugar* and *sweet* or *hot* and *cold*), or if A and B were learned at the same time, place, or situation (Aristotle, *De Memoria et Reministia*, II, 451, b18). If thoughts are analogous to atoms, then associations are the chemical bonds that underlie much of our mental life. Ebbinghaus hypothesized that in learning a randomly arranged series of syllables, he was forging associations between neighboring items in the list.

In his experiments, Ebbinghaus wrote the syllables on small pieces of paper, randomly ordered them in a row across his desk, and then recited them in order

2. Later researchers quantified the degree to which people ascribe meaning to random consonant-vowel-consonant syllables (Glaze, 1928). For example, whereas only 7% of American research participants attached meaning to *XUL*, 83% attached meaning to *WAM*.

at a rapid pace (2.5 syllables per second), keeping his beat to the tick of a watch. He would recite the series over and over again until it was no longer necessary to read the syllables because they had been committed to memory. This was determined by intermittently testing himself; that is, reciting the series without looking at the syllables. Ebbinghaus considered the list learned when he could recite it without error. The number of trials required to master the list (*trials to criterion*) served as a measure of the difficulty of memorization.

While carrying out his experiments, Ebbinghaus led a highly regulated life. He tried to maintain consistent dietary and sleeping habits and took careful note of the times at which he learned the lists and how that influenced his performance. Consistent with more modern research (Blake, 1967, e.g.,), he found it far easier to learn in the morning (e.g., 10:00–11:00 a.m.) than in the evening.[3] Ebbinghaus also took note of the variability in how well he could learn sequences of syllables from trial to trial, ascribing this variability to fluctuations in his attention.

To measure retention after a delay, Ebbinghaus did not measure the number of correctly recalled syllables. Rather, he measured the number of trials required to relearn the previously learned list. This indirect measure of retention is very sensitive—even if one cannot recall any of the syllables in a previously studied list, one may relearn the old list in fewer trials than it would take to learn a completely new list. On the other hand, this indirect measure depends on the time taken to learn the hardest part of the list and does not provide information on the detailed character of what information is retained and what must be relearned.

As an illustration of how sensitive his measure was, Ebbinghaus learned several passages in English from Lord Byron's *Don Juan* and then, 22 years later, attempted to relearn the same passages. He found that there was a significant reduction in the number of trials required to relearn the critical passages even though he could not consciously remember any of the content that he had read (not having read the text at any point during this 22-year interval). Ebbinghaus called this reduction in the number of trials to relearn *savings*.

Using these methods, Ebbinghaus was able to trace out a *learning curve* and a *forgetting curve*, which showed how savings increased with repeated study trials and decreased with increasing delays between study and test, respectively. Ebbinghaus noted (p. 89) that it was easier to learn a list when the repetitions were distributed over a space of time, as opposed to being massed within

---

3. Blake found that performance on a variety of memory and learning tasks peaked in the midmorning hours (10:30 a.m.) and dropped over the course of the rest of the day. These findings seem to generalize to performance on other cognitively demanding tasks, such as driving (Lenné, Triggs, and Redman, 1997).

a single session. He also noted that "the number of syllables which I can repeat without error after a single reading is about seven," a reference to the *span* of immediate memory that led some modern theorists to propose separate short-term and long-term memory systems, as discussed in chapters 6–8.

Ebbinghaus' contemporaries, who were not terribly surprised by his findings, were nonetheless struck by the grand scale of his experiments (Ebbinghaus submitted himself to 833 hours of experimentation over two separate one-year periods) and the rigor of his quantitative methods. Indeed, for a number of years following its publication, students of memory used Ebbinghaus' text as a primer on statistical methods.

The main theoretical advance in Ebbinghaus' work was the concept of *remote association*—that is, the idea that items are not only associated with their nearest neighbors in the list but also with their next neighbors, and next-next neighbors, albeit more weakly (this was also suggested by the philosopher Johann Herbart in 1834). To demonstrate this, Ebbinghaus introduced the notion of *transfer of training*. In this technique, Ebbinghaus would learn List 1 and then after a delay would learn List 2, where List 2 was constructed to have varying degrees of similarity to List 1. Assuming that it took N trials to learn List 2 when it was completely different from List 1, Ebbinghaus wondered how many trials it would take to learn List 2 if it was similar to List 1. As expected, Ebbinghaus found substantial savings when List 2 was identical to List 1, but he also found some savings when List 2 was composed of alternating items in List 1. That is, if List 1 was a sequence of syllables denoted $A_1, A_2, A_3, A_4, A_5, \ldots, A_L$ and List 2 was the sequence $A_1, A_3, A_5, \ldots, A_2, A_4, A_6, \ldots$, he learned List 2 more quickly than he learned a completely novel list. Ebbinghaus interpreted this as evidence for remote associations, with A_1 not only being linked to A_2 but also being linked to A_3, albeit more weakly. This became known as the *doctrine of remote associations*, according to which associations are strongest between temporally contiguous items and become progressively weaker for items that are further separated in time.

Almost immediately after its publication in 1885, the noted philosopher William James published a review of Ebbinghaus' work in the journal *Science*. Overall, James found Ebbinghaus' empirical findings to add "nothing to our gross experience of the matter." An exception, however, was Ebbinghaus' analysis of remote associations, which James regarded as evidence for the action of nonconscious mechanisms involved in the process of remembering.

1.1.2 The Work of Georg Elias Müller

In the early 1890s, Georg Elias Müller (1850–1934), a philosopher at the University of Göttingen, began a series of experiments aimed at replicating

Figure 1.2 Early memory drum. An early memory drum, based on the design of
Müller. Circa 1900.
Source: Zimmermann, E. (1903). XVIII. Preis- Liste über psychologische und
physiologische Apparate (p. 13). Leipzig: Eduard Zimmermann.

Ebbinghaus' seminal work with improved scientific methods. The first technical
hurdle was to devise methods for controlled presentation of syllables. Müller
required these methods to make the timing consistent across trials and to ensure
that the person whose memory was being tested did not also have to focus
mental energy on administering the experiment. To accomplish these goals,
he adapted a *kymograph*, which is essentially a drum that rotates at a relatively
constant speed, for the purposes of memory experimentation. The learning
material was printed on a piece of paper wrapped around the drum, which
passed through a small window (see Figure 1.2). The research participant[4]
would see the to-be-learned items at a constant rate as the drum rotated, and the
items were exposed one by one through the window. Using this *memory drum*,
Müller was able to optimize the timing of list presentation to reduce participants'
opportunities for *rehearsal*; that is, to make it more difficult for them to repeat
earlier list items to themselves during the course of list presentation. Müller
and his student Schumann also worked hard to design lists of constant difficulty

4. Throughout this text we will use the term *participant* to refer to the person volunteering
to participate in an experiment. These research participants are most often university students
who volunteer to participate in a memory experiment and receive some payment for their time
and effort. Although individuals differ in their memory capabilities, the basic characteristics of
memory function are remarkably similar across different people, so there will be little mention of
individual differences in this text.

(Müller and Schumann, 1894). This reduced the variability in learning that is due to the choice of items rather than the amount of practice.

To study how people form new associations in memory, and then later forget them, Müller and Pilzecker (1900) developed a *paired-associate learning task*: rather than having participants memorize a list of items in order, as Ebbinghaus had done, they presented randomly paired syllables to be studied (the Study Phase), and then later they gave participants one member of each pair as a cue to recall the other member (the Test Phase).[5] Rather than measuring learning by the number of trials required to relearn the material, as Ebbinghaus had done, Müller examined participants' actual recall responses. His studies of associative learning led to the important concept of *interference*: the idea that forgetting, rather than reflecting the loss of information, represents the interference of later learning with earlier learning (this concept is sometimes referred to as *retroactive interference*, as contrasted with the idea of earlier associations impeding new learning, which is termed *proactive interference*). Müller's work led to other important insights as well. Among them was the idea that when a just-experienced association is tested, it is very easy to remember, as if it were reverberating in one's mind. This notion of reverberation (*Nachklingen*) is related to the concept of short-term memory.

1.1.3 The Birth of a Science

At about the same time that Müller was carrying out his studies in Germany, major laboratories dedicated to the study of perception and memory sprouted elsewhere, particularly in the United States and in France. These laboratories began to generate data on human memory at a rapid pace, with the goal of characterizing how people performed simple memorization tasks. Early experiments were mainly aimed at studying three key aspects of memory function: the learning curve (i.e., the rate at which performance improves with practice), the forgetting curve (i.e., the rate at which performance declines with disuse or interfering activity), and the ways in which different factors influence the rates of learning and forgetting. These early researchers moved away from Ebbinghaus' single-participant model, carrying out experiments on samples of dozens, or even hundreds, of participants. In all, more than 50 scientific reports concerning memory were published in the 20 years following Ebbinghaus' monograph. Many of these early studies were conducted in the newly established laboratories at Harvard, Princeton, Cornell, and Clark universities. Perhaps the most notable feature of these studies was the creation

---

5. This method was actually first developed by Mary Calkins in an 1894 study that was not known to Müller.

of a wide variety of memory tasks, including nearly all the major memory tasks used in the laboratory to this day, as well as the use of a diverse array of learning materials, including colors, forms, objects, numbers, words, and odors (see Newman [1987] for a detailed review of this early work). As in any burgeoning science, much of the early work was descriptive, aiming to characterize and quantify the basic data on each of the tasks that was developed.

Although the descriptive approach of Ebbinghaus, and the methodological rigor of Müller, set the stage for the modern experimental study of memory, many early scholars criticized them for emphasizing behavior over experience (e.g., Titchener, 1916). Indeed, the prevailing approach among early psychologists was to develop their ideas about memory by carefully reflecting on their own thought processes. This introspectionist school of psychology, dominated by the students of Wilhelm Wundt, a founding father of the field, carried out experiments in which people studied and attempted to remember materials under controlled conditions. However, they assigned great value to the participant's description of his awareness of inner mental processes involved in remembering. One of the ideas that emerged from this introspectionist school was that remembering an item can give rise to different phenomenological experiences. For example, when judging whether a test item was previously studied, people may sometimes experience a recollection of specific details associated with the learning episode, whereas at other times people may be similarly sure that the item was previously studied on the basis of a sense of familiarity that is not accompanied by any specific details. As we will discuss in chapter 2, this distinction has turned out to play a central role in modern theories of recognition memory (e.g., Yonelinas, 2002). The introspectionists also argued for a distinction between memory for items and memory for associations (Titchener, 1916). Here, too, their ideas presaged modern work on memory (e.g., Murdock, 1974, 2006).

Far more than Ebbinghaus, Müller deserves credit for challenging the then-dominant introspectionist school and providing early psychologists with a "methodological conscience" (Katz, 1936; Kroh, 1935). Although the absence of English translations of his work somewhat limited Müller's direct lines of influence on contemporary scholarship, his indirect influence on the field was enormous. He mentored a large number of influential scholars who brought his methodological rigor to the many areas of psychology in which they worked.

1.2 ASSOCIATION, CONTEXT, AND EPISODIC MEMORY

Association served as the major theoretical construct used by early memory researchers. Consider two items that are presented in a memory experiment— these may be random syllables, as used by Ebbinghaus, words, pictures, or anything else. These two items are said to be associated if presentation of one item leads to thinking of (or responding with) the other. According to Ebbinghaus, as each new item is experienced, it becomes associated with the preceding items primarily in the forward direction, but also in the backward direction. That is, if you studied the words *car, baby, carriage, pen,* and *tree,* you would store a forward association from *car* to *baby,* a weaker backward association from *baby* to *car,* a forward association from *baby* to *carriage,* and so forth. In addition to storing associations between nearest neighbors, you would also store remote associations between words, with the strength of the association decreasing with the number of intervening words. These associations may be visualized as arrows connecting the word representations in memory, as shown in Figure 1.3A. In drawing arrows between neighboring items, we are illustrating Aristotle's principle of *association by contiguity,* the idea that experiences that take place in close temporal proximity become associated (see also Hume, 1739). Associations may also reflect shared meaning, as in the case of the words *baby* and *carriage.* As discussed in later chapters, both types of associations—those representing temporal contiguity and those representing shared meaning—play a crucial role in the function of human memory.

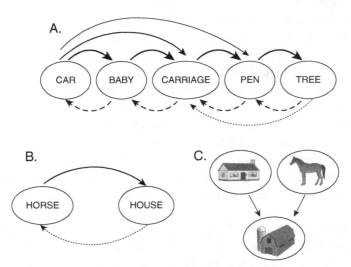

Figure 1.3 Classic notions of association. A. Illustration of Ebbinghaus' view of forward, backward, and remote associations. Associations are indicated by arrows connecting different memories, which may be words presented in a list. Solid lines denote forward associations; dotted lines denote weaker backward associations. Thinner lines denote even weaker, remote associations (only a subset of these are shown). **B.** Forward and backward associations for the pair *horse–house.* **C.** Holistic association for the pair *horse–house* into the concept *barn.*

Rather than conceiving of an association as a link connecting two mental representations (Figure 1.3B), one can conceive of the association as a new representation that combines elements of the two item representations. For example, in studying the words *horse* and *house*, one might think of a *barn* as a house for a horse (Figure 1.3C). This type of association is holistic, in that the two parts combine to form a new whole. According to some memory scholars, all associations are formed in a holistic manner (e.g., Asch and Ebenholtz, 1962).

Modern theories of association make far more specific statements about how each individual item is represented in memory, how they become associated, and how different associations interact with one another (see chapter 5). In contrast to these modern theories, which concern themselves with inner mental processes, most early memory scholars avoided speculations about the inner workings of the memory system.

It has long been recognized that an experience can never be repeated exactly on two separate occasions (e.g., Guthrie, 1935; McGeoch, 1932). For example, every time you meet a friend, watch a movie, or hear a melody, the information is experienced in a somewhat different context, where context can include the surrounding experiences, the setting, or even simply the time of occurrence. McGeoch (1932) wrote, "The learner is forming associations, not only intrinsic to the material which is being learned, but also between the parts of this material and the manifold features of the context or environment in which the learning is taking place" (p. 365). In subsequent writings, McGeoch (1942) elaborated this view by distinguishing between two kinds of context, which are sometimes referred to as *external* and *internal* context. External context refers to the physical environment and situation in which the material is being learned, including the sounds, smells, and sights that surround you as you read this material. Internal context, which is more difficult to define in concrete terms, refers to your inner mental experience as you read this text, including your inner thoughts, whether or not they are consciously accessible. The internal context associated with an experience defines the experience with respect to a mental chronology of events.

External context has long been recognized as an important factor in memory formation and retrieval (e.g., Robinson, 1932). For example, many researchers have reported that information learned in a given environment (e.g., a specific room) is better recalled in that same environment than in a different environment (see Smith and Vela, 2001, for a review). In a dramatic demonstration of environmental context effects on learning, Godden and Baddeley (1975) had scuba divers study and recall a list of words on land and under water. There were four conditions: the divers studied words on land and recalled them on land; they studied words on land and recalled them under water; they studied words under water and recalled them under water; and, finally, they studied words under water and recalled them on land. Surface-to-diver telephone cables, along with weighted Formica boards, allowed for audio list presentation and written recall (both on land and under water). Godden and Baddeley found recall to be nearly 70% greater when the context at test (on land vs. under water) was the same as the context at study.

Godden and Baddeley carried out an additional study in which participants who studied and recalled words in the same environment moved to the opposite environment and back again between study and test. For instance, participants who studied and recalled words on land (same context) dived under water during the delay. If the costs associated with changing context were caused by diving under water, then this group's ability to recall should have been similar to that of the groups whose context changed between study and test in the first experiment. Instead, Godden and Baddeley found that diving between study and test did not significantly reduce recall performance; thus, the differences in recall observed in the first experiment primarily reflect the change in context between study and test.

The idea that associations are learned not only among items but also between items and their situational context was widely recognized in the first half of the twentieth century (Carr, 1931; Hollingsworth, 1928; McGeoch, 1932; Robinson, 1932; Underwood, 1945). Despite its widespread recognition among early memory scholars, the idea of context did not find favor among the behavioristically oriented learning scholars who dominated in the postwar period (McGeoch and Irion, 1952). Whereas associative learning could be defined as an experimentally determined increase in the probability of a stimulus evoking a response, internal context is not easily tied to experimental manipulations. To scholars of a strictly empirical orientation, the difficulty of controlling and manipulating internal context greatly limited its utility as an explanatory construct. These scholars feared the admission of an ever-increasing array of hypothesized and unmeasurable mental constructs into the scientific vocabulary (e.g., Slamecka, 1987).

The notion of internal context regained respectability in the memory literature after the appearance of Gordon Bower's temporal context model in 1972 (also, Bower, 1967).[6] According to Bower's model, contextual

---

6. A model of memory is a set of equations that describe some aspects of memory function. Because the model is described in the language of mathematics, the implications of the model can be derived by the laws of mathematics. Although one may try to derive implications from theories cast as verbal arguments, for all but the simplest of arguments, it is impossible to fully understand the implications without the use of mathematics. For a model to be useful to advancing the scientific process, it is important that its implications be testable through experimental observation.

representations are composed of many features that fluctuate from moment to moment, slowly drifting through a multidimensional feature space (we will consider this idea in more detail in chapter 3). These contextual features form part of each memory that is formed, combining with other aspects of externally and internally generated experience. Because each remembered experience is marked by its unique contextual state, and because context changes slowly over time, the state of context can convey information about the time in which an event was experienced (hence the term *temporal context*). Whereas previous investigators had noted the importance of temporal coding (e.g., Yntema and Trask, 1963; Tulving and Madigan, 1970), Bower's model, which drew heavily on the classic stimulus-sampling theory developed by Estes (1955), placed the ideas of temporal coding and internally generated context on a sound theoretical footing. The Bower-Estes model provided the basis for more recent computational models of temporal context and its central role in human memory (Mensink and Raaijmakers, 1988; Howard and Kahana, 2002a; Sederberg, Howard, and Kahana, 2008; Polyn, Norman, and Kahana, 2009). These models are discussed in chapter 7.

In 1972, Endel Tulving coined the term *episodic memory* to refer to the form of memory that allows us to associate the many different types of information constituting an event into a spatio-temporal context and to later use the content of the event to retrieve its context. Episodic memory places "us" in the memory, marking the memory's position on our personal, autobiographical timeline. Retrieval of episodic memories constitutes a form of time travel in which we recover the encoding context of the previously experienced event. Other important forms of memory, such as perceptual priming and semantic memory do not have this feature.

Episodic memory not only supports the vivid recollection of formative life events, it also enables us to remember where we parked our car in the morning, whether we took our medicine, and whom we met at a social engagement. Dramatic failures of these everyday aspects of episodic memory can result from damage to the medial temporal lobe of the brain (Spiers, Maguire, and Burgess, 2001) (see Figure 1.9). More subtle impairments of episodic memory accompany the normal aging process (Kausler, 1994; Salthouse, 1991).

1.3 METHODS USED IN STUDYING MEMORY

The modern study of human memory employs methods that are similar in many ways to those pioneered by Ebbinghaus and Müller. Lists of items (often words) are presented for study, and responses are collected and measured. In some cases, participants are asked to recall the studied items. In other cases, the experimenter presents test items and asks for some type of judgment or rating of that item's occurrence in the list (e.g., Was the item on the list? Was the item in the first half or second half of the list?).

Modern computers have replaced the memory drums and response sheets of the past. By using the digital clocks built into all modern computers it is now trivial to present a series of items in a given order and at a prescribed rate and to measure the timing of participants' responses. Some investigators have begun collecting data on the Internet, using computer programs that can easily be downloaded through an Internet browser and that will later upload data to the host computer. Although such Internet experiments provide far less control over the experimental situation than testing in a laboratory testing room, they enable researchers to rapidly collect data on thousands (rather than dozens) of participants.

The major methodological advance beyond these techniques is the now-widespread use of devices to measure physiological responses during learning and memory experiments. These technologies have enabled researchers to discover the degree to which different brain regions become active during various aspects of memory function and the timing of physiological responses following a stimulus exposure. Although these physiological techniques are beginning to yield a large database of facts concerning the biological correlates of memory, the major theories of memory are still being tested primarily against behavioral data. This state of affairs is likely to change in the near future, as our understanding of the neural basis of human memory continues to rapidly mature.

Recognition and *recall* are the two most commonly used methods for studying memory. Here we introduce these two major methods. We then briefly describe *indirect* memory tasks, which measure memory without explicitly asking participants to remember a previously studied event.

1.3.1 Recognition

Consider a police lineup in which the witness to a crime is later faced with the task of judging whether a suspect in the crime is the actual perpetrator. This is an example of a recognition task. Someone has experienced some information (e.g., having seen a person commit a crime) and must later decide whether a test item (the appearance of a suspect in the lineup) matches the memory of the person seen committing the crime.

Recognition judgments are commonplace. In watching a rerun of a favorite television program, you may ask yourself whether you have seen this episode before. If the answer is yes, your level of interest may be reduced (unless you remember it as being particularly good). If you forget to bring your shopping list to the store, you may walk the aisles trying to recognize particular items as being among those you planned to purchase. Daily life contains numerous such circumstances that call upon our ability to make recognition judgments.

In studying recognition memory, scientists would like to exert greater control over the conditions prevailing both when an item is first studied and when memory for the item is later tested. Thus, in a laboratory recognition task, participants study a list of items presented in a highly controlled manner. These items are usually words, but other nonlinguistic stimuli such as complex scenes may also be used. During the test phase of the experiment, participants are shown a mixture of items that were presented as part of the study list and items that were not presented as part of the study list. For each item they must indicate whether or not it was on the just-studied list (Figure 1.4 illustrates the basic recognition procedure).

Recognition-memory judgments can be made for any attribute of an item, not just its membership on the list. For example, one might ask people to judge which of two items was most recently presented, how many times a given item was presented, or whether an item was presented in a male or female voice. Recognition can also be tested in a multiple-choice format. In this case, two (or more) test items are shown and participants have to judge which appeared on the list. There are almost an infinite number of variations on the basic recognition paradigm, some of which we will discuss in chapters 2 and 3.

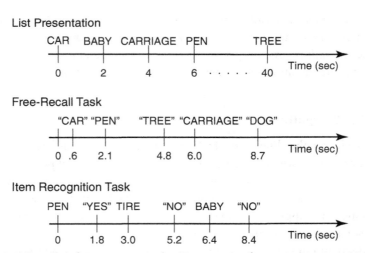

Figure 1.4 Recall and recognition tasks. Top: timing of item presentation. Middle: sample responses during a free-recall task. Bottom: sequence of test probes and *yes-no* responses in an item-recognition test. The words *pen* and *baby* appeared on the studied list, whereas the word *tire* had not. Quotes denote participants' responses.

1.3.2 Recall

Recall is a more active form of memory in which we actually remember information that is distinct from the test cue itself. In taking an essay exam, a student must recall previously studied information that is relevant to the specific question (and hopefully organize that information in a coherent and insightful manner). In meeting an old friend, one would hope to be able to recall their name, when you last met, and other shared experiences. We have all experienced the frustration of trying to recall something that we feel we should remember, but at a given occasion we are unable to do so (and then, when it is hardly needed, the information easily pops into mind!).

In the laboratory, we can study recall in a variety of different ways. After studying a list of words, participants may be asked to recall the items freely, in any order (*free recall*), in order of study (*serial recall*), or even backward. Figure 1.4 illustrates the free-recall task. Participants may also be probed to recall specific items. For example, the fifth word in the list may be given as a cue, and the participant may be asked to recall the prior or the subsequent item (*probed recall*).

One of the most widely used recall tasks involves the study of paired items followed by a memory test in which one member of each pair is shown as a cue for recall of its mate. As an example, you might study randomly paired common nouns, such as *carriage–dog, tree–pen, ribbon–diamond, horse–house*, etc. At the time of the test, you might first be asked to recall the word paired with *pen*, then the word paired with *ribbon*, and so on. This task, discussed in chapter 4, is alternatively called *paired associates* or *cued recall*. Pairs can be probed either in the forward direction (e.g., *ribbon* as a cue to recall *diamond*) or in the backward direction (e.g., *pen* as a cue to recall *tree*). Although one might expect forward recall to be easier than backward recall, research has shown that people's ability to recall an individual pair does not depend on the order in which the pair was studied (Kahana, 2002). Yet, despite this fact, people can remember which item was first and which item was second (Mandler, Rabinowitz, and Simon, 1981).

Although words are the most commonly used stimuli in recognition and recall tasks, one can also use nonlinguistic materials, such as abstract pictures or shapes. One reason why memory researchers have emphasized the use of linguistic materials is that adults are very likely to attempt to code confusable nonlinguistic materials, such as complex shapes, in a linguistic manner. In the case of recall tasks, it is also difficult to measure the recall (reproduction) of nonverbal materials such as pictures. On the other hand, perceptual imagery plays a critical role in the encoding of linguistic materials, and visual imagery can greatly facilitate many forms of learning (Paivio, 1986).

1.3.3 Indirect Memory Tasks

Although recognition, recall, and their variants are the methods most commonly used in the study of human memory, there are other important classes of memory tasks as well. For example, one can measure memory without directly asking people to remember a previously studied item. Suppose, for example, that participants studied a list of items for a later memory test. However, before giving them the memory test, one asks them to view a list of word stems in succession (e.g., *as____*, *me____*) and to complete each stem with the first word that comes to mind (e.g., *assume, memory*). Although participants are not trying to recall items from the list in the *word-stem-completion* task, research has shown that they are more likely to complete the stems from words that they have recently encountered. The increased tendency to complete stems with recently experienced words is called *priming*, because prior exposure to a given set of words has primed participants to reproduce them in the stem-completion task.

Word-stem completion is just one example of a cognitive task that can be used to demonstrate priming. In *lexical decision* (another commonly used indirect memory task), participants must decide, as quickly as possible, whether a sequence of letters is a valid word. Participants rarely make errors at this task, but they will respond more quickly to words that were recently encountered. In a *perceptual identification* task, participants see a degraded version of a word or picture that they have to identify. Again, identification is usually faster and more accurate if the item has recently been encountered, though there are important exceptions to this general observation (Huber, 2008).

The direct–indirect distinction refers to the way in which memories are retrieved. In direct memory tests, participants are asked to recognize or recall an item as having occurred in a list of previously studied items. Indirect memory tests do not make reference to a previous study episode. Rather, they reveal the memorial consequences of the study episode on a person's ability to perform some other cognitive task, such as perceptual identification or fragment completion.

A related distinction applies to the study phase of a memory experiment. When presenting participants with a set of material for study, the experimenter may instruct them to *intentionally* learn the materials for a subsequent memory test. Alternatively, the material may be presented *incidentally* by using some cover story designed to make it less likely that participants will expect a memory test. For example, participants may be asked to rate the pleasantness of each word in a series or they may be asked to judge whether the words correspond to living or nonliving things. Although intentional learning is most often studied in the lab, incidental learning may be more typical of the operation of memory in our daily lives, where we experience a variety of information without necessarily trying to learn it for an upcoming test. Even if you are not trying to remember a specific detail of an experience, you may nonetheless store that detail in memory, and later, it may pop into your mind without any specific intention to retrieve it.

1.4 THE LAWS OF REPETITION AND RECENCY

1.4.1 The Law of Repetition

The Law of Repetition[7] codifies what is perhaps the most basic observation concerning memory: memory performance increases with the number of presentations of the to-be-remembered material, as illustrated in the adage we have all heard as children, "Practice makes perfect." Although memory clearly improves with repetition, learning proceeds slowly when there is not an intent to learn. McGeoch (1942) relates:

> ... the incident described by Radossawljevitch (1907) of the subject who, because of his imperfect German, failed to comprehend the instructions.... The subject read aloud a series of eight syllables time after time, but at the forty-sixth repetition he had not yet signaled that he had mastered the list.... Radossawljevitch stopped the apparatus and asked if he could recite the series. "What! Am I to learn the syllables by heart?" was the reply. He could not recite them.... p. 275

In an early study of the role of intention in learning, Thorndike (1932) presented participants with a list of 1,304 word-number pairs (e.g., *BREAD– 29, TEXAS–78*), in which four pairs were repeated 24 times amidst other nonrepeated word–number pairs. Unbeknownst to the participants, the list was ordered so that the word in each of the four repeated pairs always followed the same number (i.e., *CHARADE* always came just after *86*; *SWING* always came just after *94*). After studying the list, participants were asked to recall the numbers that came just after certain words (e.g., *BREAD–????*). Participants were also asked to recall the words that consistently followed certain numbers (e.g., *86–????*). For word–number pairs repeated 24 times throughout the list, participants correctly recalled the target number 38% of the time. In contrast, when prompted to recall the four words that followed specific numbers 24 times

---

7. This law has also been termed the Law of Practice, the Law of Frequency, the Law of Exercise, and the Law of Use.

throughout the list, participants correctly recalled the target word only 0.5% of the time. This level of recall would be expected by chance. Thorndike thus concluded that mere temporal contiguity was not a sufficient condition for learning. Rather, participants had to do something with the pairs to forge a connection. As we will discuss in chapter 4, not all subsequent studies supported Thorndike's strong claim that associative learning does not occur in the absence of intentionality. Rather, it seems that at least some associative learning does take place under incidental encoding conditions (see Underwood, 1983, for a review).

Craik and Lockhart (1972) demonstrated that repetition (and/or study time) interacts strongly with the type of coding to determine the strength of stored memories. If to-be-learned items are processed superficially, without attention to meaning, then processing time has little effect on memory performance. When trying to learn a new association between items, motivated participants will elaborate on the meaning of the items with the goal of combining them interactively, in either an image or a story. It turns out that intention is important insofar as it leads to effective learning strategies. If you process information meaningfully and elaboratively without the intention of learning it for a later memory test, you will do about as well as if you have intended to learn it for a later recall test (Hyde and Jenkins, 1973).

There is considerable evidence that the learning due to repetition does not only occur during the study phase of an experiment. Rather, substantial learning also occurs during the test phase. The presentation of the test cue and the act of recalling or recognizing an item also act as opportunities for learning. Some evidence even suggests that in recall tasks, more learning takes place on a correct test trial than on a study trial (R. A. Bjork and Bjork, 1992; Karpicke and Roediger, 2007).

Figure 1.5 shows a learning curve for a college student who had extensive practice in learning randomly paired common words. On each of 40 training sessions, this student learned a different list of 100 word pairs by the method of alternating study and test trials (called the *study-test method*). During a study trial, each of the 100 word pairs was shown for a 2-sec study period. During a test trial, one member of each pair was shown and she attempted to recall its mate. Each pair was tested in this manner. Study and test trials alternated until the student could recall all 100 word pairs. As shown in Figure 1.5, recall probability (the fraction of correctly recalled pairs) increased nearly linearly across the first four study-test trials. By the sixth trial (not shown) all 100 pairs were recalled. The data in Figure 1.5 were averaged over many different lists. You may be surprised at how quickly the pairs were learned. With inexperienced

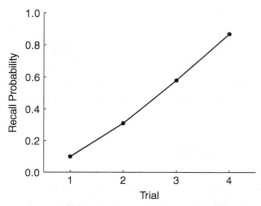

Figure 1.5 Learning curve for word pairs. Data from a highly practiced college student learning a list of 100 word pairs (Murdock, 1989).

participants,[8] the rate of learning is four or five times slower than shown in Figure 1.5.

Linear learning functions are also observed in serial-recall tasks, where participants have to recall a long list of items in order (Waugh, 1961, 1963). Linear learning curves would result if participants did not forget pairs that were previously learned and learned a constant number of new pairs on each trial. If, however, each learned pair has some chance of being forgotten from one trial to the next, then as more pairs are learned, one would expect a larger absolute number of pairs to be forgotten. Assuming that the rate of new learning does not increase over study trials, this would produce a negatively accelerated learning curve, that is, a learning curve that climbs rapidly in early trials but more slowly as learning proceeds. Such negatively accelerated learning curves are sometimes seen in memory tasks, especially in the free-recall task (Tulving, 1962). The observation of a linear learning curve implies that the difference between the number of pairs learned and forgotten does not change over trials.

As one might expect, practice not only leads people to correctly recall and recognize a greater proportion of items, it also leads them to do so more quickly. In a paired-associate task, participants may require an average of 2–4 sec to correctly recall an item during the initial stages of learning. With practice, however, participants will be able to consistently recall the same item in around 1 sec (Waugh, 1970; Anderson, 1981). Throughout this book we

8. The terms *naive* or *inexperienced participants* refers to participants who are not well practiced at the kind of list learning tasks used in the memory laboratory. Typically, these are students who are volunteering to participate in a memory experiment for the first time.

will use RT to refer to participants' response time. Initially, RTs decrease very rapidly, but the rate of decline in RT slows with practice until participants approach their fastest possible rate of responding. The decrease in RT with practice is one of the most universal properties of human and animal learning. Generally, repetition or practice leads to both faster and more accurate recall and recognition (Kahana and Loftus, 1999; Luce, 1986).

Spaced vs. massed learning

As noted above, Ebbinghaus found it easier to learn a list when the repetitions were distributed in time. This finding was later replicated by Jost (1897) in his doctoral dissertation carried out in Müller's laboratory. This observation is now known as the *spacing* or *distributed practice* effect, which refers to the general finding that learning depends on the temporal spacing of repetitions, with faster learning associated with spaced rather than massed repetitions. Figure 1.6 illustrates the spacing effect for items repeated just once in a single list (Madigan, 1969). In this study, participants studied lists containing a mixture of once-presented (1P) and twice-presented (2P) items. The 2P items were either presented successively (spacing = 0), or with varying numbers of items separating the repetitions (2, 4, 8, 20, or 40). As shown in Figure 1.6, increased separation of the 2P items improved their recall. Underwood (1970) showed that the spacing effect in free recall is obtained for both slow and fast presentation rates, for auditory and visual presentation modalities, and for items that came from different linguistic classes (nouns, verbs, etc.).

Spacing effects have also been shown in real-world situations such as learning to type (Baddeley and Longman, 1978), learning foreign languages (Bahrick

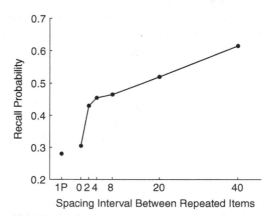

Figure 1.6 The effect of spacing repetitions in free recall. Increasing the spacing between repeated items increases the magnitude of the repetition effect. 1P indicates once presented item. Data from Madigan (1969).

and Phelps, 1987), and remembering television commercials (Singh, Mishra, Bendapudi, and Linville, 1994). In the case of commercials, companies pay handsomely to present a brief message to a large audience in the hopes that the viewers will remember that message. Thus, it is not only important to produce a compelling message, it is also important to present the message in a way that maximizes viewers' memory for this incidentally encoded material. In a study by Singh et al. (1994), 413 people, including both young and older adults, viewed a television news program during which several commercials were presented. Some commercials were presented once, and some were repeated. The repeated commercials were separated by either one or four nonrepeated commercials (spaced short and spaced long conditions). The researchers told participants that they were about to see a late-night news show taken from a network-affiliate station outside their own viewing area and that they were interested in knowing the participants' opinions about the news show. The following day, participants were brought back to the lab and tested on their memory for the commercials. They were given the name of a product category and asked to recall the brand name and claims made by the respective commercials. Participants' recall was 18% higher when the repeated commercials were spaced by four nonrepeated commercials than when they were spaced by just one commercial. This advantage of spaced learning is one of the most robust and practical findings in the human memory literature.

1.4.2 The Law of Recency

My great uncle often used to say, "I remember it as if it were yesterday" when recounting in vivid detail a salient event that took place in his youth. Whether or not his memories accurately reflected those past events, his expression captures the common observation that all other things being equal, the more recent an experience, the more easily and vividly it will be remembered. This basic characteristic of human memory has been codified as the Law of Recency (Brown, 1824; Calkins, 1896).[9] Ebbinghaus demonstrated that forgetting is rapid at first and then gradually slows, exhibiting an approximately hyperbolic decay function. This is shown in Figure 1.7, which illustrates data from a large recent study of memory for paired associates (Rubin, Hinton, and Wenzel, 1999).[10]

9. The Law of Recency is also sometimes called the Law of Disuse.

10. Rubin found that his data were significantly better fit by a more complex sum of exponential functions (i.e., $P(\text{recall}) = a_1 e^{-b_1 t} + a_2 e^{-b_2 t} + C$) than by a single hyperbolic function (i.e., $P(\text{recall}) = at^{-b}$). In these equations, t represents time and a_1, a_2, b_1, b_2, and C are free parameters that determine the shape of the function.

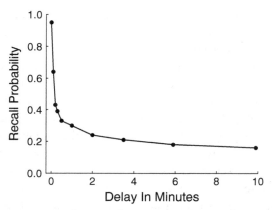

Figure 1.7 Forgetting curve for paired associates. Memory for paired associates as a function of the amount of time (and number of pairs) intervening between study and test. Data from Rubin et al. (1999).

One of the most important early findings was that the rate of forgetting depends critically on what happens between initial study and later memory tests. Forgetting tends to be greatest when the interval between study and test (the *retention interval*) is filled with high levels of mental activity. In most experiments, forgetting of a given word pair is rapid because the retention interval is filled with studying and getting tested on other word pairs.

Jenkins and Dallenbach (1924) wondered what would happen if the retention interval was filled with only minimal cognitive activity. They paid two Cornell University seniors to live in an improvised dormitory attached to the experimental psychology laboratory for seven weeks. During this time, the two students would memorize lists of 10 random syllables for a free-recall test— that is, they were asked to try to recall as many of the syllables they could in any order. The retention interval, which varied between 1 hour and 8 hours, was sometimes filled with waking activity (the students would be tested during the day), and other times it would be filled with sleep (the students would study the sequence before retiring, and then sleep would be disrupted for the recall test). When the students slept during the retention interval, there was a small amount of forgetting during the first 2 hours of sleep but virtually no forgetting during subsequent sleep lasting up to 8 hours (see Figure 1.8). During the waking condition, the students continued forgetting as the retention interval increased. Researchers are still debating the mechanism(s) underlying this effect. In particular, it has been hypothesized that sleeping during a study-test interval does more than simply reduce interfering associations. Sleep (particularly the stages known as slow wave sleep [SWS] and rapid-eye-movement [REM] sleep)

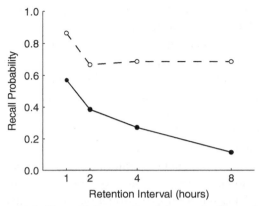

Figure 1.8 Differential effects of sleep and activity on the forgetting function.
Effects of sleep (open circles, dotted line) vs. activity (filled circles, solid line) on the
forgetting function. This figure shows data from Jenkins and Dallenbach (1924).

may actually serve a special role in consolidating previously learned memories,
making them less susceptible to interference (Walker and Stickgold, 2006;
Ellenbogen, Hulbert, Stickgold, Dinges, and Thompson-Schill, 2006) (but see
Siegel, 2001, and Rickard, Cai, Rieth, and Jones, 2008, for opposing views).

1.5 COGNITIVISM

Early students of learning and memory focused on the relation between different
aspects of the learning experience and the ability to recall or recognize the
learned items. In contrast, the cognitive approach, which sprung forward in
the late 1950s and through the 1960s, emphasized the unobservable (latent)
processes that mediate learning and memory. In 1976, William K. Estes, one of
the founders of the cognitive approach, wrote that, "Only in quite recent times
have researchers come to appreciate that rigorous testability of a theory does
not depend on conceptual elements being mapped in a one-to-one fashion onto
observable events" (Estes, 1976; p. 36).

Cognitivists, like Estes, conceived of memory as part of a computing system
that takes perceptual input and transforms it through a series of information-
processing stages that ultimately leads to overt behavioral responses. A basic
assumption underlying the cognitive approach is that the continuous stream
of sensory input is interpreted and analyzed in terms of meaningful units of
information. These units form the basic elements of memory storage. Cognitive
scientists who are interested in memory study the encoding, storage, and
retrieval of these units of information.

The question of how the stream of sensory input is interpreted and analyzed into meaningful units motivated the development of *information-processing models*. In 1958 Donald Broadbent, an Oxford University psychologist, proposed that information is separately processed by different sensory channels, each capable of holding information for a brief duration. Knowledge about the world guides the selection of information from particular sensory channels and determines what information will be further processed and stored in memory.[11] Broadbent's model emphasized the idea that people can only process a limited amount of information at any one time. The model also emphasized that an important component of information processing involves selecting either information that should be processed further or information that should be discarded. This selection of information, or *attention*, is driven both by properties of the stimulus and by one's expectations.

1.5.1 Representation, Storage, and Retrieval

As the incoming information is interpreted and stored in memory, how is the information represented in memory? Before the emergence of cognitivism, this question would not have been asked. The functionalist view held that a science of behavior should be concerned with the input–output properties of mind/brain and not with its inner workings.

Estes (1955) proposed that an item in memory is not a holistic entity but rather a bundle of smaller units called elements or features. If a molecule can be composed of atoms, which in turn are composed of protons, neutrons, and electrons, why can't an item in memory have a substructure?

Distributed representation is the idea that a memory is represented in the brain as a set of features, perhaps encoded in the pattern of activity over a large set of nerve cells (neurons). These features represent many kinds of information. This view may be distinguished from the idea of *localist representation*, in which a single unit (or a small number of localized units) represents a single memory. Evidence concerning the advantages of distributed representations is presented in chapters 3 and 4.

Once identified and represented as a collection of features, how is information stored in memory? Consider, first, the famous wax tablet analogy that Plato (429–348 BCE) constructed to describe memory storage and representation. He wrote:

---

11. According to this view, there is constant feedback between new learning and existing knowledge. An interesting question concerns whether the system has some innate knowledge that guides the learning process at the earliest stages of human development.

> I would have you imagine, then, that there exists in the mind of man a
> block of wax, which is of different sizes in different men; harder, moister,
> and having more or less purity in one than another, and in some of an
> intermediate quality . . . . Let us say that this tablet is a gift of Memory,
> the mother of the Muses, and that when we wish to remember anything
> which we have seen or heard or thought in our own minds, we hold the
> wax to the perceptions and thoughts, and in that receive the impression
> of them as from the seal of a ring; and that we remember and know what
> is imprinted as long as the image lasts; but when the image is effaced, or
> cannot be taken, then we forget and do not know.
>
> Plato, *Theaetetus* (360 BCE)

Plato posited that information is first perceived and recognized, and then
these thoughts are stored in some lasting representation that is analogous to
an imprint on a wax tablet. It is implicit that the same wax tablet might store
many different memories, but that is not made clear in Plato's text. Much later,
Sir Frances Galton (1822–1911) coined a similar analogy that emphasized his
belief that the representations for different memories are not kept distinct. He
proposed that memories blend together in the same manner that pictures may
be combined in the then recently developed technique of composite portraiture
(the nondigital precursor to morphing faces). Like Plato, Galton viewed the
process of memory storage as something separate from and subsequent to
sensation and perhaps even recognition (Galton, 1883; p. 229).

Assuming that some desired information is stored in memory, how does one
find it? This *search problem* is particularly challenging in memory tasks where
the to-be-remembered items are already well learned, such as the words in one's
own language. In such tasks, one must still remember which words appeared
on the list. To understand how people solve this search problem, one must not
only specify the representation of the items and the processes governing the
encoding of these representations in memory, but one must further specify how
items are retrieved. Hypothesized retrieval mechanisms, which are central to all
contemporary theories of memory, typically rely on the concept of association.
In these theories of memory, different stored representations can evoke one
another via associative connections formed both during the study of a target list
and during one's prior experience with the studied items. These associations
can be used to retrieve specific memories despite their being blended with many
other nontargeted memories.

The term *cognitivism* is most often used to describe research that
contemplates the mental processes believed to underlie behavior. Modern
research on memory has fully embraced the goal of uncovering these mental
processes. The new field of cognitive neuroscience is aimed at making

these mental processes more directly observable by uncovering the biological mechanisms underlying perception, learning, memory, language, and action.

As the field has marched forward in its effort to uncover hidden mental processes, some have voiced concern about whether scientists are too quick to invent constructs to explain every new fact that does not fit neatly into existing theories (Underwood, 1972). Within the field of memory research, one can see considerable variation among researchers in their tendency to stray from the data. In the next subsection, we consider two of the major approaches that characterize modern work on human memory.

1.5.2 Memory Systems and Process Models

Two major cognitive approaches predominate in the study of human memory. The first of these approaches, termed the *memory systems approach*, assumes that memory is not a singular entity, but rather is an umbrella term for a web of brain systems that each support different kinds of memory function. The goal of this approach is to determine what the different memory systems are and to identify the brain regions supporting each of these systems. Much as a biologist wants to classify the different types of organs that make up the body, the different types of cells that make up an organ, and the different types of processes that regulate cell function, memory researchers seek to identify the major subtypes of memory, the brain systems that give rise to them, and how these systems interact with one another. The second major cognitive approach involves the construction of computational models that describe the processes underlying memory function. Following this approach, researchers attempt to understand memory by specifying mathematical equations that characterize the encoding and retrieval processes underlying memory function. Having specified these equations, a computer is then used to solve the equations and thus generate predictions for what should happen in a memory experiment.[12] With these predictions in hand, scientists can ascertain where the model succeeds and where it fails to match the experimental data. These successes and failures give scientists ideas as to which of the model's assumptions are flawed and how to fix them. Sometimes, the data needed to test a crucial aspect of a model do not exist. In these cases, an experiment must be designed to test the model. This interaction between data and models helps scientists create models of human memory that can account for a broader array of known data and that can

---

12. In rare cases one can solve the equations of a memory model analytically, as you would an algebra or calculus problem. However, most memory models are too complex to solve without the aid of a computer. This is because memory models typically involve probabilistic variables (variables that represent uncertain events, see Boxes 2.1 and 2.2) and use these probabilistic variables in a nonlinear manner.

also make better predictions about new memory phenomena that are yet to be observed.

We can evaluate a memory model on at least four dimensions:

- Accuracy: A good model should agree with and reflect available, relevant data.
- Generality: A good model should ideally encompass a wide range of data.
- Testability: A good model should be framed in terms that allow for empirical tests of its major assumptions. These tests should allow researchers to distinguish one model from another. Ideally, a model should be tested on its ability to make accurate predictions about new data.
- Parsimony: If two models are equally good at fitting the known data, the less complex model should always be preferred.

One may ask how the memory systems and process modeling approaches actually differ. The main difference between the two approaches is in the style of research they represent. Scientists who follow a systems approach often compare different kinds of memory tasks, searching for patterns in the data that point to different underlying memory systems. Scientists who follow a process-modeling approach generally focus their research on one or two memory tasks and develop models that help explain detailed features of the data from those tasks. An argument for developing process models is that it is often impossible to see how a certain idea about memory will translate into precise and empirically testable predictions. Robert Lucas, a Nobel Laureate in Economics, noted that, "It is, at least for me, the working of highly abstract but explicit models that is the source of ideas for constructing new models, criticizing old ones, or reading the classics from a fresh viewpoint (Lucas, 1983)."

One may sometimes assume that multiple systems are needed to explain some data when a single system could do the job. On the other hand, process models of memory can often be myopic. They may be designed to explain a small subset of memory behavior, and even if they explain that subset perfectly, they may miss much of what is actually going on in the memory system. Researchers are beginning to bridge these two approaches by developing process models that assume a network of interacting memory systems and then using those interacting systems to explain data from a broad array of memory tasks (e.g., Humphreys, Pike, Bain, and Tehan, 1989; Norman and O'Reilly, 2003; Ashby, Alfonso-Reese, Turken, and Waldron, 1998; Nosofsky and Palmeri, 1998; Sirotin, Kimball, and Kahana, 2005; Norman, Newman, and Detre, 2007).

During the past two decades a transformative development has taken place in the study of human memory. For the first century of memory research, models and theories of memory have been aimed at explaining experimental data on behavior, such as accuracy and RT in recall or recognition-memory tasks.

Starting in the 1990s, a major emphasis in memory research has been to understand the biological mechanisms responsible for the encoding, storage, and retrieval of memories. Although a thorough discussion of the neurobiological basis of memory is beyond the scope of this text, in the next section we introduce some key ideas from neuroscience that will arise in later chapters.

1.5.3 Memory and the Brain

Modern neuroscience has taught us that the basic information processing of the brain is carried out by specialized cells, called neurons, which communicate by sending electrical signals to one another. In animal studies, the activity of individual neurons can be measured by placing an electrode (a very thin wire) near or in the neuron and measuring how the voltage differential between the electrode and a reference electrode varies over time. As a result of a complex electrochemical process, the neuron is able to produce a rapid electrical discharge, as seen in the rapid voltage fluctuation recorded from the microwire. This neural response, called an *action potential,* has virtually the same form in rats, cats, monkeys, humans, and all other mammals.

Neurons do not operate in isolation. They both receive signals from and transmit signals to other neurons by way of connections (synapses). Neurons receive signals through synapses on their dendrites and transmit signals through synapses on their axons. The number of input and output connections can vary widely across different neurons. Whereas some neurons connect to just a few other neurons, other neurons connect to thousands of neurons. The human brain possesses approximately 100 billion neurons[13] and 200 trillion connections (Buzsáki, 2006).

The neurons of the brain are not distributed in a single large mass; rather, they are organized into specialized regions, each of which may play a specific role. In the case of the brain's sensory and motor systems, we know a tremendous amount about the way neurons process information. For example, some neurons in the visual system respond most strongly to lines of a given width and orientation and some neurons in the auditory system respond most strongly to tones of a given frequency. Although much less is known about the neural basis of human memory, we do know from studies of patients with brain injuries that the hippocampus and medial temporal lobe (see Figure 1.9) are essential for storing new associations. Memory functioning also appears to depend on the frontal and parietal cortices, though the exact interplay of these regions is a topic of intense investigation.

---

13. Humans possess approximately 1,000 times as many neurons as found in rodents but only twice as many as found in monkeys.

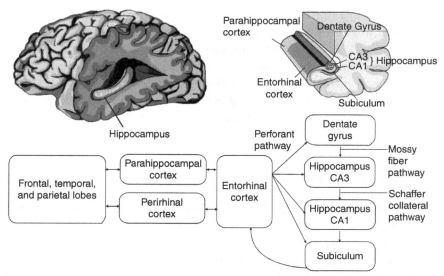

Figure 1.9 The medial temporal lobe of the human brain. Adapted from Kandel, Schwartz, and Jessell (2000).

Neurons in different brain regions can be highly responsive to distinct types of stimuli. For example, some neurons in the hippocampus have been shown to be selective to one's location in space (e.g., O'Keefe and Dostrovsky, 1971; Ekstrom et al., 2003), whereas other neurons in the hippocampus have been shown to represent associations between items (Sakai and Miyashita, 1991). Neurons in the parahippocampal gyrus have been found to respond most strongly to specific spatial views and neurons in the frontal cortex appear to respond to one's goals (e.g., what you are trying to do at a given time). These examples are not meant to suggest that neurons within a given region only represent one type of information; each neuron is part of a larger network that may encompass multiple brain regions and each brain region can contain neurons that respond to multiple behavioral variables.

From a theoretical standpoint, one could learn a great deal about human memory without being concerned with the specific brain regions involved. For biology to help us understand memory it must explain how experiences become represented in the pattern of neural activity in the brain and how those patterns of neural activity are rapidly stored, maintained, and later retrieved in the presence of an effective cue. Despite the tremendous advances in neuroscience in the last several decades, we are still lacking definitive answers to these questions. We do have some promising leads, however, as we will discuss in various points throughout the text.

Before we can attempt to understand how the brain enables us to remember, we need to understand the qualities of remembering as manifested in human (and animal) behavior. Our focus, therefore, will be on describing the major facts concerning human memory and the theories developed to explain those facts. Where possible, we will consider neuroscientific evidence that supports, or challenges, particular theories of memory. We will also consider theories of memory that are largely motivated by the nature of the brain's neural circuitry (see chapter 5).

1.6 ORGANIZATION OF THE BOOK

Much of our knowledge concerning memory derives from experimental procedures, such as the recognition and recall tasks described above. Often these quite different tasks illustrate a common set of principles or mechanisms, and it is thus tempting to organize a text around basic principles, first highlighting those principles that are common to many tasks and then focusing on the principles specific to individual tasks. However, without formal theories of the tasks in question, one cannot easily understand why certain principles have greater influence in some tasks than in others. These theories, which should make explicit assumptions about how information is represented, stored, and retrieved, can differ widely from task to task, as different memory tasks place different demands on the memory system.

An alternative organization is based on the major tasks developed to study memory in the laboratory. This organization allows us to present theory and data in an integrated fashion. This organization allows us to discuss theory and data on relatively simple memory tasks, such as recognition memory, before proceeding to more complex tasks, such as free recall. Given that the mechanisms hypothesized to underlie free recall subsume many of the same mechanisms hypothesized to underlie simpler tasks, such as recognition, this organization allows us to introduce new concepts and complexities as they are required, rather than trying to discuss all the theoretical constructs simultaneously.

We begin our analysis of human memory by discussing the recognition-memory task. Chapter 2 reviews the basic empirical data on recognition of single items and discusses these data in terms of strength theory, perhaps the simplest and oldest model of human memory. Chapter 3 introduces attribute models of recognition and the important notion of summed similarity. Attribute models are the standard modern class of memory models and will reappear throughout later chapters. Chapter 4 takes us into the domain of associative memory, presenting the major empirical findings on associative recognition and cued recall. Chapter 5 introduces attribute and neural-network models of associative memory. Chapters 6 extends the analysis of simple associations to list-wide associative memory, with an emphasis on free recall and the problem of memory search. Chapter 7 focuses on theories of memory search, including theories based on the distinction between a short-term and long-term memory system, as well as those that assume a single memory store. We next turn to the problem of serial-order memory, discussing the basic empirical data in chapter 8 and presenting the major theories in chapter 9.

One might ask whether after more than 125 years of research we have arrived at a comprehensive theory of memory, even for relatively simple tasks such as recognition memory. As we will see in the chapters that follow, much has been learned about specific memory tasks and the memory mechanisms they rely on, but we are still far from any kind of unified theory. Nevertheless, we must not despair—the science of memory is still in its infancy, especially when compared with its more mature siblings, such as physics and chemistry. Theories of memory can now provide quantitative fits to data from a wide range of experimental procedures. These theories are also moving in the direction of greater neurobiological plausibility, thus serving as a bridge between brain and behavior.

2

Item Recognition

Recognition memory refers to the ability to remember whether or not a presented item has occurred in a particular context. In a typical recognition experiment, a participant studies a list of items. Later, the participant is presented with a list of test (or probe) items, some of which were presented in the study list (*targets*, or *old* items) and some of which were not (*lures*, or *new* items). The participant's task is to discriminate between the targets and the lures. In most laboratory studies of recognition memory, both targets and lures are known items such as words, letters, or pictures of familiar objects or scenes. The participant is not being asked whether he has ever encountered a given item. Rather, the participant is being asked whether he has encountered an item in a given context, usually that of the just-presented list.

There are two standard ways to pose the recognition-memory question. In *yes–no* recognition, targets and lures are presented one at a time and the participant responds *yes* if the item was on the list and *no* if the item was not on the list. In *forced-choice* recognition, the participant is asked to choose which of two (or more) items was in the list. In using either of these methods, one can measure at least two aspects of behavior: the participant's response and the time taken to make the response (called *response time* or RT).

Because each response could be made to either a target or a lure, it is useful to classify responses into one of the following types: a *hit* is a *yes* response to a

Table 2.1
Classification of Responses in a yes–no Recognition Task.

	Response	
	"yes"	*"no"*
Target (Old)	Hit	Miss
Lure (New)	False Alarm	Correct Rejection

target; a *false alarm* is a *yes* response to a lure. A *miss* is a *no* response to a target; a *correct rejection* is a *no* response to a lure (see Table 2.1). People may also be asked to judge the quality of their memory for a given probe item. For example, they may be asked to indicate their confidence that an item was, or was not, on the study list.

The next section introduces *strength theory*, one of the most widely studied theories of recognition memory. According to this theory, people can directly assess the strength, or familiarity, of any item in memory and use this information to decide whether it had appeared on a recently studied list. Although researchers have uncovered numerous limitations of this approach, it still provides an important benchmark against which other theories are compared. Furthermore, strength theory is a particularly good starting point for discussing theories of memory in general because it introduces several important concepts that will appear in our discussion of other models throughout the text.

2.1 STRENGTH THEORY

According to strength theory, each item's memorial representation has a numerical value that represents the degree to which that item evokes a sense of familiarity. Before presenting a list of items to be studied, we can define a variable S_i to represent the memory strength of item i. Although we could assume that all items start out with strengths of zero, or with constant strength, it is more reasonable to suppose that items vary in their strength, with some items being stronger than others. If words serve as the to-be-remembered items, we would expect common words to be stronger prior to the start of the experiment than rare words; common words will have been encountered more often and more recently than rare words.

We first need to specify how items vary in their strength values; that is, we need to specify the probability, or likelihood, that a randomly chosen item will take on a particular strength value, S. Strength theory typically assumes that items take on strength values drawn from a *normal*, or *Gaussian*

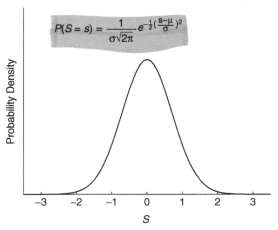

Figure 2.1 Normal probability distribution. A normal probability distribution with an average (mean) value of 0 ($\mu = 0$) and a standard deviation of 1 ($\sigma = 1$). A basic law of probability distributions is that the area under the probability distribution function, which represents the sum of the probabilities of all possible outcomes, must equal 1.0.

probability distribution.[1] A normal distribution is symmetric around a central value that represents the most likely outcome. Probabilities of other outcomes decrease as one moves away from the central values in either direction. Figure 2.1 shows a normal distribution with an average, or mean value, of 0 and a standard deviation of 1. We use the Greek letters μ (mu) and σ (sigma) to denote the mean and the standard deviation of a distribution, respectively. Because of its shape, the normal distribution is sometimes called a bell curve. Box 2.1 provides a review of basic probability concepts, and Box 2.2 provides a review of probability distributions, including the concepts of mean and standard deviation.

Having characterized the distribution of strengths for all items in memory, we can ask what happens when an item is studied (i.e., repeated). The key assumption underlying strength theory is that studying a given item increases its strength. For the moment, let us sidestep the difficult question of how repeating an item actually causes its strength to increase. The simple version of strength theory that we consider here posits that repetition of an item simply adds a constant value to its strength. Later we will consider more complex assumptions about learning and forgetting processes in recognition memory.

1. Carl Friedrich Gauss published many important results on the normal distribution in the early 1800s, but the first mathematician to use it was Abraham de Moivre, in 1734.

According to strength theory, consider what happens when a person is given a test item in a recognition task. First, the person must assess the strength of the test item, which should signal whether the item was on the list (because an item that was on the list should, on average, have a higher level of strength or familiarity than an item that was not encountered during the experiment). Strength theory assumes that people are able to read out the strength value of a given test item without that value being influenced by any other items in memory. Then, the person must decide, on the basis of this evidence, whether or not they have studied the item.

The retrieval process is assumed to depend on a *threshold* value, denoted as C. If the strength exceeds C, the person will say, "Yes, I remember the item," and if it is below C, the person will say, "No, I don't remember the item." Alternatively, we can say that the probability of saying *yes* to item i is the probability that S_i exceeds C, which we can write as $P(S_i > C)$.

This version of strength theory has four parameters that must be known if we are to solve for the predicted outcome of an experiment: the mean and standard deviation of the starting strength distribution (μ_S, σ_S), the learning increment (a), and the threshold (C).

Consider what would happen if we presented a single randomly chosen item i in the study phase of an experiment. After studying that item, its strength would be given by $S_i + a$, whereas all of the other items j would have strengths of S_j. If all the items started out with exactly the same strength (i.e. if $S = S_i = S_j$ for all i, j), then it would be easy to ensure that we could always correctly recognize the studied items from the nonstudied ones by setting C to a value between S and $S + a$. Suppose, for example, that the starting strengths were all given by $S = 1$ and that $a = 1$. In this case, the studied item would have a strength of 2, and all the nonstudied items would have strengths of 1.0. We could set $C = 1.5$ and we would never make a mistake.

We began, however, with the assumption that items start out with different strength values, with some being higher than our studied item S_i and others being lower. Assuming that there is some chance that a nonstudied item will start with a strength that is greater than $S_i + a$, our model will respond *yes* to some percentage of nonpresented (lure) items. This situation is illustrated in Figure 2.2, which shows the distributions of strength values for targets and lures in relation to the decision threshold, C. For clarity we show the same two distributions in both the upper and lower panels of the figure but with different shading to illustrate the proportion of hits and false alarms. In both panels, the x-axis indicates the strength of an item, with strength increasing from left to right. The y-axis indicates the probability, or likelihood, of a given strength value for any given target or lure.

Box 2.1

PROBABILITY AND RANDOM VARIABLES

Probability is the science of chance and uncertainty. The idea is that of an *experiment* that can have one of several *outcomes*. Although we cannot know with certainty the outcome of any given experiment, we can assess the chances of observing a given outcome by repeating the experiment many times and tallying the number of times each outcome occurs. As we repeat the experiment, the frequency of a given outcome divided by the total number of experiments will tend toward some value—this relative frequency is an estimate of the *probability* of that outcome. The more often we repeat an experiment, the more precise the *estimate* of the probability of each outcome becomes.

Suppose we give a person a list of 15 words to remember, and then we ask him to recall the words in any order. We can count the number of words he recalls on a given list, but this number is likely to vary from list to list. If we repeated this experiment many times, we could determine that 95% of the time, the number of recalled words will be between 6 and 8. Statistics is concerned with quantifying the degree of confidence one can have in these estimates.

A *random variable* is a variable that models the outcome of an experiment. Each value of the random variable represents an experimental outcome, and each outcome is associated with some probability. Consider an experiment in which we roll a single die. Let X be a random variable that can take on the values of the die. If the die is "fair," then the probability that X will take on any of the values 1 through 6 is exactly 1/6. That is, $P(X = 1) = P(X = 2) = \cdots = P(X = 6) = \frac{1}{6}$. If we roll two dice, we would have two random variables, X and Y, to represent the outcomes of each roll.

With two random variables it is helpful to define a *conditional probability*. Consider the probability of rolling a 3 on die 2 conditional on rolling a 6 on die 1. This conditional probability is simply the probability of getting both a 3 on die 2 and a 6 on die 1 divided by the probability of getting a 6 on die 1. Mathematically, we can denote the probability that X takes on the value 3 given that Y takes on the value 6 as $P(X = 3|Y = 6) = P(X = 3 \text{ and } Y = 6)/ P(Y = 6)$. X and Y are *independent* if knowing the value of Y does not provide any information about the value of X, that is, $P(X = i|Y = j) = P(X = i)$. Note that this implies that $P(X = i \text{ and } Y = j) = P(X = i) \times P(Y = j)$ and that $P(X = i \text{ or } Y = j) = P(X = i) + P(Y = j) - P(X = i) \times P(Y = j)$. In the case of two dice, the outcome of one will in no way affect the outcome of the other. Thus, X and Y are independent.

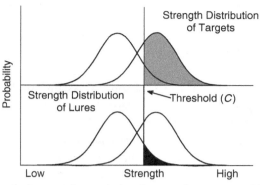

Figure 2.2 Strength theory I. Strength distributions for targets and lures. A *yes* response is given when the strength exceeds the threshold, C. The area of the light-shaded region in the upper panel represents the proportion of hits (74.2% in this example); the area of the dark-shaded region in the lower panel represents the proportion of false alarms (8.9% in this example).

The distributions shown on the right side of Figure 2.2 represent the likelihood of obtaining a particular strength value for any given target, and the distributions shown on the left represent the likelihood of obtaining a particular strength value for any given lure. The area of the light-shaded region of the target strength distribution (upper panel) represents the likelihood of a hit (74.2% in this example); the area of the dark-shaded region of the lure strength distribution (lower panel) represents the likelihood of a false alarm (8.9% in this example). The model will respond *yes* if the strength exceeds C.

The parameter σ_S represents the standard deviation of the normal distributions shown in Figure 2.2. A larger standard deviation implies broader distributions and thus more misclassifications of items as targets and lures. The ability to correctly classify test items as targets and lures thus reflects both the standard deviation, σ_S, and the difference in the means of the target and lure distributions.

Although strength theory may appear to be disconnected from real-world problems, nothing could be further from the truth. Strength theory is one example of a very general theoretical framework called either *Signal Detection Theory* or *Statistical Decision Theory* (Green and Swets, 1966; Wickens, 2002). Consider the task facing a doctor who is trying to decide if an ill patient is fighting off an infection. To do so, the physician may order a blood test so that the lab can count the number of white blood cells (and other cell types) in a cubic centimeter of the patient's blood. Each person may have a somewhat different white blood cell count when they are healthy, and even within a person, the count will vary from day to day. That is, the observed white blood

Box 2.2

PROBABILITY AND DISTRIBUTIONS

A probability distribution is the function that assigns a probability to each value of a random variable. For a random variable representing the roll of a die, each value (1–6) has the same probability 1/6. This is called a *uniform* probability distribution because all outcomes are equally likely. The distribution is also called *discrete*, because there are exactly 6 possible values, each associated with a finite probability. If the random variable could take on a continuous range of values (e.g., temperature or height), then it would be called a *continuous* random variable.

The *expected value* (or expectation) of a random variable is the sum of the products of its value and associated probability for all possible values. For the roll of a die, the expectation of X, denoted $E[X]$, is given by $E[X] = \frac{1}{6} \times 1 + \frac{1}{6} \times 2 + \frac{1}{6} \times 3 + \frac{1}{6} \times 4 + \frac{1}{6} \times 5 + \frac{1}{6} \times 6 = \frac{1}{6} \times 21 = 3.5$. In this case, the expectation works the same way as the arithmetic average. However, if the probabilities associated with different outcomes are not uniform, the expectation acts as a weighted average, weighting each outcome by its probability.[a]

The expectation is a measure of the central tendency, or "center of mass," of a probability distribution. When using random variables to describe the outcome of an actual experiment with real measured data, we typically refer to the expected value as the *mean* of the observed distribution, which is denoted by the Greek letter μ (mu).

One would often like to quantify not only the mean of the distribution but also its spread. That is, we would like to know the tendency for its values to be near or far from the center of mass. A mathematical measure of dispersion or spread is called the *variance* and is defined as the expectation of the square of the difference of each value from the expected value. Consequently, the variance of X, denoted var[X], is given by:

$$\mathrm{var}[X] = E\left[(X - \mu)^2\right] = E[X^2] - \mu^2. \tag{2.1}$$

A more easily interpreted value in dealing with actual data is the square-root of the variance, which is called the *standard deviation* and denoted by the Greek letter σ (sigma). The standard deviation thus tells us the average deviation from the mean.

---

[a] For a continuous random variable, the expectation is given by: $E[X] = \int_{-\infty}^{+\infty} xP(x)dx$

Consider a random variable, S, whose values are drawn from a normal, or Gaussian, probability distribution. In this case, the probability of S taking on the value s would be given by the formula:

$$P(S = s) = \frac{1}{\sigma\sqrt{2\pi}} e^{-\frac{1}{2}\left(\frac{s-\mu}{\sigma}\right)^2},$$

where μ is the mean, or average value, of the distribution; σ is the standard deviation, or spread of the distribution; π and e are irrational numbers whose values approximately equal 3.141 and 2.718, respectively. You may recall that the value e is given by $(1 + 1/n)^n$ in the limit as n approaches ∞.

---

cell count is a random variable. However, when fighting a disease, a person's white blood cell count will generally increase. Assuming that a single blood sample was obtained, the doctor would like to know how that white blood cell count compares with the general population of people who are healthy and how it compares with the general population of people whose bodies are fighting an infection. By setting a threshold value, the physician can decide whether to run additional tests to identify whether a particular infective process is underway.

The strength theory of recognition memory allows us to quantify the *sensitivity* of the model to differences between targets and lures, where sensitivity measures the degree of overlap between the target and lure distributions. Perfect sensitivity, corresponding to nonoverlapping target and lure distributions, implies a hit rate of 1.0 and a false-alarm rate of 0.0. Zero sensitivity, corresponding to identical target and lure distributions, implies that the hit rate is equal to the false-alarm rate.

Strength theory also allows us to quantify the model's *bias* to respond *yes* or *no* to a test item. If we assume a high value of the threshold parameter C, the model will only give a *yes* response when the strength of a test item is very high. If we want to be sure that we seldom make any false alarms, we will set a very high threshold for saying *yes*, at the expense of committing many misses. If we set a very low threshold, we will seldom miss but we will commit many false alarms.

A standard measure of sensitivity for *yes–no* recognition, called d', is the mean of the target distribution minus the mean of the lure distribution expressed in standard deviation units (σ_s). We can calculate this value in terms of the parameters of strength theory. The mean of the lure distribution is μ_S and the mean of the target distribution is $\mu_S + a$ (assuming that each of the studied items was presented just once). We can then write d' as the difference in mean strength divided by the standard deviation of the strength distribution, σ_s:

$$d' = \frac{(\mu_s + a) - \mu_s}{\sigma_s} = \frac{a}{\sigma_s}.$$

Notice that the value of d' does not depend on the threshold value, C. That is, the model allows us to conceptually separate sensitivity and bias.

In an actual recognition-memory experiment, we don't observe d' or C, but rather we observe the fraction of responses that are hits, false alarms, misses, and correct rejections (see Table 2.1). One may ask how we would map the results of such an experiment onto the parameters of the model. More generally, how can we use experimental data to test the strength theory of recognition? We will tackle this issue in the next section.

2.1.1 Testing Strength Theory

In this section we will consider one of the key predictions arising from the strength theory of recognition memory. Consider the consequences of experimentally varying the strength threshold, C, which governs the decision to respond *yes* or *no* to a given probe item. Moving the value of C up or down will change the predicted frequencies of hits and false alarms.

Consider what would happen if there were different payoffs (rewards and/or penalties) associated with incorrectly classifying a nonlist item as a list item (a false alarm) and for correctly classifying a list item as such (a hit). According to strength theory, such differential payoffs would be modeled by a change in C. If it is critical to avoid false alarms, we should raise C. Alternatively, if we want to maximize hits at all costs, we should lower C. Varying C should not affect sensitivity.

A *receiver operating characteristic* (ROC) curve shows the relation between the hit rate and the false-alarm rate as C varies. Although we could experimentally vary C by changing the payoffs for hits and false alarms, a simpler alternative involves the collection of *confidence judgments*. In this technique, people are asked to rate how confident they are that a given item was on the list. In a typical experimental procedure, participants are asked to press one of eight keys arrayed on a computer keyboard to indicate their confidence that a text item had been previously studied. The leftmost key (designated by the number 1) would represent a highly certain *no* response and the rightmost key (designated by the number 8) would represent a highly certain *yes* response. Keys near the middle of the array would represent less confident responses— the fourth and fifth keys from the left would represent highly tentative *no* and

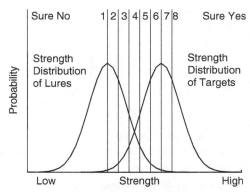

Figure 2.3 Strength theory II. This illustration is analogous to Figure 2.2, except that here we show multiple decision thresholds corresponding to the ratings given in a confidence judgment task. Although the decision thresholds appear evenly spaced in the figure, people's actual thresholds need not be evenly spaced, as the placement of these thresholds is entirely subjective.

yes responses respectively. In this configuration, the array represents an axis of confidence that an item was studied on the target list, with *no* responses on the left and *yes* responses on the right.

We can now mimic a person with a high value of *C* by grouping confidence judgments that are less than 8 into the *no* category, leaving only confidence judgments of 8 in the *yes* category. Based on this grouping, our imaginary conservative participant only responds *yes* when our real participant responds *yes* with a high degree of confidence. Similarly, we can mimic a person who is slightly less conservative by grouping confidence judgments that are less than 7 into the *no* category, leaving confidence judgments of 7 and 8 in the *yes* category. Moving the threshold further down, we reach the threshold of our real participant, with confidence judgments between 5 and 8 reflecting *yes* responses and confidence judgments between 1 and 4 reflecting *no* responses. We can continue to move our threshold even further down, all the way to the point where only a confidence judgment of 1 is in the *no* category and all other confidence judgments are grouped in the *yes* category. This hypothetical participant will only withhold a *yes* response when he is absolutely certain the item was not on the list (see Figure 2.3).

If we plot hits against false alarms for each of these hypothetical participants, we can construct an ROC curve. At the most conservative end of the spectrum, both the hit rate and the false-alarm rate will be low because the participant rarely makes *yes* responses. At the most liberal end of the spectrum, both the hit and false-alarm rates will be high because the participant almost always

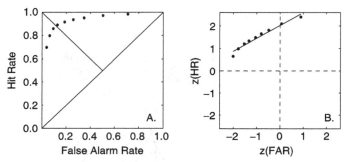

Figure 2.4 The receiver operating characteristic. A. ROC curve showing hit rate as a function of false-alarm rate for different threshold values. **B.** z-transformed ROC curve; slope of regression line is 0.57. Data from an unpublished study in my laboratory.

makes *yes* responses. The points representing hit rate and false-alarm rate for each threshold level (liberal to conservative) trace out a bow-shaped ROC curve, as shown for actual data in Figure 2.4A (See Swets, 1998, for background information on ROC curves and their applications to real-world problems, such as medical diagnosis).

Our assumption that the strengths of targets and lures are normally distributed, as shown in Figure 2.2, implies that the ROC curve should be bowed in a manner similar to that found in the actual data shown in Figure 2.4A. For a threshold of negative infinity, people will give *yes* responses to every lure and to every target item, resulting in both a false-alarm rate and a hit rate of 1.0. If we now increase the threshold, C, to the point where it equals the mean of the lure distribution, we would have a false-alarm rate of 0.5 because half of the lure items will have strengths that exceed C. If the target and lure distributions are widely separated, increasing C to the mean of the lure distribution will only cause a small decrease in the hit rate. So long as the mean of the target distribution is greater than the mean of the lure distribution, increasing C to the mean of the lure distribution will result in a hit rate that is greater than the false-alarm rate of 0.5. If we further increase C to equal the mean of the target distribution we will have a hit rate of 0.5 because half of the target items will have strengths that exceed C. The fraction of false alarms would also decrease to some value less than 0.5, the exact value depending on the separation of the target and lure distributions. Finally, if we make C infinitely large, the model will never give a *yes* response and both the hit rate and false-alarm rates would be zero. We can determine the precise shape of the ROC predicted by strength theory by calculating, for every value of C, the fraction of the target and lure distributions that exceed C. Such calculations, though difficult to carry out by hand, are easily handled by computers.

If the assumptions of strength theory are correct, then there is a statistical transformation that we can apply to the hit rate and false-alarm rate data that would turn the ROC curve into a straight line. This transformation, which is sometimes called a z-transformation, is based on a normal distribution with a mean value of zero and a standard deviation of 1. Given this distribution, we can calculate the probability, p, of obtaining a value less than or equal to z. Alternatively, we can calculate the value of z for which the probability of drawing a value less than or equal to z is exactly p. This value is the z-transformation of probability p, or $z(p)$. Mathematically, $z(p)$ is the inverse of the cumulative density function (CDF) of a normal distribution with $\mu = 0$ and $\sigma^2 = 1$. That is, $z(p)$ is the value of z that solves the equation: $\frac{1}{\sqrt{2\pi}} \int_{-\infty}^{z} e^{-x^2/2} dx = p$.

Now suppose that the standard deviations of the target and lure distributions are equal, and that the mean of the target distribution is two standard deviations above the mean of the lure distribution. If we set C equal to the mean of the lure distribution, the false-alarm rate would be 0.5; the z-transformed false-alarm rate would be zero; the hit rate would be approximately 0.975; and the z-transformed hit rate would be 2. If we then increase C to be halfway between the two distributions, then the z-transformed false-alarm rate would be -1 and the z-transformed hit rate would be 1. If we further increase C to be equal to the mean of the target distribution, then the z-transformed false-alarm rate would be -2 and the z-transformed hit rate would be 0. Thus, the z-transformed hit rate increases linearly with the z-transformed false-alarm rate, with a slope of 1.0. We refer to this relation between the z-transformed hit rate and the z-transformed false-alarm rate as a zROC curve.

The assumptions underlying strength theory thus imply that (1) that the zROC is linear, and (2) the zROC has a slope of 1.0. The linearity of the zROC results from the target and lure distributions being normally distributed. Other distributions would often imply differently shaped zROC functions (although, in practice, these shapes may not differ substantially from the ROC predicted by the normal distribution).

Studies of recognition memory have found that the zROC curves are approximately linear but have slopes that are consistently less than 1.0 (between 0.5 and 0.9 in most studies) (Glanzer, Kim, Hilford, and Adams, 1999; Koppell, 1977; Ratcliff, McKoon, and Tindall, 1994; Yonelinas, 1997; Pratte, Rouder, and Morey, 2010). This can be seen in the zROC curve shown in Figure 2.4B. The slope of the zROC reflects the ratio of the standard deviations of the lure and the target strength distributions. If the standard deviations are equal, as in the example provided above, the slope will be 1.0. If the standard deviation of the target strength distribution is larger than that of the lure strength distribution, then the slope will be smaller than 1.0, as found in the data. A slope of approximately 0.8, as observed in many experiments, implies that the variability of the target strength distribution is 25% larger than that of the lure strength distribution (Glanzer et al., 1999; Ratcliff et al., 1994).

Our theoretically motivated measure of sensitivity, d', can be expressed in terms of z-values. We first determine the position of the threshold relative to both the target and lure distributions. For example, if the false-alarm rate is 0.025, then the threshold will be two standard deviations above the mean of the lure distribution. If the hit rate is 0.84, then the threshold will be 1 standard deviation below the mean of the target distribution. (The values given above were determined by calculating the area of a normal distribution function that lies above a given threshold value.) Because there is only a single threshold that determines both the hit rate and the false-alarm rate, we know that the mean of the target distribution is three standard deviations above the mean of the lure distribution, and therefore the d' value is 3.0. More generally, for a given hit rate and false-alarm rate, the value of d' can be calculated using the equation: $d' = z(\text{hit rate}) - z(\text{false-alarm rate})$.[2] In using this formula, it is important to keep in mind that the z-scores calculated for hits and false alarms are based on a common reference distribution, not the separate distributions of targets and lures described above. In this case, $z(0.84) \approx 1$ and $z(0.025) \approx -2$, so $d' = 1 - (-2) = 3$.

The analysis presented above shows the predictions of strength theory for the relation between hit rate and false-alarm rate, as shown in the ROC and zROC curves. The shapes of these curves, in turn, reflect the shapes of the target and lure distributions. In this case, one aspect of the theory, the linearity of the zROC, is borne out in the data. But another is not: namely, the slope of the zROC. In the next section we consider some simple extensions of the simplified version of strength theory presented above.

2.1.2 Extensions and Generalizations

In our discussion of strength theory up to this point, we have made a number of unrealistic simplifying assumptions. Let us begin by considering one of these assumptions; namely, that a single study trial produces a constant increment in the strength of a studied item. Even the earliest investigations of memory by Ebbinghaus affirmed our everyday impression that attention fluctuates and that some items are easier to learn than others. Such fluctuations in attention

---

2. Although d' is a commonly used method for measuring accuracy in recognition experiments, it is important to recognize that it is based on the assumptions of strength theory as described above. Another commonly used method that does not rely on such strong (parametric) assumptions is the A or A' statistic, which measures the area under the ROC curve (Zhang and Mueller, 2005).

or in mnemonic strategy will produce variability that can be unique to a given item and to a given person. Within the framework of strength theory, it is easy to incorporate this notion of variability in goodness-of-encoding by allowing the magnitude of the increment associated with a single study trial, a, to vary across people, items, and trials (Hilford, Glanzer, Kim, and DeCarlo, 2002). Specifically, we can define a as a normally distributed random variable with mean μ_a and standard deviation σ_a (see Box 2.2).

We should take note of another simplifying assumption made in our earlier description of strength theory; namely, that the threshold used to determine whether an item is a target or a lure (C) was assumed to be unchanging from trial to trial. Although a given person may demand more or less familiarity to say *yes* to a target, the threshold value was fixed for a given person under a given set of experimental conditions. Also, we never specified how that threshold was set. Presumably, people have some control over the threshold value. They will increase it if they want to avoid making false alarms and decrease it if they want to avoid committing misses. It seems desirable, therefore, to allow the threshold to vary from trial to trial. If the threshold fluctuates randomly around some average value, then its value on a given trial could be drawn from a normal distribution with mean μ_C and standard deviation σ_C. One could easily envision more complex processes governing trial-to-trial threshold variability, but such processes are beyond the scope of the present treatment.

In allowing for variability in encoding and in the response threshold, we have replaced two parameters, a and C, with four parameters, μ_a, σ_a, μ_C, and σ_C. Each of these parameters could be set in order to achieve a good fit between the model and the data. At this point, it would serve us well to ask whether this added flexibility will enable strength theory to explain aspects of the data that could not be explained by the simpler variant described above.

We previously noted that the slope of the zROC tells us something about the relative variability of the target- and lure-strength distributions shown in Figure 2.2. Specifically, the empirical finding that the slope of the zROC is less than 1.0 implies that the variability of the target-strength distribution is greater than the variability of the lure-strength distribution. This would be a natural consequence of making the encoding parameter, a, a random variable. As an analogy, imagine a marathon in which each runner starts at a slightly different time, with the first runner starting 1 minute before the last runner. If the runners are all going at the same pace, they will all finish within a span of 1 minute. If, however, some runners are faster than others, the time range between the front runner and the one finishing last will likely be more than 1 minute (assuming that the speed of the runners is independent of their starting position). The greater the variability in running speeds, the greater the spread in finishing times. In the case of memory strength, the greater the variability in the encoding parameter, the greater the spread in the strengths of the studied items.

As a further extension of strength theory, let us reconsider our learning rule. We assumed that the first repetition of an item would act in the same manner as the hundredth repetition; in each case, the repetition would increment strength by a. One can ask whether this assumption is valid and, more to the point, whether it provides a good fit to experimental findings on the effects of repetition. Research on this issue has led to the development of alternative learning rules that provide a better description of the empirical data. One such learning rule, first proposed by Hull (1943), assumes that items can have a maximum strength of S_{max}, and that the amount of strength added on a given repetition is a fraction of the difference between the current strength and the maximum strength. That is, the strength increment is given by: $\alpha(S_{max} - S_i)$, where α is a learning rate parameter that can range from 0 to 1 and that varies from item to item, from trial to trial, and from person to person, as described above.

2.2 MULTIPLE SOURCES OF STRENGTH?

Strength theory traditionally assumes that the past history of an item's occurrence is represented by a single number—its strength. Another possibility is that several sources of information contribute to decisions about an item's previous occurrence and that these sources are somehow combined in coming up with a response (Banks, 2000). Here we will consider extensions of strength theory based on the idea that two or more dimensions of evidence contribute jointly to recognition decisions (Arndt and Reder, 2002; Onyper, Zhang, and Howard, 2010; Yonelinas, 2001; Rotello, Macmillan, and Reeder, 2004; Murdock, 2006; Wixted and Stretch, 2004). For example, in addition to assessing an item's familiarity, people may recall specific details of the item's presentation (Atkinson and Juola, 1974; Mandler, 1980). Perhaps studying the word *tree* prompted a vivid memory of a treehouse the person built as a child. When asked to judge if the word *tree* was on the list, the person, remembering having thought about their treehouse during the list presentation, is likely to say "yes."

2.2.1 The Yonelinas Familiarity-Recollection Model

Here we consider a specific two-dimensional account of recognition memory that was developed by Yonelinas (1994, 1997). The Yonelinas model assumes that when making recognition judgments, people can respond based on two distinct sources of evidence: one of these sources gives rise to a feeling of *familiarity* with an item, whereas the other source of evidence leads to the experience of *recollection*. The evidence that gives rise to a feeling of familiarity operates just like the simple version of strength theory described above. The evidence that gives rise to the experience of recollection is assumed to be all-or-none. That is, at the time of test you either recall specific details (contextual information) about the probe (with probability R, for recollection) or you do not (with probability $1 - R$). If an item is recollected, the participant will say *yes* regardless of the familiarity signal. Recollection trumps familiarity. If the item is not recollected, the participants will rely on familiarity, as specified by strength theory. This assumption implies that people can only recollect items that were studied (targets). However, the data show that people occasionally report recollecting items that they have not studied (lures) (Donaldson, 1996; Wixted and Stretch, 2004).

According to the Yonelinas model, the probabilities of responding *yes* to a target or lure are given by the equations:

$$P(\text{yes}|\text{target}) = R + (1 - R)F_{\text{target}}$$

$$P(\text{yes}|\text{lure}) = F_{\text{lure}},$$

where F_{target} and F_{lure} represent the probabilities of responding *yes* to targets and lures based on the familiarity signal and R is the probability of recollecting specific details about the item's encoding (see Box 2.1 to review the concept of conditional probability).

The assumption that people use multiple sources of evidence in making recognition decisions is just one aspect of the Yonelinas model. The model makes several additional, more specific assumptions. Most importantly, it assumes that recollection is an all-or-none process. According to the Yonelinas model, people either successfully retrieve specific details (i.e., contextual information) about an item's prior occurrence or they do not—there are no intermediate states of recollection. The model further assumes that when contextual information is retrieved (i.e., the item is recollected), participants will give a *yes* response regardless of the familiarity signal. Thus, another important assumption of the model is that people can selectively respond based on one or the other source of information and that they do so in a particular way, first checking to see if contextual information was retrieved and, if not, then consulting the familiarity signal.

The key differences between the Yonelinas model and traditional versions of strength theory lie in these additional assumptions. The predictions of traditional, *unidimensional* strength theory would look the same as an elaborated version with multiple sources of evidence so long as (a) those sources of evidence were all continuous (or nearly so) and (b) the sources combine prior to participants making a recognition decision.

2.2.2 The Variable-Recollection Model

The Yonelinas model of recollection assumes that any retrieval of source information (recollection) will trump the familiarity signal and lead people to say *yes* to a test item. Although the model does not make explicit assumptions about how recollective information is distributed (i.e., whether there are varying degrees of recollection), the assumption that recollection always trumps familiarity suggests that the participants treat even the weakest evidence from recollection as outweighing the evidence generated by the familiarity signal. As such, the recollection signal (when it is generated) acts as if it had an infinite strength value.

An alternative formulation, known as the variable-recollection model (e.g., Onyper et al., 2010; Kelley and Wixted, 2001), explicitly models recollection as a graded source of information, much like familiarity. The difference between recollection and familiarity in this model is that whereas every occurrence of a test item generates a familiarity signal drawn from a given distribution, recollection sometimes fails, resulting in a signal with zero strength. When it succeeds, recollection gives rise to a strength value drawn from a normal distribution. Figure 2.5 illustrates the strength distributions according to the variable-recollection model.

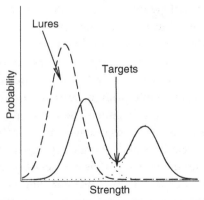

Figure 2.5 Variable-recollection model. Strength distributions for targets and lures. Note that the target distribution has two peaks: the peak centered at a lower-strength value primarily represents the familiarity signal, when recollection does not succeed; the peak centered at a higher-strength value primarily represents the recollection signal, when recollection does succeed. When a studied item is not recollected, it contributes zero strength.

2.2.3 ROC Predictions

The familiarity component of the Yonelinas model operates as a simple version of strength theory, with each presentation of an item producing a constant increment in strength. Thus, if the recollection component were absent, the Yonelinas model would predict a linear zROC with a slope of 1.0. Adding the recollection component will shift the (HR = 0, FAR = 0) point on the ROC up to (HR = R, FAR = 0). This is because the model assumes that only targets will be recollected (with probability R). This shift in the ROC will cause the zROC to curve slightly upward ("concave up") and will cause its slope to decrease. This is because for $R > 0$ the z-transformed hit rate approaches a contant value, $z(R)$, as the z-transformed false-alarm rate approaches negative infinity. Thus, the Yonelinas model predicts that the zROC will be non linear (concave up) and that the slope of the best fitting line to the non linear zROC will be less than 1. Both the nonlinearity of the predicted zROC and its reduced slope result from the hypothesized recollection process, which adds variability in the degree to which target items are learned (the increased variability arises because some target items are recollected whereas others are not). If one could selectively "knock out" the recollection process, the Yonelinas model would give rise to linear zROCs with slopes equal to 1.0.

Yonelinas has argued that patients with a disorder known as *anterograde amnesia* may suffer from a selective deficit in their ability to recollect specific details of a previously experienced episode. Anterograde amnesia most often results when the medial temporal lobe of the brain (including the hippocampus) has been damaged (see Figure 1.9). These patients often have intact memory for experiences that took place prior to their injury, but have considerable difficulty learning new information. In the most severe cases, these patients are unable to learn any new associations and rely extensively on lists to manage basic aspects of daily life. Such severe cases of amnesia have been the topic of films such as *Memento*. Patients with anterograde amnesia usually have great difficulties with recall but more mild impairments in recognition. Because the recollection component is a recall-like process, one might expect these patients to perform recognition based entirely on familiarity. Yonelinas has demonstrated that such patients exhibit zROC curves with slopes that are close to 1.0, consistent with the Yonelinas dual-process theory (Yonelinas, Kroll, Dobbins, Lazzara, and Knight, 1998).

These striking results are also consistent with the traditional unidimensional strength theory presented earlier in this chapter. According to strength theory, the slope of the zROC is predicted to vary as a function of the standard deviation of the learning parameter across items. If some items are better learned than others, then strength theory would predict that the slope of the zROC is less than 1, as observed in healthy individuals. If, however, all items receive an approximately constant strength increment, then the slope of the zROC should be approximately equal to 1 (see Wixted, 2007). Moreover, Glanzer et al. (1999) reported that for weakly encoded items, the slope of the zROC is close to 1, whereas for better encoded items, the slope of the zROC is significantly less than 1. Thus, the findings observed in amnesia are potentially consistent with both formulations of strength theory: the traditional unidimensional model with variable encoding and the Yonelinas familiarity-recollection model.

One can ask whether the observed ROC data can be fit equally well by the three models we have discussed—the Yonelinas familiarity-recollection model, the variable-recollection model, and the extended version of strength theory. Each of the three models can approximate the basic form of the ROC and zROC functions, but they differ in their predictions regarding precise shape of the curve. As such, very precise data are needed to distinguish among these models.

Onyper et al. (2010) reported extensive data comparing ROCs (and zROCs) for both words and pictures. They had 220 participants each study six lists of 64 items each consisting of either travel pictures or five to eight letter nouns. Figure 2.6 shows the zROC average curves for the words

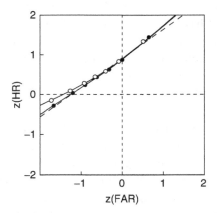

Figure 2.6 Fitting the variable-recollection model to zROCs for pictures and words. z-transformed ROC curves are shown for words (filled circles) and pictures of travel scenes (open circles). Data are from Onyper et al. (2010). The dashed line shows the best linear fit to the zROCs; the solid curves show the fits of the variable recollection model to the word and picture data.

(filled circles) and for the pictures (open circles). The zROC for the words was nearly linear—the light gray line shows the results of a linear regression to the word data (slope $= .73 \pm .02$). However, the zROC for the pictures diverges from linearity at the more conservative criteria (leftmost points in the figure). Onyper et al. (2010) found that for words, traditional strength theory provided a better fit than the Yonelinas familiarity-recollection model. However, for pictures, the Yonelinas model provided a much better fit than traditional strength theory. The variable-recollection model, however, provided a significantly better fit to both data sets than either strength theory or the Yonelinas model.

2.2.4 Remember-Know Judgments

Tulving (1985) suggested that people are aware of whether or not their recognition judgments are based on the recollection of specific details. He therefore modified the standard item-recognition task by asking people to classify probe items into three categories: (1) items they remember studying on the list (*remember*, or R judgments); (2) items that seem so familiar they "know" were on the list even though they can't remember the act of studying the item (*know*, or K judgments); and (3) items that were not on the list (*new*, or N judgments).

The version of the recognition task described above, which is often called the *RK procedure*, has been used to provide evidence for the two-dimensional models, such as the Yonelinas model. If there are two processes, it should be possible to create conditions that will *selectively influence* R and K judgments.

Consistent with the two-component models of recognition, researchers have identified conditions that have different effects on the percentages of R and K responses. For example, Gardiner and Java (1991) reported an experiment in which forgetting was assessed over a six-month period. Analyzing the recognition data in terms of R and K responses, they found that R responses declined at a significantly faster rate than K responses. In another experiment, Gregg and Gardiner (1994) had participants study words that appeared on a computer screen for a brief duration. Later they were given a recognition test in which the studied words were either presented visually (as at study) or auditorily. In both test conditions, participants gave R responses to approximately 10% of targets. In contrast, participants gave K responses to 52% of the targets in the visual-test condition but gave K responses to only 27% of the targets in the auditory-test condition. In this study, the consistent use of visual presentation at both study and test selectively increased K responses while leaving R responses unaffected. The observations of variables that selectively influence either R or K responses, as in these and other studies, led Gardiner and colleagues to conclude that R and K responses reflect distinct types of information.

Although findings of selective influence are neatly accounted for within a two-component model, such results do not necessarily contradict a one-component model. From a unidimensional-strength-theory perspective, RK judgments can be viewed as reflecting confidence, with people saying R when the familiarity exceeds a high threshold and K when it exceeds a lower threshold. Dunn (2004) presented a detailed analysis of data obtained by using the RK procedure and found that a unidimensional-strength model could provide a good overall fit to data from numerous examples of selective influence reported in the literature.

It is tempting to relate data from the RK procedure with data obtained using ROC analyses. One basic question that one can ask is whether the contribution of recollection to the ROC as derived from the Yonelinas model (i.e., the estimated hit rate when the false-alarm rate is zero) matches the rate of R responses obtained in the same experiment. Several researchers have investigated this issue and found that the proportion of R responses is often significantly larger than would be predicted from the Yonelinas analysis of the ROC. This finding could be taken as evidence that the Yonelinas model misestimates the contribution of recollection due to some error in its assumptions. Or it could mean that participants are unable to perfectly gauge whether their responses are being generated purely on the basis of recollection—that is, they may say R even when they have not actually recovered source information.

By calculating the hit rate and false-alarm rate for both R and K responses, one can generate two points along an ROC curve. As noted above, the false-alarm rate for R responses will tend to be significantly greater than zero and the overall proportion of R responses will be greater than expected according to the ROC derived from confidence judgments. Similarly, the slope of the zROC obtained using the RK procedure is often different from the slope obtained using the confidence judgment procedure (Rotello et al., 2004).

Assuming that people can access different sources of evidence in making their recognition judgments, it is possible that R-K judgments and target-lure (or confidence) judgments may reflect different weighting or combinations of these sources of evidence. For example, R-K judgments may be more sensitive to one source of evidence, and target-lure judgments may be more sensitive to another source of evidence. If the sources of evidence are recollection and familiarity, then we might hypothesize that R-K judgments largely reflect the ability to retrieve source information, whereas target-lure judgments may be weighted more toward the familiarity signal. Rotello et al. (2004) have proposed that people provide R responses when the recollection signal exceeds the familiarity signal by a certain amount. That is, when recollection is higher than familiarity, people will tend to say *remember* and when familiarity is higher than recollection they will tend to say *know*. According to this view, people have two ways of knowing that an item was on the list and their judgment reflects the degree to which the evidence favors the R source over the K source. In contrast, target-lure judgments reflect the summation of these two sources of evidence: the greater the evidence from either source, the more likely people will say that they have seen the item on the list.

2.2.5 Interim Summary

We have seen how several different theories of recognition memory make testable predictions regarding the way hit rates and false-alarm rates vary as a function of threshold (i.e., shape of the ROC). Our initial version of strength theory assumed that memorial representations varied in strength, with this variation characterized by a normal, or Gaussian, distribution. Studying an item would increase the strength of its representation in memory by a constant amount. When tested on a probe item, the model generates a *yes* response when the retrieved strength of that probe (be it a target or a lure) exceeds a threshold. This version of strength theory posits that the standard deviations of the strength distributions for targets and lures are equal and the predicted ROC curve is thus curvilinear and symmetric. The predicted zROC function is linear with a slope of 1.0. As we have seen, the data can easily reject this model because the zROC slopes, though typically linear, almost always have slopes that are significantly less than 1.0 (e.g., Figure 2.4).

Straightforward modifications of this *equal-variance* strength theory allow for the variability of the target and lure distributions to differ. Specifically, if studying an item increases its strength by a variable amount, then the target strength distribution should have a larger standard deviation than the lure strength distribution and the zROC should be linear with a slope less than 1. This unequal variance strength model is able to fit the ROC and zROC data quite well (Heathcote, 2003).

Although researchers have often described strength in these models as a unidimensional (scalar) quantity, it is also possible that strength reflects a combination of evidence drawn from various sources. The key point, however, is that these sources combine to generate a scalar strength value and this strength value in turn drives the decision process (e.g., Wixted, 2007a). A different class of multidimensional strength models assumes that people have access to multiple sources of evidence in making recognition decisions and that they can respond differently based on these different sources of evidence (e.g., Parks and Yonelinas, 2007). Although one could envision many different kinds of evidence, the major theory of this kind assumes that the two primary sources of evidence are recollection and familiarity (Yonelinas, 1994). According to this account, recollection is said to occur when people retrieve specific details regarding the source of an item's occurrence, such as the study modality (e.g., whether it was seen or heard), the surrounding mental context (Schwartz, Howard, Jing, and Kahana, 2005), or other thoughts that the item evoked at the time of study (Hall, Sekuler, and Cushman, 1969). Familiarity reflects other sources of evidence that indicate the memorial status of an item but do not include specific source information (Rugg and Curran, 2007). In addition to assuming that people can respond separately on the basis of these two types of evidence, familiarity-recollection models also assume that recollection is a threshold process that either succeeds or fails. When it fails, no source information is retrieved. When it succeeds, some amount of source information is retrieved.

We discussed two specific models based on the familiarity-recollection distinction. The Yonelinas model assumed that people always respond *yes* when they recover some source information regardless of the item's familiarity. The variable-recollection model assumed that source information provides a variable strength signal and that people give a *yes* response when the sum of the familiarity and recollection signals exceeds a threshold.

Much research has compared the ROC predictions of the unidimensional, unequal variance strength theory and the Yonelinas familiarity-recollection model. Although both models provide quite good fits to the ROC (and zROC) curves, the unequal variance strength theory often provides a fit that is numerically superior to the Yonelinas model (Heathcote, 2003; Wixted, 2007a, 2007b) (but see, Parks and Yonelinas, 2007, for an alternative view). The slight advantage that unidimensional strength theory has in predicting the ROC curves disappears when one considers the two-dimensional variable-recollection model. That model has been shown to provide significantly better fits to the ROCs than either the unidimensional, unequal variance strength theory or the Yonelinas model. This success is partially explained by its additional flexibility: the variable-recollection model has more parameters than either of the other two models and therefore it has greater flexibility in fitting data.

Given that all three major models can generate reasonable approximations to the ROC curves obtained in item recognition, it is clear that we need to explore other aspects of the data on recognition memory if we are to arrive at a clearer understanding of its underlying processes. In the next section we consider several major findings concerning item recognition and discuss these findings in light of the theoretical issues raised in the preceding sections.

2.3 MAJOR FINDINGS CONCERNING ITEM RECOGNITION

Recognition memory, like most other memory tasks, exhibits both repetition and recency effects. The more times an item has been presented on a study list, the more likely people are to say *yes* when asked to judge whether that item was studied. The hit rate for an item thus increases with the number of times the item has been studied. People also respond more quickly to repeated items (see Murdock, 1982; Hockley, 2008, for a review).

Recently studied items exhibit higher hit rates and shorter RTs than items that have not been recently studied (Murdock and Anderson, 1975). Related to the recency effect is the list-length effect. The list-length effect in recognition memory was first reported by Strong (1912), who examined people's recognition memory for magazine ads. Not surprisingly, Strong found that with longer lists, people made fewer hits and more false alarms. Thus, the more ads people were asked to remember, the worse their memory was for each of the studied ads. One may be able to explain the list-length effect as simply being a manifestation of the recency effect. Because the number of ads intervening between study and test (the study-test lag) will be greater, on average, for a long list than for a short list, one would expect worse memory for longer lists.

There would not be much interest in the list-length effect as a distinct phenomenon if it were entirely a consequence of differences in average recency. However, it is possible that long lists are harder to remember even when recency is held constant. One can address this issue by looking at the effect of the number of prior list items on memory for a given item (holding the number of subsequent list items constant). With recall tasks, such studies consistently find that adding prior items degrades performance. Thus, the list-length effect in recall is not entirely a consequence of differences in item recency. In the case of recognition memory, however, studies that have controlled for the effect of recency have not generally found significant list-length effects (Dennis and Humphreys, 2001; Ohrt and Gronlund, 1999; Goshen-Gottstein and Steinberg, 2005). When list-length effects have been found, they have generally been quite small in magnitude (Murdock and Kahana, 1993b).

The preceding discussion of list-length and recency effects has been based on studies of recognition memory that used relatively long lists. If one examines recency and list-length effects in very short lists, the patterns can be quite different. We will discuss these data in section 2.4.3.

2.3.1 The Word-frequency Effect

The frequency with which a word occurs in the English language is a reliable predictor of recognition-memory performance for that word. Recognizable, low-frequency (rare) words are easier to correctly identify as having been presented in a study list than high-frequency (common) words (Gorman, 1961). If presented with a list of words, some of which are common such as "river" and "water" and some of which are less common such as "fjord" and "jelly," people tend to make fewer false alarms to rare words than to common words (e.g., they are more likely to say "yes" to "water" than to "fjord" if neither was presented on the list). People also tend to commit more hits for rare words than for common words (e.g., they are more likely to say yes to "jelly" than to "water" if both were presented on the list).

As shown in Figure 2.7, and initially reported by Glanzer and colleagues (Glanzer and Bowles, 1976; Glanzer, Adams, Iverson, and Kim, 1993), low-frequency words have both higher hit rates and lower false-alarm rates than do high-frequency words. Glanzer and colleagues have referred to the finding that word frequency has opposite effects on hit rate and false-alarm rate as the *mirror effect*. This effect is not only seen for word frequency but is found for other characteristics of stimuli that make them easier or harder to remember (Hockley, 1996). In recognition memory, the word-frequency effect is extremely robust. It is observed both in accuracy and in RT measures (Figure 2.7) and is seen at all levels of confidence (Figure 2.8).[3]

One may ask whether the enhanced recognition of low-frequency words can be accommodated within the general framework of a strength theory of recognition memory. It is reasonable to begin by assuming that common words are more familiar than rare words before the start of the experiment. Assuming that studying rare and common words leads to an equivalent increase in strength (a), strength theory predicts that people would commit more false alarms and hits to common words (Figure 2.9A). Although the data support the predictions regarding false alarms, they contradict the predictions concerning hits. As shown in Figure 2.7, the hit rate *decreases*, rather than increases, with word frequency.

To explain this counterintuitive pattern of results, researchers have hypothesized that participants encode more information for low-frequency

---

3. In some other memory tasks, such as free recall, word frequency has the opposite effect, with people recalling more items from lists composed of high-frequency words than from lists composed of low-frequency words (Kintsch, 1970). The advantage found for recall of common words is less robust than the advantage found for recognition of rare words. The common-word-recall advantage depends on the lists being composed of either all common or all rare words. When the lists comprise a mixture of rare and common words, word frequency typically has no effect on recall (Gillund and Shiffrin, 1984; Watkins, LeCompte, and Kim, 2000).

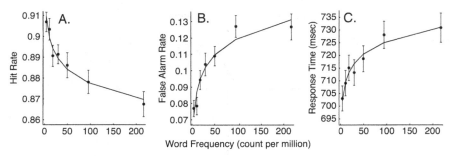

Figure 2.7 **The word-frequency effect.** Hit rate, false-alarm rate, and mean RT as a function of word frequency. Word frequency is measured as the number of times a given word occurred in a sample of approximately 1 million words taken from a wide range of books, periodicals, and newspaper articles. Data from an unpublished senior honors thesis (G. W. Schwartz, Howard, and Kahana, 2004).

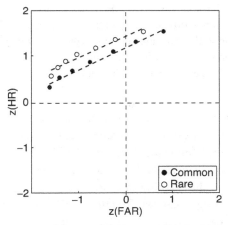

Figure 2.8 **zROCs partitioned by word frequency.** Studied words were sorted based on word frequency. Filled circles indicate common words (mean frequency = 219 occurrences per million words); open circles indicate rare words (mean frequency = 4 occurrences per million). Data from a class experiment.

words than for high-frequency words—perhaps because rare words attract greater attention than common words (Malmberg and Nelson, 2003; Rao and Proctor, 1984). Even in infancy, our attention and interest are drawn to novel items (Fantz, 1964; Fagan, 1970), and one can measure changes in brain activity for novel items just a few hundred milliseconds after the item has been displayed (Reynolds and Richards, 2005).

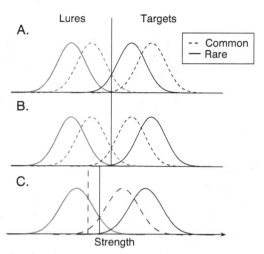

Figure 2.9 Strength theory and word frequency. A. Strength distributions of rare and common targets and lures, under the assumption that common words start out with higher strength values, on average. **B.** Strength distributions under the assumption that rare and common words also differ in their learning rate. **C.** Strength distributions under the assumption that rare and common words only differ in their learning rate, but that people can vary their decision thresholds as a function of word frequency. Dashed and solid lines indicate thresholds for common and rare words, respectively.

❧

We can implement this *elevated-attention* account of the word-frequency effect by adding a larger strength increment following the study of a low-frequency word than following the study of a high-frequency word. That is, we can allow the learning increment to be a decreasing function of word frequency. If the difference in the learning increase is large enough, then the distribution of low-frequency targets can leapfrog the distribution of high-frequency targets, leading to the situation depicted in Figure 2.9B.

It should be noted that we have used two separate processes to explain the mirror effect within the framework of strength theory. First, we assumed that rare words attract more attention and therefore get a larger strength increment than common words. Second, we assumed that low-frequency words have a lower baseline level of familiarity than high-frequency words. This assumption seems reasonable a priori, because common words, as compared with rare words, will have been encountered many more times prior to the start of the experiment and will therefore have a higher strength to start with.

To implement this assumption within strength theory, we assumed that the value of *a* was greater for lower-frequency (rare) words. Hirshman and Arndt (1997) offer some experimental support for this assumption. They reasoned that if the higher hit rate for rare words is a consequence of people naturally giving those words more attention, they could diminish the effect by making people pay more equal attention to all words—both rare and common. To show this, they used a standard technique called an *orienting task*. Rather than simply asking participants to study the words, they asked them to make a judgment about each word, such as rating it in terms of its concreteness (e.g., *hammer*–very concrete; *justice*–not very concrete). Under these conditions, which should reduce the variability in attention paid to words of different frequencies, the hit-rate advantage for rare words was significantly reduced. Criss and Shiffrin (2004) replicated these results using a wide range of orienting tasks. In every case, encoding words in a controlled manner reduced the hit-rate advantage for rare words but had no effect on the high false-alarm rates for common words.

One may ask whether these two assumptions are both required to account for the high false-alarm rate and low hit rate observed for common words. Suppose, for example, that only the first assumption (elevated attention) proves to be correct. In this case, we could still obtain the mirror effect if people adjusted their threshold based on the word frequency of a given item. As illustrated in Figure 2.9C, participants can set a high threshold for saying *yes* to a low-frequency word because they want to strike a balance between increasing their hit rate and lowering their false-alarm rate. There is evidence that people are able to make such trial-by-trial adjustments to their thresholds (e.g., Brown, Lewis, and Monk, 1977; Hirshman, 1995; Han and Dobbins, 2008, but see Stretch and Wixted, 1998, for an opposing view).

A critical problem for this account comes from studies of forced-choice recognition. In a forced-choice recognition task, participants are asked which of two items was previously studied. As expected based on the word-frequency effect, participants are more likely to correctly endorse rare targets as having been previously studied and they are also more likely to incorrectly endorse common lures. Consider, however, the case where participants are asked to choose which of two *lures* appeared on the list. In this case, people tend to endorse the common lure as having been studied. Because this task requires a discrimination between two lures rather than between targets and lures, the finding that people reliably endorse the more common lures implies the existence of separate distributions for high- and low-frequency lures (Glanzer and Bowles, 1976; Glanzer et al., 1993).

2.3.2 The RT–Distance Relation

As a general principle, manipulations that increase the accuracy of memory judgments also tend to produce shorter RTs (Kahana and Loftus, 1999; Hockley, 2008). This point is illustrated in the word-frequency-effect data

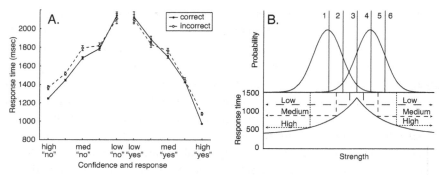

Figure 2.10 Response time as a function of confidence: data and theory. A. Mean RT, in milliseconds, is shortest for high-confidence responses and longest for low-confidence responses. This is shown for both correct *yes* responses (hits) and correct *no* responses (correct rejections) indicated by solid line, and for incorrect yes and no responses, indicated by dashed line. Analysis reported by Murdock and Dufty (1972) applied to an unpublished study from my laboratory. **B.** Predicted RTs for responses that vary in confidence according to strength theory and the RT-distance relation.

shown in Figure 2.7C, where faster responses go along with higher hit rates and lower false-alarm rates. RTs are also highly correlated with confidence; people tend to make high-confidence judgments more quickly than low-confidence judgments. In general, the more confident you are, the faster you will respond.

This RT-confidence relation is shown in Figure 2.10, where mean RT is plotted as a function of confidence for correct *yes* and correct *no* responses. If we translate this relation into the basic tenets of strength theory, it implies that RT decreases as we get further away from the recognition threshold (because we are more sure of both *yes* and *no* responses as we move away from the threshold). The finding that RT increases monotonically as the threshold is approached from either direction has been termed the *RT-distance relation* (Koppell, 1977; Murdock and Anderson, 1975). This idea is illustrated in Figure 2.10B, which shows hypothetical RT functions decreasing exponentially as one moves away from the strength threshold separating yes and no responses. Strength values associated with individual confidence responses can then be mapped onto RT values. For example, items whose strengths would lead to a highest-confidence yes response (response category 6 in the example) would have faster RTs, on average, than items whose strengths would lead to a moderate-confidence yes response.

Murdock (1985) showed that by incorporating the RT-distance relation into strength theory, one can account for many of the RT findings obtained in recognition-memory experiments. For example, there are consistent differences

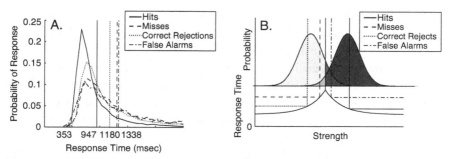

Figure 2.11 Response time for hits, false alarms, correct rejections, and misses.
A. Response time histograms, which are shown for each of the four response types, exhibit a characteristic asymmetry, often described as a "fat tail." The vertical line on each plot indicates the mean response time, which is usually shorter for correct responses than for errors. **B.** Predicted RTs for each response type according to strength theory and the RT-distance relation.

between RTs for hits, misses, false alarms, and correct rejections. RTs tend to be fastest for hits and correct rejections, and slowest for false alarms and misses. Figure 2.11A shows the RT distributions for each of these response types. Unlike the normal distribution that is symmetric around its mean, the RT distributions shown in 2.11A are skewed to the right, with a "fat tail" indicating a large spread among the slower RTs. Both the overall skew in the RT distributions and the finding of generally slower RTs for errors (false alarms and misses) follow from the RT-distance hypothesis. As illustrated in 2.11B, errors tend to occur when strength is near the decision threshold separating yes and no responses. In contrast, correct responses tend to occur when strength is far away from the decision threshold.

2.3.3 The SAT Function

When we increase the difficulty of a memory task, people tend to respond more slowly. If people can exert some control over the time they invest in their memory judgments, it stands to reason that people can compromise speed to achieve greater accuracy or vice versa. The function relating speed to accuracy is called a *speed-accuracy trade-off* (SAT) function. Consider, for example, the task of typing. If you try to type very quickly, you are likely to make many more errors than if you type very slowly. Similarly, in a recognition-memory experiment, if you try to respond as fast as possible, you are likely to make more misses and false alarms.

Schoutten and Bekker (1967) introduced an experimental technique to study the SAT function. In this technique, called the *response signal procedure*

(RSP), people are trained to respond *yes* or *no* to the test item as soon as a signal is given. A SAT function is constructed by varying the onset time of the response signal. At the very shortest delays, the person's response is essentially a guess; the information needed to make a correct response has not become available. As the signal delay increases, the person has more time, and presumably more information about the item's familiarity becomes available. Performance increases with the time of the response signal until it reaches some constant (asymptotic) value.

Figure 2.12A shows an SAT function determined by means of the RSP. These data come from a study by McElree and Dosher (1989), who had participants perform a recognition-memory task with short lists consisting of either four or six items. One can see that accuracy, as measured by d' (see section 2.1), begins to increase rapidly at around 300 ms, until it approaches a maximal value of about 4.3 for the shorter lists and 3.5 for the longer lists. Empirical SAT curves, such as those reported by McElree and Dosher, are often well fit by the equation $d'(t) = d_a'(1 - e^{-(t-T_0)/\tau})$, where d_a' is the asymptotic level of accuracy, T_0 is the time at which d' begins to rise above chance, and τ is the time constant for exponential growth. By fitting this equation to experimental data, researchers can try to identify whether a manipulation selectively influences the time when information first becomes available to the system (T_0), the rate at which information accrues (τ), or the asymptotic level of performance (d_a'). Alternatively, this analysis would reveal whether a manipulation influenced multiple components of the SAT curve.

One can see in Figure 2.12A that even though participants were faster and more accurate in responding to test items from short lists (as compared to longer lists), there was no significant difference in the time at which information first became available (the parameter T_0 in the equation above). A similar finding is observed when comparing the SAT functions for once- and twice-presented items (Figure 2.12B). Both SAT curves begin to rise at nearly the same time, but the SAT curve rises to a higher asymptotic level for the twice-presented items (Hintzman, Caulton, and Levitin, 1998). In general, researchers use the RSP to determine whether differences in accuracy also appear as differences in either the time when information first becomes available or the rate at which information accrues (parameters T_0 and τ, respectively).

Given the RSP's ability to characterize the effect of different experimental variables on the shape of the SAT function, it may seem surprising that the approach has not been widely adopted by memory researchers. There are several reasons for this. At a methodological level, the RSP is not an easy task. Considerable practice is required to ensure that participants respond almost immediately after the onset of the response signal. One of the hardest aspects of this task is withholding a correct response until the signal appears. Some people

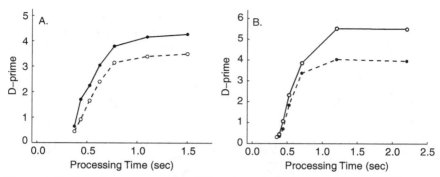

Figure 2.12 Speed-accuracy trade-off functions. A. Performance (measured by D-prime) increases with processing time (in seconds) for list lengths of four items (solid line) and six items (dashed line). Data from McElree and Dosher (1989). **B.** In item recognition, accuracy is greater for items that appeared twice (solid line) than items that appeared once (dashed line), but the accumulation of information does not begin significantly earlier. Data from Hintzman et al. (1998).

cannot do this, and consequently they must be excluded from participating. There are also conceptual difficulties in making inferences based on data obtained using the RSP. Most importantly, the response signal may alter the way in which information is processed in a given task. Essentially, the RSP turns a single task into a dual task. While participants are busy trying to derive the information needed to make a response, they must be constantly attentive to the response signal. Then, even if they are ready to respond, they must wait until the response signal arrives. This turns a fairly simple task into a relatively complex one, making the task of interest much more difficult to model.

2.4 STERNBERG'S PROCEDURE

As a final topic, we consider a variant of the recognition-memory task introduced by Sternberg (1966). Rather than presenting participants with a long list of items followed by a long series of targets and lures, Sternberg gave his participants very short lists. Following each list, a single test probe was shown, either a target or a lure, and participants had to indicate whether or not the test item was in the list by pressing one of two response levers. As an example of one such list, a participant might study a list of four consonants (B, M, F, and S). After a 1- to 2-sec delay, the participant would judge whether the letter M was in the just-presented list. With short lists, comprising one to six items, practiced participants made very few errors (often less than 3%) and responded rapidly (often in less than half a second).

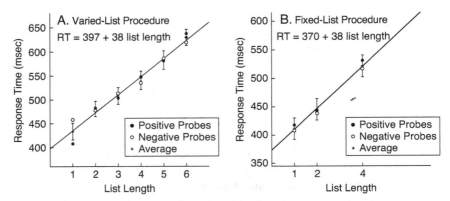

Figure 2.13 Mean response time increases with list length. Sternberg's data show that mean RT increases linearly with list length for targets and lures in both the varied-list (**A**) and the fixed-list (**B**) procedures. See text for details.

Because participants rarely made errors, their response time in judging whether a probe item was a target or a lure indicated how quickly the brain could retrieve the previously stored information. In studying people's response time in this task, Sternberg (1966) found that RTs grew linearly with the length of the studied list. He assessed this using two procedures: in the *varied-list procedure*, lists (of digits) were randomly chosen for each trial and list length varied from trial to trial. In the *fixed-list procedure*, a given list of items was prememorized and then repeatedly tested. This process was repeated for prememorized lists of various lengths. Figure 2.13A shows Sternberg's (1966) results from the varied-list procedure. Figure 2.13B shows nearly identical results from the fixed-list procedure. Three features of these data are striking. First, mean RT increased *linearly* with list length. Second, the slopes of the RT-list length function were virtually identical for targets and lures. Third, nearly equivalent slopes (38 ms/item) were obtained in the fixed-list and the varied-list procedures.

Subsequent studies by Sternberg and other investigators showed that the basic finding that RT increases nearly linearly with list length is true in a wide range of conditions and using many different kinds of materials (e.g., letters, digits, words, random polygons, etc.). The significance of these findings will become clearer when evaluated in light of serial scanning models of the short-term item-recognition task.

2.4.1 Serial Search Models

Sternberg proposed a simple model to account for mean RTs in short-term item recognition. He assumed that the probe item is serially compared with

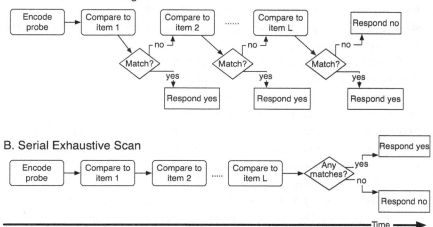

Figure 2.14 Serial search models. The stages of processing according to serial self-terminating (**A**) and serial exhaustive search (**B**) models. Comparison times across items are assumed to be independent random variables.

each of the list items stored in memory (the search set). In a *serial comparison process*, a new comparison does not begin until the previous comparison has been completed. According to Sternberg's model, the time required for each comparison is independent of the number of items in the search set (i.e., the list) and also independent of the position of each item in the search set. This predicts that RTs increase linearly with list length, as each additional item requires one additional comparison and each comparison takes (on average) the same amount of time (Figure 2.14).

Although a serial comparison process predicts a linear relation between response time and list length, it does not necessarily predict equivalent slopes for targets and lures. Consider, for example, what would happen if the memory comparison process is *self-terminating*. The probe item is compared with each stored list item until a match is detected or until all comparisons have been made. This is called a self-terminating search because the comparison process terminates as soon as a match is detected (see Figure 2.14A). Suppose that participants study a list of three items. For a randomly chosen target, there is an equal probability of finding a match after one, two, or three comparisons. On average, two comparisons are required. For a randomly chosen lure, three comparisons are always required, as all three list items must be rejected. What happens if the list length is increased from three to four? A target now requires either one, two, three, or four comparisons, resulting in an average of 2.5 comparisons. A lure requires all four comparisons to be made. Consequently, increasing the list length by one item results in an increase of 1 comparison for lures but only 0.5 comparisons (on average) for targets. Thus, the slope for lures should be twice as great as the slope for targets. As shown in Figure 2.13, this is clearly not the case.

To explain the equivalence of slopes for targets and lures, Sternberg suggested that the serial comparison process is *exhaustive*. An exhaustive search means that the probe item is compared with every list item, and a decision is not made until all comparisons have been completed (see Figure 2.14B). Although this idea may seem unrealistic at first blush, if the comparison process is extremely fast and the decision process is slow, it makes sense to do all the comparisons prior to making a decision rather than making a separate decision after each comparison (Sternberg, 1966).[4]

Sternberg (1969) presented a more complete description of the basic scanning model. The model has four processes, arranged successively in stages: stimulus encoding, memory comparison, decision, and response. The following claim is critical to the analysis of this model: a given process/stage is not initiated until the previous stage is completed. This claim is reasonable if a stage acts on information produced by a preceding stage that must be available in a fairly complete form (Sternberg, 2001). According to the model, the time required to make a comparison can be variable, with the exact value being drawn from a distribution of possible values. The shape of the distribution and its mean and variance are important in generating certain model predictions (e.g., Luce, 1986, chap. 11).

2.4.2 Parallel Search Models

In addition to examining the implications of serial search models, Sternberg (1966) also considered the possibility that the probe could be compared with the stored representations of the studied items in parallel. As with serial search models, a number of assumptions must be made in order to derive the model's implications for the behavioral data. Sternberg assumed that the comparison times could vary across items (as well as across trials and participants) and that the distribution of comparison times was independent across items and independent of the total number of comparisons being made. Given these assumptions, Sternberg considered the implications of both exhaustive and self-terminating variants of this class of parallel search models. In a self-terminating parallel search (illustrated in Figure 2.15A), a response is made as soon as

4. In support of this argument, when participants are asked to make the more difficult judgment of identifying the digit that followed the probe digit in a list, the slope of the RT-list length function is nearly twice as great for lures as it is for targets (Sternberg, 1967).

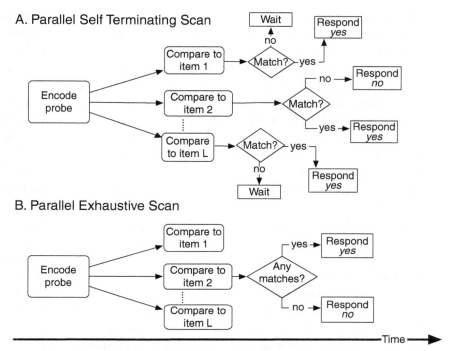

Figure 2.15 Parallel search models. The stages of processing according to parallel self-terminating (**A**) and parallel exhaustive search (**B**) models. Comparison times across items (indicated by the variable widths of each box) are assumed to be independent random variables.

any comparison returns a match. In an exhaustive parallel search (illustrated in Figure 2.15B) a response is only made after all of the comparisons are completed, even though a match may have been found early in the comparison process.

Assuming that exactly one of the studied items matches the test probe, the total comparison time for a self-terminating parallel search should be determined entirely by the distribution of comparison times for the single matching item. The comparison of the probe to other items should not influence the time for the comparison process to be completed, and therefore the mean RT should not increase with the number of studied items, contrary to Sternberg's experimental findings.[5]

5. When the test probe is a lure, however, there is no matching item among the items being compared in memory. Therefore, the process must wait until all of the comparisons are completed before a response can be made. Thus, the mean RT should increase with the number of list items, as in a parallel exhaustive search model.

In the case of an exhaustive parallel search process, a response can only be made once the last comparison has been completed. Thus, the total comparison time will depend on the slowest of the individual comparison times. As the number of comparisons increases, the slowest comparison will also increase on average. This is because there is always some chance that the added comparison will be slower than all of the others. As such, the mean RT is predicted to increase with list length. However, Sternberg showed that this model does not predict a linear increase in the total comparison time with list length. Rather, the rate of increase should slow as the list length increases. Sternberg showed that the negatively accelerated function predicted by this parallel model departs significantly from the data obtained in both the fixed-list and varied-list procedures.

Not all parallel search models give rise to the predictions described above. For example, Murdock (1971) considered a version of the parallel exhaustive search process in which the distribution of comparison times was not independent of the number of comparisons being made. He proposed that each comparison draws on a finite pool of cognitive "resources" and that the greater the fraction of resources available for a given comparison, the faster it will be carried out. As such, increasing the number of comparisons would reduce the resources available to each comparison, thus slowing the time it takes to complete the comparisons. Under certain assumptions, this type of model can mimic both the linear increase in RTs observed in the Sternberg task and the equivalence of slopes for targets and lures. It should be noted, however, that addition of assumptions concerning the way resources are shared and how they influence RTs provides a model with greater flexibility, which allows it to accommodate a larger range of possible data patterns.

2.4.3 Testing the SES Model

According to Sternberg's *serial exhaustive scanning* (SES) model, a response cannot be made until every comparison has been performed (Figure 2.14B). Consequently, the time required to perform the scanning process should be independent of serial position. Contrary to this prediction, people are significantly faster at recognizing recently presented items. Using Sternberg's procedure, significant recency effects are often obtained, but they may be small in magnitude (see McElree and Dosher, 1989; Sternberg, 1975). In one of the clearest cases, Monsell (1978) found substantial recency (i.e., faster and more accurate *yes* responses to recent list items) by presenting either letters (experiment 1) or words (experiment 2) as stimuli. In Monsell's study, the test probe followed the last list item either immediately or after a brief delay. The delay condition required participants to name a vowel presented immediately

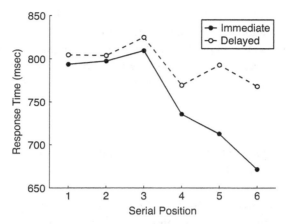

Figure 2.16 Recency and the delay interval. When tested immediately, RTs are much shorter for recent targets than for remote ones. However, this RT-recency effect is greatly reduced when there is a 3.5-sec delay between the end of list presentation and the test probe. Data from Forrin and Cunningham (1973).

after the last list item (this took an average of 500 ms). This was done to prevent participants from *rehearsing* the list items during the delay period. By rehearsal, we mean the strategy of repeating previously presented items, either aloud or quietly, to keep those items in mind until the time of test. In an earlier study, Forrin and Cunningham (1973) showed that increasing the length of an unfilled delay between study and test greatly reduced the recency effect in short-term item recognition (Figure 2.16). In general, experimental conditions that reduce or eliminate rehearsal tend to produce large recency effects, and those that encourage rehearsal yield relatively flat serial-position curves (Sternberg, 1975).

The marked recency effects obtained by Monsell (1978) and Forrin and Cunningham (1973) present a challenge to the SES model. In response to this critique, Sternberg (1975) noted that recency effects could arise outside of the comparison stage of the model. For example, if recently studied targets are *encoded* more quickly, then one would observe recency effects in overall RT even though the comparison process is independent of serial position (for a similar argument in the literature on same–different comparisons, see Proctor, [1981]).

However, if one assumes that a recently studied item will be encoded more quickly, then one might predict that lures that were studied on recent prior lists should be rejected more quickly than lures that have not appeared on any recent lists. This prediction is inconsistent with the data. People have significantly greater difficulty (i.e., they are slower and exhibit more errors) in rejecting lures that have appeared on recent study lists (e.g., Monsell, 1978). Although this finding is difficult to reconcile with Sternberg's SES model, it is exactly what you would predict on the basis of strength theory. This is because lures will have greater familiarity if they are studied on recent lists as compared with remote lists. Owing to their greater familiarity, people will be more likely to incorrectly endorse recent lures as targets, and when they are correctly rejected, people will have longer RTs because these items tend to be closer to the decision boundary.

Another challenge to the SES model comes from studies that examine list-length effects beyond the *span of immediate memory*—the maximum number of items that can be recalled in order from beginning to end on an immediate recall test. Burrows and Okada (1975) used a *prememorized-list* technique to study RTs in an item-recognition task with lists much longer than those used in Sternberg's studies. To achieve nearly errorless performance on long lists, Burrows and Okada gave their participants sufficient training so that they had memorized the list before the probe testing phase began. Figure 2.17 shows that for lists of two to six items, the slope of the best-fitting line was 37 ms per item, replicating the classic Sternberg effect (see Figure 2.13). However, a separate line fit to lists of eight or more items yielded a much shallower slope (13 ms/item). According to the SES model, each additional item in the memory set should result in a constant increase in mean RT for both targets and lures. These data indicate that the increase in mean RT is not a constant and that it varies with list length. This finding can be reconciled with the SES model if we assume that the model only applies to short (subspan) lists. As tempting as it is to interpret these data as reflecting separate search processes for short and long lists, it turns out that a single logarithmic function provides a relatively good fit to the full set of data points in Figure 2.17.

Studies of repetition effects present yet another challenge to the SES model. Baddeley and Ecob (1973) and Young (1979) found that participants were significantly faster in saying *yes* to a target item when it was presented twice in the study list (see Figure 2.18). According to the SES model, however, each item must be scanned before a response can be made, so it should not matter how many times an item is presented in the list. Repetition effects, like the recency effects discussed above, are thus difficult to reconcile within the SES framework. This critique of SES assumes that other stages are not influenced by repetition. It is not unreasonable to suppose that repeated items are encoded more quickly or that the decision process is executed more quickly when two matches have been registered than when only a single match has been registered.

In summary, Sternberg's findings of a linear relation between list length and RT, and of similar slopes for both targets and lures, have been replicated hundreds of times in studies that manipulated dozens of experimental variables.

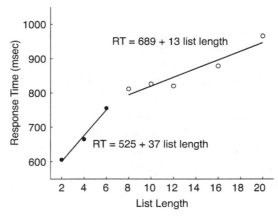

Figure 2.17 The RT-list length relation for subspan and supraspan lists. Separate linear functions are shown for subspan and supraspan list lengths. Data from Burrows and Okada (1975). See text for details.

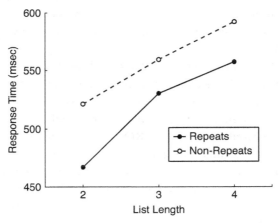

Figure 2.18 Repetition effects in subspan lists. Participants respond more quickly when probe items are presented twice (repeated) in the study list. Mean latencies for correct responses to lists both with and without repeated items are plotted as a function of the number of items in the list. Data from Baddeley and Ecob (1973) and Young (1979).

Although these findings are highly reliable, there has been a long debate about their meaning and interpretation. Many models have been proposed to account for data on short-term item recognition, yet none of these models have succeeded in capturing all of the major results described above (Sternberg, 1975).

Although the simplest version of any model can easily be rejected, the model's creators can often patch things up to correct the most serious problems. By the 1970s it became clear that many different types of models can produce identical predictions for data on mean RTs (Anderson, 1973; Townsend, 1976, 1984). More recently, attention has shifted from looking at mean RTs to examining the shape of the RT distribution. It turns out that although very different types of models can explain the same pattern in the mean RTs, explaining the exact shape of the distribution and how it changes with manipulation of experimental variables is more difficult. Memory theorists have begun to tackle this issue with promising results (Ashby, Tein, and Balakrishan, 1993; Hockley and Murdock, 1987; Ratcliff, 1978; Townsend and Fific, 2004).

2.5 SUMMARY AND CURRENT DIRECTIONS

The strength theory of recognition memory is based on the idea that items possess a variable degree of familiarity prior to the start of an experiment and that studying an item increases its familiarity (e.g., Wickelgren and Norman, 1966). By reading out the familiarity (or strength) of a test item, one can decide whether or not the test item appeared on the target list. Strength theory makes specific predictions about how the hit rate and false-alarm rate should change as we alter our decision threshold. In particular, the standard one-dimensional strength theory, with Gaussian variability in item familiarity, requires a linear relation between the z-transformed hit and false-alarm rates (Figure 2.4). Whereas the data are consistent with this linear relation, the slope of the empirically determined zROC suggests that the variance of the target distribution is significantly greater than the variance of the lure distribution. This latter result can be accommodated by an extended version of strength theory in which the strength increment is variable from item to item and from trial to trial, perhaps reflecting fluctuations in participants' attention to items during study.

A number of researchers have proposed the addition of a second informational dimension to the standard strength theory of item recognition (e.g., Arndt and Reder, 2002; Howard, Bessette-Symons, Zhang, and Hoyer, 2006; Rotello et al., 2004; Yonelinas, 1994). This second dimension (termed *recollection*) is designed to formalize the idea that people can sometimes recollect specific details about the encoding experience of that item and that recognition responses may be based on this arguably more certain information about an item's prior occurrence. Familiarity-recollection models have enabled researchers to explain some intriguing facts about how the shape of the ROC curve is affected by aging and by damage to the medial temporal lobe (Howard et al., 2006; Yonelinas et al., 1998). These models have also been used to explain data from recognition experiments in which people are asked to give remember-know judgments. These studies have shown that remember and know judgments are selectively influenced by different experimental variables (Gardiner, Ramponi, and Richardson-Klavehn, 2002).

Researchers have proposed several variants of the basic familiarity-recollection model. According to the Yonelinas model, successful recollection always trumps familiarity. As such, the model is sometimes considered an all-or-none model in which the recollection signal either has infinite strength or zero strength. According to the variable-recollection model, successful recollection yields a signal of varying strength, though the strength of recollection is assumed to be greater, on average, than the familiarity signal (Howard et al., 2006). If both recollection and familiarity signals are weak (but recollection is successful), this model could generate a *no* response. Under these same conditions, the Yonelinas model would generate a *yes* response based on the recollection signal. Both familiarity-recollection models, along with variable-encoding strength theory, can produce reasonable fits to the observed ROC and zROC functions. However, detailed quantitative tests appear to favor the variable-recollection model over the other two variants (Onyper et al., 2010; Howard et al., 2006).

All of the theories discussed above can account for the finding that rare (low-frequency) words are better recognized than common (high-frequency) words as having been studied on a recent list. To accommodate this word-frequency effect, one-dimensional strength models assume that rare words attract more attention and are thus better encoded in memory and that people use this knowledge to adjust their decision threshold to optimally separate target and lure items. Familiarity-recollection models account for the greater hit rate for rare words by assuming that they are more easily recollected than common words. The higher false-alarm rate for common words arises, according to these models, from their increased familiarity. Familiarity-recollection models are able to account for recent findings that the hit-rate component of the word-frequency effect can be selectively influenced by experimental variables (Criss and Shiffrin, 2004).

Unfortunately, neither the one-dimensional strength theory nor the two-dimensional models that incorporate a recollection process have been successfully fit to detailed data on repetition effects, recency effects, or similarity effects. To account for such data, one needs more complex models of the kind that we will discuss in chapter 3.

Scholars are actively debating the relative merits of strength theory and familiarity-recollection theory as accounts of recognition memory (e.g., Wixted, 2007a; Yonelinas and Parks, 2007). Given that variants of both models can provide a good approximation to the observed ROC curves in item recognition,

Box 2.3

NEUROSCIENCE AND THE FAMILIARITY-RECOLLECTION DISTINCTION

Using functional magnetic resonance imaging (fMRI) to measure the activity of different brain areas, Yonelinas, Otten, Shaw, and Rugg (2005) showed that distinct regions activate when successful recognition appears to reflect familiarity as compared with recollection. Analysis of the fMRI signals revealed that when participants' judgments appeared to be based on recollection, neural activity increased in a network of brain regions that included the hippocampus—a structure known to support the encoding and retrieval of associations (Suzuki, 2007). During familiarity-based judgments, fMRI analyses revealed decreased hippocampal activation and increases in a distinct network of regions that included areas of the parietal and prefrontal cortex. In an attempt to control for overall differences in confidence, Yonelinas and colleagues compared fMRI signals for test items that participants judged as having been remembered with test items that participants judged as targets *with high confidence*.

Other studies have used electroencephalographic (EEG) recordings to assess differential brain responses to familiarity and recollection. These studies have found that the electrical activity recorded at the scalp exhibits distinct waveforms for target items that elicit subjective judgments of recollection and those that exhibit high levels of confidence without an experience of recollection. Specifically, recollective responses are associated with an increased positive voltage potential around 500–700 ms post target onset (as compared with high confidence nonrecollective responses). This potential appears primarily at electrodes over the left parietal cortex. In contrast, increasing item familiarity (as indexed by participants' confidence in recognizing a target item that was not recollected) appears to be related to the amplitude of a negative EEG waveform around 400 ms post target onset. This potential appears primarily at left-frontal electrodes (see Rugg and Curran, 2007, for a review).

Countering the dual-store interpretation of these findings, Squire, Wixted, and Clark (2007) have argued that neural dissociations between recollection and familiarity really reflect differences in how the brain processes stronger and weaker memories. They argue that despite efforts to compare recollection judgments with highly confident familiarity judgments, it is still likely that recollection reflects an even higher degree of confidence and that differences in brain activity between recollection and familiarity simply reflect differences in how the brain processes stronger and weaker memories.

the appeal of parsimony (i.e., a preference for simpler models, all else being equal) has led some to eschew the familiarity-recollection approach in favor of traditional strength theory (e.g., Wixted, 2007a). On the other hand, proponents of familiarity-recollection models have pointed to neural evidence as providing strong support for their dual-process view (see Box 2.3).

The recent arguments for and against familiarity-recollection models can be interpreted in light of a much older distinction within the psychology of human memory, namely, the distinction between item and associative information (see Murdock, 1974). This classic distinction was motivated by the many differences between item recognition and associative memory tasks such as cued recall (the focus of chapter 4). It is interesting that findings in the recognition literature that point most strongly to the role of recollection come from data from associative-recognition tasks, in which participants are tested on their memory for some relation between two items or between the parts of a single item (Parks and Yonelinas, 2007). For example, the zROC curves generated in associative recognition often exhibit significant departures from linearity, thus making them hard to explain within the standard one-dimensional strength framework. One possible reconciliation of the two perspectives is that item recognition involves recollection to the degree that the task depends on the storage and retrieval of associative information. Thus, when recognition does not significantly engage associative memory processes, the traditional strength framework neatly explains the observed data. However, in tasks that encourage and even rely on associative processes, recollection (i.e., associative memory retrieval) plays a more prominent role (e.g., Murdock, 2006).

Response-time (RT) data provide an important additional source of information on recognition memory. Shorter RTs tend to accompany more accurate and more certain responses. In the case of the word-frequency effect, participants respond more quickly and with greater accuracy to rare targets. Similarly, participants respond more quickly and more accurately to recent targets and to targets that have been repeated multiple times within a study list.

One can perhaps make best use of RT data in studying recognition memory for very short lists, where participants make few if any errors. In a series of landmark studies, Sternberg (1966) demonstrated that mean RT increases linearly with list length and that the slope of this increase is nearly identical for targets and lures. Sternberg argued that these findings suggest that people sequentially compare the test probe, be it a target or a lure, with each of the studied items and that they only respond once the probe has been compared with all of the studied items. A key difference between Sternberg's serial-exhaustive scanning (SES) model and strength theory is that SES assumes that the probe is compared with all of the list items in memory and strength theory assumes that people directly assess the strength of the probe item. Another difference is that strength theory has little to say about RT data, whereas the SES model has little to say about accuracy data.

The SES model offers an elegant and parsimonious account for the linear RT-list length relation and for the parallel slopes observed for targets and lures. These two findings are difficult to explain using variants of strength theory. However, the SES model does not explain other aspects of the data, such as recency and repetition effects, and the difficulty of rejecting lures that were studied on recent lists. It may be that people have access to two strategies: one that is characterized by the SES model and another that is characterized by strength theory. When strength differences between targets and lures are minimal and when items are easily rehearsable, people may opt for SES strategy. On the other hand, when the list is too long to permit an exhaustive scan, or when items cannot easily be rehearsed, or when the scan fails for some reason, people may rely on the noisier but less fragile strength-based memory signal. It is easy to imagine that the memory system encompasses multiple sources of information and that we use whichever source is most appropriate in a particular situation. In chapter 3 we will consider another important class of models that combines key elements of both strength theory and the SES model.

2.6 STUDY QUESTIONS

1. Draw an ROC function given the following confidence judgments given to 10 targets and 10 lures. Confidence judgments are on a 6-point scale where 1 corresponds to *sure no* and 6 corresponds to *sure yes*.

Trial Number	1	2	3	4	5	6	7	8	9	10
Target/Lure	L	L	T	L	T	L	T	T	L	T
Confidence Judgment	1	2	2	4	4	3	4	6	2	5
Trial Number	11	12	13	14	15	16	17	18	19	20
Target/Lure	L	T	L	L	T	T	L	L	T	T
Confidence Judgment	2	6	3	2	5	3	5	1	5	5

2. Describe the strength theory of item recognition and how it can be used to generate hits, misses, false alarms, and correct rejections. Next, describe the word-frequency effect in item recognition and the mirror effect. How would you modify the standard strength theory of item recognition in order to explain the mirror effect?

3. Compare the findings obtained in Sternberg's short-term recognition paradigm with those obtained in recognition studies using longer lists. Why is the SES model inadequate as an explanation for recognition of

long lists? What are the strengths and weaknesses of the SES model as an account of recognition memory for short lists?

4. Recency is a ubiquitous feature of human memory. In the Sternberg task, one typically observes faster response times for targets that appeared at the end of the study list. How might one explain this result within the framework of the serial self-terminating scanning model?

5. Assume that it takes 150 ms to identify the probe item, 40 ms to compare the probe with each of the stored list items, and 200 ms to execute a response. Draw a graph of the RT-list length relation for the serial exhaustive scanning and the serial self-terminating models.

3

Attribute Models

The physiological basis of memory is simple enough in its broad outlines. Whenever any group of brain elements has been excited by a sense impression, it becomes, so to speak, tender, and liable to be easily thrown again into a similar state of excitement. If the new cause of excitement differs from the original one, a memory is the result. Whenever a single cause throws different groups of brain elements simultaneously into excitement, the result must be a blended memory.

Sir FRANCIS GALTON, *Inquiries Into Human Faculty and its Development* (1883) p. 229

According to the strength theory of recognition memory, every learned item is characterized by a scalar value, called strength (see chapter 2). Presentation of a test item retrieves the strength of the matching item in memory, and that strength value is then used to make a recognition decision. The information driving the recognition decision thus depends solely on the strength of the stored representation of the test item. Therefore, if a person is shown a lure item that is highly similar to one or more studied items, it should be rejected just as easily as a lure item that is unrelated to any of the studied items.[1] Contrary to this prediction, it is easy to show that people are significantly less likely to reject a lure when it is similar to one or more studied items (Hintzman, 1988; Kahana and Sekuler, 2002). To explain such similarity effects, we need to go beyond strength theory in considering how items in memory are represented and how a test probe interacts with these representations. We begin by introducing the conception of a memory as a list of attributes.

3.1 ATTRIBUTES

Our experiences, which are transformed into memories, can have many different attributes. In remembering an experience, we are remembering some record of these varied attributes, some of which may be learned more efficiently than others. For example, in reading a complex story, we will exhibit some degree of memory for the ideas, perhaps less for the exact wording, and even less for the position of the text on the page or the font in which it was printed. We will remember something about the context in which we did the reading—more or less depending on the degree to which the context was distinctive and/or meaningful. If someone is reading a story to us, we will have some memory for the voice in which the story was read, even if we have no specific reason for learning that attribute. The finding that people can remember specific attributes of a studied item (with varying degrees of fidelity) lends support to this general view (e.g., Underwood, 1969).

To make concrete the notion of attributes, consider the task facing a person who has to study a list of pictures of houses for a later recognition-memory test. Although it is possible that people will encode a literal image of each house, it is also likely that they will abstract certain features of each image, such as the size of the house, the number of floors, the number of windows, the age of the house, whether it is made of wood or brick, and whether it is of a particular architectural style (e.g., colonial, Victorian, contemporary, etc.). These attributes need not be independent of one another. That is, knowing something about the number of floors and windows may indicate something about the likely age or style of the house. Nonetheless, we could start by writing down a list of dimensions along which houses vary, and then for each picture of a house, fill in the value along each dimension. Such a tabulation is given in Table 3.1 for five sample houses.

1. Wickelgren and Norman (1966) proposed a solution to this limitation of traditional strength theory. Specifically, they proposed that learning an item (i.e., incrementing its strength) caused partial learning of related items, based on their similarity. Wickelgren and Norman's version of strength theory includes a number of other major refinements, including the distinction between short-term and long-term memory representations.

Table 3.1

Attributes of houses. According to attribute theory, each item in memory is
represented by a list of attribute values, one value for each attribute. Here we illustrate
some possible attributes of houses, including those that take on continuous values
(e.g., square footage) and those that take on binary values (e.g., Victorian). In the case
of binary valued dimensions, we use a value of 1 to indicate that the attribute is true and
a value of zero to indicate that the attribute is false.

Dimension	House 1	House 2	House 3	House 4	House 5
size (sq ft)	3,000	2,200	1,800	4,700	8,500
floors	2	2	1	3	2.5
windows	6	5	4	12	10
age (in years)	25	15	70	97	3
wood	0	1	0	0	1
brick	1	0	0	0	0
stone	0	0	0	1	0
colonial	1	0	1	0	0
Victorian	0	0	0	1	0
contemporary	0	1	0	0	1

In thinking about this example, it may have occurred to you that certain
memories are not easily described in terms of specific nameable attributes. In
the case of common words, there are a myriad of attributes that characterize
the meaning of a word, and many of these are not easily named. In contrast,
if one were studying memory for simple geometrical forms, it would be
straightforward to list their attributes. For example, rectangles are described
by two numbers: one for their height and one for their width. If the objects were
three-dimensional blocks, they would be described by three numbers: their
length, width, and height. In the case of more complex objects, like pictures of
houses or faces, or even words, they would vary along many attributes, where
the nature of the specific attributes are hard to define. For now, we will consider
the simple case of rectangles and develop an intuition for the way such simple
objects may be represented in memory. Later, we will show how these ideas can
be extended into the realm of more complex objects.

3.1.1 Vectors

As noted above, a rectangle can be easily described by two numbers, one
representing its length and the other its width. Geometrically, we can think of
a pair of numbers as denoting a point on a standard two-dimensional graph. In
this case, we might say that the x-axis represents the dimension of length and
the y-axis represents the dimension of width. Every possible rectangle may thus

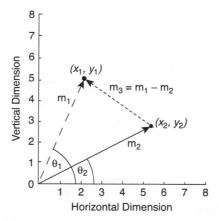

Figure 3.1 Graphical depiction of vectors. A pair of two-dimensional vectors are shown in both Cartesian coordinates, (x_1, y_1) and (x_2, y_2), and in Polar coordinates (r_1, θ_1) and (r_2, θ_2). A third difference vector is drawn between the first two vectors. See text for details.

be mapped onto an x, y coordinate on our graph, and every point on our graph corresponds to a specific rectangle. Figure 3.1 illustrates the coordinates of two rectangles represented by the points x_1, y_1 and x_2, y_2.

A point in a two-dimensional space may also be called a two-dimensional *vector*. If we draw a line from the origin $x = 0, y = 0$ to a given point with coordinates x, y, that line may be thought of as having an angle (denoted θ) and a magnitude, or distance from the origin (denoted r). The relation between the x, y coordinates, the distance, r, and the angle, θ, is given by the trigonometric equations: $x = r \cos \theta$ and $y = r \sin \theta$.

In elementary physics, where you may have used vectors to think about quantities such as *force*, r would denote the magnitude of a force, while θ would denote its direction. If we know the x, y coordinates of a vector, we can calculate r using the Pythagorean theorem: $x^2 + y^2 = r^2$. The quantity r is known as the length, or *norm*, of the vector.

Vector notation The vector representing a rectangle with length $x = 2$ and width $y = 5$ is denoted $\begin{pmatrix} 2 \\ 5 \end{pmatrix}$. Thus, we order the numbers in a column, going from top to bottom, and enclose the column of numbers within parentheses. Just as a single rectangle can be represented by a single two-dimensional vector, a set of rectangles can be represented by a set of two-dimensional vectors. We can thus represent a set (or list) of rectangles as a set of points in a two-dimensional space. Rather than writing down the set of coordinates every time we wish to refer to a vector, we will adopt the convention of using an arbitrary boldface letter to denote a vector. For example, the ith rectangle in the set may be written as $\mathbf{m}_i = \begin{pmatrix} x_i \\ y_i \end{pmatrix}$. Another common notation is to put an arrow above a letter to indicate that it refers to a vector, as in $\vec{m}_i$.

Distance   The distance between two vectors will turn out to be quite important in thinking about the role of similarity in memory. The distance between $\mathbf{m}_1 = \begin{pmatrix} x_1 \\ y_1 \end{pmatrix}$ and $\mathbf{m}_2 = \begin{pmatrix} x_2 \\ y_2 \end{pmatrix}$ equals the length of the difference vector, $\mathbf{m}_3 = \mathbf{m}_1 - \mathbf{m}_2$. The length, or *norm*, of a vector, $\mathbf{m}_i$, is denoted as $||\mathbf{m}_i||$. Using the Pythagorean theorem, we can show that $||\mathbf{m}_3|| = \sqrt{(x_1 - x_2)^2 + (y_1 - y_2)^2}$. As shown in Figure 3.1, $\mathbf{m}_3$ starts at coordinates x_2, y_2 and ends at coordinates x_1, y_1.

Vectors with more than two dimensions   Vectors are mathematical objects that can represent more than two dimensions; indeed, they can represent any number of dimensions. Thus, an object with three attributes can be represented by a three-dimensional vector, an object with four attributes can be represented by a four-dimensional vector, and an object with N attributes can be represented by an N-dimensional vector. A three-dimensional vector can be represented geometrically by a point in three-dimensional space, as in the case of a block, which is described by its height, width, and depth. Although one could think of N-dimensional vectors as points in N-dimensional space, we are not able to visualize such mathematical objects in a geometric way. Mathematically, we can denote a vector $\mathbf{m}$ with N dimensions as:

$$\mathbf{m} = \begin{pmatrix} m(1) \\ m(2) \\ m(3) \\ \vdots \\ m(N) \end{pmatrix},$$

where $m(1), m(2), m(3)$, etc., are the values for each dimension. In indexing the dimensions, or elements, of a vector, we will usually use a number or variable in parentheses, but we may also use a number or variable as a subscript. That is, we could write $m(N)$, or m_N, to refer to the Nth element of vector $\mathbf{m}$. If we want to use indices to refer to different vectors, we will typically use a subscript after a bold variable name, as in $\mathbf{m}_i$.

3.1.2 Distributed Representation

The theories we will consider in this chapter assume that an item is represented in memory as a list of attribute values, i.e., as a vector. We will call this the *Distributed Memory Hypothesis*, because it assumes that the information representing a single memory is distributed over multiple attributes, features, elements, or dimensions (these varied terms are used interchangeably in the literature). This basic idea can be found in the memory theories of scientist/inventor Robert Hooke (1969), philosopher/biologist Richard Semon (1923), and early learning theorist Edwin Guthrie (1935). Hintzman (2003) and Schacter (2001) provide fascinating discussions of the work of Hooke and Semon, respectively (see also Gomulicki [1953]). The distributed representation recording a particular experience in memory is sometimes called the memory *trace* or, after Semon (1923), the *engram*.

For simple geometric forms (e.g., two-dimensional rectangles), the dimensions of the items can be specified explicitly, and these physical dimensions often turn out to be the same as the psychological dimensions along which the items vary (e.g., Nosofsky, 1992; Kahana and Bennett, 1994). In the case of memorizing words or complex pictures, however, the theories assume that the items vary along a great number of physical and psychological dimensions whose identities may be difficult, or impossible, to fully identify.

One way to conceptualize the vectors representing complex stimuli is to think of them as characterizing the pattern of brain activity evoked by processing a given stimulus. Ultimately, all stimuli must be represented by the electrical activity of neurons in the brain. Some of these neurons may be very active, exhibiting a high firing rate, whereas others may be quiet. The firing rate of each neuron can be thought of as representing the value along the attribute coded by that particular cell (in reality a large number of neurons are likely involved in the coding of any attribute, not a single cell). Together, these cells can represent many kinds of information, including perceptual, contextual, and semantic aspects of an experience. Much as an image on a television screen is a pattern of brightness values distributed across the display, a memory may be thought of as a pattern of neural activation values distributed over a large array of neurons.

3.2 A MULTITRACE DISTRIBUTED MEMORY MODEL

In the strength theory of item recognition, each item in memory was represented by a single value (a scalar). Thus, all of the items in memory could be thought of as an array of scalar values. With distributed memories, each item is represented by a vector of values, one for each dimension or attribute, and the set of all items in memory can be thought of as an array where each row represents one dimension and each column represents a different item. Such an array of values is called a *matrix* and is usually denoted by a capital letter. For example, the matrix encompassing the three item-vectors, $\mathbf{m}_1$, $\mathbf{m}_2$, and $\mathbf{m}_3$, would be given by:

$$M = \begin{pmatrix} m_1(1) & m_2(1) & m_3(1) \\ m_1(2) & m_2(2) & m_3(2) \\ m_1(3) & m_2(3) & m_3(3) \\ \vdots & \vdots & \vdots \\ m_1(N) & m_2(N) & m_3(N) \end{pmatrix}$$

$$= \begin{pmatrix} \mathbf{m}_1 & \mathbf{m}_2 & \mathbf{m}_3 \end{pmatrix}.$$

3.2.1 Multiple Traces

According to strength theory, repetition of an item increases its strength. With distributed memories, there is no strength value to increment. This raises the question of how a given distributed representation is reinforced, or strengthened, by repetition of an item.

For the moment let us consider a very simple model for the learning process: a model in which each studied item lays down a new trace in a large and ever-growing array representing all of the traces stored in memory. This idea, which is referred to as the *multiple trace hypothesis*, implies that each encoded presentation of an item leaves its own memory trace (Hintzman, 1976; Moscovitch, Nadel, Winocur, Gilboa, and Rosenbaum, 2006). By allowing each studied item to lay down a unique trace, and by further assuming that each trace can consist of many attributes, we can easily accommodate the important idea that a given item (e.g., the word *cat*) will lay down somewhat different traces when studied on different occasions. Indeed, it seems strange to think that the encoding of a given word will be precisely the same at any two occasions. A much more natural assumption is that the stored attribute values vary based on the context in which a word occurred, such as the words that preceded it or the thoughts that it evoked.

The multiple trace hypothesis implies that the number of traces can increase without bound. Although the limits of information storage in the human brain are not currently known, it seems implausible for the brain to have an infinite storage capacity. The presence of an upper bound need not pose a problem for the multiple-trace hypothesis so long as traces can be lost/erased, similar traces can merge together, or the upper bound is large relative to the scale of human experience. To this point we have only considered how information is stored in memory; we have said nothing about retrieval. The next section considers how we can use a matrix representation, as described above, to determine whether a given probe item was or was not on a target list.

3.2.2 Memory Search and Summed Similarity

When a person encodes a test item, we assume that it is converted into a vector representation, which can then be compared with all the vectors stored in the memory matrix. One way to recognize an item is to search the memory matrix, serially comparing the probe vector with each of the stored vectors. This is analogous to the serial search process assumed by Sternberg (1966) in his serial-exhaustive scanning model. Although such a search process may be plausible for a very short list of items, it has difficulty accounting for RT data when people are asked to recognize test items drawn from long study lists. Although people do tend to respond more slowly when making recognition judgments on longer lists, the rate at which RT increases with list length slows considerably as the list lengthens (Burrows and Okada, 1975) (see Figure 2.17).

As an alternative, one can search the memory matrix in *parallel*, comparing the probe item with each of the stored vectors at the same time. In carrying out such a parallel search, we would say *yes* if we found a perfect match between the test item and one of the stored memory vectors. However, if we required a perfect match to say *yes*, we may never say *yes* because a given item is likely to be encoded in a slightly different manner on any two occasions. Thus, when an item is encoded at study and at test, the representations will be very similar, but not identical. To circumvent this problem, we could accept partial matches so long as they exceeded some threshold of similarity. Alternatively, we could calculate the similarity for each comparison and sum these similarity values to determine the *global match* between the test probe and the contents of memory. Models that adopt this approach are called either *summed-similarity* or *global matching* models.

Several versions of the summed-similarity approach have been proposed in the literature, and these models have proven to be quite successful in accounting for a wide range of recognition-memory data. Before we consider these models in greater detail, however, we need to address the issue of how to focus the search process on those items learned within a given context. In most memory experiments, this context is the most recently presented list.

3.2.3 The Role of Context

As noted in chapter 1, numerous experimental findings show that changes in situational context between study and test reduce memory performance on a wide range of tasks. These findings led to the view that contextual change is one of the major factors underlying forgetting (Carr, 1931; Hollingsworth, 1928; McGeoch, 1932; Robinson, 1932). Within the framework of attribute theory, it is easy to imagine that some attributes represent the context in which an item was learned and that items within a given list will have more overlap in their contextual attributes than items studied on different lists, or indeed items that were not part of an experiment (Bower, 1972; Crowder, 1976). If the contextual change between lists is sufficiently great, and if the context at time of test is similar to the context encoded at the time of study, then recognition judgments should largely reflect the presence or absence of the probe item within the most recent (target) list and not the presence or absence of the probe item on earlier lists.

Hintzman and Block (1971, Experiment 3) used a *judgment of frequency* (JOF) task to examine the effect that studying an item in one list has on participants' memory for the item's occurrence in another list. The JOF task is a generalization of the *yes–no* recognition task in which participants judge the number of times a test item appeared on a list, rather than judging whether or not the item was on the list. In a JOF task, lures would have been presented zero times, whereas targets could have been presented one or more times. People are surprisingly good at making such judgments.

Hintzman and Block (1971) gave their participants two study lists separated by a 5-minute break in which the participants performed an unrelated task. Each list contained 104 words, half of which were presented twice while the other half were presented five times (the order of item presentation was random so that the repetitions of a given item were interspersed among other items). The lists were designed such that a given item could have appeared zero, two, or five times on List 1 and zero, two, or five times on List 2. Thus, some of the words that appeared five times on List 1 did not appear on List 2 (condition 5–0), whereas some words that appeared twice on List 1 appeared five times on List 2 (condition 2–5), and so forth, for all possible combinations.

After seeing both lists, participants were given an unexpected JOF test, in which they were shown items and asked to separately judge the number of times the items occurred on each of the two lists. As shown in Figure 3.2, the mean judged frequency on List 1 was largely determined by the List 1 frequency of the items, and the mean judged frequency on List 2 was largely determined by the List 2 frequency of the items. There was only a small effect of List 1 frequency on List 2 judgments, and vice versa. On the basis of these data, it is clear that people can retrieve information about memories on the basis of their list membership.

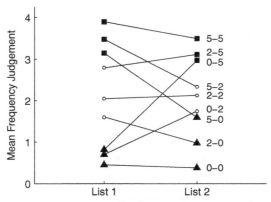

Figure 3.2 List-specific frequency judgments. Mean frequency judgments for words presented in List 1 and List 2 as a joint function of the frequency of occurrence in the two lists. Filled squares, open circles, and filled triangles denote items presented five, two, and zero times in a given list respectively. The two-digit labels designate the frequency of an item on List 1 and List 2, respectively. Data from Hintzman and Block (1971, Experiment 3).

3.2.4 Summed-similarity Computations

Within the framework of attribute theory, two memories are identical if they share the same values along each attribute. Intuitively, the similarity of two vectors should decrease as the distance between them increases. We have already seen how we can calculate the distance between two vectors in two dimensions using the Pythagorean theorem. We can extend this calculation to N-dimensional vectors, where the distance between two such vectors, $\mathbf{m}_1$ and $\mathbf{m}_2$, is the length of the difference vector, $\mathbf{m}_1 - \mathbf{m}_2$, which is

$$\sqrt{\sum_{i=1}^{N} (m_1(i) - m_2(i))^2}.$$

Now that we know how to calculate distances, we need some way of calculating similarities. When two vectors are identical (i.e., the distance between them is zero), their similarity should be set to some maximal value. As the distance between the vectors increases toward ∞, their similarity should approach zero. The exponential decay function,

$$\text{similarity} = e^{-\tau \, \text{distance}},$$

has exactly this property: it is equal to 1.0 when distance = 0 and it approaches zero as distance $\rightarrow \infty$. The variable τ (Tau) determines how quickly similarity decays with distance. Figure 3.3 shows the form of an exponential-decay function for several values of τ (see Box 2.2 for a definition of e).

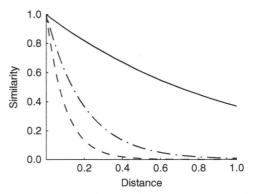

Figure 3.3 Exponential similarity-distance function. Exponential similarity-distance function for three values of τ: 1 (solid line), 5 (dash-dot line), and 10 (dashed line). The value of τ determines how quickly similarity decays with distance.

A related measure of similarity is the cosine of the angle between two vectors, $\cos\theta$. If the two vectors are identical, the angle will be zero and $\cos\theta = 1$. If the two vectors are perpendicular to one another, the angle will be 90° and $\cos\theta = 0$. If we were to select random values for each of the attributes, we would find that $\cos\theta = 0$ in expectation.[2]

Armed with measures of similarity, we can sum the similarity between the test item and each of the stored vectors in our memory matrix. As with strength theory, we can assume that the person will say *yes* if the summed similarity exceeds a threshold value.

To formalize these arguments, suppose that $\mathbf{m}_i$ represents the *i*th item of an *L*-item list. Following study of the list, the matrix *M* would represent the list in memory.

$$M = \begin{pmatrix} \mathbf{m}_1 & \mathbf{m}_2 & \mathbf{m}_3 & \dots & \mathbf{m}_L \end{pmatrix}$$

2. In many applications it is reasonable to assume that the two vectors, $\mathbf{m}_1$ and $\mathbf{m}_2$, are of approximately equal length. Supposing that the length of both vectors is given by *L*, the $\cos\theta$ measure of similarity equals $(1/L)\sum_{i=1}^{N} m_1(i)m_2(i)$. The latter term in this equation, $\sum_{i=1}^{N} m_1(i)m_2(i)$, is termed the *dot product* of $\mathbf{m}_1$ and $\mathbf{m}_2$ and is denoted as $\mathbf{m}_1 \cdot \mathbf{m}_2$. More generally, for vectors of unequal length:

$$\cos\theta(\mathbf{m}_1, \mathbf{m}_2) = \frac{\mathbf{m}_1 \cdot \mathbf{m}_2}{||\mathbf{m}_1||\;||\mathbf{m}_2||}.$$

Let $\mathbf{g}$ represent a test item, either a target (i.e., $\mathbf{g} = \mathbf{m}_i$ for some value of i) or a lure. The summed similarity between the test probe and the items stored in memory can be written as:

$$\sum_{i=1}^{L} \text{similarity}(\mathbf{g}, \mathbf{m}_i), \qquad (3.1)$$

where the similarity between $\mathbf{g}$ and $\mathbf{m}_i$ is defined as:

$$e^{-\tau\|\mathbf{g}-\mathbf{m}_i\|} = e^{-\tau\sqrt{\sum_{j=1}^{N}(g(j)-m_i(j))^2}}. \qquad (3.2)$$

The summed-similarity model dictates that a person will respond *yes* when the summed similarity between the test item and each of the stored items in memory (Equation 3.1) exceeds a threshold value C; otherwise the person responds *no*. As with strength theory, the threshold value can be set to simultaneously maximize hits and minimize false alarms. The model predicts that the probability of saying *yes* to a test item is given by the equation:

$$P(yes) = P\left(\sum_{i=1}^{L} e^{-\tau\sqrt{\sum_{j=1}^{N}(g(j)-m_i(j))^2}} > C\right). \qquad (3.3)$$

The probability of a *no* response is simply $1 - P(yes)$.

Variable encoding.   In the previous equation, we assumed that each item was stored perfectly in memory. A more realistic variant of the basic summed-similarity model involves the addition of a random "noise" vector, $\epsilon = (\epsilon_1, \epsilon_2, \ldots, \epsilon_N)$, to the stored items, and also perhaps to the test probe. Each element of the noise vector (ϵ_i) would simply be a random number drawn from a normal distribution with mean $\mu = 0$ and standard deviation σ, where σ is a model parameter. Larger values of σ imply a greater perturbation of the stored representation and thus worse memory performance.

Figure 3.4 is a schematic of the application of a summed-similarity model to a trial consisting of three study stimuli followed by a nonstudied probe item (a lure). By adding a noise vector to each item vector stored in memory, we can ensure that no two memories are ever exactly the same. Given the variability in people's responses from one occurrence of an item to another, this is a desirable property.

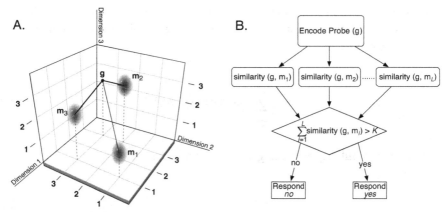

Figure 3.4 Illustration of the summed-similarity model. A. Schematic showing the memorial representations of three list items in a three-dimensional attribute space. Each item ($\mathbf{m}_1$, $\mathbf{m}_2$, and $\mathbf{m}_3$) is depicted by a shaded ellipse representing the noise associated with the coding of the item. Also shown is the relatively noiseless representation of a nonstudied test probe (g). **B.** Diagram of the information-processing stages in the summed-similarity model. First, the test probe is encoded. Then, its similarity to the memorial representations of each list item is computed. If the summed similarity exceeds a threshold, C, the model responds *yes*.

Forgetting.   We can simulate the forgetting process in a number of different ways. Two common methods are to assume that recent items count more than older items in the summed-similarity calculation or to assume that older items accrue more noise. A third method is to assume that forgetting is due to contextual drift. If context is stored as part of each vector, and if context drifts over time, then the context at the time of test will best match the context of recently experienced items, thereby making it easier to remember recent items (G. D. A. Brown, Neath, and Chater, 2007; Kahana, Zhou, Geller, and Sekuler, 2007). We will further develop this idea in section 3.4.

ROC implications.   Using Equations 3.1–3.3 we can derive the hit rate and false-alarm rate and determine the shape of the ROC curve (see chapter 2). The ROC curve predicted by summed-similarity models is bow shaped (concave down) and the z-transformed ROC curve (zROC) is approximately linear, consistent with experimental observations. The slope of the zROC predicted by summed-similarity models depends critically on assumptions regarding the positioning of lure items within the stimulus space shown in Figure 3.4A. If lures are drawn randomly throughout the stimulus space, the model predicts a zROC with a slope that is greater than 1 because the variance of the summed-similarity distribution is greater for randomly chosen lures than for targets. Because experimental zROC functions are typically measured for word lists,

---

Box 3.1

EXAMPLE CALCULATION: SUMMED-SIMILARITY

Consider a memory array in which we have stored three items:

$$M = \begin{pmatrix} 1 & 0 & 1 \\ 1 & 0 & 0 \\ 1 & 1 & 1 \\ 1 & 1 & 0 \end{pmatrix}$$

$$= \begin{pmatrix} \mathbf{m}_1 & \mathbf{m}_2 & \mathbf{m}_3 \end{pmatrix}.$$

According to the summed-similarity models, people respond *yes* when the summed similarity of the probe to the stored items exceeds a threshold. On average, the summed similarity for a target item should exceed that of a lure.

If the probe is the target item $\mathbf{m}_1$, then the distance between the probe and $\mathbf{m}_1$ is zero. Using the Pythagorean theorem, the distance between the probe and $\mathbf{m}_2$ is:

$$|\mathbf{m}_2 - \mathbf{m}_1| = \sqrt{(0-1)^2 + (0-1)^2 + (1-1)^2 + (1-1)^2} = \sqrt{2}.$$

The distance between the probe and $\mathbf{m}_3$ is:

$$|\mathbf{m}_3 - \mathbf{m}_1| = \sqrt{(1-1)^2 + (0-1)^2 + (1-1)^2 + (0-1)^2} = \sqrt{2}.$$

Because the similarity between any two vectors $\mathbf{m}_i$ and $\mathbf{m}_j$ is defined as $e^{-|\mathbf{m}_i - \mathbf{m}_j|}$, the summed similarity is given by: $e^{-0} + e^{-\sqrt{2}} + e^{-\sqrt{2}} \approx 1.48$.

Consider the summed similarity for the lure given by:

$$\begin{pmatrix} 1 \\ 0 \\ 1 \\ 1 \end{pmatrix}.$$

In this case, the probe's distances to $\mathbf{m}_1$ and $\mathbf{m}_2$ and $\mathbf{m}_3$ are each equal to 1, and the summed similarity is therefore given by: $3e^{-1} \approx 1.1$. If the decision threshold were set at 1.3, then the model would generate a *yes* response for the target and a *no* response for the lure.

---

testing the ROC implications of the summed-similarity model depends on having a good model for the vector representations of words. We will examine similarity effects in more detail in the following sections.

3.3 SIMILARITY EFFECTS

According to strength theory, recognition-memory errors arise because some lures have higher strength values than some targets. In summed-similarity theory, errors arise because some lures have higher summed similarity than some targets do. In both strength and summed-similarity theories, the variable governing people's recognition decisions has a probability distribution for targets and for lures, and these distributions overlap one another (see Figure 2.2). In strength theory, the overlap occurs because of variability in the preexperimental strengths of items. By chance, some lures will have high preexperimental strengths and will therefore be incorrectly judged as targets. In summed-similarity theory, a target will always be a good match to one of the stored items but may also partially match other stored items. If a lure partially matches enough items in memory, it can yield a large enough summed-similarity value to be judged as a target. Moreover, because we assume that the attributes of an item are not coded in exactly the same manner on any two occasions, it is possible that a target item shown at test will not yield a very high similarity with the target item's stored representation in the memory array.

Summed-similarity models predict that the presence of multiple list items that are similar to a specific target item should increase a person's likelihood of saying *yes* to that target item. This is because each related list item will contribute to the summed-similarity signal. Similarly, the presence of list items related to a lure should increase a person's likelihood of saying *yes* to the related lure.

Partially supporting these predictions, Anisfeld and Knapp (1968) found that participants were more likely than not to commit a false alarm to a word that was a synonym or a common associate of a word from the study list. Their study did not, however, examine whether having a target word that matched other studied words increased participants' tendency to say *yes*. This latter question was examined in a more thorough analysis of similarity effects reported by Hintzman (1988).

Hintzman had participants study a list of common nouns. The study list was constructed by drawing words either from common taxonomic categories (e.g., gemstones, occupations, common first names) or from a pool of common nouns that were not organized according to category. The lists were randomly ordered but for the constraint that no two items from a given category were presented in close proximity. The key manipulation in the experiment was the number of words in the list that came from a specific category; this number was

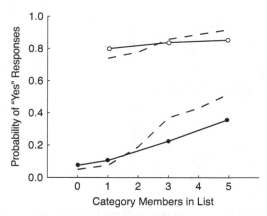

Figure 3.5 Similarity effects in recognition of categorized words. Percent of *yes* responses to targets (open circles) and lures (filled circles) as a function of the number of categorically related words present on the study list. Solid lines represent the data; dashed lines represent the predictions of a summed-similarity model. Data from Hintzman (1988).

either 1, 3, or 5. The question was whether participants would be more likely to say *yes* to targets if the list also contained other items from the same category. The data, shown in Figure 3.5, reveal that the probability of saying *yes* to a target and to a lure increased with the number of category members in the study list. This result is consistent with the predictions of summed-similarity theory, which posits that the presence of similar items on the study list will add to the total similarity of a given test item, be it a target or a lure.

One can more directly investigate similarity effects by examining recognition memory for visual forms, such as the textures shown in Figure 3.6. Using these stimuli, Kahana and Sekuler (2002) asked participants to remember short lists, comprising one to four textures. As in Sternberg's procedure, participants were then shown just one test probe that was either a target or a lure. Figure 3.6B illustrates how the probability of a *yes* response increased with summed similarity for both targets and for lures. Similar results have been found for lists composed of colors (Nosofsky and Kantner, 2006) and faces (Lacroix, Murre, Postma, and Herik, 2006; Yotsumoto, Kahana, Wilson, and Sekuler, 2007).

3.3.1 Application to Photo Lineups

The central role that similarity plays in recognition memory can also be seen in real-world situations, such as police lineups. Clark and Tunnicliff (2001) studied the effects of visual similarity on the way people identify suspects in

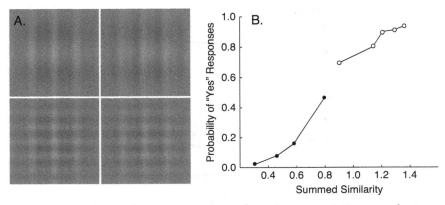

Figure 3.6 Similarity effects in recognition of visual textures. A. Four sample textures used in the study of Kahana and Sekuler (2002). **B.** Probability of a *yes* response to targets (open circles) and lures (filled circles) increases with the summed similarity of the probe item with the items in the study list.

police-style lineups. In their experiment, Clark and Tunnicliff set up two lineups. The first lineup consisted of five suspects, all chosen to be visually similar to an eyewitness's description of a robber. The second lineup included one suspect who was visually similar to the eyewitness's description of the robber along with four other suspects who were chosen to be visually similar to the first suspect. Therefore, in the first lineup each suspect had the same similarity to the robber, but in the second lineup, the first suspect was more similar to the robber than the other suspects. Hence, when picking from the first lineup, participants tended to pick each suspect with a somewhat equal distribution, while in the second lineup, the first suspect was chosen with a much higher probability than the rest of the suspects.

These results have important practical implications. Imagine a criminal case where there are two lineups. In one lineup, both the innocent suspect and lures match the eyewitness report. A second lineup has an innocent suspect (matched to an eyewitness description of the criminal) and lures matched to the suspect. Based on Clark and Tunnicliff's data and the summed-similarity model, we would expect the innocent suspect to be falsely identified/chosen much more often in the second lineup than in the first. Therefore, out of fairness to the suspect, when police need to form a lineup, they should match all of the lures to the eyewitness report.

3.4 THE DIFFUSION MODEL OF RESPONSE TIME

We have seen how attribute models assign *yes* or *no* responses to test items. A further question is how to use this class of models to predict RT data.

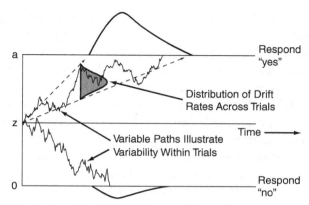

Figure 3.7 Diffusion model of RT. Schematic of how information accumulates over time for targets and lures. The *y*-axis indicates the strength of the memory signal at a given point in time (time is increasing along the *x*-axis from left to right). Starting from a value of *z*, the memory drifts upward (for a target) or downward (for a lure), with the rate of drift varying from item to item. A "yes" response is made whenever memory strength reaches the upper decision bound (*a*). The resulting RT distribution is shown at the top of the figure. A "no" response is made whenever the memory strength reaches the lower decision bound (0), with the resulting (inverted) response time distribution shown at the bottom of the figure.

As we saw in section 2.1, RTs decrease with increasing response confidence (see the discussion of the RT-distance relation in chapter 2). By determining the mathematical form of the relation between RT and the distance between summed similarity (or strength) and the decision threshold, we can predict the mean RT to any given test item. This RT-distance model can also account for the distribution of RTs to hits, false alarms, misses, and correct rejections.

Ratcliff (1978) proposed a more sophisticated model of the decision process to explain RT data in recognition memory (and in other choice tasks). In his *drift diffusion model*, decisions are not based on a direct readout of the memory signal (e.g., summed similarity or item strength). Instead, the memory signal influences the accumulation (or diffusion) of a decision variable over time.[3] As shown in Figure 3.7, the decision variable is set to a value, *z*, at the start of the decision process (this value may vary from trial to trial). Response boundaries are set at values 0 (for *no*) and *a* (for *yes*). The memory signal readout at a given

3. The diffusion model is named after the mathematical model of Brownian motion. In Brownian motion, a particle submerged in a body of water would undergo random impacts due to the motion of the water molecules. These impacts would have variable strengths and directions, causing the particle's position to fluctuate over time. This type of process is also sometimes called a random walk.

time is assumed to be noisy. However, by summating this noisy signal over time, one can see that evidence accrues toward either the *yes* or the *no* boundary. This is illustrated in the variable paths shown in Figure 3.7. If the memory strength is above a certain threshold value, the decision variable will rise at a fast rate. Conversely, when the memory strength is far below the threshold value, the decision variable will rapidly decline. This threshold value thus separates stimuli into those with positive and negative drift rates. Intermediate memory strength values will lead to more gradual changes in the decision variable. Furthermore, the diffusion model assumes that the rate of information accumulation (the drift rate) varies across trials. This variability in the drift rate is indicated by the shaded normal distribution in Figure 3.7. According to Ratcliff's diffusion model, variation in RTs is assumed to represent variation in the decision process, as characterized above, plus variation in nondecisional processes, such as those associated with stimulus encoding and response execution.

Because the accumulation of information is a noisy process, the same drift rate and decision boundaries will nonetheless lead to variable RTs and even variable responses. In this way, the diffusion model will predict the shape of the RT distributions for hits, false alarms, misses, and correct rejections, and the predicted shapes are in good agreement with the experimental data (Ratcliff, Gomez, and McKoon, 2004). In modeling recognition RTs, one must assume that the drift rate varies with factors that influence recognition difficulty. This is why it is important to link the diffusion model to a memory model (e.g., summed similarity) that specifies the memory signal provided by a given test probe following a given study list (e.g., Lamberts, 2000; Lamberts, Brockdorff, and Heit, 2003; Nosofsky and Palmeri, 1997).

3.5 CONTEXT REVISITED

In this section we consider the role of context in models of recognition memory. Attribute theories of memory lend themselves well to incorporating context into memory models. This is accomplished by partitioning a vector into two parts: one part representing the content of a memory and the other part representing the context. For example, the vector **m** might consist of 10,000 attributes, half of which represent its content while the other half represent its context. *Content attributes* refer to those attributes that are expected to be encoded in the same manner on each presentation of a given item. Conversely, *context attributes* refer to those that differ from presentation to presentation.

If the contextual attributes within a list are similar to one another but very different from the contextual attributes stored in a prior list, a test item can only be highly similar to an item in the just-studied list. As such, one can limit the influence of the prior experience on new learning, consistent with experimental results, such as those shown in Figure 3.2, and with data on short-term item recognition. One can also use contextual attributes to explain the recency effect (e.g., Figures 1.7 and 2.16). If the contextual attributes change slowly as each new item is presented, a test item will have a context that is more similar to recent items than to ones studied a long time ago (Bower, 1972; Howard and Kahana, 2002a).

Hintzman (1988) used contextual attributes to explain the finding that participants can make fairly accurate list-specific judgments of frequency. He did this by constructing two sets of contextual attributes, one for each of the two lists. He then assumed that in making judgments about a given list, participants would be able to invoke the contextual attributes of that list. By implementing these ideas within a summed-similarity model, he was able to show that the model fit the experimental data shown in Figure 3.2.

In Hintzman's model, there was a fixed context for each list. A more sophisticated view of context would have the contextual attributes change slowly as each new item is presented (e.g., Estes, 1950, 1959). How might such a contextual-drift process work? Let us first denote the set of attributes representing context as the vector $\mathbf{t}$, which we define as:

$$\mathbf{t} = \begin{pmatrix} t(1) \\ t(2) \\ t(3) \\ \vdots \\ t(N_{context}) \end{pmatrix}.$$

In this equation, $N_{context}$ is the number of attributes representing context. Now suppose that each time a new item is presented, we change the context by a small and variable amount. Symbolically, we can add or subtract a small random number from each contextual attribute, such that $t_i(j) = t_{i-1}(j) + \epsilon$, where ϵ represents a random number drawn from a normal (Gaussian) distribution, i is an index variable that counts each item presentation, and j is the index of the attribute being incremented. Using vectors, we would write the following equation to describe this contextual-drift process:

$$\mathbf{t}_i = \mathbf{t}_{i-1} + \epsilon. \tag{3.4}$$

We will assume that context changes according to Equation (3.4) following any item presentation, either during study or during test. In this implementation of contextual drift, the amount of drift does not depend on the nature of the items that are being processed. In chapter 7 we will discuss more sophisticated models in which the change in context is determined by the item or event being experienced (e.g., Howard and Kahana, 2002a; Sederberg et al., 2008).

Assuming that context changes gradually over the course of an experiment, the amount of change in context between the study of an item and its later test will increase with the number of items intervening between study and test. This is how context can be used to explain the recency effect. Recent targets will have higher summed similarity than remote targets.

To fit the data from Hintzman and Block's study, our attribute model needs to separately compute the probe item's similarity to the average List 1 context and to the average List 2 context. Otherwise, the model would make judgments reflecting the occurrence of items in the more recent list and would not care much about items in the earlier list. One can potentially solve this problem by assuming that people can somehow retrieve earlier contextual states. To do so, it is helpful to have a model that forms associations between items and context and between context and items. Chapter 7 presents an analysis of these types of context models and shows how they can be used to explain a variety of data obtained in recall tasks.

Memon, Hope, Bartlett, and Bull (2002) examined the importance of context in recognition memory for police mug shots. They had two groups of people watch a video of a staged crime. Immediately after viewing the crime video, participants in the "mug book" group viewed mug books that contained photos of several suspects including one who was highly similar in appearance to the perpetrator. Participants in the "control" group did not view the mug book. Forty-eight hours later, all of the participants viewed a lineup that excluded the perpetrator but included the suspects who were in the mug book. Participants were asked to identify the perpetrator from the lineup. Before making their recognition judgments, half of the participants in the mug book condition were told to think back to the video and to try to base their decision only on what they saw in the video and not on any photographs they looked at afterward. They found that overall, participants in the mug book condition were more likely to endorse the similar suspect as the perpetrator. This tendency was significantly reduced when the participants were asked to relive their experience before making their memory judgments. Thus, people's ability to focus their memory on a particular context has significant consequences for memory tasks designed to emulate real-world situations.

3.5.1 Word Frequency Revisited

Here we reexamine the recognition word-frequency effect within the framework of attribute theories of memory. In the summed-similarity calculation used to determine whether or not to say *yes* to a given test item, those terms in which the content information stored in memory matches that of the test probe will have the greatest similarity. In the case of a lure, all the stored items with matching content information will be outside the experimental list. In the case of targets, there will also be one matching item in the experimental list for each time the target was presented. High-frequency (common) probe items, be they targets or lures, will result in higher levels of summed similarity than low-frequency (rare) probes because they will have occurred more times in the memory array.

Unless we assume that rare words attract greater attention than common words, the absolute difference in summed similarity between targets and lures will be the same for both rare and common words. However, because the overall level of summed similarity will be higher for common items, the *relative* change in summed similarity will be greater for rare words than for common words. Whereas presenting a rare word in the study list may increase summed similarity by 10%, presenting a common word might only increase summed similarity by 5%. By allowing the model to optimally choose a threshold that separates the summed-similarity distributions of common and rare probe words, the summed-similarity model can produce a word-frequency effect.

A very different explanation of word-frequency effects has been offered by Dennis and Humphreys (2001), who present a model of recognition judgments based on the idea that recognition is fundamentally a problem of list (or context) discrimination. In their context-based model of recognition, items are associated with context, and context is also associated with items. Presentation of a test item retrieves the contextual attributes stored when the item was previously studied. For targets, this retrieved context will include attributes from the study list as well as preexperimental exposures to the word; for lures it will only include contextual attributes from preexperimental exposures. For each test probe, the retrieved contextual information is compared to the state of context vector at the time of test. This retrieved contextual information will be a better match to the test context for rare words than for common words. This is because rare words have been encoded in fewer preexperimental contexts, and these preexperimental contexts will be a poor match to the current test context.

Dennis and Humphreys' analysis suggests that the word-frequency effect is not simply a consequence of the frequency with which a word occurs in the English language. Rather, the word-frequency effect reflects the tendency for common words to occur in more varied contexts than rare words. To test this hypothesis, Steyvers and Malmberg (2003) used a computerized database of text documents (comprising more than 10,000,000 words) to calculate separate measures of (1) a word's frequency of occurrence and (2) the number of different documents in which a word occurred, as a measure of contextual variability. They were then able to show that recognition performance decreased with the number of contexts in which a word occurred, even when the level of word frequency was held constant. As an example, the words *tornado* and *outlook* have the same word frequency, but *outlook* occurs in many more varied contexts than *tornado* and is harder to recognize, as predicted by Dennis and Humphreys' model.

3.6 SUMMARY AND CURRENT DIRECTIONS

Summed-similarity models go beyond strength theory by providing an explanation for the similarity effects observed in recognition memory (see Figure 3.5). Summed-similarity models can also reproduce the linear zROC functions described in chapter 2 (Shiffrin and Steyvers, 1997). As with strength theory, summed-similarity models can account for the word-frequency effect by assuming that rare words attract more attention than common words. The increased attention can be implemented by adding less noise to the stored representation of rare words. Finally, summed-similarity models have also been successful in explaining other memory and learning phenomena. In particular, summed-similarity models can account for how people learn new categories (e.g., Nosofsky, 1986) and for the kinds of errors made in medical diagnoses (Estes, 1994).

In discussing the strength theory of item recognition, we presented data suggesting that there may be a second process, in addition to strength (or familiarity), that contributes to recognition decisions. This second process, termed *recollection*, involves the recall of contextual or source information about a previously learned episode (see section 2.2). Within the framework of attribute theory, we can reformulate the concept of recollection and its distinction from familiarity in more precise terms. According to attribute theories, recollection occurs when the retrieval process recovers a vector of attribute values about the studied item and its context. Such a process is clearly different from summed similarity, which returns a single number (or scalar) representing the overall match of the test probe with the entire contents of memory. If recollection is a process that retrieves a vector of attribute values, we need to introduce some mechanism that would allow for such a retrieval process to occur. As we will see in the next chapter, the recollection process is associative. To better understand this process we need to take a detailed look at data and theories of association.

Although we presented a specific form of summed-similarity theory, largely built on ideas developed by Douglas Hintzman, William K. Estes, and Robert Nosofsky, there are other recent specifications that add important dimensions to our analysis. The use of noise in the encoding of items to model the learning process has been separately advanced by both Murdock (1989) and by Shiffrin and Steyvers (1997) in their similarity-based models of item recognition.

The Shiffrin and Steyvers (1997) REM model bases recognition decisions on a *likelihood ratio*: when the strength of evidence that a probe item is a target divided by the strength of evidence that a probe item is a lure exceeds 1, the model generates a *yes* response; otherwise, the model generates a *no* response. This turns out to be an optimal decision rule under many assumptions and it enables the model to fit the word-frequency mirror effect along with many other phenomena.

Temporal coding is another important theoretical construct used in modeling recognition memory. If each memory is tagged according to its time of occurrence, or perhaps if the items are associated with a context representation that changes gradually over time, then retrieving this temporal information can be used to estimate the time that has elapsed since the item was previously studied. Because items encountered on a just-presented list will be more recent than lure items, one can use this temporal information as a basis for making judgments of list membership, or judgments of recency for items presented on a given list. In their context-noise model of recognition, Dennis and Humphreys (2001) proposed such an account to explain various phenomena in the literature on item recognition.

Much work has also focused on modeling RT distributions in recognition memory. The most successful approach to this problem builds on work by Ratcliff (1978), who modeled the detailed time course of information accumulation as a random walk, or diffusion, process. The basic idea is that memory strength, or summed similarity, determines the rate at which familiarity information accumulates. A *yes* response is made when the familiarity information reaches a decision threshold. Ratcliff's *drift diffusion model* offers a nice account of the RT distributions in both recognition and categorization tasks (Ratcliff et al., 2004; Nosofsky and Palmeri, 1997). This class of models has recently been shown to provide an elegant account for the accumulation of neural evidence in studies of the neural basis of perceptual decision making, both in humans and in animals (Bogacz, 2007; Philiastides, Ratcliff, and Sajda, 2006; P. L. Smith and Ratcliff, 2004). In a recent tour-de-force, Nosofsky, Little, Donkin, and Fific (2011) has shown that a summed similarity model coupled with a diffusion model of the decision process can account for the major findings concerning both RT and accuracy data obtained in Sternberg's short-term item recognition (memory-scanning) paradigm.

3.7 *LIST-STRENGTH EFFECT

Here we consider the effect of repeating a subset of list items on people's memory for the nonrepeated items. We will use the term *mixed list* to refer

---

*As mentioned in the preface, sections noted by the asterisk, like this one, require some additional mathematics background. These sections may be omitted without losing the thread of the text.

to a list that contains a mixture of repeated and once-presented items; the repeated (and therefore better learned) items are called *strong items*, and the once-presented items (which are not learned as well) are called *weak items*. We will use the terms *pure strong* and *pure weak* to refer to separate lists in which all the items are either strongly or weakly encoded. Strong items are better remembered than the weak items. The question is whether mixing repeated (strong) and nonrepeated (weak) items together in a list exaggerates or attenuates the repetition effect.

In recall tasks, memory is better for strong items in a mixed list as compared with a pure strong list, and memory is better for weak items in a pure weak list as compared with a mixed list (Ratcliff, Clark, and Shiffrin, 1990; Tulving and Hastie, 1972). In other words, the strong-to-weak item recall advantage is greater in a mixed list than in pure lists containing only strong or only weak items. This finding is known as the *list-strength effect*.

We can understand the list-strength effect observed in recall tasks in terms of interference or competition. If strong and weak items are competing for recall, the stronger items will win out, being recalled first, and the weaker items will be less likely to be remembered. In a pure strong list, the strong items compete with other strong items, so they have a harder time being recalled. In the pure weak list, the weak items are better recalled because they do not have to compete with any strong items.

One can show mathematically that summed-similarity models predict a list-strength effect in item recognition. This is because the variance of the summed-similarity distribution increases with the number of matching items in the list, and the number of matching items in the list increases when items are strengthened by repetition. To really understand how this works, we need to present mathematical derivations for one type of summed-similarity model. This is done in the next two sections.

Ratcliff, Shiffrin, and colleagues (Ratcliff et al., 1990; Shiffrin, Ratcliff, and Clark, 1990) conducted a series of experiments to test for the list-strength effect in item recognition. They consistently failed to find any evidence for a list-strength effect. In fact, they found a small effect in the opposite direction. Weaker items were better remembered in mixed lists relative to pure lists, and stronger items were less well remembered. This failed prediction has been a major challenge to the summed-similarity framework.

Although there are some potential fixes for the summed-similarity models (Murdock and Kahana, 1993a), these fixes are not entirely satisfactory (Shiffrin, Ratcliff, Murnane, and Nobel, 1993). To make matters more interesting and complex, recent studies have shown that when recognition is performed with high levels of recollection, a small but significant list-strength effect can be observed (Diana and Reder, 2005; Norman, 2002; Verde and Rotello, 2004).

3.8 *A UNITRACE ATTRIBUTE MODEL

Rather than assuming the existence of a memory array that holds each memory as a separate entity (the multiple trace hypothesis; section 3.2.1), one may prefer to construct a model in which all memories are stored in a single composite representation. We will refer to this alternative view as the *Unitrace Hypothesis*.

In a series of influential articles, Murdock and colleagues developed an attribute model of recognition memory in which all studied items add together to form a composite memory vector (Murdock, 1982; Hockley and Murdock, 1987; Murdock, 1989). At test, the model compares a test item with the memory vector and responds *yes* if the similarity exceeds a threshold.

Mathematically, the storage equation in Murdock's model is given by:

$$\tilde{\mathbf{m}}_t = \alpha \tilde{\mathbf{m}}_{t-1} + \mathbf{B}_t \mathbf{m}_t \tag{3.5}$$

where $\tilde{\mathbf{m}}$ is the memory vector and $\mathbf{m}_t$ represents the item studied at time t. The variable α is a forgetting parameter. It takes on a value between 0 and 1 and is used to weight recently stored items more heavily than older items. $\mathbf{B}_t$ is a diagonal matrix[4] whose entries $\mathbf{B}_t(i, i)$ are independent Bernoulli random variables ($\{0, 1\}$). These random variables are assumed to take the value of 1 given by model parameter p.

The attributes of a given memory vector ($\mathbf{m}_t(i)$) are assumed to be independent and identically distributed normal random variables with $\mu = 0$ and $\sigma = \sqrt{1/N}$ where N is the number of elements in the vectors.

The two parameters of the model, α and p, determine the forgetting rate and the learning rate, respectively. A high value of α ($0.95 < \alpha < 0.99$) provides a good fit to the experimental data. The value of p determines the average proportion of attributes stored in memory when an item is studied. On a given exposure to an item, one adds each of the item's attributes to the memory vector with probability p. For example, if $p = 0.5$, each attribute has a 50% chance of being added to $\tilde{\mathbf{m}}$. If the same item is repeated, it is encoded again. Since some of the attributes sampled on the repetition were not sampled previously, the representation in memory is enriched. After many repetitions of an item, the representation becomes complete and each attribute is approximately of equal strength. Probabilistic encoding, as described above, has an effect that is quite similar to adding noise to each attribute value (as discussed in section 3.2).

---

4. A diagonal matrix is zero except for the elements $\mathbf{B}_t(i, i)$.

Retrieval. If the similarity (measured by the vector dot product) of the probe item, $\mathbf{g}$, with the memory vector exceeds a threshold, the model classifies the item as a target; otherwise, it classifies the item as a lure. That is:

$$P(yes|\mathbf{g}) = P(\mathbf{g} \cdot \tilde{\mathbf{m}} > k) = P\left(\sum_{i=1}^{N} g(i)\tilde{m}(i) > k\right),$$

where k is a fixed threshold. If two vectors are of unit length, the dot product is equal to the angle between the vectors.

3.8.1 Deriving d'

We can now derive the value of sensitivity, or d', in Murdock's unitrace model. Recall that d' is the difference between the means of the target and lure distributions, expressed in standard deviation units. That is,

$$d' = \frac{E[\mathbf{m}_i \cdot \tilde{\mathbf{m}}] - E[\mathbf{g} \cdot \tilde{\mathbf{m}}]}{\sqrt{\frac{1}{2}\left(\text{var}[\mathbf{m}_i \cdot \tilde{\mathbf{m}}] + \text{var}[\mathbf{g} \cdot \tilde{\mathbf{m}}]\right)}}. \tag{3.6}$$

Following the study of a list of length L, with no repetitions, the memory vector would be given by:

$$\tilde{\mathbf{m}} = \sum_{i=1}^{L} \alpha^{L-i}\mathbf{B}_i\mathbf{m}_i. \tag{3.7}$$

We can now solve for the expected dot product (similarity) of a lure $\mathbf{g}$, with the memory vector.

$$E[\mathbf{g} \cdot \tilde{\mathbf{m}}] = E\left[\sum_{k=1}^{N} g(k)\tilde{m}(k)\right]$$

$$= E\left[\sum_{i=1}^{L}\sum_{k=1}^{N} \alpha^{L-i}g(k)\mathbf{B}_i(k,k)m_i(k)\right]$$

$$= \sum_{i=1}^{L} \alpha^{L-i}pNE\left[g(\cdot)\right]E\left[m_i(\cdot)\right] = 0$$

The second line follows from Equation 3.7. This result depends on modeling items as independent (random) vectors with mean zero. That is, $E[\mathbf{m} \cdot \mathbf{g}] = 0$. In the third line, $g(\cdot)$ and $m_i(\cdot)$ denote arbitrary elements.

The expected dot product of a target, $\mathbf{m}_j$ (where $j \in \{1..L\}$), with the memory vector given by:

$$E[\mathbf{m}_j \cdot \tilde{\mathbf{m}}] = E\left[\sum_{k=1}^{N} m_j(k)\tilde{m}(k)\right]$$

$$= E\left[\sum_{i=1}^{L}\sum_{k=1}^{N} \alpha^{L-i} m_j(k)\mathbf{B}_i(k,k)m_i(k)\right]$$

$$= p\alpha^{L-j}\sum_{k=1}^{N} E\left[m_j^2(k)\right]$$

$$= p\alpha^{L-j}.$$

The second line follows from Equation 3.7. The third line follows from the first line by separating the sum into the matching, $j = i$, term and the nonmatching, $j \neq i$ terms and then noting that nonmatching terms equal zero. In the fourth line, the expectation is given by $\sigma^2 = 1/N$.

Now we need to compute the variances. First, let us compute the variance of the dot product between a new item and the memory vector.

$$\mathrm{var}[\mathbf{g} \cdot \tilde{\mathbf{m}}] = \mathrm{var}\left[\sum_{i=1}^{L}\sum_{k=1}^{N} \alpha^{L-i} g(k)\mathbf{B}_i(k,k)m_i(k)\right]$$

$$= \sum_{i=1}^{L}\sum_{k=1}^{N} \alpha^{2(L-i)}\mathrm{var}[g(k)]\mathrm{var}[m_i(k)]\mathrm{var}[\mathbf{B}_i(k,k)]$$

$$= \sum_{i=1}^{L}\sum_{k=1}^{N} \alpha^{2(L-i)}p(1-p)\sigma^4$$

$$= \sum_{i=1}^{L} \alpha^{2(L-i)}p(1-p)/N \tag{3.8}$$

The second line follows from the fact that the covariances between independent random variables are zero. If we allow for correlated random variables, these derivations become more involved. If $\alpha = 1$, then the last term simplifies to $p(1-p)L/N$.

To calculate the variance of a target's similarity (dot product) with the memory vector, we first separate the single matching term from the remaining nonmatching terms in the sum. Because we are assuming that the vectors representing different items are uncorrelated, all of the covariances will equal zero.

$$\mathrm{var}[\mathbf{m}_j \cdot \tilde{\mathbf{m}}] = \mathrm{var}\left[\sum_{k=1}^{N} \alpha^{L-j}\mathbf{B}_i(k,k)m_j^2(k) + \sum_{i \neq j}\sum_{k=1}^{N} \alpha^{L-i}m_j(k)\mathbf{B}_i(k,k)m_i(k)\right]$$

$$= \sum_{k=1}^{N} \alpha^{2(L-j)}p(1-p)\,\mathrm{var}[m_j^2(k)] + \sum_{i \neq j}\alpha^{2(L-i)}p(1-p)/N$$

$$= \alpha^{2(L-j)}2p(1-p)/N + \sum_{i \neq j}\alpha^{2(L-i)}p(1-p)/N \tag{3.9}$$

The last line follows from the fact that $E[X^4] = 3\sigma^4$, where $X \sim \mathcal{N}(0, \sigma)$.

We can see that the variance for the resemblance of an old item with the memory vector is slightly larger than the new item. This effect is going to be on the order of $1/L$. Although it is in the right direction, this difference is not large enough to explain the 0.8 slope of the zROC functions.

3.8.2 Derivations for the List-Strength Effect

Consider the predictions of Murdock's model for the list-strength effect. To simplify the calculations, we will make five simplifying assumptions: (1) The memory vector is set to zero at the start of each list. (2) No forgetting ($\alpha = 1$). (3) No probabilistic encoding ($p = 1$). (4) Uncorrelated item vectors (i.e., $E[\mathbf{m}_i \cdot \mathbf{m}_j] = 0$). (5) Equal variances of target and lure similarity distributions. Under these assumptions, the expression for d' simplifies to:

$$d' = \frac{E[\mathbf{m}_i \cdot \tilde{\mathbf{m}}]}{\sqrt{\mathrm{var}[\mathbf{g} \cdot \tilde{\mathbf{m}}]}}. \tag{3.10}$$

We can now derive d' for items in pure strong (PS) and pure weak (PW) lists and for strong and weak items in mixed lists (designated as MS and MW). A significant list-strength effect implies that the ratio of strong item to weak item d' should be greater for mixed lists than for pure lists. That is $d'_{MS}/d'_{MW} > d'_{PS}/d'_{PW}$, which implies that $d'_{MS}d'_{PW}/d'_{MW}d'_{PS} > 1$. We can rewrite this latter expression as:

$$\frac{E[\mathbf{m}_i^S \cdot \tilde{\mathbf{m}}^M]}{\sqrt{\mathrm{var}[\mathbf{g} \cdot \tilde{\mathbf{m}}^M]}} \frac{E[\mathbf{m}_i^W \cdot \tilde{\mathbf{m}}^W]}{\sqrt{\mathrm{var}[\mathbf{g} \cdot \tilde{\mathbf{m}}^W]}} \frac{\sqrt{\mathrm{var}[\mathbf{g} \cdot \tilde{\mathbf{m}}^M]}}{E[\mathbf{m}_i^W \cdot \tilde{\mathbf{m}}^M]} \frac{\sqrt{\mathrm{var}[\mathbf{g} \cdot \tilde{\mathbf{m}}^S]}}{E[\mathbf{m}_i^S \cdot \tilde{\mathbf{m}}^S]}. \tag{3.11}$$

where $\mathbf{m}^S$ and $\mathbf{m}^W$ are strong and weak target items and $\tilde{\mathbf{m}}^S$, $\tilde{\mathbf{m}}^W$, and $\tilde{\mathbf{m}}^M$ represent the memory vectors for strong, weak, and mixed lists, respectively.

Given that $E[\mathbf{m}_i \cdot \mathbf{m}_j] = 0$ (by assumption 4), the expected dot product of a target item with the memory vector will not depend on any nonmatching items in the list. Thus, $E[\mathbf{m}^S \cdot \tilde{\mathbf{m}}^M] = E[\mathbf{m}^S \cdot \tilde{\mathbf{m}}^S]$ and $E[\mathbf{m}^W \cdot \tilde{\mathbf{m}}^M] = E[\mathbf{m}^W \cdot \tilde{\mathbf{m}}^S]$. Equation 3.11 thus simplifies to:

$$\sqrt{\frac{\mathrm{var}[\mathbf{g} \cdot \tilde{\mathbf{m}}^S]}{\mathrm{var}[\mathbf{g} \cdot \tilde{\mathbf{m}}^W]}}.$$

If strong items appear r times and weak items appear only once, then:

$$\sqrt{\frac{\mathrm{var}[\mathbf{g} \cdot \tilde{\mathbf{m}}^S]}{\mathrm{var}[\mathbf{g} \cdot \tilde{\mathbf{m}}^W]}} = \sqrt{\frac{\mathrm{var}[\mathbf{g} \cdot \sum_{i=1}^{L} r\mathbf{m}_i]}{\mathrm{var}[\mathbf{g} \cdot \sum_{i=1}^{L} \mathbf{m}_i]}} = r.$$

Thus, under the assumptions outlined above, Murdock's model predicts a strong positive list-strength effect in item recognition. Murdock and Kahana (1993b) show that a more general version of Murdock's model will still predict a strong positive list-strength effect unless one drops assumption 1 and allows memories to accumulate continuously across successive lists.

3.9 STUDY QUESTIONS

1. Calculate the three pairwise distances between the vectors: $(1, 2)$, $(3, 1)$, and $(2, 4)$.
2. Consider a memory array, M, representing a list of five items, as defined below. Calculate the summed similarity for the target $\mathbf{m}_2$. Assume $\tau = 1$ in your calculations.

$$M = \begin{pmatrix} 2 & 7 & 1 & 0 & 3 \\ 0 & 9 & 6 & 4 & 3 \\ 0 & 3 & 7 & 4 & 7 \\ 7 & 0 & 8 & 5 & 9 \\ 9 & 1 & 6 & 6 & 6 \\ 3 & 4 & 5 & 8 & 9 \\ 7 & 8 & 9 & 10 & 10 \\ 4 & 5 & 5 & 6 & 7 \\ 9 & 10 & 11 & 11 & 11 \\ 0 & 0 & 0 & 1 & 1 \end{pmatrix}$$

$$= \begin{pmatrix} \mathbf{m}_1 & \mathbf{m}_2 & \mathbf{m}_3 & \mathbf{m}_4 & \mathbf{m}_5 \end{pmatrix}$$

3. Consider the memory array, M, given above. Note that this array includes both content attributes (top 5 rows) and context attributes (bottom 5 rows). Find the highest threshold that will ensure that the model responds *yes* when probed with either of the two most recent vectors stored in the array ($\mathbf{m}_4$ and $\mathbf{m}_5$).

4. Consider an experiment in which participants are shown two rectangles, which vary in their length and width, and are then given a recognition test. First, participants see Rectangle A, and then they see Rectangle B. A single test item is then shown. The test item may either be a target (Rectangle A or Rectangle B), or one of five possible lures, designated by the numerals 1–5 (see Figure 3.8). Assuming that a summed-similarity attribute model of recognition is correct, rank, from lowest to highest, the probability that participants will say *yes* to each of the seven possible test items. If the probabilities for two test items are exactly equal, then indicate their equality with an equal sign.

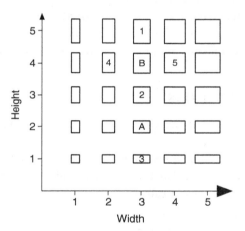

Figure 3.8 Illustration of stimuli used in study question 4.

5. Describe attribute theory and how the summed-similarity version of attribute theory has been used to explain data on recognition memory. What are the key experimental data supporting the notion of summed similarity?

4

Associations and Cued Recall

> It is evident that there is a principle of connexion between the different thoughts or ideas of the mind, and that in their appearance to the memory or imagination, they introduce each other with a certain degree of method and regularity. In our more serious thinking or discourse this is so observable that any particular thought, which breaks in upon the regular tract or chain of ideas, is immediately remarked and rejected. And even in our wildest and most wandering reveries, nay in our very dreams, we shall find, if we reflect, that the imagination ran not altogether at adventures, but that there was still a connexion upheld among the different ideas, which succeeded each other.
>
> DAVID HUME, *An Enquiry Concerning Human Understanding* (1777)

As discussed by philosophers since ancient times, our memories appear to be organized in terms of associative structures formed between items that are contiguous in space and time. Two items are said to be associated if presentation of one leads to thinking of (or responding with) the other. Examples of such associations abound in daily life. We are often faced with the challenging task of learning a new person's name, which involves at a minimum associating the representation of their name and their facial appearance. Other common examples include word learning in a second language, remembering who you are scheduled to meet for lunch, or remembering where you parked your car. At least it was the case that prior to our present era of personal-data assistants and Google's vast searchable databases, the ability to rapidly learn and later retrieve novel associations was an important tool in coping effectively with one's environment.

Laboratory studies of associative memory are concerned with people's ability to encode a relation between two items (these items are often known and thus represented in memory) and to later use one of the items as a cue to retrieve the other item. In considering associative tasks, we not only explore how people forge a memory representation that combines or links information from two previously learned representations, but we also investigate associative recall: the ability of a cue item to help people recall a target item. Thus, we add two new dimensions beyond our prior analysis of recognition memory for items: the dimensions of association and recall.

As noted in chapter 1, associations have been conceived in two quite different ways over the last century. According to the classical view, associations are links connecting two distinct knowledge representations. According to the Gestalt school of psychology, associations are new representations that combine elements of the constituent item representations (Köhler, 1947; Asch and Ebenholtz, 1962). In either of these two views, one must also consider the associations as being stored in relation to their unique situational and/or temporal context (Carr, 1931; Hollingsworth, 1928; McGeoch, 1932; Robinson, 1932; Underwood, 1945).

We begin this chapter by reviewing the basic experimental methods for studying memory for associations. Understanding these methods is crucial for deciphering the experimental studies on memory for associations. We then discuss studies of how people learn new associations, how people retrieve those associations, and how associations interfere with one another in memory.

4.1 MAJOR ASSOCIATIVE TASKS

The *cued-recall* task is the classic experimental procedure used to study associative memory. Participants study a list of paired items (termed *paired associates*), which we denote as A_1-B_1, A_2-B_2, ..., A_L-B_L, where L represents the number of pairs in the list. (We will use the notation A_i-B_i to denote the ith pair in the study list.) In contemporary studies these items are usually common words, but in early work these items were often consonant-vowel-consonant sequences (e.g., *BEZ*, *VOF*).

There are two basic versions of the cued-recall task: the *study-test method* and the *anticipation method*. In the study-test method, participants study a list of word pairs, presented one pair at a time. Either immediately following the study phase, or after some delay, participants are sequentially tested on each of the studied pairs. During this test phase, one member of each pair is presented and the participant is asked to recall the item that was paired with it. The order of testing is usually a random permutation of the order of study. At test, one can either present A_i as a cue for B_i (*forward recall*) or B_i as a cue for A_i (*backward recall*). Although forward and backward recall are sometimes contrasted, most experiments just ask for forward recall. Presentation of the pairs and test items can be either visual or auditory, but visual presentation (controlled by a computer) is the most commonly used method.

In the anticipation method, study and test are combined within a single phase. On each trial, participants are shown A_i and given a few seconds to *anticipate* (guess or recall) B_i. When participants are uncertain of the correct B_i item, they can simply wait until the B_i item is revealed. Participants repeatedly cycle through all of the A_i–B_i pairs in a given list until they can correctly recall a certain percentage of the B_i items.

Although recognition procedures are typically used to test memory for individual items, they can also be used to test memory for associations between items. In an *associative-recognition* task, participants first study a list of A_i–B_i pairs. Later, in the test phase of the experiment, participants are shown a mixture of *intact pairs*, A_i–B_i, and *rearranged pairs*, A_i–B_j. They are asked to respond *yes* to the intact pairs and *no* to the rearranged pairs. For example, if a participant studied the pairs *absence–hollow, despair–pupil, journey–worship*, and *sacred–harness*, then *journey–harness* would be a rearranged pair and *despair–pupil* would be an intact pair. Because both types of pairs comprise recently studied items, participants are required to discriminate pairs based entirely on their memory for the associations among the studied items.

Considerable attention has focused on comparing standard item recognition (as discussed in chapters 2 and 3) with associative recognition (e.g., Hockley, 1992; Nobel and Shiffrin, 2001). Although both are simple recognition tasks, the differences between them are seen to reflect the fundamental differences between memory for items and memory for associations, respectively. We will discuss the differences between item and associative recognition toward the end of this chapter.

In both cued-recall and associative-recognition tasks, participants are asked to remember a previously learned association. One can also study associative memory *indirectly*, that is, without asking participants to try to remember the studied pairs. In a classic study of indirect memory for associations, McKoon and Ratcliff (1979; Experiment 3) had participants study a list of paired associates. But then, rather than asking them to recall or recognize the previously studied pairs, McKoon and Ratcliff gave participants a lexical decision task in which they judged whether individual letter sequences were words or nonwords (see section 1.3.3). The sequence of test items was designed so that successively tested letter sequences were sometimes words that were previously paired together in the study list. Participants responded more quickly if the previously tested word was its pair from the study list, as compared to when the previously tested word belonged to a different pair. McKoon and Ratcliff's study demonstrates that memory for episodic associations can be measured without requiring people to think back to the time when the item was studied.

One can also study the nature of people's preexisting *semantic* associations among known items, as in the way that *salt* makes us think of *pepper* or *king* makes us think of *queen*. These preexisting semantic associations have been studied using a variety of tasks; prominent among these are semantic priming tasks and free-association tasks.

Before McKoon and Ratcliff's study of associative priming, Meyer and Schvaneveldt (1971) showed that the lexical decision task could be used to study semantic priming, that is, priming caused by preexperimental semantic associations. They found that participants were faster (and more accurate) at judging a word such as *butter* to be a word if the previously tested word was a semantic associate of butter, such as *bread*, as compared with an unrelated word, such as *tree*. The stronger the semantic association between two words, the shorter the RT (and the higher the accuracy) in judging the subsequently tested item to be a word. The difference between the RTs in these two conditions, the *priming*, could then be used to measure the strength of the semantic association between any two words. Unlike the McKoon and Ratcliff study, which measured priming as a function of words prior to being paired in the study list, semantic priming, as studied by Meyer and Schvaneveldt, measured priming as a function of the meaning of the words themselves.

In the *free-association* task, participants are tested on their semantic associations more directly. They are given a cue word and asked to say the first word that comes to mind. Consider the free associates that people might give to the word *dinner*; these might include *supper, eat, lunch, food,* and *meal* (Figure 4.1). The number near each line gives the relative frequencies of each of these responses derived from a large database of free-association data developed by Douglas Nelson at the University of South Florida (Nelson, McEvoy, and Schreiber, 2004). (In total, Nelson's database includes measures of associative relatedness for more than 72,000 distinct word pairs.) Whereas 11% of participants said *eat* in response to *dinner*, fewer than 1% gave *dinner* as a response to the word *eat*. Instead, the primary response to *eat* was *food*.

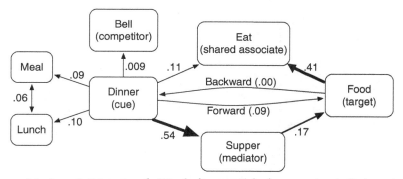

Figure 4.1 Associative network. Words *dinner* and *food* represent a studied word pair in which *dinner* later serves as the cue for recall of *food*. The other words illustrate an associative network surrounding the *dinner–food* pair, as derived from free-association data. Paths indicate the proportion of participants who gave a given response on a free-association task.

Looking more carefully at this figure, one can see that a participant could transition from one word to most other words by way of mediated associates. That is, although *dinner* may not evoke *food* directly, it may evoke *supper*, which in turn evokes *food* (see Figure 4.1). Such indirect associations, called *mediators*, have been shown to play an important role in associative-memory processes (Nelson, McKinney, Gee, and Janczura, 1998). Figure 4.1 also shows other kinds of preexperimental associations with the *dinner-food* pair, such as competing associates (e.g., *bell, meal, lunch*) and shared associates (e.g., *eat*).

4.2 ENCODING AND REPETITION

Learning a new association between two items generally requires attention to and elaboration of the relation between the items. Effective strategies that may be used to encode the relation between two words include creating a mental image in which the two words are interacting in some way, creating a phrase that links the two words, or thinking of another word (a mediator) that is meaningfully related to both words (see Murdock, 1974).

If you had to learn the word pair *ring–ladder*, you might create a mental image of climbing a ladder to ring a large bell, you might think of the phrase "she dropped her ring next to the ladder," or you might think of a mediator, as in *ring–rung–ladder*. For some word pairs, it may be easy to form an image; for others, it may be easy to form a phrase or find a mediator word; and for others, it may be extremely difficult to invoke any of these strategies. Becoming proficient in the use of these strategies can enable one to easily learn long lists of random pairs and retain those pairs over an extended period of time. In a study of the effect of interactive imagery on recall of concrete nouns, Wallace,

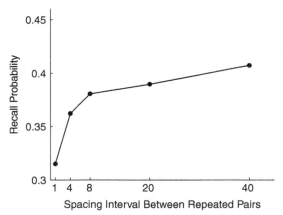

Figure 4.2 The effect of spacing repetitions on memory for associations. Recall probability increases with the spacing of the interval between repeated pairs. Data from Glenberg (1976).

Turner, and Perkins (1957) found that practiced participants could remember 664 out of 700 random pairings after a single study trial. In general, the more experience you have in learning pairs of items, the better you become at it. This finding, which is generally true in terms of all kinds of memory, is often termed the *learning-to-learn* effect (Thune, 1951; Postman, 1969).

The spacing of repetitions also plays an important role in associative learning. The *spacing effect* (see section 1.4) refers to the finding that spaced repetitions are generally better remembered than massed repetitions. This finding has been documented extensively in memory for paired associates, where the advantage of spaced practice increases steadily out to at least 20 intervening pairs (Figure 4.2). An exception to the spacing effect is that recall can be better for massed repetitions than for spaced repetitions if a pair is tested immediately after its second presentation (Peterson, Hillner, and Saltzman, 1962). This is because the recency effect can override the spacing effect when both presentations occur very close to the time of test.

4.2.1 All-or-none Associative Learning?

The fact that the learning curve increases systematically with the number of study trials (see Figure 1.5) suggests that learning is incremental, with each repetition of a pair strengthening the associative link between them (e.g., Hull, 1943). But this inference is not the only possibility. It is also possible that learning is accomplished in a single trial and that the continuous increase in performance over trials is a consequence of averaging over different items, some of which are learned on early trials and others of which are learned on later trials.

This latter view is sometimes called the *all-or-none learning hypothesis* and was advocated by Rock (1957) (see, also, Rock and Heimer (1959), Rock and Steinfeld (1963), and Clark, Lansford, and Dallenbach (1960)). Rock argued that in associating a pair of items, people attempt to find a reliable mnemonic to connect the two items. If successful, the association is established in a single trial. The more trials you have, the greater the likelihood of coming up with a reliable mnemonic. In terms of strength theory, this model posits two states for a given pair: a learned state and an unlearned state. Items start out in the unlearned state. On each trial, there is some probability that the pair will switch to the learned state. Once learned, there is some small probability a pair will revert from the learned state to the unlearned state. Rock proposed this two-state model to explain how associations are initially established to the point where they can resist interference from other pairs learned in the same context. Rock acknowledged that once established, associations can be further strengthened through repeated subsequent presentations of the pair.

In support of this view, Rock had participants study a list of letter–number pairs (e.g., *L-89, B-15, Z-22, M-19*) by the method of anticipation. As each letter appeared, the participants' task was to say the two-digit number before the correct number was shown. There were two groups of participants in Rock's experiment: The *control group* repeated the same letter-digit pairs until they could correctly recall all of them; the *experimental (substitution) group* had new pairs substituted for any pair they failed to recall on a given trial. If learning is incremental, the association between two items is strengthened even when the pair is not correctly anticipated. Further repetition increases the strength until it reaches a threshold needed to produce an overt response. Participants in the experimental group do not benefit from the repetition of nonremembered pairs. They are always faced with the task of learning a new pair in one trial. If learning is incremental, participants in the control group who *are* given repeated attempts to learn the pairs should perform much better than participants in the substitution group.

Experimentally, there was little difference between learning rates for the two groups (both groups required 4.75 trials to learn the pairs, and both groups made between 17 and 18 total errors during the learning process). Rock argued that the failure to observe a significant difference between the two groups supports an all-or-none view of association formation.

Rock recognized, but downplayed, a potential confound in this experiment; perhaps the nonrecalled pairs that were replaced (for the substitution group) were not recalled because they were actually harder to learn. These nonrecalled pairs would then be replaced with potentially easier-to-learn pairs. For example, if a participant was unable to learn the pair *L-89* on its first presentation, it might have been replaced with an easier-to-learn pair such as *C-33* or *I-95*. By the end of the experiment, the substitution group might have learned an easier set of pairs than the control group.

Williams (1961) demonstrated that the confound caused by Rock's substitution technique is serious, and therefore this technique cannot adequately address the incremental nature of learning. This was shown by having a new group of participants study lists consisting of the pairs that the experimental (substitution) group finally learned. These participants learned the experimental pairs more quickly than the control group, thus demonstrating that in the substitution procedure, harder pairs tend to be replaced by easier pairs, thus making the list easier to learn (see also Underwood, Rehula, and Keppel, 1962; Postman, 1962).

Following Rock's initial report, a number of other researchers replicated Rock's substitution experiment and attempted to control for the item difficulty confound. The results were mixed. In some studies, controlling for item difficulty did not lead to significantly slower learning in the substitution condition, while in other studies it did. For several years after these early studies, researchers tried to devise more sophisticated ways of testing the all-or-none idea, but in the end, these studies did not lead to any firm conclusions (e.g., Estes, 1960; Restle, 1965).

Although it is unlikely that learning is strictly an all-or-none process, it is probably the case that the amount of learning resulting from a single trial is quite variable, with some trials producing large strength increments and others producing smaller increments. You may recall that we came to a similar conclusion in our analysis of the recognition-memory paradigm, where models that assume variability in goodness of encoding provide a much better fit to the ROC curves (see section 2.2).

This variant of the incremental-learning hypothesis is supported by the finding that even long after a single pair, A_i–B_i, is learned, as measured by accuracy, the RT to recall B_i decreases with continued learning trials (Anderson, 1981; Waugh, 1970). The debate surrounding the all-or-none learning hypothesis brought to the foreground the idea that associative learning is not a mechanical process of strengthening simple links between item representations, but rather it is a complex process that depends on people's use of mnemonic strategies to relate new information to existing knowledge structures (Rock and Ceraso, 1964).

4.2.2 Incidental Associative Learning?

One may ask whether there is some associative learning between a pair of items simply due to their contiguity (i.e., their co-occurrence in time). To test this idea, Crowder, Serafine, and Repp (1990) asked whether the simultaneous presentation of spoken text with a hummed melody would induce an association between the two. They asked half of their participants to listen to simultaneously presented spoken text and hummed melodies (the text was spoken in rhythm with the melody). We will call these *novel songs*. The other half heard true *known songs* being sung (e.g., "Twinkle, Twinkle, Little Star"). Both groups were given an associative-recognition test. They listened to three types of stimuli: (1) *intact* songs—those that the participants had previously listened to (either novel or known), (2) *rearranged* songs created by combining the melody of one song with the lyrics of another song, and (3) *new* songs created by pairing previously heard lyrics with completely novel melodies.

Later, participants in both groups were asked to rate their confidence in having previously heard each of the melodies (ignoring the lyrics). To the extent that participants forged associations (or, in their words, *integration*) between the melodies and the lyrics, one would expect to observe higher confidence judgments for the intact songs than for the rearranged songs, which in turn would show higher confidence judgments than the new songs. This is exactly what Crowder et al. found. For the novel-song group, mean confidence ratings (with 6 being maximally confident) were 4.56, 4.04, and 3.33 for intact, rearranged, and new songs, respectively. For the known-song group, confidence ratings were 4.35, 3.96, and 3.25. Thus, even though participants were told to judge their memories for the melodies, they could not help but make use of the lyrics in their recognition judgments. Moreover, the similarity of the confidence ratings across the two groups indicates that participants in the novel-song group were able to forge associations between lyrics and melodies based on their temporal contiguity in a single experimental trial.

Crowder et al. used an associative-recognition procedure to demonstrate that we automatically store associative information due to the simultaneous processing of lyrical and melodic information. However, in studies that used distinct words as stimuli and recall as the testing procedure, evidence for incidental associative encoding has not always been observed. Whereas some studies have found evidence for associative learning in the absence of an intention to learn the pair, other studies have not.

Underwood (1983) noted that there have been sufficient demonstrations of positive effects of incidental associative learning to believe that such learning can happen (for another specific illustration, see section 4.5). But the effects of incidental, contiguity-based associations are small relative to the powerful influence of intentional associative encoding (see Greene, 1987). Nonetheless, the very existence of incidental associative learning is theoretically significant because it suggests that the brain continuously and automatically stores associative information even when we do not employ elaborative encoding strategies such as mediation or interactive imagery.

4.2.3 Associative Symmetry

An association between two items can be tested in either the forward or backward direction (direction is defined by the order in which the items were studied). One might expect that after studying a list of A_i–B_i pairs, it would be easier to recall B_i given A_i than to recall A_i given B_i. This expectation is consistent with the observation that after participants learn long sequences of items (like the alphabet), forward recall is easier than backward recall. For example, when asked to name the letter that precedes or follows a probe letter in the alphabet, backward retrieval is typically 40–60% slower than forward retrieval (Klahr, Chase, and Lovelace, 1983; Scharroo, Leeuwenberg, Stalmeier, and Vos, 1994) (see section 8.5). Similarly, in free recall, after recall of an item from position i, participants next recalled an item from list position $i + 1$ twice as frequently as an item from list position $i - 1$ (Kahana, 1996) (see section 6.2.2).

Early discussions of associative memory assumed that the strength of an association would be sensitive to the temporal order of encoding (Ebbinghaus, 1885/1913; Robinson, 1932). That is, forward associations were hypothesized to be stronger than backward associations. Furthermore, the strengths of forward and backward associations were hypothesized to be independent (the *independent-associations hypothesis*, see Wolford, 1971). An alternative view, the *associative symmetry hypothesis*, considered associations to be new representations formed by incorporating elements of each to-be-learned item into a new composite representation (Asch and Ebenholtz, 1962; Köhler, 1947). According to the associative symmetry hypothesis, the strengths of forward and backward associations are approximately equal and highly correlated.

Although many experiments have been carried out to assess the differences between forward and backward recall, most studies have found little or no difference (e.g., Ekstrand, 1966; Murdock, 1965, 1966). In the few cases where differences were found, they tended to be small in magnitude (see Kahana, 2002, for a review). Theorists who believed in the independent-associations hypothesis took any demonstration of a forward advantage to be strong support for their view. They also noted that failures to find differences between forward and backward recall were still compatible with the independent-associations hypothesis because it would be possible to form forward and backward associations that are independent but also of equal strength. Proponents of the associative symmetry hypothesis noted that their account was more parsimonious and that the failure to consistently find forward asymmetries implied that their position was most consistent with the data. We will return to the question of associative symmetry after we introduce theories of association in chapter 5.

4.2.4 Learning During Test Trials

A basic principle in human memory is that one cannot measure memory without changing it. That is, the very act of remembering (and perhaps of trying to remember) creates new memories. It is interesting to ponder the question of how much one's memory of an event is in fact memory of earlier memories of that event and not of the event itself.

Turning to the more mundane case of learning a list of paired items over many study-test trials, we can ask how much of the learning process takes place when people attempt to recall the previously studied pairs during the test trials and how much of it takes place on the learning trials themselves. In reviewing the literature on this question, R. A. Bjork and Bjork (1992) noted that ". . . the act of retrieving an item of information is considerably more potent in terms of facilitating its subsequent successful recall than is an additional study trial on that item. The actual extent to which a *successful* retrieval facilitates later retrieval appears to depend on how difficult or involved that act of retrieval is, with the subsequent benefits being a positive function of retrieval difficulty." The Bjorks' conclusions were based on an extensive body of empirical research dating back to the 1960s (e.g., Allen, Mahler, and Estes, 1969; Izawa, 1966).[1]

Although the benefits of testing are clear-cut in the basic research literature, insufficient attention has been paid to these findings in the educational literature. In fact, teachers often recommend repeated studying to students (see Rawson and Kintsch (2005), for a discussion) despite the greater benefits of testing. It is also not surprising that students prefer to study than to take tests.

An important variable that contributes to the beneficial effects of testing is the probability of retrieval success. If one makes the test trials so difficult that people cannot recall any of the to-be-remembered items, and if people are not told the correct answers on the items they fail to recall, there will be little or no learning during the memory test. On the other hand, if retrieval success is moderately high, giving people a test on the paired associates will often lead to better learning than giving people an additional chance to restudy all of the pairs.

To control for this variable, Carrier and Pashler (1992) compared the benefits of a study-only phase with a test-study phase. In the study-only phase participants were shown A_i-B_i pairs, where each A_i item was an English word and each B_i item was a corresponding word in the Siberian Eskimo Yupik language. In the test-study phase participants first attempted to recall B_i given A_i as a cue; then they were shown the A_i-B_i pair together. This test-study

---

1. The first empirical study of the beneficial effects of testing was reported by Gates (1917).

procedure is an implementation of the method of anticipation discussed in section 4.1. Following three presentations of each pair, participants were given a final cued-recall test. Carrier and Pashler found approximately 10% fewer errors in the test-study condition than in the study-only condition, even though both conditions were matched for total study time.

Roediger and Karpicke (2006) reported a far more dramatic demonstration of the beneficial effects of testing. In their study, several overlapping theoretical accounts have been proposed to explain the beneficial effects of test trials. According to the *transfer-appropriate processing* view, study trials are most effective when they require mental operations that are similar to those required at time of test. If part of your memory is not just for the association between A_i and B_i, but also for the retrieval process of using A_i to pull B_i out of memory, then practicing the retrieval will help in a later recall test more than simply studying the items. McDaniel and colleagues (McDaniel and Fisher, 1991; McDaniel, Kowitz, and Dunay, 1989) have argued that testing enhances learning by enabling people to better elaborate and re-encode the relation between the A_i and B_i items. That is, the act of recalling, as compared with restudying, produces new and more lasting connections between A_i and B_i. It is likely that both of these accounts play an important role in explaining the benefits associated with test trials. Mozer, Howe, and Pashler (2004) developed a computational model in which testing, as compared with studying, provides the brain with a more reliable *error signal* that is used to tune the way neurons wire up to each other during the learning process. They show how this model can account for some of the key findings concerning the testing effect.

An interesting and unresolved question related to the testing effect is whether testing has positive benefits on later memory when recall fails. That is, does one learn faster through the act of trying to remember even when the retrieval attempts do not succeed?

Another factor that seems to modify the beneficial effects of testing is the delay between study and test. The main benefit of testing accrues when memory is not tested immediately but rather after some delay. On an immediate test, study trials either confer a greater advantage than test trials (Hogan and Kintsch, 1971; Roediger and Karpicke, 2006) or they produce comparable levels of recall (Karpicke and Roediger, 2008). However, on a delayed test, the beneficial effects of testing can be quite dramatic (Karpicke and Roediger, 2008).

4.3 RECENCY AND LIST LENGTH

The law of recency captures the ubiquitous finding that recent experiences are more easily remembered than remote ones. For newly learned word pairs, forgetting is very rapid. If tested immediately, the last pair is almost always

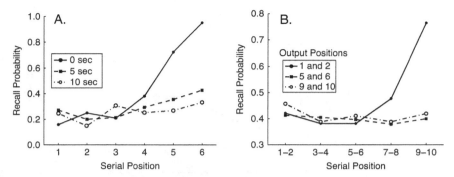

Figure 4.3 Recency and paired associates. People are very good at remembering the
last couple of pairs in a list when they are tested immediately after study. **A.** Recency is
greatly reduced after a delay of 5 sec (Murdock, 1967). **B.** Forgetting occurs during the
recall phase itself. Items tested early in recall (output positions 1 and 2) show marked
recency, whereas items tested late in recall do not exhibit recency because of the
increased lag between study and test (Tulving and Arbuckle, 1963). (Note: Murdock,
[1967] tested a single pair following study, so output position is always 1.)

correctly recalled and the next-to-last pair is recalled more than 50% of the time.
Earlier pairs, however, are recalled less well, and the level of recall of these pairs
decreases very slowly with increasing study-test retention intervals (Murdock,
1967). This can be seen for data from two different experiments, as shown in
Figure 4.3.

The recency effect for paired associates is larger for auditorily presented lists
than for lists that are presented visually. This *modality effect* is usually limited
to the last two or three studied pairs (Murdock, 1972).[2] Because people know
that they will easily remember the last few items, they may not attend to these
items as intently as they do the earlier list items. As a consequence, if one gives
people a surprise test after a long delay, the last few items may actually be
remembered less well than the items from earlier list positions (Madigan and
McCabe, 1971).

Forgetting of paired associates is very rapid at first but then becomes quite
slow (Figure 4.3). This contrasts the pattern of results obtained for recognition
of single items, where forgetting is far more gradual (e.g., Murdock and Kahana,
1993b). This difference in the form of the forgetting function could reflect
the fundamentally different responses required in recognition and recall tasks,
with recall requiring that the person generate the target item and recognition
requiring that the person judge the memorability of the target item. Hockley

---

2. The recency effect is also larger for auditorily presented items in other recall tasks, such as free
and serial recall (see chapters 6 and 8).

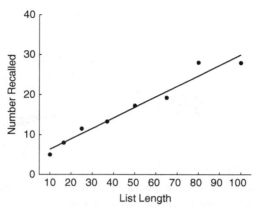

Figure 4.4 The effect of list length on the number of pairs recalled. Data from Murdock (1960).

(1992) controlled for this difference between recognition and recall by directly comparing long-term forgetting rates for word pairs and single words when he tested both using a recognition procedure. He found that pairs remembered after a short interval were still remembered after a long delay. In contrast, single items were initially remembered better than pairs but were quickly forgotten. These findings suggest a fundamental difference between memory for single items and pairs, even when the method of testing is controlled.

Related to the recency effect is the list-length effect. In studying a list of paired associates presented at a constant rate (e.g., 2 sec for each pair), participants will recall a smaller percentage of pairs in longer lists than in shorter ones. At the same time, however, participants will recall a larger absolute number of pairs as the list length increases. This is shown in Figure 4.4, which plots the number of pairs recalled for lists ranging from 10 to 100 pairs in length. It is striking that the number of pairs recalled increases approximately linearly with list length. This type of linearity would be expected if there is a set probability that a given studied pair would be recalled and if that probability does not change as additional pairs are added to the list. If adding additional pairs interferes with one's ability to recall previously studied pairs, we would expect the slope of the function to decrease with increasing list length.

4.4 RETRIEVAL ERRORS

When given an associative (cued) recall test on a previously studied pair, people typically withhold a response when they are unsure of the correct answer. Occasionally, however, people make errors, which we call *intrusions*. We can analyze people's intrusions to better understand the recall

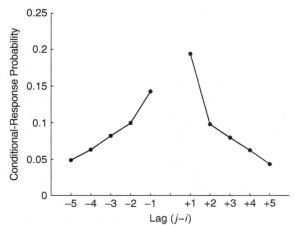

Figure 4.5 Temporal contiguity and intralist intrusions. This figure shows that the probability of incorrectly recalling a word from the jth pair in response to a cue word from ith pair (an intralist intrusion) decreases with the separation (lag $= j - i$) between the pairs (data for correct responses, i.e., lag $= 0$, are not shown). Most intralist intrusions thus come from pairs that were studied in temporal proximity to the target pair. Data from Davis et al. (2008).

process. The intrusions that people commit in associative recall exhibit three major characteristics.

First, intrusions tend to share semantic attributes with the correct response. For example, if the correct response is *dinner*, people will sometimes mistakenly recall a semantically related word such as *supper* or *meal*.

Second, people are more likely to mistakenly recall items if they have been recently studied, either on the current list (intralist intrusions) or on a prior list (prior-list intrusions). For example, Davis, Geller, Rizzuto, and Kahana (2008) found that 32% of participants' prior-list intrusions came from the preceding list, whereas 19% and 15% of prior-list intrusions came from two and three lists back, respectively. That is, intrusions exhibit a recency effect, just like correct recalls.

Third, intrusions tend to come from pairs that were initially learned close in time to the cue item. This tendency is shown in Figure 4.5, which plots the probability of an intrusion as a function of the distance in pairs from the cue item.[3]

---

3. In determining the relation between intrusion probability and distance, it is important to consider only intrusions that the participant could have made. Otherwise, one would (artifactually) observe an effect of distance simply because there are more valid transitions at shorter distances than at longer distances given the finite nature of the list. For this reason, Davis et al. computed the probability of committing an intrusion from a given lag *conditional* on that intrusion being a valid transition within the list.

Although intralist intrusions constituted only 5% of participants' responses, these intrusions exhibited a strong tendency to come from neighboring pairs. The conditional probability of an intralist intrusion decreased monotonically with the number of pairs (lag) separating the intrusion from the probed item. This effect was not limited to an increased tendency to commit intrusions from adjacent pairs. Even when adjacent pairs were excluded, a regression analysis demonstrated that the across-pair contiguity effect was highly reliable.

Because the order of test was randomized with respect to the order of study, there was no reason for participants to adopt a strategy of learning interpair associations. Indeed, such a strategy would have been counterproductive insofar as it would induce high levels of associative interference between pairs (Primoff, 1938). This demonstration of associative tendencies in participants' intralist intrusions suggests that temporally defined associations arise from a basic and most likely obligatory memory process that causes items studied in nearby list positions to become associatively connected. Even though participants did not intend to link the items in one pair with items two or three pairs away, their intrusions reveal the brain's tendency to automatically form those connections.

4.5 RETROACTIVE INTERFERENCE AND RECOVERY

Associative recall has long been used to probe the mechanisms underlying forgetting. In early investigations, participants were asked to learn a list of pairs to a criterion of one (or more) perfect recitation. Then, their memory for the same pairs was tested at delays (*retention intervals*) ranging from minutes to days, and a forgetting function was traced out.[4] One would like to know what caused the decline in performance: was it simply the passage of time or some consequence of the events that intervened during the retention interval? McGeoch (1932) noted that when the retention interval is filled with conflicting associations, performance declines more rapidly than when the retention interval is filled with an unrelated activity (such as solving puzzles). This phenomenon, known as *retroactive interference* (RI), depends critically on the nature of the intervening material being learned.

4.5.1 Briggs' Study

In a classic study of retroactive interference, Briggs (1954) asked participants to study a list of 12 paired adjectives for a subsequent cued-recall test (we will

---

4. A different participant group is tested at each retention interval to avoid transfer effects across multiple recall tests.

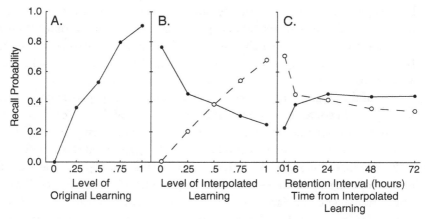

Figure 4.6 Interference and the AB/AC paradigm. A. Learning curve for A_i–B_i pairs during the first phase of the experiment. Level of original learning corresponds to the fraction of responses correctly anticipated on the trial preceding recall. **B.** During the course of A_i–C_i learning, participants were shown A_i and asked to recall whichever item first came to mind. Over A_i–C_i learning trials, B_i responses decreased (solid line) while C_i responses increased (dotted line). **C.** Recall performance on a final test as a function of the retention interval, which ranged from seconds to days. As the retention interval increased, C_i responses decreased while B_i responses increased. Data from Briggs (1954).

designate these pairs as A_1–B_1, A_2–B_2, ..., A_{12}–B_{12}). Over repeated *anticipation* trials, participants mastered the pairs, as seen in their increased probability of recalling B_i given A_i as a cue (see Figure 4.6A).

Following this initial learning phase, participants were asked to learn a new list of paired adjectives in which the A items from the first list were paired with new C items (e.g., A_1–C_1, A_2–C_2, ..., A_{12}–C_{12}). To test participants' memory, Briggs used a modified recall procedure developed by Underwood (1948). Rather than explicitly instructing them to recall only the C_i items, Briggs asked participants to recall the first item they could think of when given A_i as a cue. Thus, they might recall B_i, C_i, or some other item (an intrusion). Participants were permitted to give only one response to each pair.

Early in the process of learning the new A_i–C_i pairs, participants often recalled the B_i response items from the first list (solid line in Figure 4.6B). As learning of the A_i–C_i pairs progressed, C_i responses (dotted line in the figure) came to exceed B_i responses, thus demonstrating the interference between the newly learned pairs and the original pairs. To better understand the nature of this interference effect, Briggs retested participants at varying delays. Of particular interest was whether the superior recall of the newly learned pairs would persist over a broad range of retention intervals. As shown in Figure 4.6C, participants' tendency to recall C_i decreased with length of the retention interval. Surprisingly, however, the tendency to recall the original B_i responses actually increased with increasing delays, with the level B_i recall actually exceeding that of C_i recall at delays of 24–72 hours.

The finding that B_i responses decreased so rapidly as participants learned A_i–C_i pairs illustrates the RI phenomenon. The rate of decline of B_i responses would have been much slower had participants been given unrelated pairs (asked to learn C_i–D_i) in the second phase of the experiment. The rapid decline in B_i responses following A_i–C_i learning was taken to support the view that new competing associations did something to make it harder to recall the old associations. The standard explanation was in terms of *competition* (Webb, 1917; McGeoch, 1942). The new associations would compete with the old associations at the time of test and would win out in the competition. That is, A_i would evoke both B_i and C_i, and if C_i was stronger even by a small amount, it would be impossible to recall B_i. Another possibility was that the new A_i–C_i associations somehow overwrote or eroded the original A_i–B_i associations, making them weaker. This latter possibility is known as the *associative unlearning* hypothesis.

Recovery of Old Associations

The most interesting feature of Briggs' study, however, was the finding that the original B_i responses actually overcame the C_i responses when tested after a delay of one day or longer. Although the finding of an absolute increase in B_i recall over time is not always found, the finding of a relative superiority of B_i over C_i recall at long delays appears to be robust (Brown, 1976). This finding is referred to as *spontaneous recovery* of the A_i–B_i associations, by reference to an analogous finding in animal associative learning. In fact, the entire pattern of results shown in Figure 4.6 mimicked what had been seen in animals when two conflicting habits (associations) were formed. Initially, the second habit overrode the first one, and then after a long delay, the first habit returned as the second habit was forgotten (Pavlov, 1927; Rescorla, 2004).

Briggs' study demonstrated spontaneous recovery of previously learned associations. What was not clear, however, was whether associative unlearning or response competition was responsible for the loss of B_i responses with A_i–C_i learning. According to the response competition account of forgetting, people tended to recall C_i instead of B_i because the stronger A_i–C_i associations overcame the older, and hence weaker, A_i–B_i associations. Alternatively, the learning of the A_i–C_i associations might have extinguished the A_i–B_i associations learned earlier, as predicted by associative unlearning.

To explain the strange phenomenon of spontaneous recovery, consider that as time passes, the A_i-C_i associations somehow become weaker (perhaps due to interfering information learned during the delay period). If A_i-B_i and A_i-C_i associations are learned at times 0 and 1 hour, respectively, and then are tested 24 hours later, both will have been unlearned to an approximately equivalent degree or they will compete to an approximately equivalent degree. In either case, when cued with A_i, both B_i and C_i responses should be produced with comparable frequencies. Although this accounts for the convergence of B_i and C_i recall at long delays, it does not explain the finding that recall of B_i surpasses that of C_i at retention intervals longer than one day. The superior recall of B_i would be expected to occur if participants retrieve the B_i items during trials of A_i-C_i learning. This is because each retrieval of A_i-B_i during A_i-C_i learning constitutes an additional learning trial for A_i-B_i, making the first list associations easier to retrieve on a final recall test.

4.5.2 Competition vs. Associative Unlearning

In an attempt to decouple competition and associative unlearning, Barnes and Underwood (1959) repeated the main part of Briggs' experiment. However, instead of asking their participants to recall just one item (either B_i or C_i), they gave participants ample time to recall *both* items and encouraged them to do so. For historical reasons, the Barnes and Underwood technique is referred to as *modified modified free recall*, or simply MMFR.[5]

In their study, Barnes and Underwood had participants first learn a list of A_i-B_i pairs to some criterion level (e.g., one trial without errors). Then they asked their participants to learn a second list of A_i-C_i pairs. After varying degrees of A_i-C_i learning, they tested their participants' memory for both B_i and C_i.

As shown in Figure 4.7, participants' tendency to recall B_i gradually declined as they were given more trials of A_i-C_i learning. These data mirror the pattern of results obtained by Briggs (see Figure 4.6B). If the MMFR procedure actually eliminates response competition, as Barnes and Underwood argued, then the decrease in B_i responses with A_i-C_i learning must reflect something other than competition. Barnes and Underwood argued that these results provided support for the idea that the newly learned A_i-C_i actually weakened the stored representations of the A_i-B_i associations. Much discussion in the literature surrounds the nature of this weakening—for example, are the associations permanently eroded or just temporarily inhibited (e.g., Postman, Stark, and Fraser, 1968)?

---

5. This unfortunate terminology arose because Briggs' procedure was already known as modified free recall.

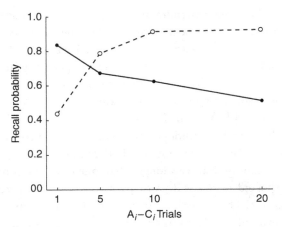

Figure 4.7 Associative interference: response competition or associative unlearning? Participants first learned an A_i–B_i list (not shown) and then, as they learned a second list of A_i–C_i pairs, they were given A_i and asked to recall both B_i and C_i. As the proportion of C_i responses (dotted line) increased (with A_i–C_i trials), the proportion of B_i responses (solid line) decreased.

A number of subsequent investigators used the MMFR procedure to assess the recovery of A_i–B_i associations under conditions of minimal response competition. Consistent with the earlier findings of Briggs (1954) and Underwood (1948), participants tended to remember more of the first list than the second list responses when tested following a delay (Brown, 1976; Wheeler, 1995). This finding was seen as support for a temporary inhibition account of unlearning in retroactive interference paradigms (Postman and Underwood, 1973).

In her 1960 dissertation, Barnes reported a far more extensive analysis of the interference theory of forgetting (published as McGovern, 1964). She assessed retroactive interference in four experimental paradigms. Following learning of A_i–B_i pairs, Barnes had participants learn either completely new C_i–D_i pairs, rearranged A_i–B_j pairs, A_i–C_i pairs (as described above), and C_i–B_i pairs. She identified at least three types of information that must be learned and then potentially unlearned: forward associations, backward associations, and contextual associations (the latter being associations between the items and the experimental context; a topic that will be further discussed below). She found the greatest levels of interference in the A_i–B_j condition (i.e., participants had greater difficulty learning those associations, and after learning, exhibited greater forgetting of the originally learned associations) and the least interference in the C_i–D_i condition. Interference levels were intermediate in the other two conditions but somewhat greater in A_i–C_i than in C_i-B_i. Given that A_i-B_j requires unlearning of both forward and backward associations it is not surprising that interference was greatest in that condition. Under the view that either (a) forward associations are stronger than backward associations or (b) repeatedly recalling C_i leads to greater response learning, it is not surprising that learning A_i-C_i was more difficult than learning C_i-B_i. In using the MMFR procedure to assess recall, McGovern interpreted the forgetting of the original associations following new learning as reflecting unlearning rather than interference.

4.6 PROACTIVE INTERFERENCE

Interference effects can occur both forward and backward in time; that is, later items can interfere with earlier items and earlier items can interfere with later items (Whitely, 1927; Underwood, 1957). Consider an experiment in which two groups of participants, Group A and Group B, learn lists of word pairs. Group A studies three distinct lists: List 1, List 2, and List 3. Group B only studies two lists: List 2 and List 3. If both groups are tested on their memory for List 2 at some later time, Group B will exhibit better recall. Studying List 1 somehow impaired Group A's ability to learn and/or recall List 2. The finding that earlier learning can interfere with new learning is termed *proactive interference* (PI).

If RI and PI both reflect competition between associations learned in similar contexts, then the magnitude of PI should reflect the number of prior competing associations learned by the participant. Similarly, the magnitude of RI should reflect the number of subsequent competing associations learned by the participant. If we (unrealistically) assume that the list items are unencumbered by associations with items learned outside of the experimental setting, and if the number of prior and subsequent pairs are equated, then the RI and PI effects should be of equal magnitude. However, the data show that RI effects are typically larger than PI effects (Melton and von Lackum, 1941). This finding is consistent with the view that both RI and PI reflect response competition and that RI also reflects an additional process such as unlearning.

Melton and von Lackum's (1941) finding that RI exceeds PI in the case of two lists should not be taken as evidence against the overall importance of PI in forgetting. Indeed, in a situation where participants learn multiple lists, PI can have a huge impact on performance. In an early study of PI in paired-associate learning, Greenberg and Underwood (1950) had participants learn a list of 10 paired adjectives to a criterion of 8 of 10 correct on a single trial. When asked to recall the same pairs after a 48-hour retention interval, participants correctly recalled ~70% of the paired associates. On the next day, Greenberg and Underwood (1950) had their participants learn a new list of 10 adjective pairs that were unrelated to the prior list. When tested on these pairs following a 48-hour delay, participants were only able to recall ~40% of the paired associates. This process was repeated for two further lists of adjectives, and recall steadily declined, falling to ~25%. It is remarkable that learning just three prior lists of paired associates, without any overlapping items, resulted in such a sharp decline in recall of the target list. The importance of PI in the analysis of forgetting became widely recognized after a seminal analysis by Underwood (1957) who showed that the pattern of results described above appeared in many other memory studies using diverse methods and materials.

In Greenberg and Underwood's (1950) experiment, substantial PI was observed even though there were no overlapping items across the studied pairs and even though no two lists were learned in a single session. To interpret PI as resulting from competition, one must therefore broaden the notion of competition to include items learned in the shared context of the experiment rather than simply items sharing direct associates or even those learned in a single session. If one were to broaden the notion of competition even further to include all previously stored memories for adjectives, then it is hard to see how learning a few dozen words in an experiment would add much interference to the vastly greater quantity of previously stored memories outside of the laboratory.

Proactive interference is a remarkably general phenomenon, appearing in nearly every type of recall and recognition task. Its effect is greatly reduced, however, when the retention test is immediate and when the target list is dissimilar from previously studied lists. A number of lines of evidence suggest that PI results from competition among memories learned in similar contexts. For example, Postman and Keppel (1977) found higher levels of PI to be associated with poorer list discrimination (assessed by asking participants to judge which of several lists a pair, or item, had appeared on). Underwood (1983) found that PI effects were far greater when successive lists contained items that were conceptually (or categorically) related to one another. The joint influence of both proactive and retroactive interference can also be seen within a single list, where recall of a given pair is reduced by increasing either the number of prior or subsequent pairs in the list (Murdock, 1963b).

4.7 CONTEXT AND INTERFERENCE THEORY

Building on earlier theorizing by McGeoch (1932), Underwood (1945) suggested that context is a crucial mechanism at work in interference studies.[6]

---

6. Despite his early recognition of context as a major factor in forgetting, Underwood made relatively little use of this construct in his many influential papers on interference theory over the following three decades.

When participants perform MMFR, even if they can only remember one of the items, they often know which list the remembered item came from. Although you might be asked to associate *apple* with *chair* in List 1 and *apple* with *car* in List 2, when tested, you would not likely recall *orange*. Somehow, you not only know that *chair* and *car* are associated with *apple* but you also know that they are associated in the context of the lists used in the experiment.

Both Underwood (1945) and Estes (1955) used the concept of context to help explain spontaneous recovery. When testing occurs close in time to the study lists, they are easily discriminable, as evidenced by Hintzman and Block's work on list discrimination (see Figure 3.2). If we assume that context drifts over time, then the contextual attributes at the time of test will be very similar to the second list and far less similar to the first list. However, when testing follows a long delay, the two lists become difficult to differentiate because the test context is very different from both of the studied contexts. This helps to explain why recall levels for A_i–B_i and A_i–C_i tend to converge after a long delay. The finding that A_i–B_i actually surpasses A_i–C_i in some experiments would be expected to arise if people think of A_i–B_i during A_i–C_i learning, as this would result in additional opportunities to encode A_i–B_i.

Contextual drift can also be used to help explain findings of proactive interference. In that case, memories from earlier experiences tend to crowd later ones, especially when tested after a long delay. This is consistent with Postman and Keppel's (1977) finding that proactive interference was related to failures of list discrimination.

As we have already seen in the last chapter, the idea of contextual attributes has become an important theoretical construct in the analysis of human memory. Within the framework of interference theory, context serves to focus retrieval on the appropriate associations, thus limiting competition from other associations. In the next chapter we will describe how this process might actually work.

4.8 SIMILARITY AND INTERFERENCE

Interference effects depend strongly on similarity. Although PI and RI effects are substantial when pairs are constructed to produce competing associations, these effects are much smaller when pairs are distinctive from one another (as in the case of an A_i–B_i list followed by a C_i–D_i list).[7] The strongest interference effects are seen when participants are asked to learn pairs formed by rearranging

---

7. Pairs can be made more distinctive through imagery or the use of mediators. In such cases, they become less susceptible to RI (Adams and Montague, 1967).

the A_i and B_i items to form a new list of A_i–B_j pairs (Martin, 1965). In these rearranged lists, competition is at work both from A items to B items and from B items back to A items.

One can also think of interference operating within a single list, whereby later list items interfere with earlier ones and vice versa. In this case, one would expect to see interference manifest itself in a list-length effect: The longer the list, the lower the probability of recalling any given item. Although such effects are clearly evident in the data, they are small in magnitude for lists of randomly paired items (see Figure 4.4).

Similarity and Memory for Name-Face Associations

Consider the common occurrence of meeting a new person and hearing their name. In such circumstances, it is highly desirable to be able to quickly learn the name-face association. Successful learning of this association allows us to address people by their names when we next meet them. Given the social significance of this ability, it is unfortunate that name-face pairings are often very difficult to learn.

Briefly reflecting on the challenge of learning to associate names and faces reveals several potential factors that make this task particularly difficult. First, associations between names and faces are very hard to elaborate in a meaningful way. Whereas with word pairs one can often come up with a verbal mediator or an interactive image, faces are far less amenable to such elaborations, and names are rarely related to faces in any meaningful way. Second, the attributes representing the appearance of a face are likely to differ from one encounter to the next. For example, the person may have styled their hair differently or they may be wearing sunglasses or a hat. Here we consider a third factor that is less obvious but is theoretically quite interesting and important. More than virtually any stimuli studied in the laboratory, faces are extremely similar to one another. They all have the same basic shape, structure, organs, etc. When you consider a set of faces representing a single gender and age range and you remove all other superficial cues (e.g., hair styling, eyeglasses, etc.), it is amazing how visually similar they are. The fact that faces are structurally so similar means that for a given name-face pair, there will be other pairs whose faces are quite similar to that of the target pair. Pantelis, van Vugt, and Kahana (2007) asked whether such similarity relations could account for why some faces are significantly easier to learn than other faces.

In a previous study, participants rated the similarity of 16 monochromatic faces, such as those shown in Figure 4.8A. Using a technique called *multidimensional scaling* (e.g., Steyvers, 2004), they used the pairwise similarities among the faces to find a vector representation of each face in a four-dimensional space, where each dimension roughly corresponded to one of the major attributes of

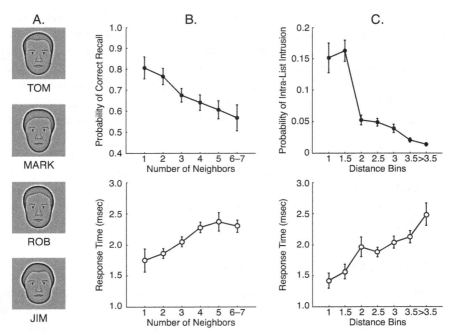

Figure 4.8 Similarity and memory for name-face associations. A. Examples of name-face pairs presented at study. A multidimensional scaling experiment indicated that the 16 faces used in the experiment could be characterized as varying primarily along four dimensions. **B.** Neighborhood effect. The upper panel shows the probability of recalling the correct name when cued with a face at test as a function of how many neighbors that face had within the study list. Two faces within a study set were considered neighbors if their distance was below a threshold value. The lower panel shows the RTs for correctly recalling the names of faces as a function of the number of neighbors. **C.** An intralist intrusion occurs when a participant, cued with a face at test, mistakenly recalls the name of a different face that was also presented during study. Each possible intrusion name corresponded with a study face, for which the distance from the cue face in four-dimensional face space was calculated. The upper panel shows the probability of making an intralist intrusion of a particular distance, given that an intrusion of that distance was possible during that trial. The lower panel shows the RTs for intralist intrusions of various distances from the cue face. Error bars represent the standard errors of the means.

the faces (e.g., the shape of the hairline, the width of the nose). Defining each face as a vector allowed them to calculate the subjectively perceived distance between any two faces.

Pantelis et al. (2007) hypothesized that people would have greater difficulty associating names with faces that had many "neighbors" in the four-dimensional face space (where neighbors are defined as the number of other faces that lie within a small radius around the target face). To test this hypothesis, they asked participants to study eight faces that were paired with common American male names. At test, participants were presented with each of the eight studied faces, one at a time. As each face appeared, participants attempted to recall the name that was previously paired with the face. This study-test procedure was repeated 10 times so that participants could learn the names of all of the faces.

When cued with a face at test, participants' accuracy at recalling the correct name decreased as the number of also-studied neighboring faces increased. RT data showed the inverse effect (see Figure 4.8B). Also, when participants made intralist intrusions, these errors tended to be names associated with faces that were similar to the target face (see Figure 4.8C).

4.8.1 Associative Symmetry and the Fan Effect

One's ability to learn and/or recall an A_i–B_i association is clearly influenced by the presence of competing associations in memory. This can be seen in the data on RI, where learning a new A_i–C_i association makes it harder to recall A_i–B_i. It can also be seen in data on PI, which show slower learning of A_i–C_i resulting from the prior learning of A_i–B_i. Associative-interference effects can also be seen in the influence of preexperimental associations on new learning. Thus, in learning a new A_i–B_i pair, if A_i has a large number of strong preexperimental associates (X_i), it will be hard to recall B_i because of competition from X_i. The general principle that interference is related to the total number of distinct associations with a given item is often called the *fan effect* (Anderson, 1974).

Figure 4.9 shows an associative network that illustrates a symmetric, bidirectional association between A_i–B_i and competing associates with both A_i and B_i. In this example, recalling B_i given A_i as a cue will be harder than the reverse, due to the increased number of associations fanning out from A_i. This shows that even if you had a perfectly symmetric association between A_i and B_i, you might still observe asymmetries in recall (Kahana, 2002).

4.9 UNLEARNING AS INHIBITION

The finding of substantial retroactive interference in the MMFR paradigm (which was intended to eliminate response competition) suggested that another forgetting process must be at work. Postman et al. (1968) suggested that the entire repertoire of first-list associations and first-list responses was temporarily inhibited during second-list learning. Dissipation of this inhibitory process

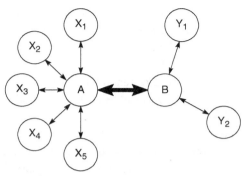

Figure 4.9 A simple associative network. The thick arrow depicts the experimental association between A and B. In this example, A has five preexperimental associates (marked $X_1, \cdots X_5$), whereas B has only two preexperimental associates (marked Y_1 and Y_2).

led to spontaneous recovery (i.e., the increase in retrievability of first-list associations following a long delay).[8]

Anderson and Spellman (1995) developed a novel empirical method for assessing the locus of the inhibitory effect. They argued that if the inhibitory process acts upon the attributes of B_i itself, then the inhibition should also reduce the retrievability of any item that is similar to B_i. To demonstrate a distinct role for the inhibition of B_i, beyond any inhibition of the A_i–B_i association, Anderson and Spellman assessed memory for B_i using an independent probe that is unrelated to A_i.

To demonstrate this attribute-level inhibition, Anderson and Spellman developed a variant of the MMFR procedure involving three distinct phases. In Phase I, participants study a list containing a mixture of both A_i–B_i and A_i–C_i pairs, where the B_i and C_i items are both conceptually related to the A_i item. Thus, the list might include the pairs, *red–blood, red–tomato, tool–pliers,* and *tool–drill,* where the words *blood* and *tomato* are both conceptually related to the word *red,* etc.

In Phase II (termed the *retrieval practice,* or RP, phase), participants are given extensive practice recalling some of the A_i–C_i pairs (e.g., *red–blood*). For these pairs, the first two letters of C_i were presented along with A_i (e.g., *red–bl____*) to ensure that participants recall C_i and not B_i. The retrieval practice phase is analogous to the learning of the A_i–C_i list in traditional MMFR experiments

8. Postman's distinction between associative and response inhibition is not widely recognized in the recent literature. Most writers assume that he had only considered associative unlearning as a factor in RI, where in fact he argued forcefully for the importance of response inhibition as well (Postman and Underwood, 1973; Postman and Gray, 1977).

except that rather than simply studying A_i–C_i, participants are asked to practice retrieving C_i given A_i as a cue. The prediction is that practicing retrieval of A_i–C_i should inhibit not just A_i–B_i but also B_i itself (and, to a lesser degree, any items that are conceptually similar to B_i).

Memory for all of the pairs is tested in the third phase of the experiment using an MMFR procedure. During this phase, which is usually given after a delay of approximately 20 minutes, participants are given each of the A_i items as cues and they are asked to recall both B_i and C_i.

On the basis of Barnes and Underwood's MMFR findings, one would expect to find better recall of C_i than B_i for those A_i–C_i pairs that were practiced in Phase II. For the A_i–C_i pairs that were not practiced, recall of B_i and C_i should be approximately equivalent and should fall midway between the levels of B_i and C_i recall for the practiced pairs. Not surprisingly, the data supported these expectations.

However, Anderson and Spellman wanted to go beyond previous MMFR studies in identifying the locus of the unlearning effect with the B_i representation. They therefore designed their lists so that for half of the pairs, B_i was semantically related to A_j (the *related* condition); for the other half of the pairs, B_i was not semantically related to A_j (the *unrelated* condition). In the related condition, participants might learn the pairs *red-blood, red–tomato, food–strawberry,* and *food–cracker* in Phase I. Figure 4.10 gives examples of A_i–B_i and A_i–C_i pairs in the related and unrelated conditions. Then, in the retrieval-practice phase, participants would practice a subset of the pairs, including *red-blood.* As a consequence of practicing *red-blood,* participants would be less likely to recall *tomato.*

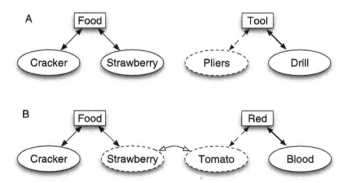

Figure 4.10 Associative structures in the retrieval-induced forgetting paradigm. Panels A and B illustrate associative structures resulting from the unrelated and related conditions, respectively. Arrows indicate associations and dashed lines indicate inhibited representations.

Anderson and Spellman's critical finding was that retrieval practice of *red-blood* not only impaired recall of *tomato* but also impaired recall of *strawberry*, a word that shares semantic attributes with *tomato* (being both red and a food). This latter result was not predicted by standard interference theory. Anderson and Spellman argued that this result demonstrates something more than associative competition or even associative inhibition. They suggested that the impaired recall of related items implies an inhibition or suppression of the nonpracticed attributes, which thereby reduces recall of other related items in memory.

Anderson and colleagues have shown that retrieval practice of A_i–C_i not only reduces A_i–B_i recall but also makes it difficult to recall (or even to recognize) B_i or items similar to B_i, regardless of whether the item is cued by A_i or by an independent probe item. Although this result has been replicated numerous times in different laboratories, it depends on providing participants with retrieval practice on the A_i–C_i pairs: if participants study A_i–C_i without repeatedly attempting to recall C_i, then the effect is often not observed (Anderson, 2003).

4.9.1 A Test of the Specific-Unlearning Hypothesis

Anderson and Spellman (1995) proposed that learning (especially retrieval practice) inhibits the attributes of competing associations in memory. That is, recalling A_i–C_i causes an inhibition of the attributes representing A_i–B_i, including the attributes of B_i itself and any items that are closely related to B_i. They thus proposed a specific mechanism for associative unlearning, as measured in the MMFR procedure (see Figure 4.7).

Both the inhibition mechanism and earlier notions of unlearning were believed to be *specific* to a given pair (Postman, 1961). That is, learning A_i–C_i would cause unlearning/inhibition of A_i–B_i but not necessarily unlearning of A_j–B_j. According to this *specific, unlearning hypothesis*, people should be less likely to recall B_i if they could recall C_i and vice versa. That is, recall of B_i and C_i should be negatively correlated.

Table 4.1 gives hypothetical data for an MMFR experiment showing the usual advantage for C_i over B_i recall and the hypothesized negative relation between B_i and C_i recall. As you can see, recall of B_i is usually associated with a failure to recall C_i and vice versa. To quantify the relation between B_i and C_i recall, we can create a *contingency table* , as shown in Table 4.2. A contingency table shows all possible combinations of outcomes: recall of both items, recall of none of the items, recall of B_i but not C_i, and recall of C_i but not B_i. From such a table we can easily compute the degree to which the two variables are correlated. For variables such as recall, which can only take on one of two values

Table 4.1
Hypothetical data comparing B_i and C_i recall in an
MMFR experiment.

item	Recall B_i	Recall C_i
1	no	no
2	no	yes
3	no	yes
4	yes	yes
5	no	yes
6	yes	no
7	no	yes
8	yes	no
⋮	⋮	⋮
Mean	0.37	0.63

Table 4.2
Contingency table for hypothetical data shown
in Table 4.1.

		Recall B_i	
		Yes	No
Recall	Yes	1	4
C_i	No	2	1

(recalled or not recalled), the correlation is often referred to as contingency, as it is calculated from the cells in a 2×2 contingency table. Yule's Q is a popular measure of correlation for 2×2 contingency tables (Bishop, Fienberg, and Holland, 1975).[9] Like standard measures of correlation, Q varies from -1.0 (perfect negative correlation) to $+1.0$ (perfect positive correlation). For the hypothetical data shown in Table 4.2, $Q = -0.78$, indicating a strong negative correlation between B_i and C_i recall.

---

9. Yule's Q is defined as $Q = (ad - bc)/(ad + bc)$, where a is the number of times a participant recalled both B_i and C_i, d is the number of times a participant recalled neither B_i or C_i, b is the number of times a participant only recalled B_i, and c is the number of times a participant only recalled C_i. For a 2×2 contingency table, Q is the same as Goodman and Kruskal's Gamma statistic.

DaPolito (1967) tested the specific-unlearning hypothesis by measuring the correlation between B_i and C_i recall. Unlike the hypothetical data shown above, DaPolito found that the probability of recalling B_i did not depend on whether C_i was recalled and vice versa. That is, he found that recall of B_i and recall of C_i are independent with the value of Q being approximately zero. Numerous subsequent studies have replicated this result (see Kahana, 2000, for a review). The failure to observe a significant negative correlation between recall of B_i and C_i in MMFR experiments suggests that any inhibitory effect of A_i–C_i learning on memory for A_i–B_i must take place at the level of the entire AB list rather than at the level of the specific *i*th pair. These results pose a serious challenge to the specific-unlearning hypothesis.[10]

A potential complicating factor makes it difficult to interpret the correlation between successive recall tests. As noted by Hintzman (1981), the correlation between successive recall tests can be influenced by variability in the difficulty of individual pairs. If, for example, A_i is a word that is very easy to associate with other words, then both A_i–B_i and A_i–C_i will be well learned, whereas if A_i is a word that is hard to associate with other words, then neither A_i–B_i nor A_i–C_i will be well learned. Thus, variability in ease of learning can induce a positive correlation between B_i and C_i recall. Because the predicted correlation is negative, it is possible that the variability in ease of learning will induce a positive correlation that exactly offsets the predicted negative correlation. As noted by Martin and Greeno (1972), however, it seems strange to assume that these two factors would precisely offset one another.

4.10 INTERFERENCE THEORY: CONCLUDING REMARKS

In his seminal 1932 paper, McGeoch argued that associative competition and contextual change were the two primary causes of forgetting. Because competition could be easily manipulated by the numbers of shared associates and the similarity of items learned within and across lists, a great deal of early work focused on testing the competition hypothesis. Melton and Irwin's (1940) observation that the degree of forgetting could not be explained by the rate of intrusion errors and Barnes and Underwood's (1959) demonstration that forgetting was substantial under conditions designed to minimize competition suggest another unlearning factor.

10. Not all studies find a near-zero correlation. A notable exception is the series of experiments reported by Tulving and Watkins (1974). They found significantly positive correlations between recall of B_i and C_i. One possible explanation is that participants were encoding the two pairs as an ABC triple (Tulving, 1997, personal communication).

In addition, early researchers were inspired by the striking parallels between human associative memory and Pavlov's (1927) analysis of the acquisition and extinction of responses in classical conditioning procedures. Drawing on these parallels, the view was that human forgetting may be akin to extinction of the conditioned response and that recovery of first-list associations following a delay may result from the same mechanisms that underlie spontaneous recovery of responses in animal studies. Given that recovery of A_i–B_i associations is seen under conditions assumed to produce minimal competition, unlearning was seen as a temporary inhibition-like process, operating at the level of associations, at the level of items, or both (Postman and Underwood, 1973; Anderson, 2003).

The Melton-Underwood-Postman interference theory conceived of forgetting as resulting from competition and inhibition of forward associations, backward associations, and associations between items and the experimental context (McGovern, 1964). For the 30-year period between 1940 and 1970, their theory occupied center stage in research on human memory. Whereas a major focus of early research on interference theory was on relating human and animal studies, the 1960s saw a shift toward modeling the underlying memory processes and extending the analysis of associative interference to the study of short-term memory tasks, where participants are tested on their immediate memory for relatively short lists of items.

Summarizing the state of interference theory, Postman and Underwood (1973) highlighted a number of major challenges facing the theory. One major problem concerned the evidence against the notion of specific unlearning of associations. It was not clear what mechanism would give rise to inhibition of the entire ensemble of first-list responses. This, along with the finding of significant retroactive interference even when completely unrelated lists were learned, suggested that perhaps inhibition was operating on the context of the first list items, but context was not a well-defined concept in the theory. The finding that inhibition is not specific to individual B_i responses, but rather operates at the level of the ensemble of A_i–B_i items, together with the finding that interference is also observed when there are no common associates between lists, suggests that perhaps it is the first list context that is being inhibited.

Another problem concerned the existence of proactive interference in the Barnes and Underwood MMFR paradigm, which is very hard to explain if one assumes that the MMFR procedure eliminates response competition. Although most interference theorists assumed that response competition was eliminated in MMFR, the logic for this view is highly questionable: just because you are permitted to recall two things does not mean that one cannot compete with the other, making it harder to remember. A third major problem was that many retroactive interference phenomena disappeared when memory was tested using an associative-recognition procedure. This finding is incompatible with the notion that unlearning (or inhibition) is a major cause of retroactive inhibition because unlearning should affect recognition as well as recall.

The emerging problems for interference theory coincided with several major concurrent developments in the study of memory. One major development during this period was the emphasis on encoding and retrieval processes. Whereas interference theorists focused on how learning one set of information impaired retrieval of another, they did not delve very much into the way in which encoding conditions (during learning) and retrieval conditions (at test) influence performance. In a series of influential papers, Tulving demonstrated how the types of retrieval cues provided at test can greatly reduce or enhance the effects of interference (e.g., Tulving and Osler, 1968; Tulving and Psotka, 1971; Tulving, 1974). There was also a major shift in focus from measuring changes in aggregate recall and recognition performance after long delays to a much more detailed analysis of performance on short-term memory tasks. Alongside the emphasis on immediate recall was the development of computational models of how encoding and retrieval operate, as well as the ascendance of models that posited separate short-term and long-term memory mechanisms (Atkinson and Shiffrin, 1968). In subsequent chapters we will address each of these topics in depth.

4.11 ITEM AND ASSOCIATIVE INFORMATION

In the previous section we contrasted inhibition of items and of associations. Item and associative information are two basic kinds of information that can be stored in memory (Murdock, 1974). Both refer to information that is learned within a given context, typically that defined by an experimental list. Memory for item information is most often measured by asking people whether they recognize a probe item as having occurred in a target list (i.e., the item recognition task discussed in chapters 2 and 3). Memory for associative information can be tested using either cued recall or associative recognition. In an associative-recognition task, people are asked whether a test pair matches one they have previously seen. To ensure that participants base their judgments solely on memory for the learned associations, the experimenter will construct lures by rearranging items from previously studied pairs to form new pairs. Thus, both the targets and lures will have been items seen in the experimental list.

There are thus two basic differences between item recognition and cued recall. Whereas recognition tasks provide participants with the target item and ask them to *judge* their memory for its prior occurrence, associative recall tasks require people to *produce* the target item in response to a retrieval cue. A second difference between item recognition and cued recall is that whereas successful recall depends on people's memory for the association between the cue and the target (associative information), successful item recognition depends on people's memory for the occurrence of the target item in the list, without reference to any specific cue (item information).

Strength theory provided the earliest account of the relation between recognition and recall. According to this view, the study of the items on a list increases their memory strength. Outcomes of both recognition and recall tests depend on an item's memory strength. Consistent with the observation that recognition is usually easier than recall, this view held that the essential difference between these tasks is that the strength threshold for recall was higher than the threshold for recognition.

Despite its heuristic value, strength theory offered an overly simplistic view of recognition-recall differences. This theory was abandoned after researchers found that experimental variables had opposing effects on recognition and recall. For example, as compared with common words, rare words are easily recognized as having been presented in a recent list but are more difficult to recall (Gregg, 1976; Kinsbourne and George, 1974; MacLeod and Kampe, 1996). A second example is the effect of intentionality on memory encoding (Glenberg and Bradley, 1979; Schwartz and Humphreys, 1974): intentional (as compared with incidental) encoding has a far greater effect on learning in a cued-recall task than in an item-recognition task. A third example is the effect of context change on memory retrieval. Whereas context effects are often quite large in recall tasks, they are generally much smaller in recognition tasks (Godden and Baddeley, 1975, 1980). A fourth example concerns the effects of damage to the medial temporal lobe (MTL) and in particular the hippocampus. Damage to the MTL system produces much larger deficits in recall than in recognition tasks (Hirst, 1986; Vargha-Khadem et al., 1997), at least when interitem similarity in the recognition task is not very high (Holdstock et al., 2002).

Generate-recognize theory provided an alternative conception of the differences between recognition and recall (e.g., Bahrick, 1970). According to this view, recall involves two stages: people first generate possible responses and then they apply a recognition test to decide whether any of the generated responses were on the list. The recognition task differs from recall in that the generate stage is absent. A strong version of this model predicts that recallable items will always be recognized. Contrary to this prediction, Tulving and colleagues (e.g., Tulving, 1968; Tulving and Thompson, 1973) found that unrecognized items may often be subsequently recalled when prompted by an appropriate retrieval cue.

4.11.1 Recognition Failure of Recallable Words

In studying the relation between recognition and recall, Tulving adopted the *successive testing technique*, a technique that had been used previously to assess the role of specific unlearning in RI. In Tulving's procedure, participants studied a list of A–B word pairs and were then tested successively, first by item recognition and then by cued recall. In the item-recognition test, participants saw B items from each of the studied pairs intermixed with nonlist items. Participants responded "yes" to items if they remembered seeing them in the study list. In the cued-recall test, participants attempted to recall the B items when given the A items as cues. In this manner, memory for each of the B items was tested twice—first by recognition and then later by recall. Tulving and colleagues observed that some items that participants failed to recognize as having been presented in the study list were nonetheless correctly recalled on the cued-recall test—a finding they referred to as the "*recognition failure of recallable words.*"

Tulving and Wiseman (1975) measured the statistical *contingency* (or association) between item recognition and cued recall at the level of individual items. Their analysis revealed a simple relation between the conditional probability of recognition given recall, $P(R|C)$, and the probability of recognition itself, $P(R)$. This relation, known as the *Tulving-Wiseman function*, describes a moderate degree of dependency between item recognition and cued recall. Expressed using Yule's Q—a measure of association for 2×2 contingency tables—one finds values ranging from 0.45 to 0.65 across a wide range of experimental conditions (Kahana, 2000; Nilsson and Gardiner, 1991).

The moderate degree of dependence between recognition and recall contrasts with tasks in which the same information is probed on two successive tests. For example, Kahana (2002) had participants study a list of 12 A–B pairs. All the studied pairs were then tested twice, once in each of two test phases (designated as Test 1 and Test 2). On Test 1, half of the studied pairs were cued in the forward order and the other half were cued in the backward order. On Test 2 (which was given after a brief delay), half of the pairs were tested in the same order as in Test 1 (forward on both tests or backward on both tests) and half were tested in the reverse order (e.g., forward on Test 1 and backward on Test 2). The correlation between successful recall of pairs tested in an identical manner on the two retrieval occasions was 0.99. More surprisingly, the correlation was 0.97 for pairs tested in the forward order on one of the tests and the backward order on the other (e.g., A–? on Test 1 and ?–B on Test 2). Kahana (2002) interpreted the similarity of these correlations as evidence for the associative symmetry hypothesis (Asch and Ebenholtz, 1962), which sees A–B associations as a holistic conjunction of both A and B items, rather than independent forward and backward links (Wolford, 1971). The preceding example illustrates that the moderate correlation between successive recognition and recall ($Q \sim 0.5$) must say something about the information processing that underlies these two memory tasks.

The moderate correlation between item recognition and cued recall, coupled with numerous experimental dissociations in which manipulated variables selectively influence either recognition or recall, led theorists to advocate for a distinction between *item-specific* and *relational* (or associative) *information* (Humphreys, 1978; Hunt and McDaniel, 1993; Murdock, 1974) with *familiarity-based* retrieval of item-specific information and *recollection* of relational information (Yonelinas, 1997; Yonelinas et al., 1998).

4.11.2 Speed–Accuracy Trade-off for Items and Associations

Nobel and Shiffrin (2001) asked whether the rate of information accumulation following the appearance of a test probe differs for item and associative information. To answer this question, they used the response signal procedure described in chapter 2. In this procedure, participants are required to respond as soon as a tone is heard. By varying the timing of the tone following the presentation of the test cue, one can track the rate at which memory performance increases over time (the speed–accuracy trade-off, or SAT, function).

Figure 4.11A shows SAT functions for item recognition, pair recognition, and associative recognition. One can see that the rate of information accumulation was significantly faster for item and pair recognition than for associative recognition. Figure 4.11B shows that for cued recall, the rate of information

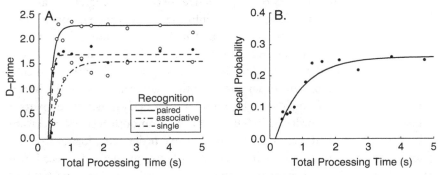

Figure 4.11 Speed-accuracy trade-off functions for item and associative information. A. SAT functions for three recognition conditions: paired-recognition, in which participants discriminated between intact and new pairs (solid line); associative recognition, in which participants discriminated between intact and rearranged pairs (dash–dot line), and standard single-item recognition (dashed lines). **B.** SAT functions for cued recall. Data from Nobel and Shiffrin (2001).

accrual was similar to that of associative recognition. These data provide further evidence concerning the different retrieval processes underlying memory for item and associative information.

In the next chapter we will discuss computational models of associative memory. These models are principally designed to explain how associative recall works. An important issue that must ultimately be addressed is how our memory system can perform cued recall, item recognition, and associative recognition. This has been a topic of intensive research efforts and is beginning to yield some impressive results (Kahana, Rizzuto, and Schneider, 2005b; Murdock, 1997; Metcalfe, 1985; Humphreys et al., 1989; Hintzman, 1988; Mensink and Raaijmakers, 1988; Norman and O'Reilly, 2003).

4.12 SUMMARY AND CURRENT DIRECTIONS

In this chapter we have surveyed some of the major experimental findings concerning associations and cued recall. The next chapter will present some of the major theories of associative memory and will evaluate those theories in terms of their ability to account for the data presented here.

The first major distinction in the study of associative memory is that of episodic vs. semantic associations (Tulving, 1972). A given pair of items may be associated prior to their co-occurrence in a study list. These preexperimental associations, which generally relate to the meaning of the items, are referred to as semantic associations. Examples include *bread–butter* and *king–queen*. When faced with the task of learning to associate a pair of unrelated items, people form a new, episodic, association. In most cases, however, even randomly paired items share some attributes in common.

Cued recall is the primary task used in the study of episodic associations. However, one can also measure episodic associations using recognition and priming procedures. Semantic associations can be measured directly with the free-association task or indirectly using a priming task.

Associative learning depends critically on intentional encoding strategies such as mediation and interactive imagery. People can learn to use these strategies to rapidly memorize very large numbers of randomly paired items. In his influential *substitution* study, Rock (1957) argued that associative learning is not incremental but rather takes place in a single trial. This view would be consistent with the idea that people either succeed or fail in finding a mnemonic to link the to-be-associated items. If they succeed, then they are very likely to learn the pair; if they fail, then they do not benefit from the co-occurrence of the paired items. Unfortunately, there are confounds with the original substitution studies that are difficult to entirely rule out.

A related, and theoretically significant, question is whether people automatically encode the association between temporally contiguous items without having any intention to learn the association. The existing evidence supports the idea that associative learning does take place automatically but at a very slow rate. This suggests a weaker form of all-or-none learning; perhaps it should be called strong-or-weak learning.

As with other types of learning, associative learning benefits from spaced (as compared with massed) practice and from intermixing study and test trials (as compared with just giving study trials). Under many circumstances test trials are actually more effective than study trials, especially in assuring long-term retention of the to-be-learned items.

People's ability to correctly recall randomly paired items exhibits a marked recency effect: recall accuracy is very high when a studied pair is tested immediately following its presentation but then falls rapidly when just one or two other pairs intervene between study and test. This very strong recency effect in cued recall contrasts with a much shallower recency effect seen in associative recognition.

Following study of a list of A_i–B_i pairs, each presented sequentially (A_i then B_i), people are about as good at recalling A_i given B_i as they are at recalling B_i given A_i. This finding has been taken by some to support the view that associations are formed symmetrically and not as separate connections from A_i to B_i and from B_i to A_i. Of course, one could have independent forward and backward associations that are still of equal strength, on average. Thus, the finding of symmetric recall does not necessarily imply symmetric associations.

To test the idea that forward and backward associations are independent but of equal strength, Kahana (2002) devised an experiment using the successive testing technique. Kahana reasoned that according to Wolford's independent-associations view, the correlation between forward recall and subsequent backward recall of the same pair should be significantly lower than the correlation between pairs tested in the same direction. Contingency analyses revealed that contrary to this view, forward and backward recall were highly correlated and were as highly correlated as pairs tested in the same direction. This finding was taken to support the associative symmetry hypothesis (Asch and Ebenholtz, 1962), which sees associations as a holistic conjunction of both A and B items. Using the same approach, Caplan, Glaholt, and McIntosh (2006) also found support for holistic associations but showed that for recall of triples and serial lists, the correlation between forward and backward probes was significantly reduced (see also, Madan, Glaholt, and Caplan (2010)). Sommer, Rose, and Büchel (2007) found evidence for holistic associations in recall of object-location associations.

Intrusion errors in cued recall exhibit three basic regularities: they tend to be semantically related to the correct response, they tend to come from recent lists (and from recent pairs in the current list), and when they come from the current list, they tend to be members of pairs studied near to the target pair. Any complete theory of associative memory must not only account for how people produce correct recalls but must also account for the factors that give rise to retrieval errors (intrusions).

Finally, the cued-recall task has provided the major testing ground for an analysis of those factors that give rise to forgetting in episodic-memory tasks. The major theoretical idea to come out of these studies is the notion that forgetting arises not from decay of memories but rather from interference among memories. We have already seen how interference arises in recognition memory as a consequence of summed similarity (see chapter 3). In recall tasks, interference effects can be studied more directly by having people learn pairs that contain competing associates, as in the A_i–B_i—A_i–C_i paradigm (see Figure 4.6). Later pairs interfere with earlier pairs (retroactive interference, RI) and earlier pairs can also interfere with later pairs (proactive interference, PI). A critical question is whether these interference effects are due to competition between the overlapping associations or, in the case of RI, are also due to a specific unlearning or inhibition of the older associations (or response items) that is caused by learning the new associations. Support for the unlearning account came from the Barnes and Underwood (1959) finding of substantial RI under conditions designed to minimize response competition. Additional evidence for an inhibitory process operating at the level of the B_i responses comes from Anderson and Spellman's (1995) study. However, the finding of independence between B_i and C_i recall challenges any specific inhibition or unlearning model. If better learning of A_i–C_i entails greater inhibition of B_i or A_i–B_i, then one would expect to find a negative correlation between recall of B_i and C_i in the MMFR procedure—a finding that was not observed experimentally. Moreover, the observation of significant RI in the A_i–B_i—C_i–D_i paradigm suggests that inhibition may not depend on specific overlap of associations at all. Rather, RI may arise from inhibition of the first-list contextual representation during second-list learning. This would give rise to a deficit in first-list recall that operates at the level of the entire ensemble rather than specific items or associations.

Mensink and Raaijmakers (1988) showed that the contextual fluctuation ideas of Estes (1955) (see section 3.4), as implemented in a computational model of cue-dependent retrieval (Raaijmakers and Shiffrin, 1980), could be used to explain nearly all of the major findings concerning forgetting of paired associates. Estes' ideas of contextual fluctuation have also been used to explain data on spacing effects (Raaijmakers, 2003) and on the dynamics of retrieval in the free-recall task (Howard and Kahana, 2002a). We will discuss these models in greater detail in chapter 7.

4.13 STUDY QUESTIONS

1. Compare the recognition and recall tasks. Discuss the ways in which these two tasks reveal shared and unique aspects of memory function.
2. Describe the all-or-none claim about the learning process and the experiment by Rock that supports it. Discuss the confounds inherent in Rock's method and how you might address them experimentally.
3. Why is it important to know whether learning by contiguity can occur without an intention to learn the connection between the neighboring items?
4. Associative memory has been a fertile ground for theorizing about the forgetting process. Three of the major ideas are: (1) response competition, (2) associative unlearning/inhibition, and (3) contextual change. Discuss the data on forgetting in terms of these three mechanisms. Which mechanisms are particularly helpful in explaining which facts? How can one use these ideas to explain the phenomenon of spontaneous recovery?
5. What is the significance of Anderson's finding of retrieval-induced forgetting and how does it relate to DaPolito's (1967) finding of independence between competing associations?

5

Models of Association

> The regularity of activity of certain association tracts will correspond to the regularity of things happening outside. The associations are not, however, a picture of the connection of the things themselves, but only the traces left by them in the sensory fields; hence their subjective character.
>
> CARL WERNICKE, *Outline of Psychiatry* (1894/1906)

In this chapter we examine models of human associative memory. In modeling associative memory we must consider both how associations are represented and stored and also how an item can be used to recall its associates. Both of these issues require us to go beyond the attribute-similarity framework introduced in chapter 3.

Historically, early models of association distinguished between encoding and retrieval phases. Early theorists also assumed that learning a novel association (e.g., A_i–B_i) involved learning about the items and their context and learning the forward and backward associations (e.g., McGovern, 1964). These ideas were closely related to the development of interference theory, as discussed in chapter 4.

A major advance in our understanding of associative memory took place in the 1970s when computer scientists, neuroscientists, and psychologists discovered mathematical methods for describing how associations could be represented in memory and retrieved in a cue-dependent manner. These models of associative memory were inspired by the circuitry of the brain itself, where connections between neurons appear to play a crucial role in associative learning and recall. This class of models developed a strong following among scientists in diverse fields, and the research that grew out of this work is known as connectionism or *neural networks*.

Neural-network models see associations as being stored in a network of connections among highly simplified model neurons. In the models we consider in this chapter, the "neurons" bear only a faint resemblance to real biological neurons: they are highly simplified computational "units" that integrate and transmit information. The activity levels of these artificial neurons represent the vector of attribute values describing an item's cognitive representation. New experiences modify the strength of the connections between the network neurons in a way that enables the network to store multiple associations across a single set of network connections.

Before discussing neural-network models, however, we first introduce a simpler class of associative models that builds closely on the multitrace attribute-similarity model of item recognition. These array models of association (Estes, 1986) have been particularly successful in accounting for data on category learning—a type of associative memory (Nosofsky, 1992). Array models posit that whenever an association is encoded, it is stored by adding a new vector to an ever-growing memory array (or matrix). Cued recall is then based on the similarity of the test cue with each of the stored vectors in the memory matrix.

5.1 THE ATTRIBUTE-SIMILARITY FRAMEWORK

The attribute-similarity model developed to explain data on item recognition can be extended to account for data on associative recall. The model is based on three core assumptions. First, each memory is represented by a list of attribute values that are modeled as a vector in a high-dimensional space. Second, each of these memory vectors is stored as a unique entry in a large and ever-growing memory matrix. Third, memory decisions are based on the similarity of a test vector to the vectors stored in the memory matrix.

In considering how to extend this modeling framework to memory for associations, we must first address the question of how two (or more) vectors combine to form an association. Perhaps the simplest approach is to stack the attributes of the vectors representing the to-be-associated items, along with their contextual attributes, into a larger memory vector. If $\mathbf{m}_i$ represents the ith pair in a list of paired items, we can write:

$$\mathbf{m}_i = \begin{pmatrix} \mathbf{a}_i \\ \mathbf{b}_i \\ \mathbf{t}_i \end{pmatrix}.$$

In this equation, $\mathbf{a}_i$ and $\mathbf{b}_i$ are the vector representations of items A_i and B_i; $\mathbf{t}_i$ is the vector representation of the context in which the A_i–B_i pair was studied. As discussed in chapter 3, we assume that the context vector drifts slowly over time according to the equation $\mathbf{t}_i = \mathbf{t}_{i-1} + \epsilon_i$, where ϵ_i is a random vector representing the moment-to-moment fluctuations in context.[1]

drift of context vector

5.1.1 Associative Recognition

Building associations as described above allows us to use summed similarity to decide whether a given pair was on a target list. The similarity of a test pair to the target list is greatest for an intact pair, A_i–B_i, whose attributes match one or more stored pairs in memory. As with attribute-similarity models of item recognition, we can define the similarity between two vectors in terms of their distance in multidimensional space. Specifically,

$$\text{similarity} = e^{-\tau \text{ distance}},$$

where τ determines how quickly similarity decays with distance and distance is calculated using the Pythagorean theorem. Figure 3.3 shows the form of an exponential-decay function for several values of τ.

For a rearranged test pair, A_i–B_j, some of the attributes will match A_i–B_i and some will match A_j–B_j. The sum of these two partial matches will generally count less than the full match of the intact pair because of the nonlinear form of the similarity-distance function, which gives greatest weight to very close matches. Box 5.1 provides an example calculation.

---

1. Rather than assuming that context is driven by random noise, one can assume that contextual change reflects the items being presented or recalled or, more precisely, the thoughts they evoke. Such experience-driven context models offer a number of advantages over the traditional randomly drifting context approach (see Howard and Kahana, 2002a; Sederberg et al., 2008; Polyn et al., 2009). We will consider these models in our discussion of free recall in chapter 7.

Box 5.1

EXAMPLE CALCULATION: ASSOCIATIVE RECOGNITION

Suppose that we have stored two pairs of items in memory, along with their temporal contexts, and that each item and context are two-element vectors:

$$M = \left(\begin{matrix} \mathbf{m}_1 & \mathbf{m}_2 \end{matrix} \right) = \left(\begin{matrix} \mathbf{a}_1 & \mathbf{a}_2 \\ \mathbf{b}_1 & \mathbf{b}_2 \\ \mathbf{t}_1 & \mathbf{t}_2 \end{matrix} \right) = \left(\begin{matrix} 1 & 0 \\ 0 & 0 \\ 0 & 1 \\ 1 & 0 \\ 0 & 0 \\ 0 & 1 \end{matrix} \right).$$

According to the summed attribute-similarity models, people respond *yes* when the summed similarity of the probe to the stored items exceeds a threshold. On an associative-recognition test, we probe memory with either an intact pair or a rearranged pair. Ideally, the summed similarity for an intact pair exceeds that of a rearranged pair.

Consider the intact probe given by:

$$\left(\begin{matrix} \mathbf{a}_2 \\ \mathbf{b}_2 \\ \mathbf{t}_3 \end{matrix} \right) = \left(\begin{matrix} 0 \\ 0 \\ 1 \\ 0 \\ 1 \\ 1 \end{matrix} \right).$$

Applying the Pythagorean theorem, the distance between the probe and $\mathbf{m}_1 = \sqrt{5}$ and the distance between the probe and $\mathbf{m}_2 = 1$. Applying the similarity distance equation with $\tau = 1$, the summed similarity is given by: $e^{-\sqrt{5}} + e^{-1} = 0.47$.

Now consider the rearranged probe given by:

$$\left(\begin{matrix} \mathbf{a}_1 \\ \mathbf{b}_2 \\ \mathbf{t}_3 \end{matrix} \right) = \left(\begin{matrix} 1 \\ 0 \\ 1 \\ 0 \\ 1 \\ 1 \end{matrix} \right).$$

The distance between the probe and $\mathbf{m}_1 = \sqrt{4}$ and the distance between the probe and $\mathbf{m}_2 = \sqrt{2}$. Thus, the summed similarity for the rearranged probe is given by: $e^{-2} + e^{-\sqrt{2}} = 0.38$. If the decision threshold were set to a value between 0.38 and 0.47, the model would correctly generate a *yes* response for the intact pair and a *no* response for the rearranged pair.

5.1.2 Cued Recall

Whereas the foregoing analysis shows how to use the attribute-similarity framework to do associative recognition, it is not yet clear how this model can account for data on cued recall. What is missing from our analysis is some way of using the attributes representing item A_i to retrieve the attributes of item B_i, and vice versa.

Perhaps the simplest approach to modeling cued recall would be to search through the memory matrix for the vector that is most similar to the test probe (think of the parallel and serial search models discussed in relation to the Sternberg task in section 2.4). If A_i is given as a cue, B_i will tend to be recalled because the vector a_i matches the attributes of the vector representing the A_i–B_i pair in memory. However, if the context of the test probe is a much better match for the context associated with another pair, A_j–B_j, and if the A_i partially matches A_j, then the probe could be more similar to the incorrect pair than to the correct one. The model would then predict that people would incorrectly recall B_j instead of B_i.

A problem with this formulation is that it will only make errors when the context of the probe strongly favors an incorrect response. Otherwise, it will always recall the correct item. The model does not allow for memory confusions based on item similarity, yet we know that such errors are common.

We can easily modify the model to generate similarity-based intrusions by assuming that the vector of attributes representing an item varies across different occurrences of the item. That is, the item is not encoded in exactly the same manner on each occurrence. This idea can be incorporated into the attribute-similarity model by adding a random "noise" vector to the vector representing the attributes of an item prior to storing the item in the memory matrix.

Using the Greek letter xi (ξ) to denote our noise vector, the stored representation of the ith pair would be given by the equation:

$$\mathbf{m}_i = \begin{pmatrix} \mathbf{a}_i + \xi_i^{\mathrm{a}} \\ \mathbf{b}_i + \xi_i^{\mathrm{b}} \\ \mathbf{t}_i \end{pmatrix}.$$

The result of adding a random vector to the stored representation of each study item is that the similarity of a matching probe will be somewhat less than 1.0. Thus, it is *possible* that a similar item in memory will be a better match to the test probe than the corresponding list item itself.

Although people sometimes commit intrusions, they are more likely not to recall anything at all. Once we have included noise in our attribute-similarity model, we can use a similarity threshold to control whether or not an item is recalled. That is, we can require that the similarity between the test probe and the best matching item in memory exceeds a threshold value, C, in order for the pair to be recalled.

Although similarity governs what is remembered in the attribute models of recognition and of recall, the recall model that we have outlined above does not rely on the summed similarity of the test probe to the contents of memory. Instead, the item that is recalled is the one that is *most similar* to the test probe.

Instead of always recalling the pair that was most similar to the probe, we could have chosen which pair to recall in a probabilistic manner, with the probability being proportional to the similarity. Specifically, we could have said that the probability of recalling $\mathbf{m}_i$ when cued with $\mathbf{p}$ is given by the equation:

$$P(\mathbf{m}_i|\mathbf{p}) = \frac{Sim(\mathbf{m}_i, \mathbf{p})}{\sum_{k=1}^{N} Sim(\mathbf{m}_k, \mathbf{p})}.$$

where *Sim* is a function that defines the similarity of two vectors.

According to this rule, every pair has some chance of being recalled, but more similar pairs have a higher probability of being recalled than less similar pairs. This type of probabilistic choice rule is often used in models of categorization, free-recall, and serial-recall tasks.

5.1.3 Repetition, Recency, Contiguity, and Interference

Consider the consequences of the attribute-similarity model for the basic empirical findings concerning cued recall. The attribute-similarity model predicts that repeated pairs will have a higher probability of being recalled because there will be multiple copies of each pair stored in memory. Because the vectors representing both the studied items and the test probe are coded in a noisy manner, having more noisy copies of the test probe in memory increases the likelihood that one of those stored copies will be the best match. Within this model, the effect of repetition will be gradual rather than all-or-none (see section 4.2). Without adding some additional assumptions or mechanisms, this model will not account for the beneficial effects of spacing on subsequent recall.[2]

As in the case of recognition memory, recency results from contextual drift. Because contextual attributes drift over time, recently studied pairs will be more similar to the test context than pairs studied at longer lags. Intrusions will result when a nontarget pair is the best match for a test probe. This

---

2. See Raaijmakers (2003) for an in-depth analysis of the various ways one can simulate the spacing effect using computational memory models.

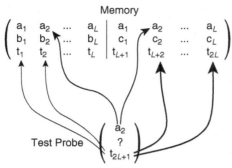

Figure 5.1 Illustration of the attribute-similarity model applied to the A_i–B_i, A_i–C_i **learning procedure.** The thickness of the arrows indicates the similarity between the item and contextual portions of the test probe and the item and contextual portions of the vectors stored in memory. The contextual portion of the test probe is most similar to the contextual portion of the most recently studied pair.

is most likely to happen when the target and nontarget pair have similar attribute values and when the contextual attributes of the test probe overlap with the non-target pair. Thus, the attribute-similarity model predicts that intrusions will reflect semantic similarity and recency. The model will not predict an effect of temporal contiguity on intrusions, as found in the data (see Figure 4.5).

Consider the attribute-similarity model's predictions for Briggs' (1954) experiment. In this experiment, participants first study a list of A_i–B_i pairs. Then, participants study a list of A_i–C_i pairs. After studying the second list, participants are probed with the A_i items to recall either B_i or C_i.

Figure 5.1 illustrates the similarity of a test probe representing item A_2 to the vectors stored in the memory matrix. In this example, we use L to denote the length of each list (in pairs). The test vector contains two subvectors: $\mathbf{a}_2$ represents the attributes of A_2 and $\mathbf{t}_{2L+1}$ represents the contextual attributes at the time of test (the subscript $2L + 1$ indicates that context has been updated $2L + 1$ times since the beginning of the first list). The subvector $\mathbf{a}_2$ should be equally similar to the vectors representing the stored A_2–B_2 and A_2–C_2 pairs, and $\mathbf{a}_2$ should be more similar to these vectors than to those in any of the other stored pairs. On the other hand, the contextual attributes in the test probe, $\mathbf{t}_{2L+1}$, should be most similar to the contextual attributes in the most recently encoded pair A_L–C_L and less similar to older pairs.

Basing recall on the total similarity of the test probe to each of the stored pairs implies that C_2 is most likely to be recalled in response to A_2. In general, memory for a target pair will be adversely affected by the presence of a highly similar pair or overlapping pair in a recently studied list. Although the attribute-similarity framework provides a natural account for a number of associative interference phenomena, other aspects of interference, such as the finding of inhibition in the retrieval-induced forgetting paradigm (see section 4.9), are more difficult to explain within this framework.

5.1.4 Categorization

Here we consider how one might use attribute-similarity models to account for data on category learning. Category learning is an associative-memory task that has been used extensively in the development and testing of similarity-based models. In this task, participants learn to assign category labels, or names, to groups of items that come from some contiguous region of the attribute space. As an example, Figure 5.2 shows a two-dimensional space representing rectangles that vary in their width and height. Suppose that participants are taught to associate the labels A, B, and C with the rectangles in the three marked regions. In the study-test version of this task, participants alternate study and test phases. In the study phase, images of rectangles are paired with their labels. In the test phase, the studied rectangles are shown and participants are asked to respond with the appropriate label. In the anticipation procedure, participants are given a fixed time to recall (anticipate) the response label and are then given the correct response as feedback. These two methods parallel the study-test and anticipation procedures used in cued recall.

Successful categorization requires that people associate the category label with each item in a given region of the stimulus space. A paired-associate task is much like a categorization task in which the mapping between items and categories is one-to-one, that is, where a unique label is associated with each studied item.

In category learning experiments, we are often interested in knowing which pairs are the easiest to learn and which are the hardest. We are also very interested in the misclassifications people make during the learning process. These misclassifications are akin to intrusions in cued recall. To better study the pattern of misclassifications, researchers often require participants to provide a category response for every test item.

Similarity-based models have been used extensively to study people's misclassifications. The most sophisticated work on these models has been carried out by Nosofsky in a series of influential papers (1986, 1987, 1992). In Nosofsky's attribute-similarity model of categorization, the probability of giving a category label as a response to a test item increases with the summed similarity of the test item to the other members of the category and decreases with the summed similarity of the test item to members of the

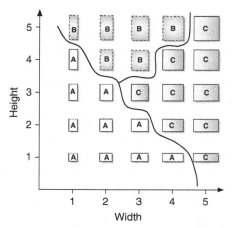

Figure 5.2 Categorization task. Rectangles in each of three regions of the stimulus space are associated with the category labels A, B, and C.

other categories. Nosofsky's model can account for data on both accuracy and RT in categorization for a wide range of different stimulus types (e.g., Nosofsky and Palmeri, 1997).

Nosofsky's model can also explain how people respond when asked to categorize new items that were not part of the studied list. In the example shown in Figure 5.2, suppose that the rectangle with *width* = 2 and *height* = 5 was never paired with the label B and that all of the other rectangles were studied with their category labels. According to the model, people will be very likely to give a B response when tested with rectangle (2,5). This is because rectangle (2,5) is highly similar to several rectangles that were associated with B and substantially less similar to rectangles associated with the other category labels.

Because all items within a category come from a single region of stimulus space, categorization tasks can sometimes encourage participants to use a very different strategy from associative learning. Rather than storing and retrieving each vector representing the association between the attributes of an item and its label, as in Nosofsky's model, people can abstract a *rule* from the stored memories (termed *exemplars*) and use that rule to solve the category-learning problem (Ashby and Maddox, 2005). Suppose, for example, that people could learn the category boundaries (shown as lines) in Figure 5.2. In that case, people would not need to compute the similarities between a test item and all of the stored examples to make a decision. Instead, they would need to remember the association between each category and the boundaries that define the region of stimulus space corresponding to that category (Ashby and Maddox, 1993).

Although complex category boundaries such as those in our rectangle example are very difficult to learn (Ashby, Queller, and Berretty, 1999), one could imagine a much simpler categorization problem in which the boundaries between regions were determined by a single value, such as the height of the rectangle. For example, one could design an experiment in which rectangles whose heights were below some value were in category A, those whose heights exceeded some other value were in category C, and those with intermediate heights were in category B. In such a case, it would seem easier to learn this rule than to store and retrieve the associations between every example rectangle and its category label. Whether or not people are able to abstract such rules depends critically on how the regions of the stimulus space map onto category labels. If people do not need to combine information from multiple dimensions while classifying items, they will be more likely to adopt a rule-based strategy. When simple rules define the categories, the similarity-exemplar approach does not provide a good fit to the classification data (Ashby and Maddox, 2005).

Several recent theories of category learning have embraced the view that people can make use of multiple learning mechanisms in categorization tasks. So long as people are provided with the appropriate mappings between exemplars and categories, there is little doubt that those associations will be learned. However, if a simple rule provides a way to categorize the items, learning that rule will usually be more efficient than memorizing all of the exemplar-category associations. Yet, when rules require integrating information across multiple dimensions, exemplar learning often constitutes the more efficient strategy. In cases where a rule accounts for most of the classifications, a hybrid strategy can be used: people can learn the rule and also learn the exceptions as specific exemplar-category associations (Ashby and Maddox, 2005). Finally, when a tightly grouped cluster of highly similar items is associated with a single category, people may not bother to store each new repetition as a separate exemplar-category association. Rather, they may simply strengthen a common representation of the *prototype* (or center of mass) of the cluster. Evidence for such prototype representations comes from the finding that presenting learners with an unstudied item that is located at the center-of-mass of a cluster will sometimes yield a stronger category response than presenting the learner with any of the previously studied exemplars (Smith, 2002).

5.1.5 Limitations

Although the attribute-similarity model can be applied to a wide range of recall phenomena, it appears to be limited in several ways. First, the model's assumption that every item is stored separately in an ever-growing memory matrix seems implausible. Consider, for example, how large the storage capacity of the brain would need to be if it contained a separate detailed record of every time a person saw the face of their friend or parent or of every occurrence of the word "the" encountered when reading text. You would need to store literally billions of entries in your memory array, each possibly consisting of thousands of features.[3]

Second, the attribute-similarity model assumes that to recall an item you must search through every single instance of every item experienced in your entire life, looking for a best match. Such a search process could not reasonably take place in a serial manner, so it would have to happen in parallel. But in that case, the search process would have to involve matching the probe item simultaneously with hundreds of millions (and perhaps billions) of stored patterns. It would be more desirable if one could have memories that were *content addressable*—that is, memories that could be evoked directly by the cue item without requiring any kind of search process. The neural-network models that we will consider in the next section largely overcome both of these limitations while retaining many of the attractive features of the attribute-similarity framework.

5.2 NEURAL-NETWORK MODELS

Neural-network models assume that each neuron (or node) is connected to many other neurons. Together, these neurons (nodes) form a highly interconnected network. In our model system, each neuron can be characterized by its *activation* value, and each connection is characterized by its strength value, = *weight* or *weight*. At a given time, the vector of activations for the neurons in the network is called the *state vector* of the network. The state vector, which can represent the attributes of a memory, is not static. It changes from moment to moment as our mind wanders or as new information is being experienced. So, although the state vector can represent a previously stored memory vector, it does not store any memories[Rather, memories are stored in the connections between neurons, and these connections enable the network to recover previously stored memories.]The connection strengths are also not static. They change during learning to allow the state vector to recall previously learned memories. An important property of neural-network models is that they can store a large number of distinct memories in the pattern of connections among the nodes of the network. As we explain below, these properties of neural networks allow

---

3. Gallistel and King (2009) present behavioral evidence in support of the brain having enormous computational abilities—far more than would be expected based on the idea that information is stored in simple neural networks. They challenge the scientific community to consider the possibility that humans possess biological systems for storing and retrieving far more information than previously suspected.

them to overcome the two key limitations of the attribute-similarity models described above.

5.2.1 Network Dynamics

Each node, or neuron, in a neural network gets input from other nodes and sends output to other nodes. A scalar value, termed <u>activation</u>, describes the <u>output of each node</u>. The <u>activation of node</u> i, denoted $\underline{a(i)}$, is related to the input that it receives from other nodes in the network. The input that node i receives from node j is the product of $a(j)$ and the weight of the connections between i and j, denoted $w(i, j)$. Putting this together, we can write:

activation$_i$ = function$g$ $\left(\Sigma(weight\ of\ i \cdot j)(activation_j) \right)$

$$a(i) = g\left(\sum_{j=1}^{N} w(i, j)a(j) \right) \tag{5.1}$$

where the function $g(\text{input})$ transforms the unit's input into its activation value. In many of the examples that follow, we assume, for simplicity, that the activation is equal to the input (i.e., we assume that $g(\text{input}) = \text{input}$). Later we consider cases where a unit's activation is a nonlinear function of its input.

In modeling the behavior of a neural network, it is useful to define a neuron's activation as being either above or below its average activation level. This is done by defining an activation of zero as the average activation of a neuron: positive activation values would denote above-average activity and negative activation values would denote below-average activity.

Equation 5.1, proposed by McCullough and Pitts (1943), is called the *dynamical rule* of the network. This rule provides a simplified description of the behavior of neurons, whereby <u>activations map onto the neurons' firing rates</u> and <u>weights map onto the strength</u> of the synaptic connections between the neurons. Figure 5.3 illustrates the McCullough-Pitts dynamical rule.

5.2.2 Hebbian Learning

Hebb (1949) proposed that learning results from changes in the connection strengths, or weights, between neurons. Specifically, he hypothesized that the weight of the connection between neurons i and j (denoted $w(i, j)$) is increased by the product of their activity at each time-step t. Mathematically, we can write the Hebb learning rule as:

$$w(i, j)_t = w(i, j)_{t-1} + a(i)_t a(j)_t \tag{5.2}$$

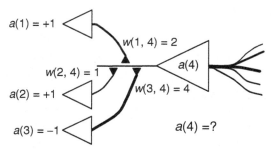

Figure 5.3 McCullough-Pitts model neuron. In this illustration, each open triangle represents a neuron, with neurons receiving input from the left and sending output to the right (this arrangement is arbitrary). The activation of Neuron 4, $a(4)$, is determined by the weighted sum of the inputs coming from Neurons 1, 2, and 3. In this example, the weighted sum of inputs is -1. Thus, $a(4) = g(-1)$. If using a linear-activation function, as defined by $g(x) = x$, then $a(4) = -1$.

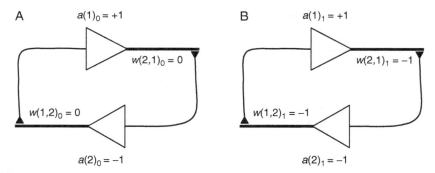

Figure 5.4 Hebb learning rule. The weight between two neurons is incremented based on the product of their activations. If the weights in this example were initially set to zero at $t = 0$ (left panel), application of the Hebb rule would update the weights to both equal -1 at $t = 1$ (right panel).

where $a(i)_t$ denotes the activation of neuron i at time t. Although it is convenient to assume that all of the weights are initially set to zero (when $t = 0$), one could also assume that the weights are initially set to some random values.

According to the Hebb rule, if neurons i and j both have above-average (i.e., positive) activations, their connection is strengthened. Similarly, if they both have below-average (i.e., negative) activations, their connection is also strengthened. But, if one neuron's activation is positive while the other's is negative, their connection is weakened. Figure 5.4 illustrates the Hebb learning rule for a network with just two neurons.

5.2.3 Modeling Cued Recall

Anderson (1970) showed that the combination of the Hebbian learning rule and the McCullough-Pitts dynamical rule enables a network to simulate associative memory, storing associations between multiple patterns (vectors) in a single set of connection strengths (a weight matrix).

To see how this works, consider two sets of neurons: one set represents the attributes of item A and the second set represents the attributes of item B. Let $a(i)$ denote the output of the ith unit representing A and let $b(j)$ denote the output of the jth unit representing B. (We again assume that items are vectors of attributes, but we now assume that each attribute value is coded by the firing rate of one of our simplified neurons.) Suppose, further, that each neuron representing attributes of A is connected to each neuron representing attributes of B.

We can now write the weight matrix as:

$$w(i,j)_t = w(i,j)_{t-1} + a(i)_t b(j)_t. \tag{5.3}$$

That is, the increase in the weight between each neuron representing A and each neuron representing B is just the product of their activations (outputs).

We can now see how association might work. Suppose that we set the activations of the neurons representing A to their appropriate values and allow Equation 5.1 to determine the activations of the neurons representing item B. The output (activation) of the jth node of B is given by:

$$\tilde{b}(j) = g\left(\sum_{i=1}^{N} w(i,j)a(i)\right) = g\left(\sum_{i=1}^{N} a(i)b(j)a(i)\right), \tag{5.4}$$

where $\tilde{b}(j)$ is the new value of $b(j)$ after it has been updated by applying the dynamical rule. Anderson assumed that a simple linear function, $g(x) = x$, related a neuron's input to its output. Thus, we can rewrite Equation 5.4 as:

$$\tilde{b}(j) = b(j) \sum_{i=1}^{N} a(i)^2. \tag{5.5}$$

Showing that $\tilde{b}(j) = b(j)$ would prove that applying Equation 5.1 enables the network to recall the desired vector. Anderson assumed that the activation values of the neurons $a(i)$ and $b(i)$ were independent, normally distributed, random numbers with mean, $\mu = 0$, and variance, $\sigma^2 = 1/N$ (this assumption on the variance simplifies the derivations that follow). Using the formula that relates the expectation and variance of a random variable (see Box 2.2), we can write $\text{var}[a(i)] = E[a(i)^2] - \mu^2$. Given that $a(i)$ has a mean value of zero (i.e., $\mu = 0$) and a variance of $1/N$, we can see that $E[a(i)^2] = 1/N$ and therefore $E[\sum_{i=1}^{N} a(i)^2] = 1$.

The preceding analysis shows that the sum of the squared activations of $a(i)$ equals 1 *on average*. However, to achieve perfect recall of $b(i)$, we need to show that $\sum_{i=1}^{N} a(i)^2 = 1$ (without the expectation). This latter equality is true in the limit as N approaches infinity. That is, using elementary probability theory, we can show that $\text{var}[\sum_{i=1}^{N} a(i)^2] = \sum_{i=1}^{N} \text{var}[a(i)^2] = 2/N$, so as N grows larger and larger, the variance gets smaller and smaller. If N is very large, as would be expected in a real network of millions of neurons, then the variance would become negligibly small.

Thus, we can thus see that, following the application of the Hebb learning rule, the McCullough-Pitts neurons can "retrieve" B when "cued" with A. However, with multiple associations stored in memory, and with vectors that are not independent of one another, the linear-associator model can only retrieve an approximation of the desired target memory. Ideally, we would like our network to be able to reconstruct, or *deblur*, the retrieved information so that we could recall the actual stored target memory. This can be accomplished using a nonlinear-activation function, as described in the next section.

5.2.4 The Hopfield Network

The Hopfield model (1982) is perhaps the simplest and most well-studied network model of associative memory. This network stores a memory vector in such a way that we can use part of the vector, or a noisy version of the vector, to retrieve the most similar vector stored in the network. This type of operation, in which a vector is associated with itself, is called *autoassociation. Heteroassociation* refers to the storage of an association between two different vectors.

A Hopfield network is designed to store, or autoassociate, individual vectors. To store a heteroassociation—an association between two different vectors— all we need to do is create a vector that combines the attributes of the to-be-associated items. We will consider heteroassociation in the next section. For now, let us examine the behavior of the Hopfield network in storing and retrieving individual vectors.

As with Anderson's linear neural-network model, we can describe the Hopfield model by specifying the representation of the items and the equations used to modify the weights and to change the activations of the nodes. Hopfield found it convenient to use vectors of binary-valued attributes to represent items. These attributes take on values of either $+1$ or -1, with equal probability. A value of $+1$ would correspond to a neuron whose firing rate, or activity level, is above its average value; a value of -1 would correspond to a neuron whose activity level was below its average value. The learning rule used in the Hopfield model is the same as the Hebb learning rule given in Equation 5.3. If we have stored L vectors, $\{\mathbf{a}_1, \ldots, \mathbf{a}_L\}$ in the network, we will have weights given by:

$$w(i, j) = \sum_{k=1}^{L} a_k(i) a_k(j). \tag{5.6}$$

Strictly speaking, the equations we have used for the Hebb rule imply that the weight between a neuron and itself is also modified (i.e., $w(i, i) = a(i)^2$). For reasons that are beyond the scope of our treatment, it is advantageous to set the self strengths, $w(i, i)$, to zero. We have done so in the following example.

Suppose that we want to store three vectors, $\mathbf{a}_1$, $\mathbf{a}_2$, and $\mathbf{a}_3$, in a Hopfield network with five nodes.

$$\mathbf{a}_1 = \begin{pmatrix} +1 \\ -1 \\ -1 \\ +1 \\ +1 \end{pmatrix} \quad \mathbf{a}_2 = \begin{pmatrix} -1 \\ +1 \\ -1 \\ -1 \\ +1 \end{pmatrix} \quad \mathbf{a}_3 = \begin{pmatrix} +1 \\ +1 \\ +1 \\ -1 \\ -1 \end{pmatrix}$$

Storing these three patterns in the Hopfield network yields the weight matrix:

$$W = \begin{pmatrix} 0 & -1 & +1 & +1 & -1 \\ -1 & 0 & +1 & -3 & -1 \\ +1 & +1 & 0 & -1 & -3 \\ +1 & -3 & -1 & 0 & +1 \\ -1 & -1 & -3 & +1 & 0 \end{pmatrix}$$

where the value given in the ith row and jth column of the matrix corresponds to the weight, $w(i, j)$, between neuron i and neuron j. One can see that $w(2, 4) = -3$ because the second and fourth attributes have opposite signs (one is -1 and the other is $+1$) in each of the three vectors, $\mathbf{a}_1$, $\mathbf{a}_2$, and $\mathbf{a}_3$. One can also see that the weight matrix is symmetric; in every case, $w(i, j) = w(j, i)$.

Retrieval in the Hopfield model is accomplished by applying the McCullough-Pitts dynamical rule (see Equation 5.1) in an iterative fashion. Whereas Anderson used the activation function $g(x) = x$ in his linear-network model, Hopfield used a nonlinear-activation function, $g(x) = \text{sgn}(x)$, where

$$\text{sgn}(x) = \begin{cases} +1 & \text{if } x > 0, \\ -1 & \text{if } x < 0. \end{cases}$$

If $x = 0$, then the sgn operation would return either a value of -1 or $+1$ with equal probability.

Hopfield's dynamical rule is therefore given by:

$$s(i) = \text{sgn}\left(\sum_{j=1}^{N} w(i, j)s(j)\right) \qquad (5.7)$$

where $\mathbf{s} = s(1), s(2), \ldots, s(N)$ represents the current state of the network (this is sometimes called the *state vector*). Hopfield was able to prove that with the sgn activation function, the dynamical rule will always modify the values of the state vector in the direction of one of the stored patterns (Hertz, Krogh, and Palmer, 1991).

As an illustration of how retrieval works in the Hopfield model, consider the evolution of the network if we set the state vector, $\mathbf{s}$, to be equal to the test vector:

$$\mathbf{a}_{\text{test}} = \begin{pmatrix} -1 \\ -1 \\ -1 \\ -1 \\ +1 \end{pmatrix}.$$

Figure 5.5 provides a graphical illustration of the activation values of the nodes and the connection weights. During the recall process, we would pick a random node, calculate its activation, pick another random node, calculate its activation, and repeat the process until the activation values stabilize on a given pattern.

Updating the activation of node 1 requires that we apply the dynamical rule, Equation 5.7, to the weight matrix, W, and the probe vector, $\mathbf{a}_{\text{test}}$. The weighted sum of the inputs to this node is -2, and therefore the node's activation will remain at -1. Applying the same process to node 2 gives us an input of $+2$ and therefore indicates that the nodes' activations will flip from -1 to $+1$. Similarly, the activations of the remaining three nodes remain the same after applying the dynamical rule.[4] Thus, the input pattern $\mathbf{a}_{\text{test}}$ evolves into the memory pattern $\mathbf{a}_2$.

By counting the number of times the dynamical rule has to be applied before the network activations stabilize, one can estimate a "response time" of the

---

4. After applying the dynamical rule to a given node, the activation of that node may change and then influence the activations of other nodes in the network.

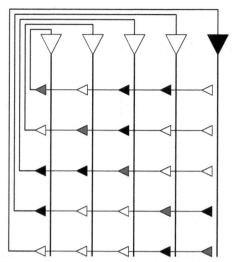

Figure 5.5 Schematic of the Hopfield network. The five large triangles at the top of the figure represent the five nodes (or neurons) in the network. The output from each of these nodes (lines connecting to the top of each large triangle) connects to the input line going into each of the other nodes by way of a weighted synapse (small triangle). Positive activations and positive weights are indicated by filled (dark) triangles; negative activations and negative weights are indicated by open (white) triangles. Small gray triangles indicate zero weights. The activations of the nodes correspond to the activation of the test vector, $\mathbf{a}_{test}$, and the weights correspond to the matrix formed after storing the three vectors, $\mathbf{a}_1$, $\mathbf{a}_2$, and $\mathbf{a}_3$. Note that the activations of the nodes will change each time the network updates.

memory retrieval process (Plaut, 1995; Ratcliff, Zandt, and McKoon, 1999). This response time is not in units of actual time unless we specify the amount of time that each update would require. Our ability to come to a realistic estimate at this stage of our knowledge is rather limited. However, what we can do is examine whether the model predicts differences in RT among conditions that mimic those found in the data. Figure 5.6 shows a sample RT distribution generated by the model.

Using Equation 5.7, the network is able to deblur the retrieved information to one of the stored items with reasonable success. But this debluring process is not perfect; sometimes the model will recall a mixture of two item vectors or it will fail to converge on any memory, getting stuck in some indeterminate state. It turns out that one can improve the performance of the model, and prevent it from getting stuck in a partial-recall state, by adding a small amount of noise to the activations before applying the dynamical rule.

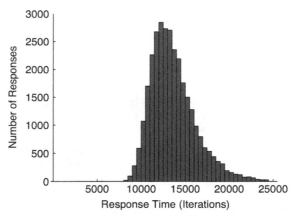

Figure 5.6 "Response time" in a Hopfield network. This histogram shows the distribution of the number of network updates required for pattern convergence. The number of updates for convergence can be thought of as a measure of the "response time" of the network.

5.2.5 Cued Recall in a Hopfield Network

Rizzuto and Kahana (2001) modified the Hopfield model to simulate forward and backward cued recall. Although auto-association is generally used to encode a single representation, it is possible to store both auto-associative and heteroassociative information within a single memory matrix if the representation being stored is the combination of two items. This is done by concatenating the vectors representing $\mathbf{A}_k$ and $\mathbf{B}_k$ to form a new vector that is given by:

$$\mathbf{m}_k = \left(\begin{array}{c} \mathbf{a}_k \\ \mathbf{b}_k \end{array} \right),$$

where $\mathbf{a}_k$ and $\mathbf{b}_k$ are binary (± 1), N-dimensional vectors representing the items to be associated.

The learning rule for a list of L pairs can then be written as:

$$w(i, j) = \sum_{k=1}^{L} m_k(i) m_k(j), \tag{5.8}$$

where $W = w(i, j)$ is a $2N \times 2N$ weight matrix with four quadrants, as illustrated in Figure 5.7. Quadrants 1 and 3 of the matrix contain autoassociative information, while quadrants 2 and 4 contain heteroassociative information.

Rizzuto and Kahana (2001) showed that a probabilistic-learning algorithm enabled their network model to account for the effect of repetition on

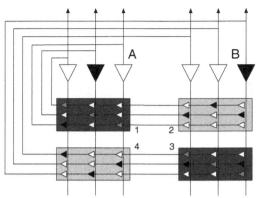

Figure 5.7 Hopfield network for cued recall. The six triangles represent Hopfield-model neurons (in a real simulation there would be many more than six). Half of the neurons represent the attributes of A_i and the other half represent the attributes of B_i. The lightly shaded rectangles indicate quadrants of the weight matrix that store the A_i to B_i and the B_i to A_i heteroassociations; the darker rectangles indicate autoassociative A_i to A_i and B_i to B_i associations. Arrows indicate the output of the neurons.

recall accuracy. In their formulation, each weight, $w(i, j)$, has some probability of being updated on a given trial. Thus, for a given pair k, the rule for storing each weight would be:

$$\Delta w(i, j) = \begin{cases} m_k(i)m_k(j) & \text{with probability} \quad \gamma \\ 0 & \text{with probability} \quad 1 - \gamma \end{cases} \tag{5.9}$$

where γ is a random variable taking a value between 0 and 1 that determines the learning rate of the model. The mean and the variance of the distribution are parameters of the model that represent the mean probability of encoding a weight and the variability around that mean.[5]

Retrieval in this model follows the approach of Hopfield (1982). To recall pair k, we update each node of the state vector $s(i)$ according to the equation:

$$s_{t+1}(i) = \text{sgn} \left(\sum_j w(i, j) \, s_t(j) \right), \tag{5.10}$$

5. Rizzuto and Kahana actually proposed separate learning parameters for forward and backward associations. By varying the correlation between them, they could make the model simulate independent associations (correlation of zero) or symmetric associations (correlation of 1). They then showed that the symmetric model provided the best fit to behavioral data on the correlations between forward and backward recall of a single studied pair.

where t denotes the time step of the dynamical rule. At each time step we randomly choose a node to be updated, but the updating of that node will depend on the combined input it receives from all of the other nodes in the network. Thus, the entire network contributes to the change in the activation of any single node. It is also important to keep in mind that during the retrieval process, no learning occurs (i.e., the weights of the network remain fixed). The network must be able to switch between its learning mode and its recall mode. Given the empirical data on learning during recall, this feature of the model is unattractive. It is possible, however, to set up the model so that it can learn the recalled state once retrieval is complete.

The initial state of the network is set to

$$s_0 = \begin{pmatrix} \mathbf{a}_k \\ \mathbf{x} \end{pmatrix}$$

for forward recall, and to

$$s_0 = \begin{pmatrix} \mathbf{x} \\ \mathbf{b}_k \end{pmatrix}$$

for backward recall, where $\mathbf{x}$ is an N-dimensional, random, binary (± 1) vector. The state of the cue vector ($\mathbf{a}_k$, in the case of a test in the forward direction) is held constant throughout retrieval because the cue is continuously present until the person makes his or her response.

Table 5.1 shows that this network model can simulate experimental data on learning and on the equivalence of forward and backward recall. The model predicts symmetric recall (see section 4.4) because studying a pair of items produces an equivalent increment in the weight matrices representing the forward and backward associative connections.

Table 5.1

Modeling learning. A Hopfield network that uses Equation 5.9 as a learning rule can fit experimental data on forward and backward cued recall of pairs studied once (1P), three times (3P), and five times (5P). Results from Rizzuto and Kahana (2001).

	Recall Probability			
	Forward		Backward	
	Data	Model	Data	Model
1p	0.35	0.35	0.36	0.35
3p	0.65	0.65	0.65	0.65
5p	0.75	0.75	0.73	0.75

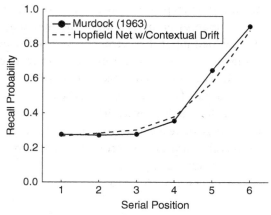

Figure 5.8 Modeling recency. Contextual drift enables the Hopfield model to account for the recency effect found in cued recall. For this simulation, half of the network's nodes represented context. A randomly chosen subset of these context nodes changed signs each time a new pair was studied. Data from Murdock (1963a). Simulation is courtesy of D. Rizzuto.

5.2.6 Context and Recency

Contextual attributes play an important role in memory processing. Thus, it is important to represent context in some way within network models of association. As with attribute-similarity models, it is straightforward to represent context within a network model. This is done by designating a subset of the nodes as context nodes, which are set to a random pattern of $+1$ and -1 values at the start of training. Then, as each item (or pair) is encoded, a small portion of the context nodes change their activation value from $+1$ to -1 or from -1 to $+1$. In this way, the vector of attributes representing context changes slowly as new information enters the network. Figure 5.8 shows that adding contextual drift to a standard Hopfield network enables the model to account for the very rapid initial forgetting found in cued-recall experiments.

5.2.7 Network Capacity

The number of nodes (neurons) and connections (synapses) in a network largely determines the number of memories it can store. In a Hopfield network, each memory is a binary vector of $+1$ and -1 values. If the vectors are chosen at random, the model can accurately recall approximately 138 vectors stored for every 1,000 nodes (Hertz et al., 1991). If you try to store a larger number of vectors in the network, it will start to make many errors during recall.

The connectivity (topology) of the Hopfield network is similar to that of a brain region in the human hippocampus known as CA3. This region has approximately 350,000 neurons, and recent neurobiological studies suggest that it plays an important role in associative memory function (Gilbert and Kesner, 2003). If region CA3 were wired just like a Hopfield network, it would be able to store approximately 45,000 unique memories, where each of these memories is a binary vector in 350,000 dimensions. One such vector could represent as much information as is found on an average page of text in this book.

The ability of a neural network to deblur a pattern depends on factors other than the size of the network. For example, the network's ability to recall a pattern will depend on the quality of the test cue and the number of similar patterns stored in the network. If the test probe is very similar to a single stored memory, the network will have an easy time recalling that memory. Conversely, if a test probe is similar to multiple memories, the network will have a harder time recalling the best match.

The hypothesized ability of the hippocampus to store and retrieve memories does not imply that all of our memories are stored in that one brain region. Indeed, patients who have substantial damage to the hippocampus still retain much of their ability to remember information learned prior to their injury or the onset of their disease. The major consequence of hippocampal damage is an impaired ability to store new memories and, more specifically, to store new associative memories (see Squire, Clark, and Bayley, 2004, for a review). This finding would be consistant with the hippocampus being critical for associating item and context representations (Polyn and Kahana, 2008).

5.2.8 Intrusions

When the Hopfield model recalls the wrong pattern, it is most likely to be that of a similar item in memory. Thus, the model can account for the fact that intrusions are most likely to be items that are semantically related to the desired target item. If the model employs contextual nodes to differentiate items in different lists, it also tends to make intrusions to items from recent as opposed to remote lists (see Figure 5.9). Thus, the Hopfield network can explain two of the key factors that predict intrusion errors: semantic similarity and recency.

When intrusions come from other pairs within a list, they tend to be from pairs studied close in time to the target item. The Hopfield model can also explain this effect because the A_i probe will tend to recall the vector of context features t_i, and this vector is similar to the context of neighboring pairs, such as $A_{i-1}-B_{i-1}$ and $A_{i+1}-B_{i+1}$. Thus, the model can simulate the effect of temporal contiguity on intrusions (Figure 5.10).

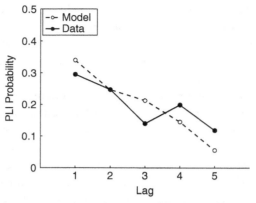

Figure 5.9 Modeling recency across lists. A Hopfield model with contextual drift predicts that prior-list intrusions (PLIs) will exhibit a recency effect across lists, as seen in data reported by Davis et al. (2008). Simulation courtesy of A. Geller.

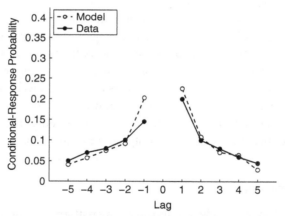

Figure 5.10 Modeling the contiguity effect in cued recall. A Hopfield model with contextual drift predicts that intralist intrusions will exhibit a contiguity effect, as seen in the data from Davis et al. (2008). Simulation courtesy of A. Geller.

5.3 SUMMARY AND CURRENT DIRECTIONS

This chapter presented information about models of human associative memory. These models are built on the core ideas developed in chapter 3, namely, that memories can be modeled as vectors of attributes and that these vectors can comprise both stimulus information and contextual information.

The first class of models we discussed builds directly on the attribute-similarity framework used to explain recognition memory. In this framework, associations are created by concatenating the vectors representing two (or possibly more) items, along with contextual attributes, into a single vector. This vector, in turn, is stored in a memory array, along with all previously stored memories. A vector representing a recall cue can then be compared with each of the stored vectors in the memory array. Assuming that the most similar vector stored in the memory array exceeds a similarity threshold, that vector will be recalled.

Despite its simplicity, this similarity-based model can explain a number of basic facts about cued recall, such as the effects of similarity and competition. By incorporating contextual fluctuation into the model, it can also generate a recency effect, recovery of previously learned associations following a long delay, and a number of other related phenomena. The model's primary limitations concern the plausibility of separately storing every experienced item in an ever-growing memory matrix and the assumption that recall involves separate comparisons of the probe item to each and every one of these stored representations.

Neural-network models overcome many of the limitations of array models by proposing that many memories can be stored together in a composite representation. Inspired by the computational properties of actual neurons, these models allow memories to be evoked directly by a cue item without requiring a conventional search process. As such, the stored memories are referred to as being "content addressable."

Neural networks store memories, defined as patterns of neural activity, in the strengths or weights of the connections between neurons. One of the most important and attractive features of neural networks is that they can store a multitude of memories in a single set of connections. As each new memory is experienced, the weights connecting the network's neurons are updated according to a learning rule. We focused on one such learning rule, known as Hebbian learning, whereby the weight between two neurons increases or decreases as a function of the product of the neurons' activations. As with array models, the memories are vectors of attributes, but in the case of neural networks, each attribute corresponds to the activity level of a neuron.

Rather than directly comparing a probe item with each of the stored memories, the retrieval (or recall) process in a neural network occurs as a natural process of the network's dynamics. When the network is not in a learning mode, each neuron's activity depends on the activity of the other neurons in the network and the connection weights to those neurons. The simple dynamical rule illustrated in Figure 5.3 and defined by Equation 5.1 allows the network to "recall" previously learned patterns. This recall process unfolds over time, with the activity levels of the neurons fluctuating until the network settles into a stable state. In modeling laboratory studies of memory, this stable state would typically correspond to recalling a particular item, but not necessarily the target item. Occasionally, the network will not reach a stable pattern, thus generating response omissions.

As with array models, one can incorporate contextual features into neural networks to distinguish between identical items encoded on distinct occasions or in different contexts. Assuming that context changes slowly over time, the network will give rise to a recency effect, as seen in the data. However, without adding some additional assumptions or mechanisms, neural-network models can not account for the beneficial effects of spacing on subsequent cued recall.

A major challenge for memory theories is to explain data on both recognition and recall. One possibility is that both tasks rely on common brain mechanisms or, minimally, that they can both be explained within a common computational framework. Alternatively, the two forms of memory may be quite distinct, relying on different brain systems and requiring different types of explanatory models.

We have already seen that the array framework can be used to describe data obtained in both recognition and recall tasks. Array models of recall and recognition are not identical: recall relies on somehow selecting a single matching vector, whereas recognition relies on the summed similarity of the test item to all of the stored memories (Hintzman, 1988). However, given the attractive features of neural-network models of recall, one may ask whether a similar framework can be used to help understand item and associative recognition.

Murdock (1982) showed how one could integrate similarity-based models of recognition and network-type models of recall within a single computational framework. As with neural-network theories, Murdock assumed that multiple items could be stored in a single memory representation. He also assumed that associative information was encoded in the products of the activations of individual attributes. However, to store both items (vectors) and associations (matrices) in a single representation, Murdock transformed the associative matrices into vectors using a mathematical operation known as convolution. The convolution of two vectors, $\mathbf{a}$ and $\mathbf{b}$, is defined by the equation $(\mathbf{a} * \mathbf{b})(m) = \sum_i \mathbf{a}(i)\mathbf{b}(m - i)$, where m is the index to the elements in the convolution vector, i indexes the elements in the item vectors $\mathbf{a}$ and $\mathbf{b}$, and the asterisk ($*$) denotes the convolution operator.[6] Retrieval also involves a special mathematical operation to recover one of the stored items given the other item as a retrieval cue. If a single association is stored as $\mathbf{m} = \mathbf{a} * \mathbf{b}$, then computing the inverse operation, $\sum_i \mathbf{a}(i)\mathbf{m}(m + i)$, will retrieve an approximation of $\mathbf{b}$.

---

6. If each of two item vectors has N elements, the convolution will be a vector with $2N - 1$ elements.

This operation will work even if you store many different associations in a single vector.

The beauty of Murdock's model is that you can store both associations and individual items in a common memory vector. In this way you can do both recall, using convolution and its inverse, and recognition, by computing the similarity of a test item to the memory vector itself. Unlike the weight matrices formed in neural-network models, which allow for separate forward and backward associations, convolution is inherently symmetrical, or commutative (i.e., $\mathbf{a} * \mathbf{b} = \mathbf{b} * \mathbf{a}$). Thus, Murdock's model formalizes the notion of associative symmetry articulated by Asch and Ebenholtz (1962).

Whereas Murdock has demonstrated the theoretical utility of combining associations and items into a vector representation, Bogacz, Brown, and Giraud-Carrier (2001) and Humphreys et al. (1989) have shown how item-similarity and associative recall can be accomplished by storing all of the items in a single neural-network (or matrix) representation.

According to Bogacz et al. (2001), recognition is based on the similarity between the matrix representation of a test item and the matrix representation of the stored memories (in a Hopfield network). This single similarity measure is very similar to the summed similarity of array models since all of the individual items are represented in the associative matrix. In an important earlier paper, Metcalfe (1985) proposed a very similar model that used convolution as the basis for associative storage (see Kahana et al., 2005b, for a more detailed analysis of different approaches to modeling recognition and recall).

The hybrid recognition-recall models described above are an extremely promising approach to understanding human episodic memory. For example, Monaco, Abbott, and Kahana (2007) showed how the Bogacz et al. (2001) model can predict the word-frequency effect in item recognition without a special elevated attention mechanism. Kahana et al. 2005b showed how the hybrid recognition-recall models described above could account for data on the recognition-failure of recallable words discussed in chapter 4. Many findings, however, are yet to be explained. For example, none of the hybrid models discussed above has yet been shown to provide an adequate account of spacing effects in recognition and recall or on the distributions of RTs and SAT functions generated in item recognition, associative recognition, and cued recall.

Despite the theoretical appeal of modeling recognition and recall within a common framework, as in the hybrid models described above, it is also possible that recognition and recall are best described by distinct models. Indeed, item recognition and cued recall exhibit a number of behavioral dissociations. In chapter 2 we discussed evidence suggesting that recognition depends on both associative and item information; cued recall on the other hand depends exclusively on associative information. Whereas both cued recall and the associative component of recognition seem to rely on the integrity of the brain structure known as the hippocampus, the item component of recognition appears to rely more strongly on neighboring brain structures, such as the perirhinal cortex (Eichenbaum, Yonelinas, and Ranganath, 2007).

Norman and O'Reilly (2003) developed a more biologically motivated neural-network model to describe the complementary roles of the hippocampus and the surrounding cortical regions in both item and associative-recognition memory. Their model simulates the functions of each of the major regions of the hippocampal formation and describes a set of rules for how the hippocampal and neocortical systems interact to support recognition performance under different experimental conditions. This model is a particularly nice illustration of an exciting new direction in neural-network models of memory. As our knowledge of the brain is rapidly advancing, neural-network models are being used to simultaneously fit behavioral and neurobiological data. In the process, they are providing ever greater insights into how brain systems implement the major functions of human memory (e.g., Grossberg and Pearson, 2008).

5.4 *MORE ON LINEAR ASSOCIATORS

In this section we illustrate how the algebra of associative memories can be simplified by rewriting our equations in terms of matrices. In particular, we consider Anderson's *linear associator* model in greater detail. Instead of writing Equation 5.2 (the Hebb rule) at the level of individual activation values, we can write it using vector notation as:

$$W = \mathbf{b}\mathbf{a}^\top \tag{5.11}$$

where $\top$ denotes the *transpose operation*, which exchanges the columns of a vector with its rows. If $\mathbf{a}$ and $\mathbf{b}$ are both column vectors (this is the convention we will use throughout), then this equation says that we are multiplying a column vector by a row vector, which results in the matrix:

$$\begin{pmatrix} b_1 \\ b_2 \end{pmatrix} \begin{pmatrix} a_1 & a_2 \end{pmatrix} = \begin{pmatrix} a_1b_1 & a_2b_1 \\ a_1b_2 & a_2b_2 \end{pmatrix}. \tag{5.12}$$

We can see that each element, or entry, in the matrix is just the product of the activations mandated by the Hebb rule.

Retrieval (the dynamical rule) is accomplished by multiplying the cue item by the weight matrix. That is,

$$W\mathbf{a} = \mathbf{b}\mathbf{a}^\top\mathbf{a} = \mathbf{b}(\mathbf{a}^\top\mathbf{a}). \qquad (5.13)$$

If each activation value is normally distributed with mean zero and variance $1/N$, we can show that $E[\mathbf{a}^\top\mathbf{a}] = 1$, the expected value of the ith attribute of the retrieved vector, will exactly equal the ith attribute of the target vector, $\mathbf{b}$.

The matrix model is not limited to storing a single association. One can add each additional association to the same weight matrix. For instance, if people study a list of L pairs, the weight matrix would be given by:

$$W = \sum_{l=1}^{L} \mathbf{b}_l\mathbf{a}_l^\top. \qquad (5.14)$$

Cuing with $\mathbf{a}_k$ will retrieve a noisy version of $\mathbf{b}_k$:

$$W\mathbf{a}_k = \sum_{l=1}^{L} \mathbf{b}_l\mathbf{a}_l^\top\mathbf{a}_k \qquad (5.15)$$

$$= \mathbf{b}_k\mathbf{a}_k^\top\mathbf{a}_k + \sum_{l\neq k}\mathbf{b}_l\mathbf{a}_l^\top\mathbf{a}_k$$

$$= \mathbf{b}_k(\mathbf{a}_k \cdot \mathbf{a}_k) + \sum_{l\neq k}\mathbf{b}_l(\mathbf{a}_l \cdot \mathbf{a}_k)$$

$$= \mathbf{b}_k + \text{error}.$$

If the item vectors are orthonormal[7] retrieval is perfect. With correlated item vectors, the matrix model retrieves a linear combination of items, with the target item being the strongest.

The matrix model we have just described is sometimes called a *heteroassociator* because each item is associated with a different item. You may notice that with the formulation given above, only forward recall is possible. To achieve

7. A set of perpendicular vectors of unit length is called an orthonormal set. Because the inner product (or dot product) of two orthonormal vectors is zero, all of the $\mathbf{a}_l \cdot \mathbf{a}_k$ terms will be zero. In addition, because the inner product of an orthonormal vector with itself is one, $\mathbf{b}_k(\mathbf{a}_k \cdot \mathbf{a}_k) = \mathbf{b}_k$. In reading these equations, it is important to know that matrix multiplication is not commutative but is both associative and distributive.

backward recall, the memory matrix must include both the forward and backward weight matrices, as given below:

$$W_l = W_{l-1} + \mathbf{b}_l\mathbf{a}_l^\top + \mathbf{a}_l\mathbf{b}_l^\top. \tag{5.16}$$

Whereas heteroassociation is used to link two different items, autoassociation (as discussed previously) can be used to create a content-addressable memory, storing individual items that can then be retrieved when given a partial input. We also use autoassociation to store associations between items. This is done by summing[8] the **a** and the **b** item vectors and then autoassociating the resulting composite vector. Symbolically,

$$\begin{aligned}
W_l &= W_{l-1} + (\mathbf{a}_l + \mathbf{b}_l)(\mathbf{a}_l + \mathbf{b}_l)^\top \\
&= W_{l-1} + \mathbf{a}_l\mathbf{a}_l^\top + \mathbf{a}_l\mathbf{b}_l^\top + \mathbf{b}_l\mathbf{a}_l^\top + \mathbf{b}_l\mathbf{b}_l^\top.
\end{aligned}$$

In this equation, the autoassociation carries item-specific information about $\mathbf{a}_l$ and $\mathbf{b}_l$, as well as the relational information needed for both forward and backward recall. Multiplying the cue item, $\mathbf{a}_k$, by the memory matrix retrieves an approximate representation of the studied pair, $\mathbf{a}_k + \mathbf{b}_k$.

$$\begin{aligned}
W\mathbf{a}_k &= \sum_{l=1}^{L}(\mathbf{a}_l\mathbf{a}_l^\top + \mathbf{a}_l\mathbf{b}_l^\top + \mathbf{b}_l\mathbf{a}_l^\top + \mathbf{b}_l\mathbf{b}_l^\top)\mathbf{a}_k \\
&= (\mathbf{a}_k + \mathbf{b}_k)(\mathbf{a}_k \cdot \mathbf{a}_k + \mathbf{b}_k \cdot \mathbf{a}_k) \\
&\quad + \sum_{l\neq k}(\mathbf{a}_l + \mathbf{b}_l)(\mathbf{a}_l \cdot \mathbf{a}_k + \mathbf{b}_l \cdot \mathbf{a}_k) \\
&= \mathbf{a}_k + \mathbf{b}_k + \text{error}.
\end{aligned}$$

Backward retrieval is accomplished in the same way, $W\mathbf{b}_k = \mathbf{a}_k + \mathbf{b}_k + \text{error}$. In both cases, if the vectors are orthonormal, retrieval is error free.

Because vector addition is commutative, this implementation of cued recall is inherently symmetrical. Even if the strengths of the **a** and **b** items are differentially weighted, the forward and backward heteroassociative terms would have the same strength. The symmetric nature of these linear models also applies to their nonlinear variants (e.g., Buhmann, Divko, and Schulten, 1989; Hopfield, 1982).

---

8. In this example, we are not concatenating the item vectors, though it would be easy to rewrite the example using concatenation.

5.5 *PROJECT: CUED RECALL IN A HOPFIELD NETWORK

For readers with some computer programming background, the following project may help achieve a deeper understanding of the models discussed in this chapter and of the techniques involved in simulating memory models. Although the project can be implemented in any programming language, such as Java, C/C++, or Python, it may be easiest to implement in a high-level matrix-oriented language such as MATLAB or R.

The goal of this project is to simulate an autoassociative neural-network model of paired-associate memory. Following Hopfield (1982), let us assume that random binary vectors ($+1$, -1 with equal probability) represent items. First create 400 random items, each consisting of 500 attributes (we will call this collection of items the model's *Lexicon*). To form a pair of items, draw two items from the lexicon and concatenate them into a single 1,000 attribute vector. To simulate a list of L pairs, choose pairs of unique items such that no item appears in more than one pair. Now store the L pairs in a Hopfield network consisting of $N = 1,000$ neurons.

To simulate cued recall, probe memory with a correct member of a pair concatenated with a noise vector (Rizzuto and Kahana, 2001). Then update the network for 10,000 iterations. At each iteration update just one randomly chosen neuron rather than updating the entire vector in one step (this is called asynchronous updating). After each neuron is updated, see how well the target vector matches each of the items in the lexicon. If the target exactly matches one item in the lexicon, then consider that item as having been recalled. Save the number of iterations up to that point (we will consider this value as being related to RT) and indicate that the network settled into the target state. It is possible that the network will settle into a state corresponding to one of the other stored items or into a mixture state corresponding to none of the stored items. Finally, it is possible that the network will not settle into any state within 20,000 iterations. Record all of this information, including the number of iterations.

Repeat the process described above for 100 simulated lists (with $L = 100$ for each list). Then aggregate the number of iterations into a frequency histogram (e.g., how many recall attempts required 1 iteration, 2 iterations, ..., 10,000 iterations). This histogram of number of iterations may be considered as the network's RT (assuming that each iteration takes a certain amount of time). Compare the shape of this histogram with the RT distributions shown in chapter 2. In addition, you should calculate and report the probabilities of correct responses, intrusions, and no responses. Examine how the performance of the network changes as you vary the value of L in these simulations. Does increasing the value of L result in lower recall rates, more intrusions, slower correct responses?

After you have successfully completed the exercise described above, try using correlated (i.e., similar) vectors. You can model similarity by keeping the first x attributes constant across all patterns and then examining how the network's performance varies with the degree of similarity (x).

5.6 STUDY QUESTIONS

1. Compute the weight matrix that would result from studying the following three vectors that are stored in a Hopfield network: $\mathbf{a}_1 = (-1, -1, -1)$, $\mathbf{a}_2 = (+1, -1, -1)$, and $\mathbf{a}_3 = (-1, +1, +1)$. Assuming that we probed memory with the test vector $\mathbf{a}_{\text{test}} = (+1, +1, +1)$, give the resulting vector after updating the activation of each node and indicate which vector has been recovered.

2. Explain how a Hopfield network can store multiple memory vectors. Include in your explanation a description, in words, of the Hebb learning rule and the McCulloch-Pitts dynamical rule. Explain how the weights change as multiple memory vectors are stored in the network and how the network can transform a noisy test vector given as an input into one of the stored vectors in memory. Explain how the network can be used to model response time in memory retrieval.

3. Describe how neural-network models can be used to fit data on paired-associate recall. Include, along with your description, a discussion of how context can be incorporated into the model and how this type of neural network can explain basic findings on paired-associate recall, such as recency effects, intrusions, and associative interference. What advantages does this model have over attribute-similarity models of associative recall?

4. Contextual drift, item similarity, and associative competition are three important ideas in the psychology of learning and memory. **a.** Describe how each of these concepts can help us to understand what happens in the A-B, A-C associative-interference paradigm (include a brief description of what these three concepts mean). **b.** Do these concepts apply to memory for names and faces and, if so, how? **c.** Describe Anderson's study of retrieval-induced forgetting and discuss which aspects of that phenomenon can, and cannot, be explained using the concepts mentioned above.

5. Consider the associative-symmetry hypothesis and the independent-associations hypothesis. **a.** Briefly describe each of these theories of associative memory. **b.** Describe the experimental data that

have been used to support either theory. **c.** Explain how you might build a neural-network model of association (either a Hopfield network or a linear associator network) to simulate symmetric associations and how you might build a neural network to simulate independent associations.

6. Consider a Hopfield-style neural-network model of associative memory in which items are represented as vectors of ones and zeros. Learning follows the Hebb rule, $w(i, j)_t = w(i, j)_{t-1} + a(i)a(j)$, and retrieval follows the McCullough-Pitts rule, $a(i) = g\left(\sum_{j=1}^{N} w(i, j)a(j)\right)$, with $g(x)$ defined as a threshold function such that $g(x) = 1$ when $x > 1.5$ and $g(x) = 0$ when $x \leq 1.5$. Assume, as usual, that $w(i, j) = 0$ at the start of the experiment and that $w(i, i) = 0$.

Suppose that we want to store the following three pairs of items, represented as vectors $\mathbf{m}_1$, $\mathbf{m}_2$, and $\mathbf{m}_3$, in our network. In each vector, the top four numbers represent the first word in the pair; the bottom four numbers represent the second word in the pair.

$$
\mathbf{a}_1 = \begin{pmatrix} 0 \\ 1 \\ 0 \\ 0 \\ 0 \\ 0 \\ 0 \\ 1 \end{pmatrix} \quad
\mathbf{a}_2 = \begin{pmatrix} 0 \\ 0 \\ 1 \\ 0 \\ 1 \\ 1 \\ 0 \\ 0 \end{pmatrix} \quad
\mathbf{a}_3 = \begin{pmatrix} 1 \\ 0 \\ 0 \\ 1 \\ 1 \\ 0 \\ 1 \\ 0 \end{pmatrix}
$$

Suppose that we "cue" the network, by setting the vector of activation values to:

$$
\mathbf{m}_{\text{test}} = \begin{pmatrix} 1 \\ 0 \\ 0 \\ 1 \\ 1 \\ 0 \\ 0 \\ 1 \end{pmatrix}.
$$

What would the resulting vector be after all of the neurons have been updated? (Show all of your work, including the weight matrix and the order in which you updated the activations.) Update the neurons in sequence from the first/top to the last/bottom. **b.** Explain how this model can make predictions about response times in associative memory tasks.

6

Free Recall and Memory Search

The stream of thought flows on; but most of its segments fall into the bottomless abyss of oblivion. Of some, no memory survives the instant of their passage. Of others, it is confined to a few moments, hours, or days. Others again, leave vestiges which are indestructible, and by means of which they may be recalled as long as life endures.

WILLIAM JAMES, *Principles of Psychology* (1890)

We are often faced with the task of remembering a collection of items that were learned in a given context or that share a certain attribute. For example, a friend might ask whom you met at a party, what you did on a recent trip, or which of Clint Eastwood's movies you have seen. In the laboratory, this type of memory search is most often studied through *free recall*, a simple variant of the basic list-memory tasks discussed in the previous chapters.

In a free-recall task, a participant studies a list of words for a later recall test. The words are presented one at a time. Then after all the words are shown, the participant attempts to recall the words from the list in any order.[1] As with other list-memory tasks, common words are convenient stimuli; they are familiar to all participants, have meanings that are generally agreed upon, and can be processed rapidly. In addition, there are enough common words in the English language that one can create many lists, all consisting of unique words.

A key feature of free recall is that the participant is allowed to recall the list items in any order. Thus, the analysis of the order in which a participant recalls the list items may give clues as to the underlying mechanisms of memory search. In particular, we may ask what factors determine the order in which participants recall words from the list, how these factors interact to determine whether a given item is recalled, and, in the end, how many items are actually recalled. In this chapter we review the basic empirical findings concerning free recall. In subsequent chapters we will draw on these basic findings to help evaluate models proposed to explain this important memory function.

6.1 SERIAL-POSITION EFFECTS

If a list is sufficiently short (e.g., fewer than five or six words), participants will have little difficulty recalling all of the words. However, with longer lists, participants will typically be unable to recall all the items and they will occasionally recall items that were not on the list. We refer to recall of a nonlist item that appeared on an earlier list as a *prior-list intrusion* (PLI) and to recall of a nonlist item that did *not* appear on any earlier list as an *extralist intrusion* (ELI).

A first step in characterizing the way participants recall list items is to calculate the probability of recalling an item as a function of its serial position in the list. This function is called a *serial-position curve*. Figure 6.1 shows serial-position curves reported in a classic study conducted by Murdock (1962). Murdock examined the effects of list length and presentation rate on the serial-position curve by visually presenting lists of 10, 15, and 20 words at a 2-sec rate (2 seconds per item) and lists of 20, 30, and 40 words at a 1-sec rate, with each list followed by 90 sec of oral free recall. As shown in Figure 6.1, these curves have a characteristic form: excellent recall of the last few items (the *recency* effect), poorest recall of the middle items, and enhanced recall of the first few items (the *primacy* effect).

---

1. In 1894, E. A. Kirkpatrick published the first study using the free-recall method. This was the same year that Mary Calkins introduced the paired-associate technique. Because of the unconstrained nature of the free-recall technique, Ebbinghaus (1908) found it to be "crude and superficial." However, interest in free recall surged following a series of influential studies published between 1953 and 1962 by Leo Postman, Weston Bousfield, James Deese, Ben Murdock, and Endel Tulving.

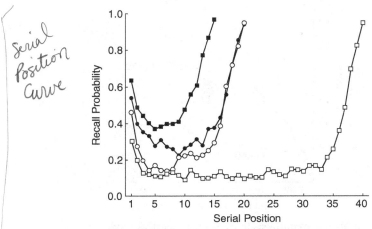

Serial Position Curve

Figure 6.1 The serial-position curve in free recall. The four curves represent lists of 15 items (filled squares), and 20 items (filled circles), both presented at a 2-sec/item rate, and lists of 20 items (open circles), and 40 items (open squares), both presented at a 1-sec/item rate (data from Murdock, 1962). To avoid overcrowding of lines and markers, we have omitted the serial-position curves for the 10-item and 30-item lists. Those two curves show identical trends.

Consider the serial-position curves for the different list lengths and presentation rates. Murdock's data show that increasing list length or speeding the presentation rate resulted in lower recall of early and middle items but did not affect recall of the last six or so items. In fact, if we were to line up the serial-position curves on the last list item, we would find that they lie virtually on top of each other for the last several items.

In addition to study time (presentation rate) and list length, other variables that boost recall of early and middle (*prerecency*) items have little or no effect on recency items. For example, lists of similar words are better recalled than unrelated words (Craik and Levy, 1970) and lists of common words are better recalled than lists of rare words (Raymond, 1969; Sumby, 1963).[2] In both of these cases, however, the improved recall is not seen for the recency items.

6.1.1 Study Time, List Length, and the Total-Time Hypothesis

Murdock's experiment illustrates how study time and list length both influence recall probability. Participants recalled a larger percentage of the study list when

---

2. Whereas in item recognition, rare (low-frequency) words are better recognized, in free recall, common (high-frequency) words are better recalled.

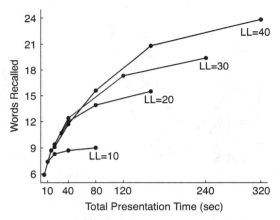

Figure 6.2 Total-time hypothesis in free recall. Recall as a function of total presentation time for lists of varying list length (LL = 10, 20, 30, or 40). Items were presented at a rate of 0.5, 1, 2, 4, or 8 sec per word. Data from Roberts (1972).

given more time to study each item or when given shorter lists. Although the percentage of words recalled is greater for short than for long lists, the absolute number of words recalled generally increases with list length. This is easy to understand because increasing list length increases the opportunities to recall list items and gives participants more total time to study items.

Early research examining the effect of study time on recall led to the *total-time hypothesis (TTH)*, which states that the number of items a participant can recall depends on the amount of time available to study (Murdock, 1960). According to the TTH, studying 20 items for 3 sec each and studying 60 items for 1 sec each should yield the same number of items recalled.

Roberts (1972) tested the TTH by examining the effects of both presentation rate and list length on the total number of items recalled in a free-recall task. Roberts gave practiced participants lists of 10, 20, 30, or 40 words at each of five presentation rates (0.5, 1, 2, 4, or 8 sec per word). In all, there were 20 different combinations of list length and presentation rate.[3] Each point in Figure 6.2 shows data for one of the combinations of the list length and presentation rate. The major result, as seen in the figure, is that participants remembered more items with fast presentation rates and longer lists than with slow presentation rates and shorter lists. These data reveal that the total-time hypothesis is not correct. For a given total presentation time, adding items to the list and shortening each of their exposures enables participants to

3. Roberts also manipulated presentation modality, with half of the lists presented auditorily and the other half presented visually.

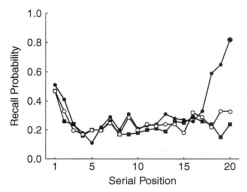

Figure 6.3 The effect of a distractor in free recall. The presence of a distractor interval eliminates the recency effect but has little effect on recall of early and middle list items (Postman and Phillips, 1965). Shown are serial-position curves for 20 item lists with 0 (filled circles), 15 (open circles), or 30 (filled squares) sec of distractor between study and test.

recall more items than does lengthening presentation rate and decreasing list length.

6.1.2 The Fragile Nature of Recency

Postman and Phillips (1965) found that the striking recency effects seen in immediate free recall disappeared when participants were tested following a brief delay during which they engaged in a distracting task. Three groups of participants were asked to freely recall a list of words after a 0-sec, 15-sec, or 30-sec retention interval. During the retention interval, participants were asked to count backward by threes starting from a three-digit number. After just 15 sec of a distracting task, the recency effect was almost completely gone (Figure 6.3), but the distractor had little or no effect on participants' memory for the early and middle (prerecency) items.[4]

The nature of the distractor task does not appear to be crucial for eliminating the recency effect, but it is necessary to give the participant something to

4. Although the general observation that the recency effect is extremely fragile in the face of distracting activity was known to early investigators (e.g., Müller and Pilzecker, 1900), the specific demonstration in free recall was a key finding in support of dual-store models that ascribed recency to retrieval from a short-term memory store. This finding was made in contemporaneous reports by Postman and Phillips (1965) and Glanzer and Cunitz (1966). Although the Glanzer and Cunitz study is more widely known, their serial-position curves exhibit much stronger primacy than recency. This atypical pattern suggests that many of their participants were adopting a serial-recall rather than a free-recall strategy.

do during the retention interval. Baddeley and Hitch (1977) reported an experiment in which participants were presented with a list of names that they were to classify as typically male or female but were not told that a memory test would follow (a technique called *incidental learning*). If participants are unaware that there will be a memory test, there is no reason to believe that they will actively try to remember the words. One group of participants was given a distractor interval of 15 sec during which they were required to copy digits. Another group was required to wait 15 sec but was not required to perform any task. A third group of participants was given the memory test immediately after the last name was presented. Although the group with the digit-copying task had an impaired recency effect, the group with the no-distractor delay produced a serial-position curve indistinguishable from that of the group with immediate test.

The finding that the recency effect can be eliminated by a short distractor paralleled contemporaneous memory findings in other studies of short-term memory. For example, giving participants a brief distractor task immediately after they have studied a list of paired associates removes the otherwise strong recency effect observed in that task (Figure 4.3).

Brown (1958) developed another memory task that has been frequently used to demonstrate the fragile nature of participants' memory for recently experienced items. In these experiments (Brown, 1958; Peterson and Peterson, 1959; Hellyer, 1962), participants studied three letters or words (e.g., *D-V-L* or *house-ribbon-railway*) and were asked to recall them in order. When the recall test was delayed by just 18 sec (during which participants were asked to count backward by threes from a three-digit number), recall dropped from more than 90% to less than 25%. List length is a critical variable in these studies: when participants only have to remember a single item, they recall that item on more than 80% of trials after 18 seconds of distraction (Murdock, 1961).

Study Modality and Recency

Modality of presentation is another factor that influences the recency effect but has no effect on prerecency items. As in the paired-associate task, one finds greater recency for lists presented auditorily than for those presented visually. Murdock and Walker (1969) were the first to demonstrate this effect in free recall. They had participants study and free recall lists consisting of 20 randomly chosen high-frequency words. Words were either presented visually or auditorily, but recall was always vocal. Examining the serial-position curves for auditorily and visually presented lists, one can see that the recency effect is enhanced in the auditory modality (see Figure 6.4). The benefit associated with auditory presentation did not extend to prerecency items.

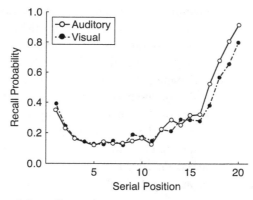

Figure 6.4 The modality effect in free recall. Recall of recently studied items is enhanced when the items are heard (auditory presentation) as opposed to seen (visual presentation). This modality effect is specific to the recency portion of the serial-position curve; earlier list items are recalled equally well for both seen and heard items (Murdock and Walker, 1969).

Thus, modality of presentation influences memory for recency but not for prerecency items.

6.1.3 Recency and Short-term Memory

Noting the fragile nature of the recency effect in free recall, cued recall, and the Brown-Peterson paradigm, memory scientists in the 1960s began to embrace a distinction between two memory stores with different properties: short-term memory and long-term memory. The basic idea, which is discussed in greater detail in chapter 7, is that items enter a short-term store (termed STS) as the list is studied. STS can only hold a few items at a time, so as new items are studied, they displace older items that are already being held in STS. While items reside in STS, their (vector) representations in long-term store (LTS) become associated with each other and with a representation of the general list context. Thus, the longer items reside in STS, the greater their associative strength in LTS.

According to dual-store models, at the time of test, the items in STS are available for immediate report. This explains the recency effect because the last few items are more likely to still be in STS. It also explains the elimination of the recency effect by an end-of-list distractor because the distractor is likely to displace the list items from STS. As discussed in the next section, the primacy effect is the result of the first few items spending more time in STS. This is because items drop out of STS probabilistically, so that the first few items have some probability of remaining in STS longer than later items. The last few items spend the shortest time in STS, which accounts for the finding that on a final free-recall test given at the end of the entire experiment, these items are actually remembered less well than items from the middle of the list (Craik, 1970).[5]

In a highly influential paper, Atkinson and Shiffrin (1968) surveyed the gathering evidence for a distinction between short-term and long-term memory and presented a computational model of memory based on the two-store distinction. This basic framework was later advanced into a more sophisticated theory of memory search by Shiffrin and colleagues (Raaijmakers and Shiffrin, 1980; Shiffrin and Raaijmakers, 1992). Their model of memory search, termed the *search of associative memory (SAM)* model, will be discussed in the next chapter.

6.1.4 Rehearsal and Primacy

In studying a list of words for a later memory test, motivated participants will actively rehearse items as the list proceeds. That is, they use the time following each item presentation to think back to earlier list items. It was noted early on that the primacy effect tends to be larger when opportunities for rehearsal are enhanced, as would be the case with a slow presentation rate and intentional learning instructions (Glenberg et al., 1980; Marshall and Werder, 1972; Rundus, 1980; Watkins, Neath, and Sechler, 1989). When lists are presented at a fast rate or when participants are not informed that they will be given a memory test, primacy effects are greatly diminished (though not completely eliminated). Because these manipulations are likely to minimize rehearsal, findings such as these led to the view that primacy reflects increased rehearsal of early list items, and researchers sought to develop methods aimed at directly observing and quantifying the rehearsal process.

The overt-rehearsal technique

Rundus (1971) devised an experimental technique to probe participants' rehearsal patterns. He asked participants to say, out loud, everything that came into their minds as they tried to memorize the words on the study list for a free-recall test.[6] Using this *overt-rehearsal technique*, Rundus was able to

5. The negative recency effect reported by Craik (1970) appears to depend critically on each list being recalled immediately following its presentation. When recall is not tested immediately following each list presentation, negative recency is not obtained in final free recall (Marmurek, 1983). This finding is not so easy to reconcile with dual-store models.

6. Although the overt-rehearsal method appears analogous to the free-association method discussed in chapter 4, there is an important difference. In overt rehearsal, participants are

count the number of overt rehearsals that each item in the list received.[7] He found that primacy items received the greatest number of rehearsals and that participants often continued to rehearse the primacy items until the end of the list. Rundus also demonstrated that the number of rehearsals an item received was highly correlated with that item's eventual recall. This finding, coupled with participants' preferential rehearsal of primacy items, lent support to the theory that the primacy effect in free recall is a consequence of participants' rehearsal strategies.

Rundus attempted to extend his analysis of rehearsal to explain other recall phenomena. For example, he showed that when lists contained some repeated items, the repeated items received more rehearsals when they were separated by other study items (i.e., spaced) than when they were repeated successively (i.e., massed). Rundus used this fact to argue that the spacing effect—the finding that recall of repeated items increases when they are spaced apart—was partly due to participants' tendency to devote more rehearsal to spaced items.

At this point the reader may reasonably wonder whether the analysis of rehearsals actually constitutes an explanation of the phenomena of interest or whether it merely elaborates those phenomena, adding another dimension that we must explain (e.g., why participants tend to rehearse primacy items, etc.). We will revisit this question after considering some important additional data on the relation between rehearsal and recall.

Using the overt-rehearsal procedure, Brodie and Murdock (1977) examined the relation between presentation rate and the primacy effect. Previous work had shown that slower presentation rates give rise to stronger primacy effects. Brodie and Murdock showed that with a slow (5-second) presentation rate, early list items also tend to be rehearsed later in the study list than with a fast (1.25-second) presentation rate. They argued that by rehearsing early list items later in the list, those items will benefit from greater *recency*. Thus, the rehearsal process not only leads participants to devote more time to some items than to others; it also makes items from earlier list positions appear later in the sequence of rehearsals and thus more recent at the time of test.

Brodie and Murdock proposed that rather than examining recall as a function of the position of an item in the list, one should examine recall as a function of the position in which an item was last rehearsed. They thus contrasted two types of serial positions, which they referred to as nominal serial position and functional serial position. *Nominal serial position* is the position of the item in the

trying to remember the items in the current list, so their thoughts will tend to focus on those items.

7. Although overt rehearsal is surely not the same as the covert rehearsal that participants actually do, it is a reasonable approach to gaining some insight into the covert-rehearsal process.

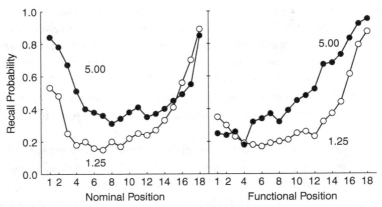

Figure 6.5 Functional and nominal serial-position curves. The left and right panels plot accuracy as a function of nominal and functional serial position, respectively, for 18-item lists presented either at a 5.0- or 1.25-sec rate. Data from Brodie and Murdock (1977).

list, as presented by the experimenter to the participant. *Functional serial position* is the position of the item in the participant's sequence of rehearsals. Because a given item may be rehearsed many times during the study period, Brodie and Murdock decided that the most relevant position is that of the last rehearsal. A *functional-serial-position curve* shows the relation between recall accuracy and functional serial position.

Figure 6.5 compares the nominal and functional serial-position curves obtained by Brodie and Murdock. For the nominal serial-position curves, primacy is especially strong in the slow presentation rate condition. For the functional serial-position curves, there is little or no primacy in the slow presentation rate condition. Rather, the curve shows a nearly continuous recency effect extending from the end of the list to the beginning. In the fast presentation rate condition, where participants have far less time to rehearse earlier list items during each item presentation, primacy is also reduced in the functional serial-position curve but it is still present to a modest degree. This analysis suggests that the primacy effect largely results from early list items being rehearsed more recently than middle items. Subsequent work by Ward and colleagues (e.g., Tan and Ward, 2000; Ward, 2002) has replicated and extended these findings by showing that in a broad range of experimental conditions, the recency with which an item has been last rehearsed is the critical variable predicting its recall.

There are several limitations to research using the overt-rehearsal procedure. Perhaps the first objection is that asking participants to rehearse out loud

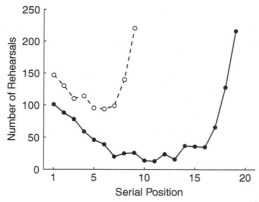

Figure 6.6 Rehearsal serial-position curve. The dashed curve illustrates the total number of rehearsals made to items in serial positions 1–9 during the encoding of the item in position 10. The solid curve illustrates the total number of rehearsals made to items from positions 1–19 during the encoding of the item in position 20. Both curves show that participants' overt rehearsals exhibit a serial-position curve that looks similar to the recall-serial-position curve. Similar curves could be drawn for items presented at other serial positions. The reason for the large number of rehearsals is that the data are aggregated over multiple study-test lists. Data from Murdock and Metcalfe (1978).

changes the task, making it less natural and leading participants to behave in a way that they would not otherwise behave in regular free recall.

Second, any attempt to explain recall data with rehearsal data suffers from the chicken-and-egg problem. Unless we know why participants rehearse items the way they do, we can't use their rehearsal to explain their recall. Instead, their rehearsal data may only provide us with one more thing that requires explanation—namely, what makes rehearsals?

Murdock and Metcalfe (1978) examined the distribution of rehearsals following the presentation of each study item. Their data, shown in Figure 6.6, reveal that rehearsals exhibit a serial-position curve that looks very much like the serial-position curve in free recall. The main difference between the recall and rehearsal serial-position curves is that when rehearsing items during the study period, participants are free to repeat items.

In an elegant analysis of participants' overt-rehearsal data, Laming (2006, 2008) argued that rehearsals are essentially mini-recalls that participants make as they study the list. In support of this view, Laming found that the sequence of recalls had the same statistical structure as the sequence of rehearsals once repeats were excluded. Laming's view turns the analysis of rehearsals on its head. Rather than trying to use rehearsals to explain recall, Laming argues that we should be using recall to explain rehearsal. The problem is that any recall task in which participants are free to rehearse is complicated by the fact that during study, participants do not merely attend to the presented stimuli; rather, participants make use of the study period to also try and recall previously studied items.

Unlike the large primacy effect attributable to rehearsal, a residual primacy effect for the very first list position does not seem to be dependent on rehearsal (Howard and Kahana, 1999; Laming, 1999). Similar first-position primacy effects have been reported in item recognition experiments involving difficult-to-rehearse items (e.g., Neath, 1993b; Neath and Crowder, 1996; Wright, Santiago, Sands, Kendrick, and Cook, 1985). This suggests that primacy, though greatly enhanced by the rehearsal process, cannot be entirely explained by it.

6.2 RETRIEVAL DYNAMICS

In thinking about recall as a dynamic process, we can go beyond the serial-position and rehearsal analyses presented above. Specifically, we can examine the order and timing of participants' recalls, their tendency to occasionally recall items that were not presented on the target list, and the way in which their transitions are influenced by experimental variables. We first consider the three main types of events in the recall process: starting, transition, and stopping.

6.2.1 Starting

As a first step, we need to specify how participants begin the recall process, that is, how they choose the first item to recall. Deese and Kaufman (1957) observed that participants begin recall with the last few list items. In fact, the tendency to begin recall at the end of the list underlies the recency effect observed in the serial-position curve (Laming, 1999). This tendency can be measured by plotting the *probability of first recall* (PFR) curve, which is a serial-position curve for just the first item recalled (Hogan, 1975; Howard and Kahana, 1999; Laming, 1999).[8]

Howard and Kahana (1999) conducted two experiments designed to analyze free recall under conditions that minimize rehearsal.[9] As expected, the recency

8. To calculate the probability of first recall, one tallies the number of times the first recall came from a certain serial position in the presented word list and then divides the tally by the number of times the first recall could have come from that serial position.

9. Rehearsal was minimized by presenting items at a fast rate (1 second per item) and asking participants to judge each presented item as either a concrete or abstract noun.

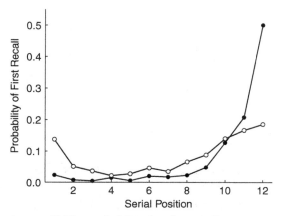

Figure 6.7 Starting recall. The probability that the very first response comes from a given serial position illustrates the striking tendency to start by recalling the last item in immediate free recall (filled circles). In delayed free recall, this tendency is greatly diminished (open circles). Data from Howard and Kahana (1999), Experiment 1.

effect was prominent in immediate free recall but was attenuated by having participants perform 16 seconds of simple arithmetic problems between study and test. Figure 6.7 shows the PFR curves for data from this experiment. In immediate free recall, participants start recalling from the end of the list, whereas in delayed free recall, they initiate retrieval from varied-list positions.

6.2.2 Recall Transitions and the Contiguity Effect

Because the order of participants' free-recall responses reflects the order in which items come to mind, recall transitions reveal the organization of memory for the list items. Consider, for example, that a participant has just recalled an item from serial position i and that the next recall is from serial position j. We can measure the relation between recall probability and the *lag* between i and j, defined as $j - i$. This measure is called the *conditional-response probability as a function of lag*, or *lag-CRP*.

Figure 6.8A shows an average lag-CRP function based on data from 18 free-recall experiments. Positive values of $lag = j - i$ correspond to (forward) transitions from earlier to later items; negative values of *lag* correspond to backward recall transitions. Large absolute values of *lag* (henceforth, absolute lag) correspond to words spaced widely in the list; small absolute values of lag correspond to words spaced closely together in the list. For example, if the list had contained the subsequence *absence hollow pupil* and a participant recalled *hollow*, then *pupil*, the recall of *pupil* would have a lag of $+1$. If, instead, the

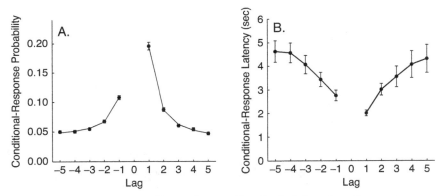

Figure 6.8 The contiguity effect in free recall. A. Probability of recalling an item from serial position $i +$ lag immediately following recall of an item from serial position i. **B.** Interresponse time between recall of an item from serial positions i and $i +$ lag. Data are averaged across 20 free-recall experiments. Error bars represent 95% confidence intervals.

participant recalled *hollow*, then *absence*, the transition to *absence* would be associated with a lag of -1. In this case, the participant is moving backward in the list; *absence* followed by *pupil* would yield a lag of $+2$.

The conditional-response probability for a transition of a certain lag is calculated by first tallying the number of times a transition of that lag was made and then dividing that tally by the number of times a transition of that lag could have been made. Possible transitions do not include those in which (a) the lag is outside the bounds of the list (e.g., negative lags following recall of the first list item) or (b) the item has already been recalled. Although participants occasionally make prior-list intrusions and sometimes repeat previously recalled items, such transitions are far less frequent than those involving target list items.

The lag-CRP function has two invariant characteristics. First, the function decreases systematically as absolute lag increases, approaching an asymptotic value at moderate lags; the asymptotic value depends almost exclusively on list length, with lower asymptotic values for longer lists. Second, for small absolute lags, the function is consistently asymmetric, with an approximately 2:1 ratio favoring forward over backward recall transitions. Although the contiguity effect is monotonically decreasing for lags ranging from 1 to 5 items, transitions to end-of-list items (and, in some cases, start-of-list items) are more frequent than transitions to items of intermediate lag, especially for the first few output positions (Farrell and Lewandowsky, 2008). Although this would appear to challenge the generality of the contiguity effect, it has been shown that this effect is exactly what you would predict if the recency effect persists through the first several recalls (Polyn et al., 2009; Howard, Sederberg, and Kahana, 2009).[10]

The contiguity effect shown in Figure 6.8A has been confirmed in experiments that use widely differing methodologies. Regardless of whether items are presented visually or auditorily, quickly or slowly, whether people study long or short lists, lists of semantically related or unrelated items, whether people are encouraged to rehearse or whether rehearsal is disrupted, successively recalled items are far more likely to come from nearby serial positions than from remote serial positions (Kahana, Howard, and Polyn, 2008; Kahana and Miller, 2013).

To understand how various experimental variables influence the contiguity effect, it is convenient to quantify the effect with a single number. Polyn et al. (2009) introduced a percentile-based measure for this purpose. This measure (called the *temporal-clustering score*) produces a percentile rank for each recall transition, which reflects the temporal proximity of the two recalled items in the study list, taking into account that already-recalled items are no longer available for recall. Participants who exhibit a strong degree of temporal organization produce strong contiguity effects (with the maximum value of 1 reflecting perfect contiguity-based organization).

The contiguity effect in free recall has been shown to be related to participants' overall ability to recall list items. For example, older adults, who recall significantly fewer correct items than younger adults, exhibit significantly reduced contiguity effects (Kahana, Howard, Zaromb, and Wingfield, 2002). Moreover, across a large sample of participants, the magnitude of the contiguity effect was significantly (positively) correlated with recall performance (Sederberg, Miller, Howard, and Kahana, 2010). This pattern is shown in Figure 6.9.

An interesting feature of the contiguity effect is the strong forward asymmetry, with recall transitions being nearly twice as likely in the forward than in the backward direction. This more pronounced tendency to make forward transitions is also seen in ordered (serial) recall and in the pattern of errors observed when participants are given a single list item as a probe to recall its successor (Kahana and Caplan, 2002; Caplan et al., 2006). However, the forward asymmetry effect in free recall contrasts with the finding that recall

---

10. In immediate free recall, the lag-CRP exhibits a much stronger contiguity effect for the first few recall transitions than for later recall transitions. This reflects bleed-in from the recency effect, where the last two or three study items tend to be recalled as a cluster prior to recall of other items. The lag-CRP function remains stable across later output positions, thus reflecting the general tendency to make transitions between neighboring items throughout recall. In delayed free recall, recency is reduced or eliminated, and the lag-CRP remains stable across all output positions.

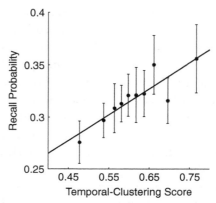

Figure 6.9 Contiguity effect predicts recall performance. Participants were ranked by the strength of their contiguity effect (indexed by the *temporal-clustering score*) and then binned into 10 equal-sized groups (deciles). There is a significant trend for recall performance to increase as the contiguity effect increases. Errors are 95% confidence intervals calculated across all participants in each decile. The line represents the regression fit to the data points (standardized $\beta = 0.88, p < .001$).

of paired associates is almost perfectly symmetrical, with subjects exhibiting nearly identical rates of forward and backward recall, and with forward and backward recall being highly correlated at the level of individual pairs (Asch and Ebenholtz, 1962; Ekstrand, 1966; Kahana, 2002). It may be that temporally segregated word pairs (as in paired-associate memory tasks) are more likely to be encoded as separate meaning units than neighboring words in a list. Associative symmetry may thus be a property of well-integrated pairs that is broken due to the interference among items from different list positions (Caplan et al., 2006).

Whereas the contiguity effect illustrates the temporal organization of memory, it is also well known that participants' sequences of recalls reflect preexisting semantic associations among list items (e.g., Bousfield, 1953; Romney, Brewer, and Batchelder, 1993). We will consider the important role of semantic organization in free recall, as well as several other types of similarity-based clustering phenomena, in section 6.3.

Interresponse times

RT data, which are routinely collected in recognition and in cued-recall tasks, can also be measured in free recall. Because participants make multiple responses, the relevant measure is the inter-response time (IRT) between successive recalls. One of the first studies to look at IRTs was carried out by Murdock and Okada (1970). By having participants speak their responses into a microphone, then amplifying the voice signal and plotting the speech signals continuously during the recall process, they were able to identify word-onset times in a relatively precise manner. This was an extremely labor-intensive study, and few investigators undertook such measures at that time. Instead, some investigators measured latencies by having participants type responses on a keyboard and measuring the time taken to type the first letter of each response (Waugh, 1970). Another method was to have an experimenter press a button each time a participant recalled an item. But today, with modern desktop computers it is possible to digitally record participants' vocal responses. Such vocal responses have the advantage of being faster and more natural than typed responses. After the data have been collected, one can use computer software to measure the times of each word onset in the recorded sound files.[11]

Recording participants' IRTs allows one to calculate a *conditional response latency* (lag-CRL) curve. A lag-CRL curve relates IRTs between successively recalled words to their proximity in the study list (i.e., their lag). As shown in Figure 6.8B, IRTs are short when neighboring list items are recalled successively, and they increase with the lag between the items' positions in the study list. The lag-CRL portrays the same basic result as the lag-CRP; namely, the more likely the transition, the faster the transition. It is likely that both lag-CRP and lag-CRL functions reflect the operation of a single underlying mechanism. Nearby items are more strongly associated with each other than are distant items. The stronger the association, the higher the recall probability and the shorter the IRT between successively recalled items.

6.2.3 Stopping Recall

At some point, participants stop recalling, either because their time has run out, because they cannot think of any other items that were on the list, or because they have finished recalling all of the items. Understanding recall termination is particularly important because whatever accounts for recall termination determines the total number of items that are ultimately recalled. Although previous research has revealed a great deal about how people initiate recall and how they transition between successively recalled items, much less is known about the conditions that influence recall termination.

The first challenge in studying recall termination is determining whether a participant is done recalling items. One can determine this either by asking participants to indicate when they cannot recall any further items or by simply looking at the last item they recall within a fixed recall period. Given that most

11. Software developed for this purpose can be freely obtained at http://memory.psych.upenn.edu.

free-recall studies give participants a fixed amount of time to recall the items that they can remember, the second approach allows one to consider a much wider range of data. Because the recall interval used in most studies (around 2 minutes) is quite long in relation to the IRTs between successive recalls, it is unlikely that participants are still making correct recalls at the very end of the recall period.

Miller, Kahana, and Weidemann (2012) defined recall termination as occurring when the time between the last recalled item and the end of the fixed recall period was both longer than all of the IRTs on the current trial and exceeded a criterion of 12 sec. This value was chosen to exceed the mean exit latency of 10 sec reported by Dougherty and Harbison (2007) in an open-ended retrieval period where participants pressed a button to indicate that they could not recall any more items. Miller et al. then analyzed 28,015 trials of free recall across 14 different published studies. Of these trials, 18,829 met their criteria for recall termination (67.2%). Using this large dataset, they examined how recall termination varied with output position and as a function of the nature of the last recalled item.

Figure 6.10 shows the conditional probability of recall termination following correct responses, prior-list intrusions, and extralist intrusions, as a function of output position during recall. The probability of stopping is very low for the first few responses, but it rises as recall proceeds. Participants are more likely to terminate recall following an intrusion (either a PLI or an ELI) than following a correct recall. This pattern holds true at all stages of the recall process, from early to late output positions (Figure 6.10; Miller et al., 2012).

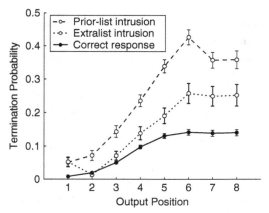

Figure 6.10 Probability of stopping recall. Probability of a response being the final response in a recall sequence for correct recalls, prior-list intrusions, and extralist intrusions as a function of output position. Error bars represent ± *SEM*. Data from Miller et al., 2012.

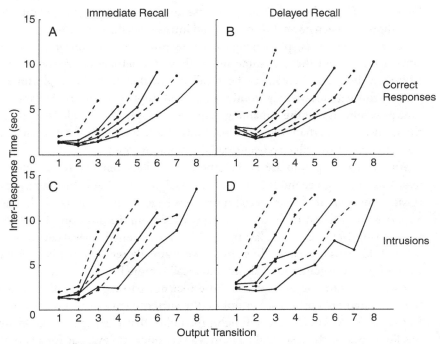

Figure 6.11 Interresponse times (IRTs) in free recall. IRT as a joint function of output position and total number of item recalls on a given trial (each line corresponds to trials on which four, five, . . ., nine items were recalled; the time between the recall signal and the first recall is not shown). Upper panels show data from transitions between correct responses; lower panels for transitions between correct responses and intrusions. Left panels show data from immediate free recall (IFR); right panels show data from delayed free recall (DFR). The IRTs for the first few transitions tend to be slower in DFR than in IFR, but otherwise the two procedures give similar patterns. Not surprisingly, participants tend to be slower in making transitions between correct responses and intrusions, but there too the data show the same basic pattern. Data from experiments in the free-recall database (Sederberg, Miller, Howard, and Kahana, 2010).

Just as the probability of stopping increases with each successive response, so do the participants' IRTs. Early responses are generally made rapidly, and as recall proceeds, the times between successive responses lengthen. This was first demonstrated by Murdock and Okada (1970), who found that in immediate free recall, IRTs increase exponentially with output position. Figure 6.11A, B shows a replication of their analysis based on data from both immediate and delayed free recall. These curves indicate that the time between successive responses is a reliable predictor of when participants will stop recalling.

Figure 6.11C, D show a similar increase in IRTs with output position for transitions between correct responses and intrusions (PLIs or ELIs).

As recall proceeds, participants become progressively slower in making correct recalls and then, at some point, they stop altogether. Assuming that additional list items remain to be recalled and that there is ample time to retrieve those items, we may wonder why recall stopped at this particular point. One possibility is that the remaining items were simply not encoded well during the study phase. Perhaps the participant was so intensively thinking about some items that he or she effectively ignored the remaining items.

An alternative possibility is that the nonrecalled items were encoded, at least to some degree, and the current retrieval cue is not effective in targeting those items. Our analysis of recall transitions suggests how this might happen. Suppose that the last three recalled items were from list positions 3, 2, and 1, respectively. In this case, the last recalled item is a strong retrieval cue for items 2 and 3. However, because those items were already recalled, the last recalled item is not a very good retrieval cue, and recall is more likely to terminate.

As a more extreme example, suppose that our participant recalled an item that appeared on a prior list but not on the current list (a prior-list intrusion). In this case, we would expect a high probability that participants would stop recalling because the just-recalled item is a very poor retrieval cue for any of the items on the target list. This is exactly what we have seen in Figure 6.10 and also in data reported by Zaromb et al. (2006).

This analysis omits many important variables, such as the semantic relatedness among the list items. Nonetheless, it suggests that participants can sometimes find themselves in a mental cul-de-sac where the recently recalled items are simply poor cues for the remaining target items. This may relate to the commonplace experience of being unable to recall some well-learned information. Although it feels as if the answer is at the "tip of our tongue," we are lacking the retrieval cues necessary to target the desired memory.

6.3 SEMANTIC CLUSTERING

The influence of preexisting semantic relations on episodic recall has been of interest to psychological researchers at least since Bartlett (1932). In free recall, participants rely upon both preexisting knowledge of the semantic relations that may be present between items in a list (*semantic memory*) and newly formed temporal associations among such items (*episodic memory*). This section considers the important role that semantic memory plays in the process of memory search.

One can easily illustrate how semantic relatedness influences recall by asking participants to learn categorized word lists—lists containing several exemplars from each of several semantic categories (e.g., animals such as cow and horse, gemstones such as emerald and amethyst, trees such as birch and maple). Even when the presentation order of the items is randomized in such a way that words from a single category do not appear in adjacent list positions, participants tend to recall words from the same natural category together (Bousfield, 1953; Bousfield, Sedgewick, and Cohen, 1954; Jenkins and Russell, 1952). Romney et al. (1993) reported that when participants recalled a list comprised of items from a single category, category members that were more closely related to each other also tended to be recalled closer together in the output sequence. These findings illustrate the phenomenon of *semantic clustering* insofar as participants' responses are clustered according to the semantic relations among the items on the target list.

Not only are recalled items reported by category, but the IRTs for within-category transitions are shorter than the IRTs for between-category transitions (Pollio, Richards, and Lucas, 1969). To the extent that long between-category IRTs reflect the time taken to find the next category in episodic memory, making category names available to participants should shorten between-category IRTs. Indeed, this is the case (Patterson, Meltzer, and Mandler, 1971). Without this aid, between-category transitions would have to rely solely on the interitem associations forged during study.

In a categorized word list, the semantic relations among items are either very strong (for the within-category items) or very weak (for the between-category items). Traditional analyses of the effect of semantic relatedness on recall have been based almost exclusively on such a binary representation of semantic similarity. In this section we will discuss recent advances that have enabled us to look at the effects of semantic relatedness on recall of lists that do not possess any obvious semantic organization.

Analyzing the effects of semantic similarity when participants recall lists of random (noncategorized) words requires a fine-grained measure of semantic similarity. Historically, attempts to measure semantic similarity for arbitrary word pairs have relied either on participants' ratings of the similarities among words (Romney et al., 1993), or on data from word-association experiments, such as those discussed in chapter 4 (Nelson et al., 1998). Using these methods, one can produce a matrix of similarities among all possible pairs of items. Although such an approach works well with a small number of items, the number of combinations increases as the square of the number of words. As such, it is simply impractical to use direct-similarity judgments or word associations to measure the semantic relations among tens of thousands of words. As we shall see, new computational methods address these problems by enabling the estimation of semantic similarity between almost any pair of words.

6.3.1 Models of Semantic Space

Using computational methods to analyze large linguistic databases, researchers have recently developed multidimensional models of semantic space. For a large number of words, these models specify each word's vector representation in a high-dimensional semantic space. In this section we will discuss two of the models: latent semantic analysis (or LSA) and word association spaces (WAS). Using either LSA or WAS we can quantify the semantic relatedness for almost any pair of English words.

Latent semantic analysis (LSA)

LSA assumes that words which are related in meaning tend to occur close together in texts. The method begins by taking a large corpus of text and counting the number of times that a given word i occurs in a given paragraph j. The resulting matrix, $L(i, j)$, has as many rows as there are words in the corpus and as many columns as there are paragraphs. A mathematical technique called *singular-value decomposition* (SVD) is then used to transform the matrix in such a way as to reduce the number of columns while preserving the similarity structure among the rows. Semantic relatedness is measured by the cosine of the angle between vectors consisting of the entries in a particular pair of rows ($\cos \theta$). Completely unrelated words would have $\cos \theta \approx 0$, and strong associates would have $\cos \theta$ values between 0.4 and 1.0. For a more thorough treatment and discussion, see Landauer and Dumais (1997) and Landauer, Foltz, and Laham (1998).

Word association spaces (WAS)

WAS starts with an associative matrix constructed from free-association norms collected at the University of South Florida (USF) (Nelson, Zhang, and McKinney, 2001). These norms have proven useful in evaluating the role of semantic factors on item recognition (Nelson et al., 2001) and cued recall (Nelson and Zhang, 2000). In particular, studies based on the USF norms have revealed the importance of indirect word associations in predicting the way people recall pairs of items (Nelson, Bennett, and Leibert, 1997; Nelson et al., 1998).

The WAS technique uses SVD to transform the USF free-association norms into a multidimensional semantic space. Each word is first represented as a vector of its associative strengths to other words.[12] SVD is then applied to reduce the dimensionality of the resultant matrix. The semantic relatedness of

---

12. The asymmetric associative strengths given by the norms are made symmetric by summing the forward and backward associative strengths (the tendency of *dog* to evoke *cat* and the tendency of *cat* to evoke *dog*).

two words can be calculated as the cosine of the angle between their vectors in WAS space, and accordingly, words that are directly associated or have similar associates have large cosine values. Words that do not directly share associations may still have high relatedness values because of their mediated associations (see chapter 4). This method is discussed in greater detail in Steyvers, Shiffrin, and Nelson (2004).

6.3.2 The Semantic Proximity Effect

Just as the lag-CRP measures the conditional probability of a recall transition as a function of an item's temporal contiguity to the just-recalled item during study, it is possible to measure the conditional probability of a recall transition as a function of an item's semantic relatedness to the just-recalled item, as measured by LSA or WAS (this function is termed the semantic-CRP).

Using study lists comprised of randomly arranged common nouns, Howard and Kahana (2002a) found that the stronger the semantic relation between two list words, the more likely it was that they would be recalled in neighboring output positions. Howard and Kahana also reported that the stronger the semantic relation between two recalled words in neighboring output positions, the shorter the IRT between the two words. We refer to these results, illustrated in Figure 6.12, as the *semantic proximity effect*. The semantic proximity effect

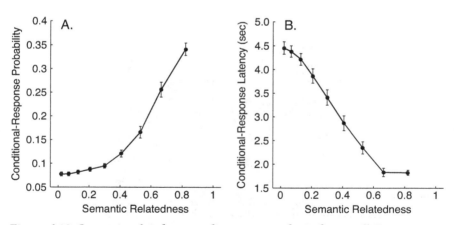

Figure 6.12 Semantic relatedness predicts output order in free recall. Participants are more likely to recall items that are semantically related to the just-recalled item (**A**) and they do so more quickly (**B**). Semantic relatedness was measured using latent semantic analysis. A word has a semantic relatedness of 1 with itself and a semantic relatedness of zero with completely unrelated items. Similar results were obtained when using WAS as the similarity metric. Error bars are 95% confidence intervals. Reproduced from Kahana and Miller (2010).

is evident even at low levels of semantic similarity (e.g., NUMBER and JOURNAL have an LSA similarity of 0.11, while PONY and FOREHEAD have an LSA similarity of 0.21). Analyses of recall dynamics reveal how even modest semantic relations can exhibit a powerful influence on the way people search their memories. Even when lists lack any strong associates or any obvious categorical organization, recall transitions are driven by the relative semantic strengths among the stored items.

Semantic proximity not only dictates the dynamics of correct responses in free recall; it also influences the kinds of recall errors people make. When recalling a list of words, participants occasionally recall items that were not on the target list, but were on a previously studied list. Assuming that these prior-list items compete with current-list items for recall and that semantic information is an important retrieval cue, we would expect PLIs to have greater semantic relatedness (a higher $\cos \theta$ in LSA or WAS space) to the just-recalled word than do correct recalls. Consistent with this prediction, Zaromb et al. (2006) reported that participants tend to commit PLIs whose recall-transition $\cos \theta$ values are, on average, higher than those for correct recall transitions (Figure 6.13). To the extent that measures such as LSA and WAS capture the semantic relatedness of words in the English language, these results suggest that semantic associations induce PLIs.

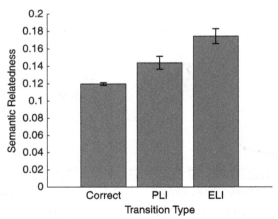

Figure 6.13 Semantic associations induce intrusions. The role of semantic association in the commission of intrusions as measured by Latent Semantic Analysis (LSA). The figure shows mean LSA semantic-relatedness values for making transitions from a correct list item to either another correct item, a prior-list intrusion (PLI) or an extra-list intrusion (ELI). Error bars are 95% confidence intervals. Data are from Miller et al. (2012).

6.3.3 The False Memory Paradigm

Recently, a great deal of attention, both in the popular press and in the laboratory, has focused on the phenomenon of false memory: mistaken memory for an event that never occurred or that occurred but not as remembered. In the case of free recall, false memory may be said to occur whenever a participant recalls an item that was not on the study list. When making such intrusions, participants are sometimes highly confident that the item they incorrectly recalled was presented as part of the study list.

A technique that has become a popular method for demonstrating and studying the phenomenon of false memory was originally developed by Deese (1959) and later refined and extended by Roediger and McDermott (1995). In this technique, known as the Deese-Roediger-McDermott (or DRM) procedure, participants study lists of items that are semantically associated with an unpresented *critical* word (Deese, 1959; Roediger and McDermott, 1995).[13] For example, participants might study the list: *sour, candy, sugar, honey, cake, nice, heart, tart, good, pie*, etc., all of which are semantically related to the critical word *sweet*. When participants are asked to recall these words, one finds that they will often recall the word *sweet*, even though it was not presented. In the example given above, recall of *sweet* is typically as high or higher than recall of the studied words. This effect has been replicated in many studies (see Brainerd and Reyna, 2005; Gallo, 2006; Roediger, Balota, and Watson, 2001, for reviews).

Although intrusions of the critical word during recall occur quite frequently in the DRM paradigm, intrusions of other words—including PLIs and ELIs— occur much less frequently (Kimball, Smith, and Kahana, 2007). The dual findings of a high rate of critical word intrusions and relatively low rates of other intrusions constitute an important puzzle for theories of memory.

A number of existing theories have attempted to explain these results in terms of basic memory principles (Brainerd and Reyna, 2005; Kimball et al., 2007; Mather, Henkel, and Johnson, 1997; Roediger et al., 2001). One leading account of false memory suggests that studying a word activates semantically associated words in memory, by way of a network of semantic associations (see chapter 4). Because it is associated with many of the studied words, the critical nonstudied word becomes strongly activated during study. Because it has been so strongly activated, there is confusion at test as to whether the critical word was internally activated or whether it was actually experienced (Mather et al., 1997; Roediger et al., 2001). This account of false memory is known as the

---

13. These lists are generated using data from word-association experiments (see chapter 4, Major Associative Tasks).

activation monitoring theory because semantic associates are activated during encoding and because internally generated responses are monitored during recall to determine whether or not they occurred in the context of the study list.

A second leading account of false memory assumes that participants encode perceptual, semantic, and contextual attributes of items. Accessing the semantic features at retrieval promotes intrusion of the critical word, whereas accessing the perceptual and contextual attributes promotes retrieval of the studied words and rejection of intrusions. According to this *fuzzy trace theory* of false memory (Brainerd, Payne, Wright, and Reyna, 2003; Brainerd and Reyna, 2005), the semantic attributes are assumed to be more robust and stable than the perceptual and contextual ones.[14]

There is evidence showing that false memory arises as a result of processes operating at both encoding and retrieval. An example of evidence implicating encoding processes is the finding by Smith, Gerkens, Pierce, and Choi (2002) that the critical word showed evidence of priming on a poststudy priming task designed to minimize deliberative, conceptually driven retrieval of list words. On the other hand, a role for retrieval processes in the occurrence of false memories is implicated by such evidence as the finding that providing a subset of studied items from a DRM list as cues during a recall test reduced false recall of the critical word (Bauml and Kuhbandner, 2003; Kimball and Bjork, 2002; Reysen and Nairne, 2002).

In chapter 7 we will discuss a mathematical model of false memory based on the dual-store SAM theory of free recall (Kimball et al., 2007). According to this model, unstudied words' associations to list context are encoded during study in proportion to their strength of semantic association to the items currently in the short-term store. During retrieval, words are activated in proportion to their strength of semantic association to the set of recently recalled words. Using these mechanisms, Kimball et al. were able to simultaneously account for many of the major findings concerning both correct and false recalls.

6.3.4 Temporal, Semantic, and Similarity-based Clustering

The contiguity effect indicates that items studied in temporally contiguous positions tend to be clustered together in the recall sequence. Similarly, the semantic proximity effect illustrates that items that share semantic attributes tend to be clustered together in recall. Although we have emphasized these two forms of clustering, one can observe clustering for other attributes of items.

---

14. In the terminology of fuzzy trace theory, semantic attributes are referred to as the *gist* representation, whereas perceptual and contextual attributes are referred to as the *verbatim* representation.

For example, Murdock and Walker (1969) had participants study lists in which some items were presented visually and others were presented auditorily. They found that participants' responses were clustered according to the modality in which the items were encoded (i.e., visually presented items tended to be recalled together). Hintzman, Block, and Inskeep (1972) had participants study lists in which some items were presented in a male voice and other items were presented in a female voice. They found that responses were clustered according to the gender by which the item was spoken. Polyn et al. (2009) had participants study lists in which items were encoded using different tasks: as each word appeared, participants were cued either to judge whether the item will fit into a shoebox or to judge whether the item is living or not living. During recall, items studied using the same encoding task tended to be clustered together. Polyn et al. (2009) showed that participants simultaneously exhibit *temporal clustering* (i.e., contiguity), *semantic clustering*, and *task clustering*.

As mentioned previously, Polyn et al. (2009) used a percentile-based measure to examine how various experimental variables influence the contiguity effect (i.e., the degree of temporal clustering). To measure the degree of semantic clustering, Polyn et al. used a similar technique to produce a percentile rank for each recall transition, reflecting the semantic similarity of the two recalled items. Participants who exhibit strong semantic organization produce high semantic clustering scores. By quantifying each form of clustering, one can determine whether the different types of clustering interact with one another. This analysis reveals that both semantic and task-clustering effects are enhanced for contiguous items (Howard and Kahana, 2002b; Polyn et al., 2009).

Just as the source characteristics of a judgment task can serve as context for a set of studied items, the elaborate network of landmarks and features of an environment can serve as context for material experienced within that environment (Smith, 1988). To elucidate the joint contributions of temporal and spatial information to memory search, Miller, Lazarus, Polyn, and Kahana (in press) asked participants to play the role of a delivery person in a 3D-rendered virtual town (Figure 6.14A,B). After an initial spatial-learning phase, participants navigated to stores throughout the town and, upon arrival at each store, the delivered item was revealed. After making a delivery to each store, participants freely recalled all of the delivered items. After the final trial, participants are asked to free recall all of stores in the town. In this task, Miller et al. observed significant temporal clustering for recalled items, significant spatial clustering for recalled stores, and significant spatial clustering in the order of recalled items themselves (Figure 6.14C). This latter effect provides insight into how memories are organized within a spatiotemporal context by demonstrating spatial organization of nonspatial memories embedded in a spatial context.

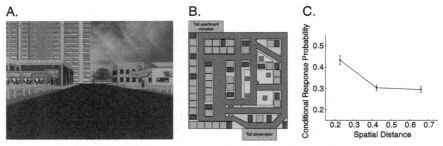

Figure 6.14 Spatial clustering in free recall of objects delivered in a virtual town.
A. View a participant may see when navigating through the virtual town. **B.** Overhead
map of the town. **C.** Objects that were delivered to nearby locations tend to cluster
during recall, as seen in the conditional response probability as a function of spatial
distance within the town. Data from Miller et al. (in press).

6.4 INTRUSIONS

Recency, temporal contiguity, and semantic proximity are three major factors
that influence correct recall of list items. In the preceding section we discussed
how semantic relatedness can influence participants to commit extralist and
prior-list intrusions. Here we delve further into the question of what factors give
rise to intrusions in free recall.

In our discussion of intrusions in cued recall (see section 4.5), we noted
that most intrusions tend to come from the most recent list, with the number
of intrusions decreasing with increasing list lag. In essence, this is a recency
effect. We tend to remember recent items. In addition, if we incorrectly recall
an item that was not on the current list, it will tend to be from a recent
prior list.

This *intrusion recency effect* is also seen in free recall, where PLIs are far
more likely to come from the immediately preceding list than from earlier
lists (Figure 6.15). The PLI-recency effect is similar in both immediate and
delayed free recall, as well as for younger and older adults (Zaromb et al.,
2006) (although older adults make a larger absolute number of intrusions than
younger adults do).

The PLI-recency effect in free recall illustrates the tendency for intrusions
to come from recent lists, which reflects the importance of recency in episodic
memory. Recent experiences are more memorable. This is true not only in
immediate terms of participants' tendency to recall the last few items in a list
but it is also true in a relative sense, wherein memory is improved for recent
items across much greater time scales.

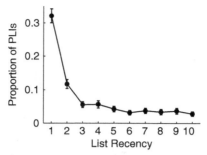

Figure 6.15 Recency of prior-list intrusions. Proportion of prior-list intrusions (PLIs) coming from lists presented from 1 to 10 lists back. Because PLIs from 10 lists back can only occur on list 11 and later, we excluded the first 10 lists from these analyses. Error bars represent 95% confidence intervals. Data are aggregated across studies in the free-recall database (Sederberg et al., 2010).

Zaromb et al. (2006) asked whether temporal contiguity can similarly induce participants to commit PLIs. By creating lists that contained mixtures of novel items and items repeated from earlier lists, Zaromb and colleagues found that recalls of repeated items were more likely to be followed by PLIs than were recalls of novel items. This finding would emerge if temporal associations forged on prior lists compete with the associations formed in the current list and if these older associations occasionally win in the competition.

When recalling a list of items in a memory experiment, participants are eager to avoid making intrusions. As such, participants may censor themselves during recall, omitting responses that they deem inappropriate. As such, the small number of *overt* intrusions that people commit during recall (typically around 5% of the total number of recalls) may significantly underestimate the influence of intrusions on the recall process. People may frequently commit intrusions *covertly*, and these intrusions may alter recall dynamics in important ways.

To study the influence of covert intrusions on recall, Kahana, Dolan, Sauder, and Wingfield (2005a) introduced an externalized recall (ER) procedure. In the ER procedure, after participants have become familiar with standard free-recall instructions, the experimenter asks them to say out loud all words that come to mind at the time of test, even if they think those words did not occur in the most recent list, which they are explicitly attempting to recall. To separately examine the internal censoring process during recall, participants are also asked to indicate when they have recalled an item they believe was not on the most recent list by pressing the spacebar immediately following recall of that item. This technique, which builds on an earlier study by Roediger and Payne (1985), was used by Kahana et al. (2005a) to study age-related differences in free recall

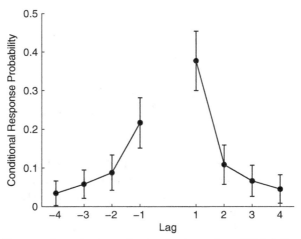

Figure 6.16 Temporal contiguity and prior-list intrusions (PLIs). Successive PLIs that came from the same original list tend also to come from neighboring serial positions. Based on studies in the free recall database (Sederberg et al., 2010) and a previous analysis reported in Zaromb et al. (2006).

and by Zaromb et al. (2006) and Unsworth, Heitz, and Parks (2008) to study intrusions more generally.

The ER procedure reveals that participants commit many more covert intrusions than overt ones. Among older adults, who recall fewer list items and make more intrusions, the ER procedure revealed that conditional on making an intrusion, older adults were more likely to accept that intrusion as a correct response than younger adults (Kahana et al. 2005a). Thus, older adults not only exhibit a greater overall tendency to sample items from outside of the experimental context; they also are less able to discriminate those items from target items.

Zaromb et al. (2006) used the ER procedure to analyze transitions between successive prior-list intrusions in free recall (in standard free recall, successive PLIs occur too rarely to be studied). They found that when two PLIs occur in succession, and when they both came from the same list, they tend to come from neighboring list positions (Figure 6.16).

6.5 REPETITION EFFECTS

In previous sections we have focused on the process of encoding and recalling a single list. In this section we consider the question of learning a list over multiple study-test trials (known as multitrial free recall). We begin by discussing a classic study of the learning process carried out by Endel Tulving in 1962.

6.5.1 Subjective Organization

In studying the learning process in multitrial free recall, Tulving (1962) noticed that the sequence in which participants recalled list items became more and more consistent over repeated trials even though the items were presented in a different and randomly determined order on each trial. Tulving quantified this tendency by showing that the correlation between the order of participants' recalls increased across successive study-test trials. One interpretation of this finding is that over repeated trials, participants created an organized representation of the list in memory. Because the organization was quite variable across participants, Tulving referred to this finding as *subjective organization*.

During the 1970s there was a vigorous debate over the best way to measure subjective organization, with numerous methods being proposed by different researchers (Sternberg and Tulving, 1977). A relatively simple method that has been shown to have nice statistical properties is called *pair frequency*. Pair frequency is defined as the number of observed intertrial repetitions of word pairs minus the number of intertrial repetitions of word pairs expected to occur by chance. An intertrial repetition is defined as a pair of studied words that were recalled successively on trials t and $t+1$. Such pairs are considered repetitions even if the order of recall differs across trials (e.g., if the participant recalls . . ., *key, rose,* . . . on Trial 4 and then recalls . . ., *rose, key,* . . . on Trial 5).

Klein, Addis, and Kahana (2005) analyzed organization over learning trials in free recall, with two major experimental conditions. In the *FR-Varied* condition, participants performed free recall on a list of words that was presented in a different random order on each of five study-test trials. In the *FR-Constant* condition, the list was repeated in the same order on each trial. Across both conditions, the degree of organization increased with the number of items recalled (Figure 6.17). Clearly, organization increases in tandem with learning. The finding that the final recall sequences differed from participant to participant implies that the way the material is organized may be unique to each individual.

Tulving (1968) argued that learning relies on participants actively organizing items in memory rather than on a mechanical process of strengthening associations. In one of his experiments, Tulving had two groups of participants learn a target list of 36 items by multitrial free recall. Prior to learning the target list, both groups were given eight study-test trials on a *practice* list consisting of 18 items. For the experimental group, the words on the practice list were a random subset of the words in the target list. For the control group, there was no overlap between the words on the practice and on the target list.

As expected, participants in the experimental group recalled more words than those in the control group on the first trial. But after several trials, the control group surpassed the experimental group. In the end, the experimental

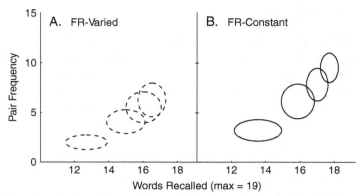

Figure 6.17 The relation between organization and recall across learning trials.
Data are from two conditions of a multitrial free-recall experiment (Klein et al., 2005).
In the FR-varied condition, the sequence of item presentations was randomized on
each trial. In the FR-constant condition, the sequence was constant across trials.
Organization is measured by pair frequency (Anderson and Watts, 1969). Ellipses
indicate regions of 95% confidence in the data.

group took considerably longer to learn the target list. Tulving took this finding
as evidence against the notion that repetition is the primary determinant of
learning in multitrial free recall.

Novinski (1969) replicated Tulving's study and further demonstrated that
the experimental group's difficulty in learning the list stemmed largely from
participants' inability to recall the items that were studied on the practice list.
Even after 12 trials of studying the experimental list, participants recalled fewer
practice list items than they did at the end of the practice list training period.

Although a participant in this type of experiment will undoubtedly realize
that some of the items on the experimental list were also on the practice
list, the participant will not know exactly how many. Consequently, this task
poses a list discrimination problem. If the participant is too casual about
reporting items from the practice list, he will commit intrusions. Slamecka,
Moore, and Carey (1972) compared experimental and control groups under
the standard instructions to recall the items from the target list with "low
criterion" instructions, encouraging participants to write down all of the words
they could think of, even if it meant guessing. As shown in Figure 6.18, Tulving's
cross-over effect (left panel) goes away under the low-criterion condition. This
is consistent with the list discrimination account of these data.

Tulving's demonstration of subjective organization in free recall of *random*
word lists had a greater impact on the scientific community than did earlier
demonstrations that semantic similarity strongly influences the order in which
we recall lists of items. This was because Tulving's demonstration suggested

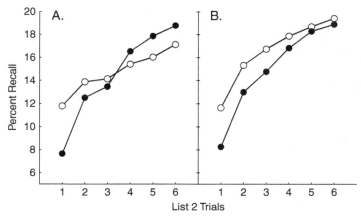

Figure 6.18 Recall probabilities. Data from Slamecka et al. (1972). Recall probabilities for the experimental group (open circles) and control group (solid circles) under standard instructions (**A.**) and under low-criterion instructions (**B.**).

that participants not only use the organization present in the material but that they impose their own organization as a key dimension of the learning process.

The appeal of organization theory led some researchers to reject association-istic models of free recall. As Tulving (1968) noted, "It looks as if the conceptual analyses of free recall have been developed not just in isolation, but almost in defiance of the traditional S[timulus]-R[esponse] models of behavior." As we shall see in the next chapter, modern versions of associative theory can easily accommodate the finding of subjective organization.

6.5.2 Temporal and Semantic Clustering

The data on subjective organization reported by Klein et al. (2005) can also be analyzed in terms of the dynamics of recall and, in particular, the contiguity effect and the semantic proximity effect. In the FR-constant condition, contiguity-based associations are reinforced across successive study-test trials, whereas in the FR-varied condition, contiguity-based associations vary from trial to trial, producing associative competition among items.

Klein et al. found a strong contiguity effect in all conditions and on all trials. As shown in Figure 6.19A, the contiguity effect (as seen in the degree of temporal clustering) decreased over trials in the FR-varied condition ($p < 0.05$) and increased over trials in the FR-constant condition ($p < 0.001$). The opposite pattern was true of semantic associations: semantic clustering increased over trials in the FR-varied condition ($p < 0.05$), but remains relatively flat in the FR-constant condition. Although the contiguity effect decreased significantly

FR Varied ↑semantic ↓contiguity(associative comp)

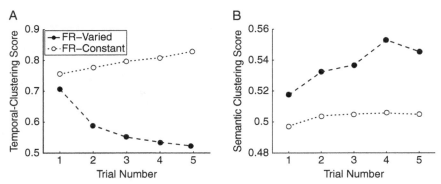

Figure 6.19 Temporal and semantic clustering across trials. When list order was randomized at the start of each learning trial (FR-varied condition), temporal clustering of recalls decreased over trials and semantic clustering increased. When list order was kept constant on each trial (FR-constant condition), temporal clustering increased slowly over trials and semantic clustering remained relatively constant. Reanalysis of data from Klein et al. (2005) carried out by L. Lohnas.

over learning trials in the FR-varied condition, it should be noted that lag was calculated based on the most recent list presentation. If the order of participants' recalls reflects both the order of presentation on the most recent list and also the orders on earlier lists, then the contiguity effect as defined based on the most recent list should decrease over trials.

Klein et al.'s study shows how associative information from prior study and test trials strongly influences the way people recall items on the current list. The finding that even in random word lists semantic clustering increases with trials in the FR-varied condition helps to explain the phenomenon of subjective organization in terms of basic associative processes (Tulving, 1966; Schwartz and Humphreys, 1973).

6.6 SUMMARY AND CURRENT DIRECTIONS

Suppose that you are trying to remember a set of experiences that share a common context, such as the places that you visited on a recent trip. If you are trying to recall these items without regard to the order in which you experienced them, this is an example of free recall. In the laboratory, we create mini-experiences by presenting lists of meaningful items in a controlled manner. We then ask participants to recall the items in any order they choose. By studying the way participants recall these lists, we hope to gain insights into the memory mechanisms underlying the recall process.

The present chapter surveyed some of the major empirical findings concerning free recall of word lists. For many years, the major empirical measure of free-recall performance was the serial-position curve (Murdock, 1962). The major theoretical question was whether recall of items from recency and prerecency serial positions reflects different memory mechanisms. The finding that a number of different experimental variables selectively influence recall of recency and prerecency items led to the view that recency items are recalled from a limited-capacity short-term store, whereas prerecency items are recalled from a semantically organized long-term store. According to this classic memory model (termed the *modal* model), the primacy effect is due to increased rehearsal of early list items, which strengthens those items' associations in long-term store. Support for this view comes from studies using the Rundus overt-rehearsal procedure, where participants say out loud any item that comes to mind as they are studying the list.

A far more detailed picture of the way participants recall lists can be obtained by analyzing the order and timing of participants' recalls. On an immediate free-recall test, participants start by recalling recent (end-of-list) items. Following their first recall, participants tend to make transitions to items that were studied near in time to the just-recalled item and to items that are semantically related to the just-recalled item. These two characteristics of recall transitions can be quantified by measuring the conditional-response probability and latency as a function of lag or of semantic relatedness. As recall proceeds, participants continue to make transitions on the basis of semantic and temporal associations, but they do so more slowly and their tendency to recall items that were not on the target list (intrusions) increases. When intrusions are committed, they tend to be items from recent prior lists that are also semantically similar to the just-recalled word. With each successive recall, the probability that participants will stop recalling items altogether increases. The probability of stopping increases significantly after participants commit an intrusion.

A good deal of recent interest has been focused on the question of why intrusions are sometimes made with a degree of certainty that parallels or even surpasses correct recalls. In the false-memory literature, researchers ask participants to study lists that have been specifically designed to induce semantic intrusions. An ongoing debate concerns whether these intrusions arise because the critical nonpresented item was rehearsed during the encoding of the study list or whether it was evoked by a convergence of semantic cues during the recall phase (see Roediger et al., 2001).

We have seen that many of the principles that govern recall of lists operate at multiple time scales. Let us return to our example of recalling all of the films you have seen, a set of experiences that is likely to span a significant fraction of your life. Most people will tend to recall films that they have seen often and that they have particularly liked, but they will also tend to recall recently seen

Box 6.1

THE NEURAL BASIS OF MEMORY SEARCH

To recall an experienced item, some component of the pattern of brain activity that accompanied its original presentation must be revived. Cognitive neuroscientists have recently begun to search for the neural correlates of memory search in free recall. Polyn, Natu, Cohen, and Norman (2005) used functional magnetic resonance imaging (fMRI) to determine whether the pattern of brain activity measured when retrieving an item from memory matches the pattern of brain activity measured during encoding of that item. For each participant, a statistical model was used to identify the neural activity associated with each of three classes of study items (celebrities, landmarks, and objects). Then, the model was applied to the recall-period data from that participant, allowing the researchers to generate a second-by-second estimate of the relative presence of each of the three category patterns during the memory search period. They found category-specific brain activity during the study of an item. During recall, they found the same pattern of category-specific activity was reinstated just prior to the recall of each item. Thus, they were able to predict the category of the recalled item based solely on patterns of brain activity recorded using fMRI. These patterns were found throughout the brain, including regions in the medial temporal lobe (MTL) and the prefrontal cortex (PFC).

Although fMRI allows researchers to noninvasively measure memory-related brain activity with good spatial resolution, it does not have the temporal resolution to tell us about the millisecond-level dynamics of neural activity during memory search. Sederberg et al. (2007) examined electroencephalographic (EEG) activity in neurosurgical patients whose brain activity was being monitored with electrodes implanted in numerous brain regions. These patients took part in a free-recall task, and the researchers analyzed the pattern of brain oscillations both during the study period and during free recall. They found that the same pattern of high-frequency (gamma, 44–100 Hz) oscillatory activity that predicts (during study) that a given item will be later recalled also activates during the recall period for correctly recalled items, versus erroneously recalled items from previous lists (Figure 6.20). The areas showing this gamma activity matched well with those revealed by fMRI investigations of subsequent memory (e.g., hippocampus, MTL and PFC), and no other oscillatory band showed such an effect.

Gelbard-Sagiv, Mukamel, Harel, Malach, and Fried (2008) asked whether reactivation occurs at the level of individual neurons. Recording neuronal responses in neurosurgical patients as they performed a free-recall task, they

Successful Encoding   Correct Retrieval

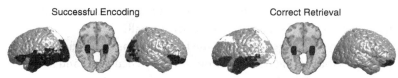

Figure 6.20 Brain oscillations associated with successful encoding and correct retrieval. During encoding (44–100 Hz), oscillatory activity was greater during the encoding of items that were subsequently recalled. During retrieval, gamma was greater during the 500 ms preceding recall verbalization for correct items (as compared with intrusions). Black regions exhibited significant increases in encoding- or retrieval-related oscillations; white regions were excluded from the analysis due to insufficient electrode coverage.

identified neurons that increased their firing rate when people viewed movie clips featuring famous people, characters, or animals. They found that neurons that responded when viewing a movie clip also responded when people were free recalling the movies they had seen. This effect was observed significantly for neurons in the hippocampus and other MTL regions.

These three studies show the reactivation of study-related patterns of neural activity during memory search for the studied stimuli and demonstrate that reactivation depends on a network of brain regions including the hippocampus, MTL, and PFC.

---

films first, and their transitions will exhibit the effects of semantic relatedness and temporal contiguity that we have discussed in this chapter. Rarely, they will recall seeing films that they had heard about from friends but had not actually seen themselves (intrusion errors). These tendencies illustrate both the generality of memory phenomena and also their ability to operate across time scales much larger than those used in laboratory studies.

6.7 STUDY QUESTIONS

1. Describe the dynamics of retrieval in free recall and how these dynamics may be quantified. In particular, describe the way people start recall, stop recall, and transition among items.
2. How has the overt-rehearsal technique been used to inform our understanding of free recall and what are its limitations?
3. Temporal association, semantic relatedness, and recency are three major factors that determine the way in which participants remember lists of items. What experimental evidence supports this claim? How would you assess the manner in which semantic relatedness and temporal association combine to determine recall?

4. What factors give rise to intrusion errors in free recall and how are they related to the factors that influence correct recall?

5. In what ways does the analysis of the free-recall task teach us memory principles that we did not learn from studying cued recall and item recognition and in what ways does free recall reveal the same principles as those simpler tasks?

6. Consider the following recall sequences shown in the table below. Each row represents recall of a 10 item list, and each number represents the serial position of the recalled item. Calculate the serial-position curve, the probability of first recall, the lag-CRP (for lags -4 to $+4$), and the probability of stopping. For the lag-CRP, remember to keep track of which transitions are possible at each output position.

Output Position	1	2	3	4	5	6	7	8	9	10
Trial 1	10	8	9	4	5	1	2			
Trial 2	8	9	10	5	7					
Trial 3	10	9	8	4	5					
Trial 4	10	5	1	2	6	9	8	3		

7

Models of Free Recall

If we can come to understand what is going on in free recall, then we can have some confidence that we understand the more basic [memory] processes ....

B. B. MURDOCK, *Human Memory: Theory and Data* (1974) p. 307

In this chapter we discuss models of free recall. We begin with dual-store models that assume separate but interacting short-term and long-term memory stores. We then present experimental evidence that is hard to reconcile with these dual-store models. Finally, we show how models of memory search based on the ideas of contextual cueing and contextual retrieval can account both for the phenomena that had initially fueled the distinction between short-term and long-term memory and for the more recent findings that had challenged that distinction.

7.1 DUAL-STORE MEMORY SEARCH MODELS

Perhaps the most influential computational model of memory is the dual-store model proposed by Atkinson and Shiffrin (1968). Their original model has undergone extensive development and refinement over the years. The modern version of this model is referred to by the acronym *SAM*, which stands for *Search of Associative Memory*. SAM has been applied to a broad range of recall phenomena, including the effects of presentation rate and list length (Raaijmakers and Shiffrin, 1980), part-set cuing (Raaijmakers and Shiffrin, 1981),[1] word frequency (Gillund and Shiffrin, 1984), interference and forgetting (Mensink and Raaijmakers, 1988), list strength (Shiffrin et al., 1990), temporal contiguity (Kahana, 1996), semantic memory (Sirotin et al., 2005), and false memory (Kimball et al., 2007).

7.1.1 STS and LTS

According to SAM, there are two types of storage: information can be in the *short-term store (STS)* or the *long-term store (LTS)*. STS is represented as a memory "buffer" that can hold a small number of items (it is thus said to have *limited capacity*). The detailed operation of this memory buffer will be spelled out in section 7.1.2, but the basic idea is that while items reside in STS (1) they can be easily recalled and (2) their representations in LTS can become strengthened. LTS is represented as a matrix containing values for the strengths of the associations formed through rehearsal, including pairwise associations among the list words, as well as associations between each list word and the list context. List context is conceptualized as the temporal and situational setting for a particular list. $S(i, j)$ denotes the strength of association between items i and j, and $S(i, context)$ denotes the strength of association between item i and the list context.

Conceptually, LTS can be viewed as a variant of the associative neural-network models described in chapter 5. The key feature of LTS is that it stores associations among items and between items and context. To simplify the computations involved in modeling memory, Raaijmakers and Shiffrin (1980) assumed that context did not change from item to item. Rather, it was fixed throughout the encoding and retrieval of a given list. More recent variants of the model (Mensink and Raaijmakers, 1988; Sirotin et al., 2005) allow context to evolve gradually over the course of item presentations and recalls.

Associations in LTS reflect newly formed connections tied to a given context (or episode). Semantic relatedness, as measured by word-association norms or latent semantic analysis (see chapter 6), was not considered in early versions of SAM. Rather, it was assumed that the words in a list were only weakly

---

1. In part-set cuing experiments, participants are given a subset of the studied items as retrieval cues at test. Rather than facilitating recall of the remaining items, these part-set cues can actually impair their recall (Slamecka, 1968).

related prior to the experiment and that the associations relevant for recall were the ones formed during study of the list. As described later in this section, Sirotin et al. (2005) incorporated semantic similarity effects within SAM by further dividing LTS into two components: one to simulate contextually bound associations (episodic LTS) and another to simulate associations in semantic memory (semantic LTS).

7.1.2 Storage

SAM assumes that list items enter STS as they are presented and that a participant rehearses the items occupying STS at any given time, thereby increasing the strengths of the items' episodic associations in LTS. STS has a limited capacity. That is, only a small number of items can be in STS at any time and, once STS is full, a newly encoded item will displace an item that is already in STS. In this way, new items enter STS and older items drop out of STS. The exact rules governing how new items displace older items will be explained shortly.

One can think of STS either as a separate store or as an active state of items in LTS. The conception of STS and LTS as two separate stores became popular in the 1970s because of its analogy to computer systems that have separate short-term and long-term storage. It was also consistent with the finding that some patients with anterograde amnesia appeared to have normal short-term memory but could not form new long-term memories even though they appeared to have good memory for life events experienced before their brain injury. In an immediate free recall task, these patients would exhibit relatively good recall of end-of-list items accompanied by severely impaired recall of pre-recency items (Baddeley and Warrington, 1970). These data were interpreted as showing that patients with anterograde amnesia had damage to the neural circuitry required to store associations in LTS. For the present purposes, however, the key issue is not the anatomical organization of STS and LTS in the human brain, but rather the role that STS plays in the processes that influence memory performance.

Figure 7.1 illustrates the storage process in SAM as a list of words is being studied for a subsequent memory test. In this example, STS is assumed to hold up to four words at any one time. As the word *house* is processed, it enters the first slot in STS, as illustrated in the leftmost array in the upper part of the figure. When the next word, *shoe*, is processed, it takes its place in the first slot, pushing *house* into the second slot. This continues until all four slots have been filled. At that point, each new studied word displaces one of the older words in STS, as in the case of the word *dog* displacing the word *house* as shown in the figure. According to SAM, the longer an item has been in the

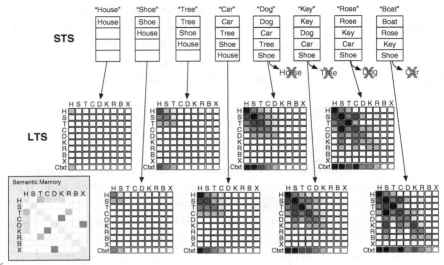

Figure 7.1 The storage process in SAM. This diagram illustrates how SAM encodes the word list *house, shoe, tree, car, dog, key, rose,* and *boat.* STS is assumed to hold up to four items. As each word is studied, it enters STS. When STS is full, each new word will *probabilistically* knock out one of the words already in STS (as indicated by the X-ed out words *House, Tree, Dog, Car*). While words reside in STS, they strengthen the associations in episodic LTS as shown in the LTS matrices. The darker shading of the associations in the lower diagonal of the LTS matrices reflects the assumption that forward associations receive a greater boost in LTS strength than do backward associations. The rows and columns of LTS are labeled by the first letter of each studied word (i.e., H = *House,* S = *Shoe,* etc.). The bottom row of each matrix (labeled *Ctxt*) represents the associative strengths between each item and the list context. Across the seven matrices, one can see the strengths of the LTS associations change as each item is encoded. The matrix labeled *Semantic Memory* illustrates the strength of the semantic associations among the studied items. For example, *Car* and *Key* are strongly associated, as are *Tree* and *House.* Unlike the episodic LTS matrix, the semantic LTS matrix does not change over the course of item presentation. Although the semantic LTS illustrates associations as being symmetric, the SAM model can accommodate either symmetric or asymmetric associations.

buffer, the more likely it is to be displaced (Phillips, Shiffrin, and Atkinson, 1967).

The matrices in the lower portion of Figure 7.1 illustrate how rehearsal in STS modifies the strengths of associations in LTS. The shading of the cells in each matrix represents the strength of a particular association between two list items (each item is denoted by its first letter), between a list item and the list context, or between a list item and itself (the darker the shading, the stronger the association).

~~A~~ SAM assumes that rehearsal increases the strength of association between each item in STS and the list context. Specifically, for each unit of time that an item, i, spends in STS, the strength of its association to context, $S(i, context)$, is incremented by some value. Rehearsal also increases the strength of the association between any two items that simultaneously occupy STS. For each unit of time that two items, i and j, spend together in STS, their forward interitem strength, $S(i, j)$, is incremented and their backward interitem strength, $S(j, i)$, is incremented by a smaller value.

The values of the strength increments described above are parameters of the model. SAM's operation depends on the values of these and other parameter values (as described below). To assess whether SAM can account for the key behavioral data on free recall, we determine whether there is some set of values for these parameters that enables the model to match the data. We do this by simulating many combinations of parameter values to determine which values minimize the deviation between model and data.

SAM uses separate learning parameters for forward and backward associations to simulate the bias in output order that favors item-to-item recall transitions in the forward direction (This is shown in Figure 7.3b later in this chapter.). SAM represents the strength of an item—conceptualized as its autoassociation (see chapter 5)—and includes parameters that determine how much to increment an item's autoassociative strength when the item occupies STS during study, and when it is output during recall. The self-strength of the items is illustrated by the shading of the cells along the diagonal. Although these autoassociative strengths play a key role in modeling recognition, they are not critical in the way SAM is used to model free recall.

The amount of time that each item spends in STS during study is determined by the presentation rate, the size of the buffer (the maximum number of items that can simultaneously occupy STS), and by the rule for displacement of items from the buffer. In early implementations of SAM, the size of the STS rehearsal buffer, r, was taken to be a single fixed value for all participants and on all trials, with $r = 4$ typically providing the best fit to free-recall data. There is no reason to assume that the size of the buffer is constant across participants and items. Allowing the size of the buffer to vary is necessary for SAM to fit detailed aspects of the data on free recall (Kahana, 1996).

As mentioned above, SAM assumes that each list item enters STS when it is presented. When STS becomes full, each new item displaces one of the old items then occupying STS. The actual rule used to describe how items are displaced from STS has varied across implementations of SAM. In general, the model assumes that the longer an item has been in the buffer, the more likely it is to be displaced (Phillips et al., 1967).[2]

7.1.3 Retrieval From STS and Search of LTS

Figure 7.2 illustrates the retrieval process in SAM. SAM posits that in immediate free recall, the first stage of retrieval reflects the output of items from the STS buffer. According to SAM, items in STS are always available for immediate recall, so the items in the buffer at the end of list presentation are output first during immediate free recall. In delayed free recall, the distractor task also relies on STS. Therefore, the items in STS are displaced by each successive distractor item. If the distractor is of sufficient difficulty/duration, the STS will have been emptied before recall, and recall will begin with a search of LTS.

The next stage of retrieval is from LTS. In this stage, SAM assumes that participants search LTS by means of a cue-dependent retrieval process driven by competition among all items associated with a given set of cues. Each cycle of the search process includes two phases: first, an item is *sampled* and then it may or may not be *recalled*.

SAM begins the search by using context as a retrieval cue, with the probability of an item being sampled depending on the strength of the association between context and that item. As illustrated by the upper dartboard in Figure 7.2, one of the words that has not already been recalled from STS is probabilistically sampled, with a probability that is proportional to the strength of the items' association with the list context. Sampling probabilistically is analogous to throwing a dart at a dartboard, where the larger the area of a given target (corresponding to a candidate item in memory), the more likely you are to hit it. In our example, the words *house* and *car* have the highest probability of being sampled, followed by the word *tree* and *dog*. This is because *house* and *car* spent more time in STS than the other items, as shown in Figure 7.1. Nonetheless, any of the four words may be sampled. In our example, we assume that *tree* is sampled at this stage.

---

2. The probability that the ith buffer item is to be displaced is given by:

$$\frac{q(1-q)^{i-1}}{1-(1-q)^r},$$

where q is a parameter of the model that determines the degree of bias favoring displacement of older items and r is the size of the buffer.

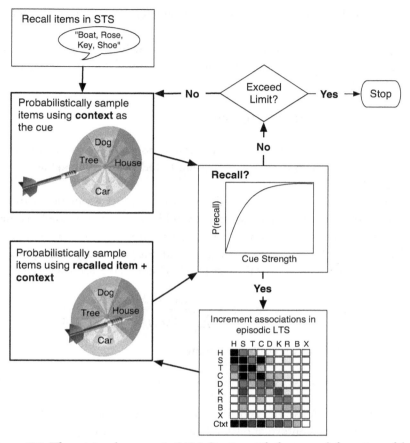

Figure 7.2 The retrieval process in SAM. Starting with the upper-left portion of the figure, the recall process begins with recall of items in STS and continues with search of LTS cued by context and previously recalled items. Recalling an item from LTS involves two stages: (1) probabilistically selecting candidate items for potential recall and (2) probabilistically determining whether the candidate item is recalled. Recall ends after a certain number of failures to recall. See text for further details.

According to SAM, the probability of sampling an item i when using *context* alone as a retrieval cue is given by the equation:

$$P_{\text{SAMPLING}}(i|\text{context}) = \frac{S(i, \text{context})^{W_c}}{\sum_{k=1}^{N} S(k, \text{context})^{W_c}} \qquad (7.1)$$

where N is the total number of items stored in LTS and W_c is a parameter weighting the contextual retrieval cue. This equation ensures that items with greater strengths of association with the list context are more likely to be sampled. The role of the weighting parameter, W_c, will become apparent in our discussion below.[3]

Once *tree* has been sampled, it is further evaluated to determine whether or not it will be recalled. The probability that a sampled item, i, is recalled is given by the equation:

$$P_{\text{RECALL}}(i|\text{context}) = 1 - e^{-W_c S(i, \text{ context})}. \tag{7.2}$$

Thus, recall also depends on the strength of association between the item and the list context. This recall equation is illustrated by the graph in the upper-right box in Figure 7.2.

Successful recall of *tree* would further strengthen its association with context in episodic LTS, and its representation would then be used, in combination with context, to cue recall of another list item. This process is illustrated in the lower left portion of Figure 7.2. According to SAM, the probability of sampling item i, given that both *context* and the just-recalled item j serve as retrieval cues, is:

$$P_{\text{SAMPLING}}(i|j, \text{context}) = \frac{S(i, j)^{W_e} S(i, \text{context})^{W_c}}{\sum_{k=1}^{N} S(k, j)^{W_e} S(k, \text{context})^{W_c}}, \tag{7.3}$$

and the probability of recalling the item is:

$$P_{\text{RECALL}}(i|j, \text{ context}) = 1 - e^{-W_e S(i,j) - W_c S(i, \text{ context})}. \tag{7.4}$$

In these equations, W_e and W_c are parameters that weight the episodic (interitem) and contextual retrieval cues, respectively. Regardless of an item's strength of association with context, with other retrieved items, or with both, SAM assumes that an item that was previously recalled cannot be recalled again. This assumption prevents the model from repeating items during recall. Although such repeats do occur in actual recall data, they are rare under most experimental conditions.[4] When retrieval cues lead to successful recall of an item, the strengths of the item's associations with the retrieval cues are incremented in LTS. This is known as output encoding. Four separate model parameters determine the degree to which interitem and context-to-item strengths are incremented during encoding and during recall.

---

3. SAM uses an exponential weighting scheme rather than a simple multiplicative one. Such a scheme has a very different effect when strengths are greater than or less than 1. In both cases, a weighting exponent of zero will yield a value of 1. Increasing the weighting exponent will increase the value for strengths greater than 1 but will decrease the value for strengths less than 1. It is likely that the SAM model would also provide a good fit to the behavioral data with simpler weighting schemes.

4. Across eight free-recall experiments, participants committed repetitions on just 3% of trials.

7.1.4 Stopping Rule

Two rules determine when a simulated participant stops searching: one governs when a participant abandons search with a particular set of retrieval cues and a second governs when the participant abandons search altogether. When there have been Max_1 consecutive failures at recall using a particular item together with context as retrieval cues, SAM assumes that the simulated participant reverts to using the context alone as a retrieval cue. Search stops altogether when Max_2 recall failures have accumulated over all sets of retrieval cues. For simplicity, Figure 7.2 illustrates a single stopping rule, with recall terminating when a total limit on the number of recall attempts has been exceeded.

7.1.5 Contextual Drift

Mensink and Raaijmakers (1988) added a mechanism to SAM that allowed for the change of context across multiple study and recall episodes. Consistent with the classic theory of Estes (1955), Mensink and Raaijmakers represented context as a vector that changes slowly over time. At a given time step, associations between context and items in STS are strengthened. At the time of test, the current state of context is used as a cue to probe memory. Thus, the probability that an item will be sampled and recalled is proportional to the distance between the time-of-test context and the encoding context of the item. By incorporating contextual drift, Mensink and Raaijmakers (1988) were able to use SAM to simulate various interference and forgetting effects observed in paired-associate experiments, such as those described in chapter 4.

7.1.6 Semantic Associations in LTS

In the original SAM model, LTS was used to describe the strengths of new associations forged during the study of a list; that is, LTS represents *episodic memory*. To account for the effects of preexperimental, semantic associations on memory search, it is important to separately represent the associations present in semantic memory. As described in chapter 6, techniques such as LSA and WAS can be used to quantify the strength of these semantic associations. Within SAM, representing these associations can be accomplished by forming a separate semantic LTS matrix. The strength of the associations in this semantic matrix remain fixed during the course of the experiment, reflecting an assumption that semantic associations are not significantly affected by episodic experience on the scale of a single experiment (see Nelson et al., 1998). From now on we will refer to the two matrices in LTS as the *episodic matrix* and the *semantic matrix*.

When context and the previously recalled item are used as retrieval cues, the sampling and recall processes involve the use of both the semantic associations in the semantic matrix and the episodic and contextual associations in the episodic matrix. Accordingly, the probability of sampling item i following the recall of item j is:

$$P_{\text{SAMPLING}}(i|j, \text{context}) = \frac{S_s(i,j)^{W_s} S_e(i,j)^{W_e} S_e(i, \text{context})^{W_c}}{\sum_{k=1}^{N} S_s(k,j)^{W_s} S_e(k,j)^{W_e} S_e(k, \text{context})^{W_c}},$$

(7.5)

and the probability of recalling the item is:

$$P_{\text{RECALL}}(i|j, \text{context}) = 1 - e^{-W_s S_s(i,j) - W_e S_e(i,j) - W_c S_e(i, \text{context})},$$

(7.6)

where $S_s(i, j)$ is the strength of the semantic association between items i and j in the semantic matrix; $S_e(i, j)$ is the strength of the episodic association between items i and j in the episodic matrix; $S_e(i, \text{context})$ is the strength of the episodic association between item i and context in the episodic matrix; N is the number of words in LTS; and W_s, W_e, and W_c are the parameters for the weighting of retrieval cues consisting of semantic interitem associations, episodic interitem associations, and item-to-context associations, respectively. The probability of recalling an item retrieved using context alone is calculated based on the item's mean semantic and episodic relatedness to other items in memory.

Consider two nonrecalled items (B and C) that have equivalently high contextual and episodic strengths of association with a just recalled item (A). Items B and C may have a higher probability of being sampled than other items because of their high contextual and episodic strengths. This advantage may increase if episodic and contextual associations are given more weight during retrieval via higher values for the retrieval weight parameters W_e and W_c. However, if the semantic association between items A and B is higher than that between A and C, B is more likely to be sampled. The multiplicative nature of the retrieval rule (as in Equation 7.5) means that each type of association— semantic, episodic, and contextual—modulates the influence of the other types of associations on sampling probabilities.[5] If the effects of semantic and episodic strengths were additive, then increasing the strengths in the episodic matrix over successive study-test trials would dilute the effects of semantic associations to the point that semantic relatedness would no longer influence recall transitions after many study-test trials. This is inconsistent with experimental findings

5. By ensuring that all of the semantic-association strengths are greater than zero, we can eliminate the potential problem that the multiplicative rule would result in a zero probability of sampling a particular item altogether. This is reasonable inasmuch as any two words are related semantically in some way when the pair is considered in isolation.

showing that semantic influences tend to remain constant or even increase over successive trials (e.g., Klein et al., 2005).

7.2 TESTING DUAL-STORE MODELS

7.2.1 Serial-Position Effects

STS plays two crucial roles in the SAM model. First, at the time of test, any item that is in STS can be recalled. Second, during study, the duration that an item resides in STS determines the degree to which associations in the episodic LTS are strengthened.

The first of these roles has been used to explain the recency effect in free recall and its disruption by a short period of distraction. Recency appears because the items at the end of the list are most likely to be in STS at the time of test. Because newly processed information displaces items from STS, SAM can account for the substantial reduction of recency by a brief end-of-list distractor task. Because of the fixed capacity of STS, SAM can account for the finding that recency is insensitive to manipulations of list length or presentation rate.

The second of these roles has been used to explain several characteristics of participants' recall of prerecency items. Let us first consider the primacy effect. According to SAM, items are displaced from STS in a probabilistic fashion (e.g., Phillips et al., 1967). The oldest item in STS is most likely to be displaced by a new item, the second oldest item is the next most likely item to be displaced, and so on. If the oldest item were always displaced, then each item would spend an equal amount of time in STS. But since the oldest item is not always displaced, some older items will spend a long time in STS and will thus have their strengths in episodic LTS increased more than other, newer items. Having stronger associations, these early list items are more likely to be recalled at the time of test. Slower presentation rates lead to higher levels of recall. This is because with longer study time, items spend more time in STS before they are displaced, thus leading to stronger item-to-item and item-to-context associations in episodic LTS.

The values of the strength increments described above are parameters of the model. SAM's operation depends on the values of a number of different parameters. We can ask whether there is some set of values for these parameters that enables the model to mimic some of the key behavioral data on free recall, such as the serial-position curve for different list lengths. Figure 7.3 shows SAM's ability to simultaneously fit the basic shape of the serial-position curve and the serial-position curves for each of these three aspects of the behavioral data. To obtain these fits, we simulated many combinations of parameter values in an effort to find the ones that provided the best fit to all these aspects of

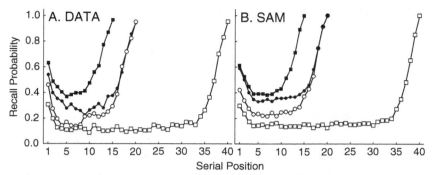

Figure 7.3 Serial-position effects in SAM. The SAM model (panel B) can account for the shape of the serial-position curve as well as dissociations between recency and prerecency reported by Murdock (1962, Panel A). Filled squares and circles denote lists of 15 items and 20 items presented at a 2-sec/item rate; open circles and squares denote lists of 20 items and 40 items presented at a 1-sec/item rate. Simulations are based on the extended SAM model described in Sirotin et al. (2005).

the data.[6] As shown in Figure 7.3, not only is SAM able to capture the pattern of results within each curve but it is also able to capture the changes in the serial-position curves across manipulations of list length and presentation rate (presentation rate is assumed to influence the encoding parameters of the model). Simulating the same version of SAM under conditions designed to mimic delayed free recall results in similar serial-position curves, except that the recency effect is eliminated because the distractor task given during the delay interval displaces the last few items from STS (see Figure 6.3).

7.2.2 Temporal and Semantic Clustering

SAM also accounts for the finding that recall of an item is most often followed by recall of another item studied in a neighboring list position, as shown in Figure 6.8. This is because neighboring items are most likely to spend time together in STS, and thus the associative bonds between those items in episodic LTS will be strengthened. As shown in Figure 7.4A, the combination of SAM's rehearsal process and retrieval process enables it to fit the contiguity effect, that is, after an item is recalled from serial position i, the next item recalled will tend to come from a nearby position $i +$ lag. To account for the forward bias in the contiguity effect, the model uses separate parameters for incrementing forward

---

6. There are a number of computer programs that can be used to search for the set of parameter values that will minimize a model's error in fitting the data. Several common methods are implemented in scientific software packages such as MATLAB.

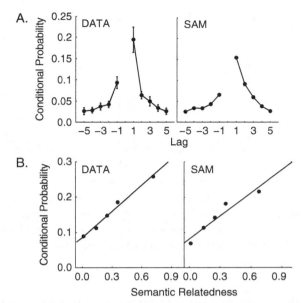

Figure 7.4 Temporal contiguity and semantic proximity effects in SAM. A. SAM's fit to the contiguity effect. **B.** SAM's fit to the semantic-proximity effect. Simulations are based on Sirotin et al. (2005).

versus backward associations during both encoding and retrieval. These fits were obtained using parameter values identical to those used in the fits to the 20-item lists in Figure 7.3.

SAM can also account for participants' tendency to make recall transitions to semantically related items (the *semantic proximity effect* shown in Figure 7.4B). This effect arises in the model because semantic similarities are used to cue retrieval. However, it is impressive that the model can reproduce the degree of semantic clustering observed in the data while simultaneously fitting contiguity and serial-position effects.

7.2.3 Category Clustering

A very reliable effect observed in free-recall studies is learners' tendency to recall categorically related words in clusters, even when the order of presentation of list items has been randomized (e.g., Bousfield, 1953; Patterson et al., 1971; Pollio et al., 1969). In a study of category clustering, Kahana and Wingfield (2000) asked participants to study lists of 20 words, each comprised of four exemplars drawn from each of five natural categories. Participants studied and recalled a list several times until they achieved perfect recall, with presentation order randomized anew for each trial. To measure category clustering on each

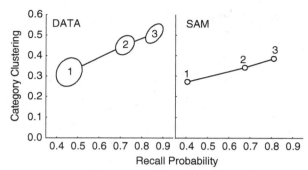

Figure 7.5 Category clustering and SAM. Increases in category clustering with list learning for categorized lists. Clustering is plotted as a function of recall probability for the first three trials of a multitrial free-recall experiment (Kahana & Wingfield, 2000). Left: Experimental data; ellipses represent the 95% confidence region around each point. Right: Simulations of the SAM model. Simulations based on Sirotin et al. (2005).

trial, they divided the number of within-category recall transitions by the total number of recall transitions (this is called the ratio of repetition [Bousfield, 1953]). They then subtracted from the observed ratio of repetition on that trial, the ratio that would be expected if the items had been recalled in a random order. This measure reflects the degree to which participants recall list items by category.

The left panel of Figure 7.5 shows the data for the first three study-recall trials. Recall probability is plotted on the horizontal axis and category clustering (as calculated based on the ratio-of-repetition measure) is plotted on the vertical axis. Ellipses represent the 95% confidence region around each point. The figure shows that both recall and semantic clustering increased across Trials 1, 2, and 3. The right panel in Figure 7.5 depicts the recall and clustering results from simulations of the SAM model (Sirotin et al., 2005). In modeling these data, the WAS metric was used to define the strengths of associations in semantic memory. Two mechanisms are likely responsible for the ability of SAM to cluster responses categorically. First, pairs of words would be recalled together due to semantic relatedness. Second, following the initial recall, these pairs would become increasingly likely to be recalled together on subsequent trials because of the strengthening of episodic associations through output encoding.

7.2.4 Prior-list and Extralist Intrusions

When participants commit prior-list intrusions (PLIs), those intrusions tend to be items that appeared on recent lists. This PLI-recency effect (see chapter 6,

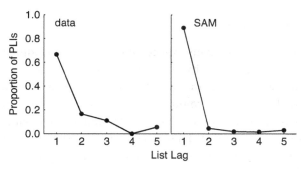

Figure 7.6 The PLI-recency effect. Left: Data from Howard and Kahana (1999) showing that PLIs tend to come from more recent lists. Right: SAM captures this basic trend.

Table 7.1
Modeling Instrusions and Correct Responses.
Average number of prior-list intrusions (PLIs), extralist intrusions (ELIs), and correct recalls during a free recall task. Data are from Howard and Kahana (1999). Modeling is based on Sirotin et al. (2005). Numbers in parentheses are 95% confidence intervals.

	Correct	PLI	ELI
DATA	5.0 ($\pm$0.5)	0.5 ($\pm$0.2)	0.2 ($\pm$0.1)
SAM	4.7	0.53	0.18

Intrusions) can be seen in Figure 7.6 (left). As Figure 7.6 (right) shows, SAM can reproduce this basic trend reasonably well. Furthermore, Table 7.1 shows that SAM reproduces correct means not just for PLIs but also for correct recalls and extralist intrusions (ELIs). Extralist intrusions can arise because the semantic matrix represents associations between list items and items from a person's broader vocabulary not presented during a simulated experiment. It is important to keep in mind that while fitting these aspects of the data, SAM is also fitting the other, more basic, aspects of the recall data shown in Figure 7.3. All of these fits were obtained using a single set of parameter values.

The ability of SAM both to simulate PLIs and to capture the PLI-recency effect arises because of contextual drift. ELIs are generated by strong semantic associations. These features of the model afford a nonpresented item some chance of being recalled, to the extent that it is semantically related to a just-recalled item that is part of the retrieval cue.

7.2.5 Interim Summary

SAM is able to simulate many aspects of recall data, including recency effects, primacy effects, the contiguity effect and the semantic-proximity effect, prior-list and extralist intrusions, and the effects of semantic organization on learning across multiple trials. To account for the semantic effects in recall experiments, it is necessary to augment the original SAM model with a semantic-associative matrix (Sirotin et al., 2005). This semantic matrix is not altered by events that occur during an experiment but rather plays a role only during retrieval, acting as an additional source of information that constrains, and is constrained by, contextual and episodic associations in guiding memory search.

Applying a multiplicative sampling and recall rule, in which semantic, episodic, and contextual information come together to predict recall, is useful because it provides a mechanism by which episodic/contextual factors constrain semantic search, thereby avoiding an explosion of semantically induced intrusions. Similarly, semantic factors constrain episodic search, so as to account for effects based on semantic properties of stimuli and/or semantic strategies. In SAM, the relative importance of the different types of associations is adjusted through variation of the retrieval weight parameters, which are exponents of the associative strengths in the sampling and recall rules.

Although the version of SAM presented here (Sirotin et al., 2005) can account for the basic data on prior-list and extralist intrusions, the only way it can account for the very high levels of intrusions observed in the Deese-Roediger-McDermott false memory paradigm (section 6.3.3) is by weighting semantic associations very heavily in the retrieval equation. However, with such high weight on the semantic associations, the model predicts that participants make far more intrusions of noncritical words (e.g., PLIs and ELIs) than observed in the data.

Kimball et al. (2007) proposed a modified set of storage and retrieval equations that allow SAM to account for the major findings in the false memory literature. They proposed that during encoding, unstudied words' associations to list context are stored in proportion to the product of their semantic association strengths to all of the items currently in STS. The basic idea is that all of the items in STS combine to cue semantic associates during the study phase of an experiment. Kimball et al. (2007) modified the retrieval rule in SAM to allow for multiple prior recalls to collectively (and multiplicatively) cue the next item being sampled. That is, rather than assuming that the one prior recall (along with list context) cues the next item, they assume that several prior recalls (as many as can be held in STS) combine to cue the next recalled item. Using these mechanisms, Kimball et al. were able to simultaneously account for the high level of critical word intrusions, the low levels of PLIs and ELIs, and many other features of data obtained in studies of false memory.

7.3 PROBLEMS FOR DUAL-STORE MODELS

Despite the impressive successes of dual-store models of free recall, there are several major phenomena that they cannot easily explain. In this section we discuss these empirical phenomena and why they are difficult to accommodate within the dual-store framework. Later we will present an alternative to dual-store theory that was largely inspired by the empirical puzzles presented here. We will also discuss ways in which dual-store theory has been revised to help address these challenges. We begin with a discussion of the recency effect, then turn to a discussion of the contiguity effect, and finally present a critique of the idea that rehearsal in STS is critical for encoding information into LTS.

7.3.1 Long-term Recency

The Law of Recency, presented in chapter 1, states that recent experiences are more easily remembered than remote ones. We have previously considered the possibility that recent events are more memorable because the context in which they were encoded has more overlap with the current context. We have also considered the possibility that new memories interfere with, or inhibit, older memories or even that memories simply decay over time. According to dual-store models, the striking recency effect that is observed for the very last few items experienced reflects a very different kind of process—namely, the operation of a special short-term store that can hold onto a small number of items until they are displaced by newer items. The data on free recall seem to support this explanation in that recency is easily disrupted by a brief distractor task.

Bjork and Whitten (1974) conducted an experiment that challenged the traditional STS-based account of recency effects in free recall. They were interested in seeing how well participants could recall a list of word pairs under conditions designed to eliminate between-pair rehearsal. Specifically, they gave their participants a difficult distractor task following the appearance of each pair, including the last one. Because the distractor task should have displaced any items in STS, the authors did not expect to find a recency effect. To their surprise, they found a strong recency effect, with the final few pairs being recalled better than pairs from the middle of the list. They called this the *long-term recency effect*.

In the years since Bjork and Whitten's discovery, the long-term recency effect has been replicated many times with varying materials and with a wide range of delay times from tenths of seconds (Neath, 1993a) to days (Glenberg, Bradley,

Kraus, and Renzaglia, 1983). The key factors in determining the presence and magnitude of the long-term recency effect are the durations of the filled *retention interval* (RI, the delay after the final list item) and the filled *interpresentation interval* (IPI, the delay between the words on the list). For a given RI, increasing the IPI results in more recency and better absolute recall of the last item on the list.

Figure 7.7 illustrates the three basic recall experiments in which recency effects have been examined. Recency effects, which are found in immediate free recall, are greatly reduced in delayed free recall but return in continual-distractor free recall (see Figure 7.8). Specifically, the amount of recency, as measured by

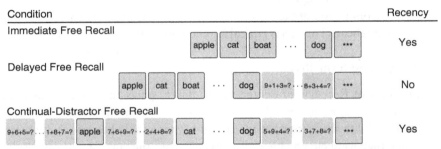

Figure 7.7 Illustration of immediate, delayed, and continual-distractor free recall. A row of asterisks signals participants to begin recall. In delayed free recall, a distractor task precedes the recall signal. In continual-distractor free recall, a distractor task is interpolated between each item and between the final item and the recall signal.

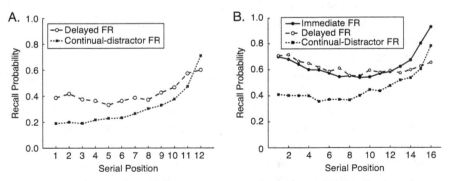

Figure 7.8 Long-term recency. A. Serial-position curves in delayed and continual-distractor free recall. Participants performed a 16-sec arithmetic distractor task that followed the last list item. In the continual-distractor condition, participants also performed a 16-sec arithmetic distractor after each study item. Data from Howard and Kahana (1999), replicating earlier studies. **B.** Serial-position curves in immediate, delayed, and continual-distractor free recall from an unpublished study by Polyn and Kahana.

the slope of the serial-position curve calculated over the last three or four items, depends on the ratio of the RI to the IPI. This relation, which is called the *ratio rule*, suggests that recency reflects the operation of a common mechanism across different time scales. If a single principle can be used to describe the recency effects observed at both short and long time scales, a theory that posits separate mechanisms for short-term and long-term recency would be unappealing. This is an example of the principle of parsimony discussed in chapter 1.

One possible explanation for the long-term recency effect is that giving distractors after each item accustoms participants to the distractor task. By the end of the list, participants may be able to rehearse list items while performing the distractor, thus producing a significant recency effect. A version of this view was put forward by Koppenaal and Glanzer (1990), who found that switching distractors at the very end of the list disrupted the long-term recency effect. But this position was subsequently challenged both by Thapar and Greene (1993) and by Neath (1993a), who found a significant long-term recency effect when participants were given different distractor tasks after every list item and only a small decrement in the recency effect when the distractor was changed after the very last item (see Figure 7.9). In addition, a robust long-term recency effect was found even when the distractor task was extremely taxing, making it unlikely that participants were surreptitiously rehearsing items during the distractor interval (Watkins et al., 1989).

Figure 7.10 illustrates the ratio rule for the recency effect in free recall. The trend line indicates that the slope of the recency effect depends on the log ratio

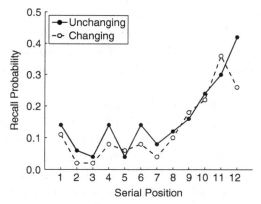

Figure 7.9 Variable distractors. Recency is observed, although slightly reduced, when the distractor task following the last list item is different from the distractor task following earlier list items (changing condition). In a condition where the same task is given following each item, the usual long-term recency effect is observed (Neath, 1993a).

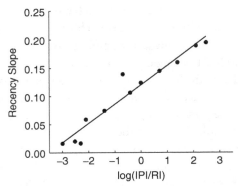

Figure 7.10 Ratio rule. The slope of the recency portion of the serial-position curve (the last three items) depends on the logarithm (log) of the ratio of the retention interval (RI) to the interpresentation interval (IPI). When the RI is much larger than the IPI, as in delayed free recall, the recency effect is very small. When the IPI and the RI have equal durations (i.e., the log ratio is zero), one observes robust recency in both immediate and continual-distractor free recall. When the IPI is larger than the RI, the recency effect is further enhanced. Data from Nairne, Neath, Serra, and Byun (1997) and from several studies in our lab. Each point on the graph represents a separate experiment or experimental condition.

of the IPI and the RI: $log(\frac{IPI}{RI})$. If the ratio of the IPI and the RI is fixed, the recency slope is the same regardless of the absolute values of the two intervals.

Analysis of the dynamics of memory search shows that recency effects in free recall arise primarily from participants' tendency to begin recall at the end of the list. This tendency is measured by plotting the probability of first recall (PFR) function, which is simply a serial-position curve for the very first item recalled. Figure 7.11 plots the PFR functions obtained in immediate, delayed, and continual-distractor free recall. Consistent with the ratio rule, the PFR functions for immediate and continual-distractor conditions are quite similar, whereas the PFR for delayed free recall shows a marked reduction in participants' tendency to begin recall with the last few list items.

Dual-store models, such as SAM, cannot easily account for the fact that recency depends on the relative (rather than the absolute) time since an item was studied. It seems that another explanation is needed to account for recency effects observed at longer time scales. One possibility is that STS explains recency on short time scales and that another mechanism, such as contextual drift or decay, explains recency on longer time scales (Davelaar, Goshen-Gottstein, Ashkenazi, Haarmann, and Usher, 2005).

Alternatively, the recency effect in both immediate and continual-distractor free recall may reflect a common mechanism. Evidence consistent with this

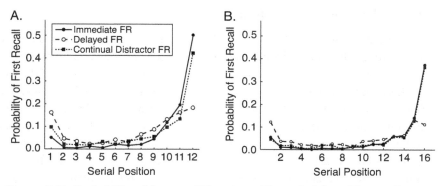

Figure 7.11 Probability of first-recall functions. The probability of first recall functions for immediate free recall, delayed free recall, and continual-distractor free recall. **A.** Data from Howard and Kahana (1999). **B.** Data from an unpublished study by Polyn and Kahana.

latter view comes from the finding that the same variables that preferentially affect recall of prerecency items in immediate free recall also preferentially affect recall of prerecency items in continual-distractor free recall. Word frequency (Greene, 1986), semantic similarity (Greene and Crowder, 1984), incidental instructions (Glenberg et al., 1980; Neath, 1993a), and list length (Greene, 1986) all have a significant effect on the retrieval of prerecency items and little or no impact on recency or long-term recency.[7] Further, the long-term recency effect probably reflects a general principle of memory that can be seen in many aspects of our daily lives. Baddeley and Hitch (1977) showed that recency effects extend over long intervals in retrieval of facts about autobiographical events, in this case rugby games and solutions to anagram puzzles.

The ratio rule implies that recency does not depend on the absolute time since an item was encoded, but rather on the relative times that different recent items have been encoded. This contradicts dual-store models, which assume that recency effects depend on the size of STS and the rules governing displacement.

According to the ratio rule, recency is observed at all time scales in a manner that depends on the relative timing of the different learned events. That is, doubling both the RI and the IPI would not affect the recency effect (Glenberg et al., 1980, 1983). Phenomena that behave in this way are said to exhibit *time-scale invariance.*

7. Davelaar et al. (2005) present several exceptions to this general principle, some of which are discussed in section 7.6.

7.3.2 The Long-range Contiguity Effect

Howard and Kahana (1999) asked whether the contiguity effect also appears when studied items are spaced apart in time and when a demanding distractor task is given between each list item. Figure 7.12 illustrates the lag-CRP curves for IPIs ranging from 0 sec (delayed free recall) to 16 sec (continual-distractor free recall). They found that the contiguity effect was relatively constant across this range of IPIs. Although 16 sec of distractor task activity between items did not disrupt the contiguity effect, the same 16 sec of distractor activity presented at the end of the list was sufficient to greatly attenuate the recency effect. This result can also be seen in the temporal-clustering scores calculated for each IPI condition (Figure 7.12B).

Prior to this finding, participants' tendency to make recall transitions among items from neighboring list positions was seen as evidence for associations formed in STS. Indeed, the SAM model provides a good fit to the contiguity effect seen in free recall because nearby items spend more time together in STS than remote items do (see Figure 7.3). However, SAM cannot predict the finding of long-range contiguity in continual-distractor free recall, because the distractor task given during the IPIs should displace items from STS and thus disrupt the contiguity effect.

As with the recency effect, STS processes can also account for the contiguity effect in both immediate free recall and delayed free recall. Items presented in contiguous list positions spend more time together in STS than items from more remote serial positions. Contiguous items are therefore more strongly associated and more likely to be recalled in nearby output positions because of cuing with interitem episodic associations. In contrast, STS cannot account for the occurrence of associations among neighboring items in continual-distractor free recall because an interitem distractor should disrupt the formation of these interitem associations in STS.

To explain the long-range contiguity effect seen in Figure 7.12, one could simply argue that participants do not store the distractors in memory, or that they are so dissimilar from the list items that people can search memory for the list items without being influenced by the distractors. The first problem with this account is that in delayed free recall, the distractor task has a very significant impact on memory as seen in Figure 7.11. In addition, one also sees long-range contiguity effects in tasks where the distractors are items that must be encoded in memory (Davis et al., 2008), and these effects can persist across several minutes of such memory encoding (Howard, Youker, and Venkatadass, 2008). The time-scale invariance of the contiguity effect therefore requires an explanation outside of the STS-LTS dual-process framework (but see Davelaar et al. (2005) and Kahana, Sederberg, and Howard (2008), for a denouement).

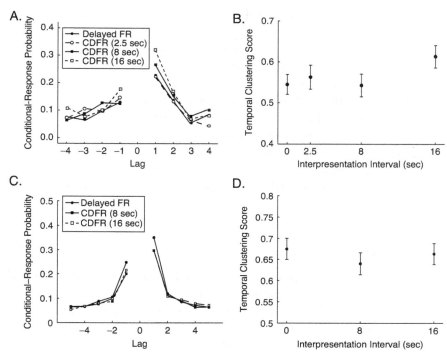

Figure 7.12 Long-range contiguity effects. A. The conditional-response probability as a function of lag exhibits a strong contiguity effect in both delayed free recall and in continual-distractor free recall (CDFR). The three CDFR conditions varied the interpresentation interval (IPI) during which participants performed an arithmetic distractor task between list items, as noted in the legend. **B.** Temporal-clustering scores for each of the four conditions shown in Panel A. Error bars represent 95% confidence intervals. **C, D.** The same analysis as in Panels A and B applied to a dataset from a replication of this study using different words, list lengths, and encoding task (Polyn and Kahana, unpublished).

Like the recency effect, the contiguity effect can span gaps much longer than the 16 seconds of arithmetic that Howard and Kahana used to study long-range contiguity. Howard et al. (2008) asked participants who had just studied and recalled many different word lists to freely recall all of the items they could remember from all of the lists. They then examined the recall transitions that participants made between items studied on different lists, and found that these transitions were significantly more likely to be made to items studied in neighboring lists. In fact, the across-list contiguity effect seen in the final free recall was found to be statistically reliable for transitions spanning as many as 6 study-test lists each containing 10 unrelated items.

In a study of memory for real life events, Moreton and Ward (2010) asked three different groups of people to freely recall autobiographical events from one of three time periods: the last 5 weeks, the last 5 months, or the last 5 years. As expected based on the contiguity effect, events were more likely to be successively recalled if they occurred close in time to one another. Furthermore, this contiguity effect for autobiographical events was quite similar across the three different time scales, with the tendency to successively recall events from neighboring weeks in the 5-week group being similar to the tendency to successively recall events from neighboring years in the 5-year group. Thus, it appears that the similarity of contiguity effect across different time scales extends well beyond the usual time scale of list memory experiments.

7.3.3 Levels of Processing

The rules governing an item's entry and exit from STS allow dual-store models (e.g., SAM) to simulate participants' rehearsal of list items. The longer an item resides in STS, the greater the strengths of the item's associations to its neighbors and to the list context. This predicts that recall depends critically on the amount of time that an item is rehearsed in STS.

Craik and Lockhart (1972) presented striking evidence against the view that time in STS is the key determinant of storage in LTS. They demonstrated that the manner of encoding can have a substantial impact on recall. Rather than asking participants to study words for a later memory test, Craik and Lockhart used an *incidental-learning* procedure: during study, participants answered a question about a target word and were later given a surprise recall test. If the study question emphasized the word's perceptual, or surface, attributes (e.g., Is the word in capital letters?), recall of the word was very poor, whereas if the study question emphasized the meaning of the word (e.g., Would it fit in the sentence '. . .'?), later recall was very good.

Craik and Lockhart distinguished two different kinds of rehearsal. Simply repeating a word without trying to elaborate its meaning is termed *maintenance rehearsal*, which is in contrast to *elaborative rehearsal*, in which the participant elaborates the meaning of the word while trying to remember it. They reported evidence showing that while elaborative rehearsal produces long-term retention, maintenance rehearsal does not. That is, repetition alone produces little learning (see chapter 4).

After Craik and Lockhart's claim that maintenance rehearsal does not produce long-term learning, a number of investigators carefully examined the effects of maintenance rehearsal on retention. These studies found that maintenance rehearsal does, in fact, produce enhanced long-term recall, but that the effect is much weaker than elaborative rehearsal (see Baddeley, 1978, for a review).

The finding that elaborative rehearsal leads to better memory may mean that participants are working harder to encode the information and/or that elaborative encoding lays down features in memory that are more suitable to the types of tasks used to test memory. On most memory tests, we ask participants to recall or recognize the items that appeared on a list without reference to their surface (perceptual) features. However, in some memory tasks, the surface features can be quite important (e.g., Kolers and Ostry, 1974). Imagine that we showed participants a set of detailed pictures of, say, the Eiffel Tower, then gave them a recognition test where all the lures were also pictures of the Eiffel Tower. In this task, attending to the appearance of the items is likely to result in a greater benefit to memory than attending to the meaning of the items. Findings along these lines have been documented by Intraub and Nicklos (1985).

7.4 SINGLE-STORE RETRIEVED-CONTEXT MODELS

In this section we discuss context-based memory models that can account for both recency and contiguity without making any distinction between short-term and long-term memory storage. In previous chapters we have already introduced the idea that each experienced item or event becomes associated with a unique temporal context and that context is a multidimensional representation that changes gradually over the course of item presentations. We also showed how cuing memory with the current state of context tends to activate recent items more strongly than remote items. This is because the state of context at the time of test is most similar to the contexts associated with recently studied items.

To use these ideas in predicting participants' responses in a memory experiment, we need some way of translating activations into recalls. Following the SAM model, we could assume that the probability of recalling an item is determined by the ratio of its activation to the summed activations of all of the potential recalls. Alternatively, using a neural-network model we would iteratively update the network until its state matched that of one of the studied items. In either case, the recall process is competitive such that an item is most likely to be recalled when its activation is substantially larger than the other candidate items.

In immediate free recall, because the current state of context is very similar to that associated with recently studied items, the model predicts a strong recency effect. When recall is delayed, and the retention interval is filled with distracting mental activity, the state of context at the time of test will have drifted away from the contextual states associated with the list items. As such, the model predicts that the magnitude of the recency effect will decrease with the duration of the retention interval. This is exactly what is observed in the data.

In continual-distractor free recall, increasing the interval between item presentations (the interpresentation interval) reduces the similarities of the contexts associated with neighboring list items. Although the context at test will have drifted away from the representation associated with the final list item, the relative similarities among list items has not changed. Neighboring items are still more similar than remote items, and the context at the time of test is still much more similar to that associated with the last item than it is to the contexts associated with earlier list items. As long as the recall process is competitive, the recency items will win the competition even if the overlap between all of the context representations has been greatly reduced. In this case, the recency effect depends on the *relative* similarity of the test context to each of the studied items, not the absolute similarity. In continual-distractor free recall, because context drifts both during item presentation and during the distractors, the relative similarity of the test context to each of the studied items will be the same as it is in immediate free recall, and the model thus predicts similar recency effects in immediate and in continual-distractor free recall.

Let us now consider how we can extend these ideas to account for the contiguity effect in free recall. Although the contiguity effect is often interpreted as reflecting direct associations between items, the contiguity effect can also arise if neighboring items are associated with similar contexts and if recalling an item (partially) reinstates the context that was present when the item was studied. In this case, the *retrieved context* will serve as a good retrieval cue for neighboring items as they will tend to have been encoded in a similar context to the just recalled item (Howard and Kahana, 1999, 2002a). If retrieval transitions are driven by the relative similarity between the temporal contexts of different list items, then one would expect to find robust contiguity effects even in continual-distractor free recall (see Figure 7.12). Moreover, one would expect to find that the tendency to make transitions among neighboring list items would be largely independent of the absolute temporal separation of the items in the list. In contrast, models that assume that interitem associations are formed through rehearsal in STS have great difficulty explaining the contiguity effects observed in both immediate and continual-distractor free recall. It would seem that interitem associations should at least be partially disrupted by a demanding interitem distractor.

Within the retrieved-context framework, the recency effect, as seen in participants' tendency to begin recalling items from the end of the list, and the contiguity effect, as seen in participants' tendency to recall nearby items successively, reflect two distinct memory processes. To *initiate* recall, the retrieval cue is the state of context at the end of the study list. This contextual state will be more similar to the states that were associated with recent list items than to those associated with earlier list items. As mentioned above, this produces the recency effect in that these end-of-list items tend to be recalled first and with the highest probability. Upon successful recall of an item, the participant retrieves the state of context that was stored in memory when that item was originally presented. This retrieved context then serves as a retrieval cue for subsequent recalls. Because the retrieved context is similar to the context of nearby list items, it serves as a stronger cue for these items, generating a strong contiguity effect.

In the next section we describe how retrieved context theories have been formalized as mathematical models that can make quantitative predictions about what should happen in recall experiments. We then discuss the success of these models in accounting for data from recall experiments.

7.4.1 The Temporal Context Model

In previous chapters we discussed models in which the evolution of context over item presentations is described as a random walk: $\mathbf{t}_i = \mathbf{t}_{i-1} + \epsilon$, where $\mathbf{t}$ is a vector representing the state of context after studying the ith item on a list and ϵ is a vector of random numbers, each drawn from a normal distribution. This equation implies that context fluctuates independently of the actual items being experienced or remembered. Departing from these earlier models, the temporal context model (TCM) proposes that context changes as a direct consequence of the sequence of experienced items (Howard and Kahana, 2002a). In TCM, the activation of item representations, either during presentation or retrieval, drives the evolution of context.

Context dynamics.

Suppose that a participant studied the list *house, shoe, tree, car, dog, key, rose, boat*. TCM assumes that when the word *house* is studied, it activates house-related information in memory. This information could include semantic information concerning the meaning of *house* (shelter), imagery of one's own house or other recently seen houses, or any other mental representations evoked by the experience of studying the word *house*. These activated representations would not be strictly limited to the concept *house* but could include related concepts activated by the concept of *house* or specific memories associated with the concept of *house*. In the terminology of the model, all of this information would be referred to as the context associated with house prior to the start of the experiment (the meaning of this terminology will hopefully become clearer further along). This house-related information would be used to update the current state of context in much the same way as random noise was assumed to update the state of context in the random walk model described above. Except now, rather than adding random features to the state of context, the features being added are those associated with the representation of house. To illustrate this idea we could rewrite the equation above as: $\mathbf{t}_i = \mathbf{t}_{i-1} + \mathbf{f}_i$, where $\mathbf{f}_i$ denotes the representation of the ith item in the studied list. It is useful to modify this equation so that the overall length of the context vector does not grow continuously as new memories are being recorded. This can be easily done by multiplying the previous state of context by a decay factor, $0 < \rho < 1$ and scaling the new input to context, $\mathbf{f}$, by a factor β whose value is set to ensure that the overall length of the vector is set at 1.0. The resulting equation for contextual evolution is then given by:

$$\mathbf{t}_i = \rho \mathbf{t}_{i-1} + \beta \mathbf{f}_i. \tag{7.7}$$

Studying the second list item, *shoe*, would activate shoe-related information, which would further update the current state of context, weakening the strength of the house-related information in the evolving context representation. This would continue for each item presentation, so that by the time *boat* is studied, the current state of context would include the information related to each of the studied items, but with the more recent items being represented more strongly than the earlier list items. In this manner, the thoughts evoked by each studied item push the internal context signal through a high-dimensional vector space.

Forming associations between items and context.
So far we have described how the sequence of experienced items can change the representation of internal context. But for this context representation to be useful in storing memories and guiding their retrieval, it must be linked to the representations of the items themselves. In TCM, as each item is studied, its attributes become associated with the current state of context, and vice-versa. These bidirectional associations are stored in an associative neural network, with one set of connections representing item-to-context associations and another set of connections representing context-to-item associations. As each item is studied, the strengths (weights) of the connections between units (neurons) are strengthened according to the principle of Hebbian learning.

In chapter 6 we saw how a network of interconnected neuron-like processing units can form associations between different vectors. This can be accomplished using a combination of the Hebbian learning rule and the McCullough-Pitts *dynamical rule*. We use the Hebb rule to store associations between the vector representations of items and contexts. We can then use the dynamical rule to simulate associative retrieval, cuing either with context to retrieve items or with items to retrieve their contexts. TCM uses separate associative matrices to link items to context (W^{FT}) and context to items (W^{TF}). The learning rule for these two matrices can be written as:

$$w^{FT}(i, j)_t = w^{FT}(i, j)_{t-1} + t(i)f(j)_t \qquad (7.8)$$

$$w^{TF}(i, j)_t = w^{TF}(i, j)_{t-1} + f(i)_t t(j)_t. \qquad (7.9)$$

Associating item and context representations turns out to be a powerful way of organizing memories. Cuing memory with the current state of context will activate items associated with similar contexts. Because context changes gradually over the course of item presentations or recalls, the current state of context will overlap most strongly with those items that were recently encoded. This will allow the model to produce the recency effect in immediate free recall and its attenuation in delayed free recall. Similarly, cuing memory with an item will activate its associated context, which will in turn activate contiguously studied list items. Before we describe this retrieval process in greater detail, we revisit the question of how exactly context evolves during the course of list presentation.

Using retrieved context to update context.

TCM assumes that the sequence of experienced items, and the thoughts they evoke, drive the evolution of context. To implement this within the model, we update context by adding the current item vector to the state of context (and weighting things appropriately so the overall length of the context vector remains constant). This raises the question of how context should be updated when recalling an item. The context-to-item associations stored during encoding allow for recall of an item to retrieve its previously associated contexts. One could then use these retrieved context representations to evolve the current state of context. Similarly, one could assume that during encoding, items also retrieve their previously associated contexts, and it is these contexts that cause the updating of the context representation. By using the retrieved context representation to update the state of context (both during encoding and during recall), one does not have to worry about the possibility that items and context have different numbers of features.

Under the assumption that retrieved context is used to update the current state of context, consider what happens during the study (encoding) phase of a recall experiment. Prior to studying the list, each item will have been associated with many prior contexts in which the item has occurred. For simplicity, TCM assumes a single preexperimental context associated with each item. This representation can be thought of as the average of all preexperimental contexts. Studying a given list item (represented as $\mathbf{f}_i$) will retrieve its preexperimental context using the matrix of weights connecting the item to the context units of the network (W^{FT}). Using the (linear) dynamical rule, the retrieved context representation is given by:

$$\sum_{j=1}^{N} w^{FT}(i, j) f(i),$$

where N is the number of neurons representing item features in the neural network. Using matrix notation, we can write this simply as $W^{FT}\mathbf{f}(i)$ (see section 5.4 for a review of matrix-vector multiplication). We can now rewrite our context evolution equation as:

$$\mathbf{t}_i = \rho_i \mathbf{t}_{i-1} + \beta \mathbf{t}^{input}, \tag{7.10}$$

where,

$$\mathbf{t}^{input} = W^{FT}\mathbf{f}(i) = \sum_{j=1}^{N} w^{FT}(i, j) f(i)$$

According to this equation the state of context is a weighted sum of the context retrieved by the studied (or recalled) item ($\mathbf{t}^{input}$) and the previous state of context, $\mathbf{t}_{i-1}$.

Recall process.
The current state of context serves as the cue for recall. Context activates item representations via the context-to-item associations stored in memory (the matrix of connection weights, W^{TF}). Specifically, the input to the set of neurons representing items is given by the vector $\mathbf{f}^{input}$ whose elements are activated according to the dynamical rule:

$$f^{input}(i) = \sum_{j=1}^{N} w^{TF}(i, j) t(i).$$

The activation of a given target item (e.g., a specific word on the list) is defined as the similarity between $\mathbf{f}^{input}$ and the target item's representation in memory.

Although cuing with context may activate many items to varying degrees, only one item may be recalled at a time. The process by which an individual item is selected for recall involves a competition among the items. This competition could be modeled in a number of ways. One could use an autoassociative neural network (e.g., a Hopfield network) to store each of the items in semantic memory and then cue that network with $\mathbf{f}^{input}$. Such a model would generate predictions about how long it takes to recall a given item (i.e., interresponse times) and it would also predict that some cues would not result in any items being recalled. Alternatively, one could simplify the calculations by using a much simpler probabilistic choice rule, such as the *sampling* rule used by the SAM model. According to such a rule, the probability of recalling a given item, $\mathbf{f}_i$, would be given by:

$$P(\mathbf{f}_i | \mathbf{f}^{input}) = \frac{Sim(\mathbf{f}_i, \mathbf{f}^{input})}{\sum_{k=1}^{N} Sim(\mathbf{f}_k, \mathbf{f}^{input})}$$

where *Sim* is a function that defines the similarity of two vectors. This approach is much simpler computationally, but it does not provide any information on how long it takes to make a given choice. A third approach, adopted by Sederberg et al. (2008) and Polyn et al. (2009), is to use each of the similarity values in the equation above to drive an accumulator that integrates evidence over time. The first item whose accumulated evidence reaches the recall threshold is recalled. Because the accumulators are assumed to be noisy, the item with the highest similarity to $\mathbf{f}^{input}$ will not always be recalled, but it is more likely to be recalled than any of the other items. Figure 7.13 illustrates the evolution of the accumulator values for five items with relatively strong activations. In this example, the item with the seventh highest activation value is

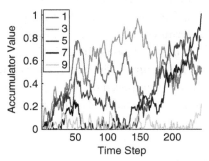

Figure 7.13 Accumulator choice model. We have chosen five items with strong activations to illustrate the choice model. Each item is illustrated by a different gray-scale line. The number in the legend indicates the rank of the item based on its initial activation value, with 1 being the most strongly activated item. The *x*-axis represents time, and the *y*-axis represents the value of the accumulator at each time step. The process terminates when one of the accumulators (item 7, shown in black) reaches the threshold value of 1.0.

the first to reach the decision boundary. One can see from this example that the accumulator model captures the probabilistic nature of memory retrieval and also generates predictions about the time it takes to retrieve a given item. The equation defining the accumulators is given by:

$$\mathbf{x}_j = (1 - \tau\kappa - \tau\lambda\mathbf{N})\,\mathbf{x}_{j-1} + \tau\mathbf{f}^{\text{IN}} + \epsilon_j, \qquad (7.11)$$

where j indexes the number of steps in the accumulation process, κ controls decay, λ controls competition between the accumulators by scaling an inhibitory connection matrix $\mathbf{N}$, τ is a rate constant controlling the overall speed of the decision process, and ϵ is a noise vector drawn from a random normal distribution with mean zero and standard deviation η (where an increased value of η leads to a noisier recall competition). In all three of the approaches outlined above, the recall period is modeled as a series of competitions. Each competition either produces a winning item, which is then recalled, or runs out of time, at which point the recall period is over and the next trial begins.

Once recalled, an item is re-presented to the network and used to update the current state of temporal context. The retrieval of an item also retrieves the state of temporal context that was present when it was first studied. Consequently, context is updated with a combination of the preexperimental and newly learned contextual representations of the just-recalled item. This new state of context now serves as the cue to recall further items. During recall, context is updated using the same mechanism as during the study period (although the rate of context updating, defined by the parameter β, can differ between study and recall events). This recall process, where the just-recalled item updates the current state of temporal context, which then provides a cue for the subsequent recall, continues until all the items are recalled or time runs out.

The criterion for terminating recall is an essential ingredient for modeling serial-position effects in recall tasks. In TCM (e.g., Sederberg et al., 2008; Polyn et al., 2009), the accumulators provide a natural stopping rule that is analogous to the time limits imposed on participants in free-recall experiments. Specifically, we assume that recall ends after a fixed number of accumulator time steps.

Modeling distractors.

The arithmetic distractor tasks typically employed in delayed and continual-distractor free recall can be modeled as random vectors that cause context to drift at some rate. Although distractor items drive context, we assume that they do not give rise to any modification of the associative weight matrices linking items to context and context to items. Participants have no reason to learn the distractors, although they presumably do remember something about them. More importantly, however, the distractor tasks used in free-recall experiments involve materials that are completely different from the material being learned (e.g., numbers vs. words). Even if the distractor items are stored perfectly in memory, they would not be expected to compete significantly with the to-be-remembered items during retrieval.

Modeling semantic similarity.

In defining the nature of preexperimental context, TCM assumes that similar items tend to occur in similar contexts over the lifetime of an individual. For example, France and Napoleon will be more likely to occur in similar contexts than two unrelated concepts. In TCM, we can represent these semantic relations between items by setting the initial weights in w^{TF} based on the similarities among list items. In this way, the temporal context retrieved by the just-recalled item supports the retrieval of semantically related items (Rao and Howard, 2008). At a practical level, this is implemented by storing the similarity values between list items in the connections of w^{TF} prior to the start of the experiment. As discussed in chapter 6, the similarities among different words can be determined using a model of semantic representation, such as latent semantic analysis (LSA) (Landauer and Dumais, 1997).

Modeling primacy.

As discussed in chapter 6, the two main sources of primacy effects in free recall are an increased tendency to rehearse items from early serial positions throughout the list presentation (Rundus, 1971; Murdock and Metcalfe, 1978; Tan and Ward, 2000) and increased attention or decreased competition during the study of early list items giving rise to better encoding (Sederberg et al., 2006; Serruya, Sederberg, and Kahana, in press). To account for primacy within a model of recall, one must either model the rehearsal process or the change in attention over the course of item presentations, or both. Whereas the SAM model characterizes the rehearsal process, TCM assumes that early list items attract more attention due to their novelty (see also Brown, Preece, and Hulme, 2000; Burgess and Hitch, 1999). This approach is supported by the observation that the major phenomena of free recall (other than primacy) do not appear to depend strongly on rehearsal.

Specifically, we introduce the scalar ϕ_i factor to describe the recall advantage for items in early serial positions (its value is determined by two manipulable parameters of the model). This factor starts at a value above 1; as the list progresses, it decays to 1, at which point it has no effect on the dynamics of the model:

$$\phi_i = \phi_s e^{-\phi_d(i-1)} + 1. \tag{7.12}$$

Here, ϕ_s is a scaling parameter controlling the magnitude of the primacy effect, and ϕ_d is a decay parameter, which controls the rate at which this advantage decays with serial position (i).

Forward asymmetry in the contiguity effect.

According to TCM, recalling item f_i retrieves (activates) its associated experimental list context t_i and its associated preexperimental context (i.e., the average of contexts experienced prior to the study list). The preexperimental context was the input to the context evolution equation when item f_i was studied; that is, the preexperimental context is the vector t_i^{input} in Equation 7.10. Following recall of item f_i, these two components of the retrieved context are added to the current state of context to form the new state of context, which in turn cues the next response. Each of these three components of the context vector will bias retrieval in a particular way. Insofar as the prior state of context contained items from the end of the list, that portion of the context vector will activate recent items. In contrast, the retrieved list context will tend to activate items studied contiguously to the just-recalled item. Because the list context is (approximately) equally similar to the items that preceded and followed it in the list, this component of context will facilitate transitions to neighboring items in a symmetrical manner. In contrast, the retrieved preexperimental context associated with item f_i was only incorporated into the context vector following the presentation of that item. As such, this component of context will provide a strongly asymmetric cue favoring transitions to subsequent list items rather than prior list items. The combined forward-asymmetric and bidirectional cue for subsequent recalls gives rise to the characteristic asymmetric contiguity effect.

7.5 TESTING RETRIEVED CONTEXT THEORY

As with the SAM model, TCM has gone through significant refinements since it was initially developed. Rather than reviewing all of the different variants of the model, we consider here the model developed by Polyn et al. (2009).[8] First let us consider Murdock's classic study of the serial-position curve in immediate free recall. As shown in Figure 7.14A, increasing list length did not change the overall shape of the curve, although it decreased the probability of recalling early and midlist items. As shown in Figure 7.14B, TCM provides a reasonable fit to all three curves with a single set of parameter values. Cuing memory with the

---

8. In their paper, Polyn and colleagues refer to their expanded version of TCM as the *context maintenance and retrieval model*. Because the broad class of retrieved context theory is often referred to as TCM, we have chosen to stick with that acronym in this text.

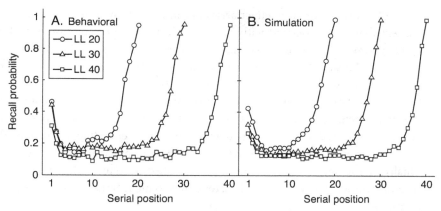

Figure 7.14 Serial-position effects in the temporal context model (TCM).
A. Serial-position curves for lists of length (LL) 20, 30, and 40 words. Data from Murdock (1962). **B.** Simulated data from TCM. Reproduced from Polyn et al. (2009).

current state of context at the time of test naturally gives rise to a recency effect in immediate free recall. This is because recently experienced items are most strongly represented in context. This effect is not dependent on the number of previously studied items. In contrast, increasing list length makes it harder to recall items from early and midlist positions because of increased competition from other list items. In the accumulator model of recall competition (see Equation 7.11), the level of activation of a given item determines the degree to which it suppresses the activations of other items, thus increasing the level of competition in the model. However, the recent items are somewhat insulated from this competition as they are strongly activated by the time-of-test context cue in immediate free recall. Items retrieved later in the recall sequence are relatively less well activated and thus feel the effects of competition more sharply.

Howard and Kahana (2002a) originally proposed TCM to account for the long-term recency and long-range contiguity effects. In delayed free recall, the distractor task will have caused the representation of context to drift away from its state at the end of the studied list. As such, TCM predicts that the recency effect should be greatly diminished following a period of distracting mental activity (e.g., Figure 6.3). In continual-distractor free recall, the distractors between item presentations will have reduced the overlap in the context representations among all of the list items. However, because recall is a competition based on the relative activations of all of the list items, time-of-test context will produce a large recency effect because all of the items will have been similarly affected by the distractor tasks.

In TCM, the contiguity effect arises because recall of an item activates the context that was associated with that item during list presentation as well as (preexperimental) contexts associated with the item prior to the most recent study list. These retrieved contextual states combine with the current state of context to serve as the retrieval cue for the next response. Because the list context associated with an item overlaps with the encoding context of the item's neighbors, a contiguity effect results. Because the preexperimental context associated with an item overlaps with the encoding context of the items' successors in the list, there is a forward asymmetry in recall transitions. Finally, to the degree that the time-of-test context overlaps with the context of recently studied items, there will be a tendency to make transitions to end-of-list items.

In continual-distractor free recall, the distractor activity interpolated between study items will diminish the degree to which the context associated with an item overlaps with the context associated with its neighbors. However, because recall is competitive, the overall reduction in the contextual overlap among items will not significantly diminish the contiguity effect. To the extent that the activations of neighboring list items are greater than the activations of remote list items, a contiguity effect is predicted. The absolute activations of the items are thus less important than their relative activations.[9]

One of the more subtle predictions of TCM concerns the difference between the contiguity effect measured for early recalls and later recalls. For the first few recalls, the contiguity effect shows a tendency for participants to make transitions not only to neighboring items but also to items from the end of the list (Farrell and Lewandowsky, 2008). As can be seen in Figure 7.15A, early recall of a midlist item (among the first three responses) tends to be followed by recall of an item from the end of the list. This tendency is not seen for later recalls, where people just make transitions to items from neighboring positions (Figure 7.15C). This pattern of experimental results is very similar to the predictions of TCM (see Figures 7.15B and D). TCM predicts this pattern because of the persistence of the recency effect after a mid-list item is recalled. Figure 7.15C shows that later in the recall sequence, the influence of the recency effect recedes, but the contiguity effect remains.

A fundamental assumption of retrieved context models, such as TCM, is that the contexts in which words on a list are studied play a critical role in the order in which those words will be recalled. If this assumption is correct, fluctuations in

---

9. The astute reader will notice that if the noise term in the accumulator decision model is not scaled by the overall activations of the list items, the model will predict that with a sufficient interitem distractor, the contiguity effect will be sharply attenuated. For this reason, Sederberg et al. (2008) scale the noise by the overall variability in the item activations.

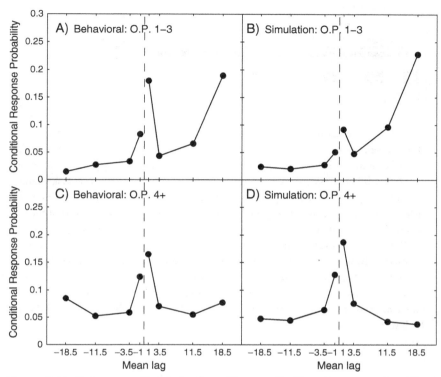

Figure 7.15 Contiguity effect for early and late recalls. Transitions originating from midlist items (serial positions 5–19 out of 24) are considered. Each point represents the aggregate probability for a set of lags, marked according to the mean lag of that bin. From left to right these are: −19 to −18, −17 to −6, −5 to −2, −1, 1, 2 to 5, 6 to 17, and 18 to 19. A: Data for output positions 1 to 3. B: TCM fits to data in Panel A. C: Data for output positions 4 and onward. D: TCM fits to data from Panel C. Reproduced from Polyn et al. (2009).

the rate of contextual drift from item to item should influence recall dynamics. Polyn and Kahana (2008) designed a variant of the continual-distractor free-recall task that attempted to explicitly control the rate of contextual drift between items. This was done by varying the duration of an arithmetic distractor task given after each word presentation. The schedule of distraction intervals increased and decreased, oscillating multiple times in a given list, as shown in Figure 7.16A.

TCM predicts that if a participant recalled an item from the *increasing* portion of the list, then it would be relatively more difficult to next recall an item studied in the forward direction, since the increasing schedule of distraction intervals will cause more context change for items in the forward direction. Thus, the

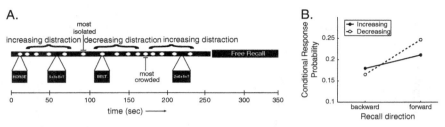

Figure 7.16 Interpolated distracting activity influences recall dynamics.
A. Representative trial of variable-duration distractor free recall. Participants studied lists of 15 items (white ellipses). Between items, participants engage in a distracting mental arithmetic task (black shading). The duration of the distracting task changes over the course of the list, ranging from 6 to 23 seconds. After the final period of the distracting task, participants engage in free recall for 90 seconds. Portions of the list where distraction intervals are getting longer are referred to as *increasing distraction*; portions where distraction intervals are getting shorter are referred to as *decreasing distraction*. **B.** When a rising distraction item is recalled, transitions are less likely to go in the forward direction than when a falling distraction item is recalled. Increasing the distractor interval following a studied item thus attenuates the forward asymmetry effect, as predicted by retrieved context theory. Data from Polyn, Burke, and Kahana (submitted).

state of context associated with the just-recalled item is less similar to the state of context associated with the following items, causing these items to be poorly supported in the retrieval competition. Similarly, if the participant recalls an item from the *decreasing* portion of the list, forward-going transitions would be enhanced, since context is quite similar between the just-recalled item and the following items. Both of these predictions were borne out in the data. Figure 7.16B shows a preserved forward asymmetry for transitions from the *decreasing* portion of the list and an attenuation of the forward asymmetry for transitions from the *increasing* portion of the list. Polyn et al. (submitted) found that the likelihood of making a forward-going transition to be significantly decreased in the increasing condition ($p < 0.005$). This finding supports the idea that periods of distracting mental activity serve to shift temporal context away from previous states and that the contextual states associated with list items directly influence the way people recall word lists.

The accumulator-based decision model used to determine which activated item will be recalled makes specific predictions concerning the way IRTs should change over the course of the recall period. We have already seen (see section 6.2.3) how the times between successively recalled items grow progressively longer throughout the recall period—the time between the first

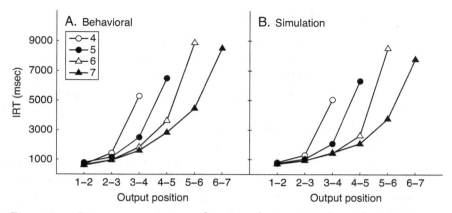

Figure 7.17 Interresponse time as a function of output position and total number of items recalled on that trial (the four lines correspond to trials on which 4, 5, 6, and 7 items were recalled). A. Behavioral data from Murdock and Okada (1970). **B.** Simulated data from the best-fitting parameter set of the Polyn et al. (2009) version of TCM.

two responses is usually on the order of 1 second, whereas the times between the last two responses is typically around 8 seconds. This pattern is shown in Figure 7.17A for data from Murdock and Okada's original (1970) study. Interresponse times increase exponentially with output position, and the rate of this growth is slower for lists in which participants recall a larger number of items (see Figure 7.17A). TCM predicts exactly the same pattern as that observed in the data (see Figure 7.17B). This pattern is predicted because of an interaction between several components of the model. First and foremost is the fact that items that are more strongly activated than their competitors will be recalled quickly, whereas items that are only marginally stronger than their competitors will be recalled slowly. Across the set of studied material there is significant variability in the degree to which items will become activated by a given context cue. This variability results both from the dynamics of the context representation over the course of retrieval and also from the varying relatedness (semantic similarity) among list items. Items that are recalled at the start of the recall interval have a tendency to be strongly activated by a given cue (e.g., the last few items being activated by the state of context at the end of the list). Later in the recall interval, after the most strongly activated items have already been recalled, the competition for recall is among items that are more likely to be similarly activated by the context cue. Choosing among these similarly activated items will take longer as they all tend to inhibit one another on their way to the decision boundary.

7.5.1 Context and Directed Forgetting

In the directed-forgetting technique (e.g,. Bjork, 1970; Block, 1971; Muther, 1965; Epstein, 1972), participants study two lists of words for a later free-recall test. Following the first list, half of the participants are told to forget the words on that list (because it was just a practice list); the remaining participants are told that those words represent the first half of the list that they will be asked to recall. Both groups then study the second list, after which they are asked to recall all of the items from both lists. Under these conditions, participants who were instructed to forget the first list recall fewer first list items and a greater number of second list items, as compared with the other group. Because the "forget" instruction doesn't arrive until after the first list has been studied, one cannot attribute this forgetting to impaired processing or rehearsal of the first list items.

On the basis of these data, Bjork and colleagues suggested that participants, when instructed to forget, somehow suppress or inhibit the representations of the first list items. The inhibition idea used here is akin to that proposed by Michael Anderson to explain retrieval-induced forgetting (see chapter 4). Bjork's account suggests that participants have active control over their ability to inhibit previously learned information.

In a twist on the directed-forgetting procedure, Sahakyan and Kelley (2002) showed that if a period of elaborative mental activity (e.g., imagine what you would do if you were invisible) is inserted between two studied lists, one observes both reduced memorability of the first list and enhanced memory for the second list. They suggested that the elaborative mental activity undertaken between the lists has the effect of disrupting temporal context, making the items studied in the first list less accessible and reducing the degree of interference between these items and the items in the second list. They further proposed that a similar mechanism underlies the reduced accessibility of materials cued to be forgotten in the directed-forgetting paradigm.

Parallel findings can also be observed with manipulations of external context. For example, Strand (1970) carried out a classic study of environmental context change using a retroactive interference paradigm (in which participants studied two lists in sequence and were then tested on their memory for the first). Participants were run in one of three conditions: a neutral condition in which participants studied both lists in the same room; a context-change condition in which participants walked to another room between lists; and a context-disruption condition in which participants walked into the hall between lists but returned to the same room. Strand found that the context-change and the context-disruption conditions elicited an equivalent degree of reduction of retroactive interference, suggesting that the primary factor at work was the disruption due to traversing the halls and not the removal of the contextual associations of the surrounding environment. Here, the novel interpolated activity involves simply walking into the hall; presumably, this drives an updating of context, which causes the two lists to be encoded more distinctly in memory.

7.6 SUMMARY AND CURRENT DIRECTIONS

The SAM retrieval model and its variants have been successfully applied to a broad range of data on free recall. According to SAM, studying an item activates its representation in a short-term store (STS) rehearsal buffer. The duration of activation in STS, in turn, determines the strengthening of associations in long-term store (LTS). Because only a small number of items can be active in STS at a given time, newly studied items displace older items in the buffer. While an item is active in STS its LTS associations to context and to other items concurrently in STS are increased.

At the time of test, any items that are active in STS are immediately recalled. Additional items are recalled from LTS via a cue-dependent search process. SAM begins by cuing with list context to retrieve an item and then uses the retrieved item along with context to cue the next item. Each attempt at cuing involves two phases. First, an item is "sampled" from memory. Sampling is probabilistic such that items are more likely to be sampled when they have a greater associative strength to the presented cue (when multiple cues are present, they combine multiplicatively see Equation 7.5). After being sampled, an item may or may not be recalled depending (probabilistically) on the absolute strength of the cues and on whether the item was already recalled (Equation 7.6). Recalling an item with a given set of cues results in a further strengthening of that item's association to its cues. Recall stops after a certain number of recall failures have occurred.

Using the mechanisms described above, SAM is able to fit a wide range of data on free recall, including serial-position effects, dissociations between recall of recency and prerecency items, rehearsal data, contiguity effects, and interresponse times.

Newer versions of SAM allow contextual associations to change gradually as items are studied or recalled (Mensink and Raaijmakers, 1988) and add a separate semantic LTS that works together with the contextually based (i.e., episodic) LTS (Sirotin et al., 2005). These additions to SAM enable the model to account for data on category clustering, semantic-CRP effects, extralist and prior-list intrusions and their modulation by semantic relatedness, spacing effects, subjective organization, and numerous other phenomena.

The ability to generate high levels of false memory in the laboratory has been a topic of considerable recent interest. As discussed in chapter 6, when people are asked to learn lists of items, many of which are strong associates of a critical nonpresented item, their rates of incorrectly recalling and recognizing those nonpresented items can be extremely high, often matching or exceeding the proportion of correct recall and recognition. Whereas SAM can easily generate

---

Box 7.1

NEURAL CORRELATES OF CONTEXT EVOLUTION AND REINSTATEMENT

Memory theorists posit that when people recall a past event, they not only recover features of the event itself, but they also recover information associated with other events that occurred nearby in time. The events surrounding a target event, and the thoughts they evoke, may be considered to represent a context for the target event, helping to distinguish that event from similar events experienced at different times. The ability to reinstate this contextual information during memory search has been considered a hallmark of episodic, or event-based, memory. A recent study by Manning, Polyn, Baltuch, Litt, and Kahana (2011) sought to determine whether contextual reinstatement may be observed in electrical signals recorded from the human brain during episodic recall.

The researchers examined electrocorticographic (ECoG) activity recorded from electrodes implanted in the brains of neurosurgical patients undergoing invasive monitoring for epileptic siezures (Figure 7.18A,B). The patients volunteered to participate in a *delayed free recall* experiment. After studying each list of words, participants performed a brief arithmetic distractor task and then attempted to recall the words in any order. After the patients had studied and recalled words from many lists, the researchers computed the similarity between the ECoG patterns recorded just prior to each recall with those recorded after the patient had studied each word.

The researchers found that, upon recalling a studied word, the recorded patterns of brain activity were not only similar to the patterns observed when the word was studied, but were also similar to the patterns observed during study of neighboring list words, with similarity decreasing reliably with positional distance (Figure 7.18C)—just as predicted by context reinstatement models of free recall. The degree to which individual patients exhibited this neural signature of contextual reinstatement was correlated with the contiguity effect as seen in Figure 7.18D. In this way, the study provides neural evidence for contextual reinstatement in humans.

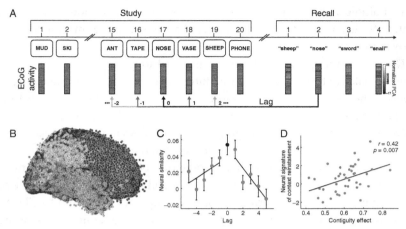

Figure 7.18 Neural evidence for contextual reinstatement in humans.
A. After studying a list of 20 words and performing a brief distraction task,
a participant recalls as many words as he can remember, in any order. ECoG
activity is recorded during each study and recall event. The similarity between
the recorded patterns is computed as a function of lag. **B.** Each dot marks the
location of a single electrode [temporal lobe (1,815 electrodes), frontal lobe
(1,737 electrodes), parietal lobe (512 electrodes), and occipital lobe (138
electrodes)]. **C.** Similarity between the activity recorded during recall of a word
from serial position i and study of a word from serial position $i + $ lag (black dot
denotes study and recall of the same word), i.e., lag $= 0$. **D.** Participants
exhibiting stronger neural signatures of context reinstatement also exhibited
more pronounced contiguity effects.

high levels of false recall under the conditions described above, the model
does so at the expense of generating far too many extralist intrusions. Kimball
et al. (2007) proposed two ways of modifying SAM to address the balance
of false recall and extralist intrusions. The first of these mechanisms pertains
to the encoding phase of the experiment. During encoding, unstudied items
may also become associated with list context if they are strong associates of
the items in STS. During recall, multiple prior recalled items may serve as a
compound cue for recall of the next item. Although each of these mechanisms
help the model to explain the benchmark data on false recall, including both
mechanisms enables the model to provide a good approximation to many of the
observed effects.

Because STS is responsible for both recency and contiguity effects, SAM
predicts that both should be disrupted in continual-distractor free recall.
Contrary to this prediction, the data show that recency and contiguity can

span multiple items and even multiple lists. Specifically, both recency and contiguity depend on the relative rather than the absolute intervals between study items.

The twin findings of long-term recency and long-range contiguity pose a serious challenge to SAM's STS-based interpretation of recency and contiguity effects. Whereas the notion of a short-term store (or working memory) may serve other useful cognitive functions, as in phonological processing or linguistic unitization (or chunking, see chapters 8 and 9), it does not appear necessary to explain recency and contiguity effects observed in free recall.

An alternative to the dual-store interpretation of recency and association is to allow drifting context to give rise to recency and retrieved context to give rise to contiguity. This view is formalized in the temporal context model (TCM), which assumes that items are associated with context and context is associated with items. Recency arises because context is a strong cue for end-of-list items on an immediate test. Contiguity arises because recalling an item retrieves its context, which in turn cues neighboring items.

Davelaar et al. (2005) criticized TCM's account of immediate and long-term recency, arguing that there are several dissociations between these two phenomena that cannot be explained by a single-component memory model. For example, they reported an experiment comparing proactive interference effects in immediate and continual-distractor free recall. When participants studied two lists of semantically similar items in succession, memory was worse for the items on the second list. In continual-distractor free recall, this interference was seen at all serial positions. However, in immediate free recall, this interference was seen only at early and middle serial positions— recency serial positions were unaffected. Davelaar et al. (2005) argued that this dissociation was evidence for a short-term buffer operating in immediate free recall: recency items were maintained in STS and read out at the start of the recall period. As such, recency items were not subject to interference from other items in memory (Davelaar et al., 2005; Davelaar, Haarmann, Goshen-Gottstein, and Usher, 2006; Usher, Davelaar, Haarmann, and Goshen-Gottstein, 2008). They proposed a dual-store model consisting of an STS and a randomly drifting context vector. By their account, immediate recency was attributable to STS, whereas long-term recency was due to context-mediated retrieval.

As further support for their dual-store model, Davelaar et al. (2005) note that the contiguity effect in immediate and continual-distractor free recall are not identical. Specifically, the magnitude of the contiguity effect is greater for the first output position in immediate recall, whereas it is constant across output positions in continual-distractor free recall (Howard and Kahana, 1999).

According to Davelaar et al., this dissociation between immediate and continual-distractor free recall arises because the first few recalled items come directly from the buffer in immediate recall (but are driven by the context vector in continual-distractor free recall).

Sederberg et al. (2008) showed that by implementing a competitive retrieval rule that is also sensitive to the absolute magnitude of the retrieved vectors, TCM can explain several of the key dissociations noted by Davelaar et al. The two models, however, are not as different as they may seem. Both assume that a persistent representation of list items is crucial for producing the recency effect. In the Davelaar et al. model, this representation is conceived of as an activation-based STS, whereas in the Sederberg et al. model, this representation is temporal context.

7.7 STUDY QUESTIONS

1. Consider the immediate free-recall task. How does the SAM model of free recall account for the recency effect, the primacy effect, and the effects of temporal and semantic similarity on recall transitions (i.e., the lag-CRP and semantic-CRP functions)?

2. It is said that both recency and temporally defined associations (as seen in the lag CRP) are approximately time-scale invariant. Explain this statement, describe the relevant empirical data in support of it, and discuss its theoretical implications.

3. Describe the effects of modality (auditory vs. visual), list length, presentation rate, and end-of-list distraction on the serial-position curve in free recall. How have these data been used to argue for the distinction between STS and LTS?

4. Consider the serial-position curves obtained in immediate, delayed, and continual-distractor free recall. What aspects of these data can and cannot be accounted for by the SAM model and by TCM? Explain your answer.

5. How does TCM account for the asymmetry in the contiguity effect? Under what experimental conditions could one eliminate or even reverse this asymmetry?

6. Consider a free-recall experiment in which there are 50 items: 10 are presented once, 10 are presented twice successively (massed), and 10 are presented twice at various points in the list. For example, the list might look like: ABCDDECFFG . . ., where each letter denotes a different word. (a) For items that are not from the primacy or recency

portions of the serial-position curve, how would recall probability differ for the three types of words? (b) Consider a variant of this experiment in which each item in the list is drawn from a single taxonomic category (i.e., all are names of common animals). How would you expect these conditions to differ according to SAM and TCM?

8

Sequence Memory

Acts of recollection happen because one change is of a nature to occur after another. If the changes follow each other of necessity, clearly a person who undergoes the earlier change will always undergo the later one.

ARISTOTLE, *De Memoria et Reminiscentia* (451b10)

One can easily think of important sequences that we have all learned, such as our phone number or the letters of our alphabet. When memorizing lyrics, poems, or the lines of a play, we rely on our ability to remember meaningful sequences of verbal information. Musical memory is another example of remembering an ordered series of items where the items are notes or chords. In some cases, such as the alphabet, the same sequence is used over the course of a lifetime. In other cases, such as memorizing a room number at a hotel, the sequence must be learned quickly and will only be relevant for a few days. In this chapter, we consider the basic experimental data on memory for sequences. In chapter 9, we evaluate those data in terms of the major theories proposed to explain serial-order memory.

Historically there have been two major lines of research on memory for sequences. The first line, which stems from the classic work of Ebbinghaus

(1885/1913), aims to characterize the information that people store and retrieve when learning to recall sequences of items. Ebbinghaus memorized long sequences of randomly arranged syllables to test the hypothesis that sequence learning involved the strengthening of associations between neighboring items (e.g., the contiguity effect). Although many early studies of serial learning supported Ebbinghaus' contiguity-based associative model, early researchers also found that people could remember the positions of the items within a list and could use this positional information as an aid during recall.

A great deal of research has focused on distinguishing between models of sequence memory based purely on interitem associations and models based on item-to-position associations (e.g., Young, 1968). In chapter 9 we will discuss both classes of models and the key data supporting each of them.

The second line of research, which focuses on immediate recall of short sequences, follows the tradition of short-term memory research. This work has focused on identifying the characteristics of short-term memory for sequences that differ from more general long-term memory processes. Of particular interest is the question of whether short sequences are maintained in a short-term store and whether the short-term representation is primarily phonological (i.e., speech based) in nature. As with dual-store models of free recall, dual-store models of serial recall have also come under considerable scrutiny in recent years. Nonetheless, the interpretation of serial-recall data as reflecting the operation of a short-term memory system has had enduring influence in the field.

8.1 SERIAL RECALL AND MEMORY SPAN

Serial recall is the classic method for studying memory for sequentially ordered materials. Participants study a series of items (e.g., words, letters, or digits) that are presented one at a time and then attempt to recall those items in order of presentation. Although participants are typically asked to recall the list in a forward order, occasionally experimenters test participants' ability to recall the list backward.

The ability to recall a given item in a sequence depends both on conditions of encoding and retrieval. During the retrieval phase of an experiment, recall of a given item will depend critically on the prior sequence of recalls leading up to that item. To simplify the analysis of sequence memory, researchers have sometimes probed for recall of a single item in a sequence. For example, if participants studied the series *house, shoe, tree, car, dog, key, rose, boat,* one might ask them to recall the fifth item in the series, to recall the item that followed *car,* or to recall the item that preceded *key.* This probed recall technique helps researchers sidestep the complex dynamics of the recall process in evaluating whether participants have encoded information about a given item's position within a sequence.

If a list is sufficiently short, people can recall a list in presentation order without making errors. Oberly (1927) found that on 50% of trials, participants could recall seven digits without error. Defining *memory span* as the maximum number of items that participants can correctly recall on 50% of trials, Crannell and Parish (1957) found a mean span of five words, six letters, and seven digits. The *modality effect* also appears as an increased memory span for auditorily presented lists (Drewnowski and Murdock, 1980).

Memory span is not only dependent on item classes (e.g., digits vs. words) and on modality (e.g., auditory vs. visual), it is also dependent on the specific features of the items. Baddeley, Thomson, and Buchanan (1975) found that memory span depends on word-articulation times, with memory span being higher for words that can be spoken rapidly (e.g., *sum, wit, hate*) than for words that take longer to articulate (e.g., *opportunity, university, aluminum*). This finding is known as the *word-length effect.*

A series of further experiments demonstrated that the word-length effect was not due to differences in number of syllables, number of phonemes, or word frequency (these are all variables that correlate with articulation time). Instead, the crucial variable was the time taken to pronounce the words. This result can also be seen in cross-language comparisons. Ellis and Hennelly (1980) noticed that Welsh speakers have significantly lower digit span than English speakers. Although digits in Welsh and English have the same numbers of syllables, Welsh digits take longer to pronounce. To test the hypothesis that the difference in digit span is a consequence of pronunciation time, Ellis and Henneley tested Welsh-English bilinguals and found that their digit span for Welsh numerals was shorter than for English numerals. However, when corrected for the time taken to articulate the digits, their spans were equivalent. These studies show that memory span is approximately equal to the number of items (e.g., words, digits) that can be articulated in 2 sec (Baddeley et al., 1975).

The word-length effect is an important source of evidence for the role of *phonological coding* (coding based on speech sounds) in immediate ordered recall. One prominent view is that immediate serial recall of short lists largely depends on retrieval from a hypothesized phonological short-term store (pSTS) in which items are coded primarily in terms of their phonological attributes, which decay rapidly in the presence of interfering information. This store has been termed the phonological loop because rehearsing items can prevent the rapid decay of the phonological trace (Baddeley, 1986). According to this view, one would expect shorter words, which can be rehearsed more quickly, to be easier to recall. This is because the time since the encoding/rehearsal of the oldest item is shorter for these words. Research by Cowan (1992) suggests that one must not only consider the role of encoding/rehearsal, but that the recall of the items themselves contributes significantly to the word-length effect. For example, recall of individual words strongly depends on the time it takes to pronounce the words recalled prior to the target item (Cowan, 1992).

The word length effect is not only observed in immediate serial recall. It is also found in delayed serial recall and in both immediate and delayed free recall. This suggests that whatever effect word length has on encoding and retrieval processes in recall tasks, they are not specific to immediate serial recall. The generality of the word-length effect could thus be seen as evidence against the interpretation that word-length effects reflect the operation of pSTS. Alternatively, the generality of the word-length effect could be seen as evidence that pSTS plays an important role in encoding and rehearsal processes that influence long-term retention of items in both free- and serial-recall tasks. Either way, the effect highlights the role of phonological attributes of items in memory encoding and retrieval processes.

Although the studies just described focus on the role of phonological coding in determining memory span, recent evidence suggests that semantic factors also play an important role in immediate memory span. Walker and Hulme (1999) found that immediate serial recall was better for concrete words (e.g., *hammer*) than for abstract words (e.g., *justice*), even when controlling for speech rate. This concreteness effect produced an advantage at all serial positions and in both forward and backward recall.

The studies described above indicate that memory span (and, more generally, serial recall) depends on properties of the studied words. Phonological characteristics of studied words appear to be particularly important in the immediate serial-recall task. These and related findings have led some researchers to argue that immediate serial recall primarily relies on the operation of STS and that the representation of these items in STS is primarily phonological.

8.2 SERIAL-POSITION EFFECTS

As in other memory tasks, we can plot a serial-position curve that indicates the accuracy of recalling items as a function of their position in the study list. Unlike free recall, where an item is scored as correct irrespective of its position in the recall sequence, in serial recall, we would like to know not only whether an item was recalled but whether it was recalled in the correct order. Two methods are possible: strict-position scoring and relative-order scoring. In strict-position scoring, an item is correct only if it is recalled in the correct position. In relative-order scoring, an item is considered to be correctly recalled if the just-recalled item came from an earlier serial position in the study list. For example, if after studying *house, shoe, tree, car, dog, key, rose, boat,* a participant recalled *"house, shoe, tree, key, rose,"* then all items would be correct by a relative-order criterion. If, however, a participant recalled *"house, shoe, key, tree, rose,"* then *tree* would be in the wrong relative order.

Figure 8.1 shows serial-position curves from vocal recall of lists consisting of 5, 11, and 19 common nouns (Kahana et al., 2010). Data were scored using the relative-order scoring method.[1] The basic characteristic of these curves is a very strong primacy effect and a much weaker but statistically reliable recency effect. One can also see a small list-length effect, where recall of items at a given serial position is better for short lists than for long lists.

The serial-position curves in Figure 8.1A illustrate recall accuracy after a single study trial. But one may also ask what the data would look like after participants have studied a list until they can recall all of the items without error. In this case, we would examine the IRTs as a function of list length and serial position.

As shown in Figure 8.1B, there are also primacy and recency effects in participants' IRTs. That is, the first few and last few responses are given more quickly than the middle responses. This finding is perhaps not surprising because over the course of learning, participants will have had more opportunities (on average) to recall the first few and the last few items than items from interior list positions. This additional practice will cause those items to become better learned and may therefore facilitate their rapid retrieval. To overcome this confound, we can examine IRTs on lists that are perfectly recalled following their first presentation. In this case, we are limited to examining IRTs obtained during recall of shorter (seven item) lists. As shown by the solid curve in Figure 8.1B, participants exhibit both primacy and recency in their IRTs even for lists recalled perfectly after a single presentation. Kahana and Jacobs (2000) observed similar results for lists of consonants.

We can also examine serial-position effects in probe-recall tasks. In these tasks, participants are typically given item i as a cue to recall either item $i + 1$ (forward-probed recall) or item $i - 1$ (backward-probed recall) or they are given position i as a cue to recall item i (positional probe). Using any of these procedures, one finds that the resulting serial-position curve looks quite similar to the serial-position curve in paired-associate recall (see Figure 4.3), with a large recency effect over the last several probe positions and a small primacy effect (see Figure 8.2 for data from forward-probed recall from Murdock, 1968).

---

1. Relative-order scoring is the preferred method for scoring serial-recall data, especially when participants study long lists (Addis and Kahana, 2004; Drewnowski and Murdock, 1980). Using the absolute scoring method, a participant who makes one error early in recall and then recalls the remaining items correctly would be marked wrong on all of the items following the error.

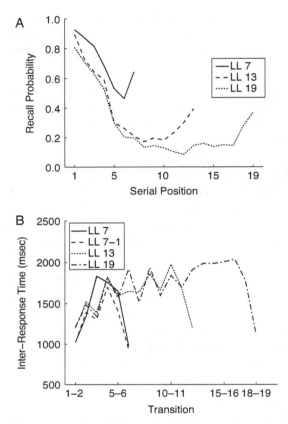

Figure 8.1 Serial-position effects. A. Serial-position curve for recall of 7-word, 13-word, and 19-word lists. **B.** Interresponse times (IRTs, in milliseconds) for transitions between successive recalls are shown for 7-word, 13-word, and 19-word lists (LL = 7, LL = 13, LL = 19). These graphs represent data from an experiment in which participants repeatedly studied each list until they could correctly recall all of the items. The IRTs thus reflect data from all trials on which the lists were correctly recalled. In the case of the 7-word list, data are shown separately for cases where the list was recalled perfectly on the first trial (LL = 7–1), and for all correct recall trials combined (LL = 7). Data from Kahana, Mollison, and Addis (2010).

This suggests that the primacy effect seen in forward serial recall is largely a consequence of the order of recall; that is, by starting recall at the beginning of the list, it is more likely that the recall process will derail or stop before the later list items are recalled. Because successful probed recall depends on participants' memory for the order of the studied items, the rehearsal patterns that tend to favor primacy in free recall (e.g., rehearsing early list items throughout the list) are unlikely to be helpful in serial or probed recall.

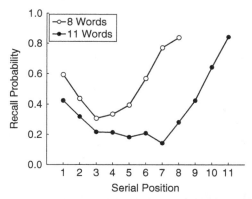

Figure 8.2 Serial-position effects in probed recall. In this scenario, the item that immediately followed the probed item in the study list is recalled. Data from Murdock (1968).

8.3 MODALITY AND SUFFIX EFFECTS: EVIDENCE FOR A PHONOLOGICAL STS?

People exhibit a larger recency effect when recalling auditorily, as compared with visually, presented lists. This modality effect is nicely illustrated in a study by Madigan (1971) that contrasted the modality effect in forward and backward serial recall. Madigan found a large modality effect in forward recall, where auditory presentation specifically enhanced recall of the last few items (Figure 8.3A). In backward serial recall, the modality effect was much smaller; notice how the serial-position curve in backward serial recall is an approximate mirror reversal of the curve in forward recall and similar to that seen in free recall (Figure 8.3B). Although not as large as in forward serial recall, modality effects have been observed in both free- and cued-recall tasks (Penney, 1975, 1989).

The modality effect observed in serial recall can be greatly reduced by ending the list with a single distractor item, or *suffix* (Dallett, 1965). Consider the following experiment: a series of items is presented auditorily and then people attempt to recall the list in order. On half of the trials, the list is immediately followed by a word or a sound that people know they do not have to recall (e.g., the words *now, end,* or *stop*). On the remaining trials, recall is immediate. As shown in Figure 8.4, performance on the recency portion of the serial-position curve is significantly impaired for the suffix lists. This occurs even though people know they will not have to recall the final suffix item. The suffix effect has been observed in many experiments employing a variety of materials, methods, and recall paradigms (e.g., Parkinson, 1978).

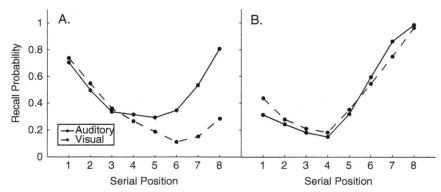

Figure 8.3 Modality effects in forward and backward serial recall. Serial-position curves are plotted for words presented auditorily (solid lines) and visually (dashed lines) for forward recall (**A.**) and backward recall (**B.**). Data from Madigan (1971).

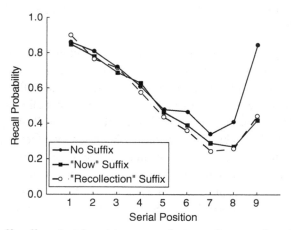

Figure 8.4 Suffix effect. Serial-position curves for immediate serial recall are shown for two suffix conditions (short suffix "now" vs. long suffix "recollection") and a no-suffix control condition. Data from Bloom and Watkins (1999).

Suffix and modality effects, and especially the finding that suffix effects are much larger for auditory than for visual lists (e.g., Greene, 1987), have lent critical support to the view that recency in immediate serial recall reflects the operation of pSTS—a short-term store that maintains a phonological representation of recently experienced items (Greene, 1992; Crowder and

Morton, 1969).[2] In the visual modality, studies of memory for rapidly presented letter arrays led researchers to postulate the existence of a visuospatial short-term store (vSTS).[3] vSTS maintains a relatively intact visual representation for about 1 sec after viewing an image (Averbach and Coriell, 1961; Sperling, 1960). In the auditory modality, similar studies suggested the existence of a pSTS that decays over a longer period (about 3 sec; see Darwin, Turvey, and Crowder [1972]). The preserved phonological representations were assumed to be largely unanalyzed in terms of their meaning or category structure. In a serial-recall task, if people are able to recall the early list items before the representations of the last items decay, the last few items will have an advantage because of the extended duration of echoic memory. The presence of a suffix will partially overwrite the representation of the last list items, making it harder to benefit from the contents of echoic memory.

The modality and suffix effects illustrate dissociations between recency items and prerecency items in the serial-position curve. In our discussion of free recall, we have seen that such dissociations appear even when the temporal spacing of the items is stretched out (as in continual-distractor free recall). Indeed, modality effects have been observed on delayed tests (Watkins and Watkins, 1980), and the suffix effect has been observed after a 20-sec delay (Watkins and Todres, 1980). These findings suggest that there is no fixed time for the operation of pSTS. Furthermore, the size of the suffix effect is particularly sensitive to participants' interpretation of the suffix. For example, if the suffix is interpreted as a nonlinguistic sound, the suffix effect is much smaller than when it is interpreted as a linguistic element (Bloom and Watkins, 1999). This suggests that the operation of pSTS does depend on the meaning of its contents.

8.4 RECALL ERRORS

As in free-recall tasks, participants in serial-recall tasks occasionally commit prior-list and extralist intrusions. In an early study, Melton and Irwin (1940) analyzed the types of errors people made in learning to recall lists of syllables (e.g., GEB, DEZ, MEK, . . . FUP). Participants first learned List 1, then learned List 2, and then relearned List 1. They found that many of the errors in relearning List 1 were intrusions from List 2. Furthermore, these intrusions

---

2. Several terms have been used to describe the type of short-term memory believed to underlie recency effects in immediate serial recall. These terms include *working memory, phonological loop, precategorical acoustic store,* and *echoic memory.* Although these terms have not been used in exactly the same manner, they all pertain to a short-term memory system specialized for processing phonological information.

3. The visuospatial short-term store has also been referred to as iconic memory.

were often syllables from List 2 that were similar to the target syllable on the relearned list *or* syllables from List 2 that came from the same serial position as the target syllable on List 1. If List 1 was the sequence *GEB, DEZ, MEK, VAY, TUD, POZ, NOM, FUP* and List 2 was the sequence *SIV, KUG, HIB, BEZ, HIJ, REB, PIF, VIT*, then upon relearning List 1, participants might recall "*GEB, BEZ, MEK, VAY, TUD, POZ, NOM, FUP,*" where *BEZ* is an intrusion from List 2 that is similar to the correct target *DEZ*, or they might recall "*GEB, BEZ, MEK, VAY, TUD, POZ, PIF, FUP,*" where *PIF* was an item in the seventh position of List 2 (see also Conrad, 1960).

Owing to the requirement that participants recall items in their presentation order, recall of an item in the wrong absolute or relative position would also be considered an error. This highlights an important difference between serial and free recall; in free recall, such errors would be considered correct responses. Here we consider the nature of order errors in serial recall and their interpretation.

8.4.1 Positional Clustering

When a participant recalls list item i in output position $i + lag$ (where $lag \neq 0$), this is referred to as a *transposition error*.[4] A particularly common type of transposition error is one in which two neighboring list items are reversed during recall. For example, if a participant studied the list *house, shoe, tree, car, . . .*, and then recalled "*house, shoe, car, tree, . . .,*" the reversal of *car* and *tree* is a transposition.

As a general rule, when a participant recalls a list item in the wrong position, the item tends to be recalled near the correct target position. The tendency can be seen by calculating the probability of an item i being recalled in position $i + lag$ for each value of lag. One would expect this probability to be highest at lag $= 0$ (representing correct recalls) and to decrease as lag increases. This tendency, which has been termed the *locality constraint*, has been documented extensively in serial-recall tasks. It is seen both in the probability of making transpositions (e.g., Lee and Estes, 1977) and also in the IRTs to making transposition errors (e.g., Farrell and Lewandowsky, 2004). This effect has also been extensively studied in reordering tasks, where following study of a list, participants are presented with the list items in a random order and are asked

---

4. When recalling a list of items, participants may skip several items that they can't remember and continue recalling further along in the list. The omission of the intervening items would lead the subsequent items to be scored as errors unless participants indicate when they know they are skipping items in the sequence. This can be done by having participants say "skip" or "pass", or by having them press a button whenever they know they are skipping an item (or items) during recall of the list.

to rearrange them into the correct order (e.g., Nairne, 1990a, 1990b, 1992). Although the locality constraint becomes less prominent as one increases the retention interval between study and test, the effect persists even after very long retention intervals (Nairne, 1990b).

Because the locality constraint implies that responses in serial recall are clustered around the position of the target item, we will use the term *positional clustering* to describe this phenomenon. The advantage of this term is that it is more easily differentiated from the well-known phenomenon of temporal clustering and from other forms of clustering that may be observed in recall tasks.

Positional clustering (the locality constraint) would be expected if the retrieval cue is a memorial representation of each item's list position. When the positional cue fails to correctly retrieve the appropriate item, it will tend to activate items from neighboring list positions. As such, positional clustering has been one of the major sources of evidence for positional-coding models of serial recall. These models assume that participants associate each item with a positional code and then use the positional codes as a cue to retrieve the items.

The basic positional-clustering result is illustrated in the top row of Figure 8.5, which shows that the probability of recalling an item decreases as a function of distance from the correct position. (For this analysis, one computes the frequency of errors at each lag divided by the frequency at which those errors could be made.) To make this clustering measure concrete, consider the example list *house, shoe, tree, car, . . . boat*. If a participant recalls *house, shoe, tree*, then *tree* is at distance 0 because it appears in the third position both in the list and in the recall sequence. On the other hand, if a participant recalls *house, shoe, car*, then *car* is at distance -1 because it appears one position early in the recall sequence compared to the list. Likewise, *shoe* in the recall sequence *house, tree, shoe* appears one position late and is at distance $+1$.

8.4.2 Temporal Clustering

In free recall we have seen how participants exhibit a strong *temporal-clustering* effect, making transitions among items studied in neighboring list positions. This effect was shown by computing the conditional probability of making a transition between item i and item $i + \text{lag}$ conditional on the possibility that item $i + \text{lag}$ could be recalled at that point (the lag-CRP analysis shown in Figure 6.8).

Applying the lag-CRP analysis to serial recall reveals that order errors are frequently items from list positions near that of the *just recalled item*, regardless of that item's serial position. This temporal-clustering (or contiguity) effect has been demonstrated in many serial-recall experiments (Bhatarah, Ward, and

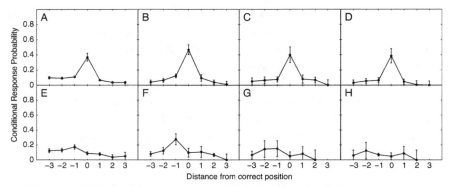

Figure 8.5 Probability of recalling an item as a function of its distance from its correct position. Negative values correspond to recalling an item too early, and positive values correspond to recalling an item too late. Missing data points indicate that the corresponding condition did not occur. Error bars indicate 95% confidence intervals computed using the method of Loftus and Masson (1994). Panels in the top row were computed based on all recalls, while panels in the bottom row were computed based only on recalls following the first order error. Each column is based on data from a different experiment. **A** and **E.** Golomb et al. (2008). **B** and **F.** Kahana and Caplan (2002, Exp. 2). **C** and **G.** Kahana et al. (2010, 13-word lists). **D** and **H.** Kahana et al. (2010, 19-word lists).

Tan, 2006, 2008; Golomb, Peelle, Addis, Kahana, and Wingfield, 2008; Klein et al., 2005). Whereas positional clustering is observed when recalled items cluster around their correct output positions, temporal clustering is observed when recalled items cluster around the position of the just-recalled item.

The top row of Figure 8.6 illustrates the temporal-clustering effect in serial recall. Here, a distance of $+1$ means the item had the same predecessor both in the recall sequence and in the list. A distance of $+2$ means there was one item in the list separating the item and its predecessor, and so on. Negative distances correspond to filling in items that were skipped over earlier in the recall sequence. Finally, a distance of 0 means that an item was repeated twice in a row. This did not occur in the data we analyzed. The probability of seeing an item at each lag was further conditioned on the lag's availability. In addition to revealing a strong contiguity effect, these data also show strong asymmetry effects, with errors in the forward direction being significantly more likely than errors in the backward direction.

8.4.3 Confounds and Interpretive Issues

Our joint findings of strong positional- and temporal-clustering effects may seem surprising given that positional clustering has been associated with

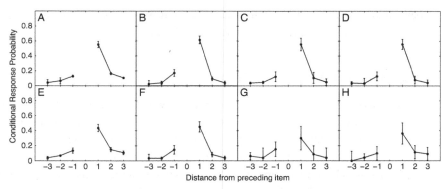

Figure 8.6 Probability of recalling an item as a function of distance from preceding recall. Negative values correspond to recalling an earlier item from the list, while positive values correspond to recalling a later item from the list. Error bars indicate 95% confidence intervals computed using the method of Loftus and Masson (1994). Panels in the top row were computed based on all recalls, while those in the bottom row were computed based only on recalls following the first-order error. Panels are based on the first trial of the studies listed in Figure 8.5.

positional-coding theories of serial recall, and temporal clustering has been associated with associative chaining theories of serial recall. However, it is important to recognize a critical confound in this comparison. Specifically, in most serial-recall studies, the majority of responses appear in their correct output positions. Consider, for instance, the correct recall sequence *house, shoe, tree* from our example list. If the next response is *car*, then its distance from the correct output position is 0 because *car* appears in the fourth list position. Its distance from the preceding response, *tree*, is +1. Correct responses appearing at the beginning of each recall sequence account for the majority of responses made, and they all fall into the 0 bin of the positional-clustering measure and the +1 bin of the temporal-clustering measure.

Fortunately, one can eliminate the confound described above by restricting the clustering analyses to items following the first-order error on each trial (Solway, Murdock, and Kahana, 2012). Positional- and temporal-clustering effects for these items are displayed in the bottom rows of Figures 8.5 and 8.6, respectively. Figure 8.5 shows that the probability of recalling an item no longer decreases as a function of distance from the item's correct position. On the other hand, Figure 8.6 shows that although weaker than before, the contiguity effect is preserved. After making their first-order error, participants tend to pick up with the item that followed the erroneous recall in the list. These analyses reveal that the asymmetrical temporal contiguity effect persists following order errors, whereas the positional-clustering effect collapses. After making an error, participants were most likely to recall the item on the list following the just-recalled item and not the item that appeared in the next position.

8.5 ASSOCIATIVE ASYMMETRY

After studying a list of A_i–B_i pairs, people are typically just as good at recalling B_i given A_i as a cue as they are at recalling A_i given B_i as a cue. This finding led Asch and Ebenholtz (1962) to advocate for the view that associations are stored as holistic representations rather than as ordered sequences of two items. Although retrieval in memory for pairs is approximately symmetric with respect to order of study, we have seen that retrieval in free recall shows marked asymmetries: forward transitions in recall are significantly more frequent than backward transitions. This result is highly robust, with the degree of asymmetry being nearly identical for long and short lists, auditory and visual presentations, and for immediate, delayed, and continual-distractor free recall. Here we consider the question of whether the forward asymmetry observed in free recall is a more general property of memory for sequential information.

Although one can assess associative asymmetry by comparing forward and backward recall performance, this comparison is confounded by the nature of the serial-recall task. Because people begin recall at the start of the list, the number of possible backward transitions following recall of a given item will typically be far smaller than the number of available forward transitions (this is because many more prior items will have already been recalled). One can overcome this problem by using the probed-recall procedure to compare forward and backward recall. In this procedure, participants are given a single randomly chosen item as a cue to recall either its successor or predecessor in the list.

Forward asymmetries appear in probed recall of well-learned sequences. For example, when naming the letter that precedes or follows a probe letter in the alphabet (e.g., what letter precedes/follows D?), backward retrieval is typically 40–60% slower than forward retrieval, with this asymmetry effect especially pronounced toward the end of the alphabet (Klahr et al., 1983; Scharroo et al., 1994). For randomly arranged sequences of words learned in an experimental session, differences between forward and backward recall tend to be small but statistically significant for both auditorily and visually presented sequences (Kahana, 1993; Kahana and Caplan, 2002).

Kahana and Caplan (2002) further examined the question of associative symmetry in a serial-learning experiment. Their participants learned lists of 19 items, presented auditorily, to a perfect recall criterion. Then, after a distractor task, they attempted to recall individual items when cued in either the forward or

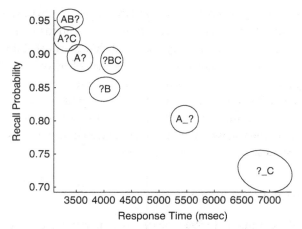

Figure 8.7 Accuracy versus RT for probed recall of serial lists. Cue types are represented by the corresponding symbols in each ellipse (e.g., A? indicates forward-probed recall with a single-item cue; AB? indicates forward-probed recall with a double-item cue). Each ellipse marks the 95% confidence bound around the mean accuracy and the mean RT for the corresponding condition. Data from Kahana and Caplan (2002).

backward order, using either single-item cues or pairs of adjacent items as cues. Their comparison of single-item and compound (i.e., two-item) cues allowed Kahana and Caplan (2002) to ask whether multiple prior items combine to form the cue for the next item.

As shown in Figure 8.7, Kahana and Caplan found higher recall accuracy and faster response times when participants were cued in the forward, as compared with the backward, direction. This forward asymmetry was evident both when participants were cued with a single item (the error ellipses denoted as A?, B?, ?B and ?C) and when participants were cued with a pair of adjacent items (the error ellipses denoted as AB? and ?BC). The asymmetry effect was especially pronounced when participants were cued with a single item to recall the item following or preceding its immediate neighbor (the remote cues denoted as A_? and ?_C).

Kahana and Caplan (2002) also found a significant advantage for compound cuing over single-item cuing. Prior evidence for compound cuing has been obtained in probed recall. For example, Posnansky (1972) cued participants for recall of a given target item in three ways: with a position cue, with the prior item as the cue, or with the prior three items as a cue. Cuing with three prior items sometimes enabled recall even when cuing with a single prior item or position did not.

If the probe item is from position i and the target is from position $i + 1$, people sometimes mistakenly recall either subsequent list items $(i + \text{lag})$ or prior list items $(i - \text{lag})$. Kahana and Caplan found that the probability of incorrectly recalling $i + 2$ is significantly greater than that of incorrectly recalling $i + 3$. Similarly, the probability of incorrectly recalling item $i - 1$ is greater than that of incorrectly recalling item $i - 2$. These error gradients also reveal a forward asymmetry $(i + 2$ is more likely than $i - 1)$. They found that when participants were probed in the backward direction (i.e., given item i and asked to recall item $i - 1$), the same forward asymmetry is obtained.

8.6 GROUPING EFFECTS

Müller and Schumann (1894) observed that practiced participants tend to rhythmically group items during serial learning (see also Müller and Pilzecker [1900]). Because it is difficult to study participants' *grouping* strategies in an unconstrained learning situation, researchers have devised methods to encourage specific grouping strategies whose consequences can be reliably measured. Such experimenter-imposed grouping is typically achieved by inserting pauses at regular intervals during list presentation.

There are four major consequences of experimenter-imposed grouping. First, consistent grouping leads to better serial recall, with the highest levels of recall observed for group sizes of three or four items (Wickelgren, 1967). Second, the grouping effect is largest for auditorily presented lists (Ryan, 1969). Third, transpositions of items in grouped lists tend to preserve the within-group position of the item (Johnson, 1972; Brown et al., 2000). Fourth, people's IRTs during recall are longer at group boundaries (Maybery, Parmentier, and Jones, 2002). As discussed in chapter 9, these and related findings inspired the development of hierarchical associative models that have been applied with great success to data on serial recall (e.g., Estes, 1972; Lee and Estes, 1977; Murdock, 1993, 1997).

Even without imposing grouping experimentally, one can see evidence for grouping processes in people's IRT patterns. Figure 8.8 shows IRT serial-position curves for 19 participants studied by Kahana and Jacobs (2000). Each participant learned lists of 11, 12, or 13 consonants to a perfect recall criterion (for clarity, only the data from the 11-consonant lists are shown; other list lengths exhibited very similar patterns). Because grouping could be idiosyncratic to individual lists, one would only expect to see evidence for grouping in these IRT serial-position curves if the grouping pattern was consistent across lists.

One can see that most of the participants' serial-position curves are not smooth; rather, they exhibit consistent pauses at certain list positions.

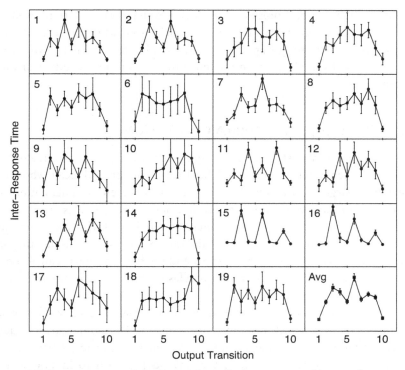

Figure 8.8 Inter-response times in serial recall of consonants. Data are from one of several experimental conditions reported in Kahana and Jacobs (2000). Nineteen participants learned lists of 11, 12, or 13 consonants to a perfect recall criterion. The data come from the 11-consonant condition, with lists containing no repeated items.

These pauses are exactly what one would expect if participants were grouping the items. Consider, for instance, participants 15 and 16 who consistently paused after recalling items 3, 6, and 9 or participants 1, 13, and 19 who consistently paused after recalling items 2, 4, 6, and 8. These IRT serial-position curves are consistent with participants forming groups of either two or three items. The hypothetical process of grouping items, which has been termed *chunking*, may explain how collections of elements become unitized into single-item representations.

The notion of grouping in serial recall is closely related to the idea of *organization* that we discussed in the context of free recall. In both cases, the data suggest that participants' memories are organized according to their similarity along various dimensions. When communicating linguistic information, we naturally group sounds into words, words into phrases and sentences, sentences into paragraphs, etc. Musical compositions also make extensive use of grouping to help communicate to the listener. Grouping processes operate in (visual and auditory) perception to form higher-order representations from more primitive constituents. In the case of serial recall, when there is no obvious basis on which to group the items, people invent their own grouping schemes and exhibit a strong tendency to form groups (chunks) of three or four items.

8.7 SUMMARY AND CURRENT DIRECTIONS

In the serial-recall task, people attempt to recall a sequence of studied items in a constrained order. Most research has focused on forward recall, where people exhibit a large primacy effect and smaller recency effect. This pattern is the opposite of that observed in free recall, where recency effects are much larger than primacy effects. The strong primacy in serial recall is largely a consequence of participants initiating retrieval at the start of the list (we discuss this further in the next chapter). Both the primacy and the recency effects can also be seen in participants' IRTs, which are shorter (faster) both at the beginning and at the end of the list.

The characteristic extended primacy effect and small recency effect observed in serial recall of word lists can also be observed in nonlinguistic sequential behavior in both human and nonhuman primates (Terrace, 2010). A striking example of this can be seen in the way people learn to imitate sequences of motor actions. Agam, Bullock, and Sekuler (2005) asked participants to observe a disc moving along a multisegment trajectory on a computer monitor (Figure 8.9A). After a 4-sec retention interval, participants were asked to reproduce the trajectory using a computer stylus (Panel B) and researchers observed the degree to which the reproduced sequence of movements matched the presented sequence (Panel C).

Agam and colleagues found that the error in the orientation of the first reproduced segment (of the complete path) was around 10–20 degrees and that the error increased with each segment in the series until the last segment, which was typically more accurate than the second to last segment. Their findings, shown in Figure 8.9D, closely resemble the serial-position curve for serial recall of words. Each line in the figure represents sequences of different numbers of segments.

As with other recall tasks, studying participants' errors in serial recall can help us understand the recall process. Intrusion errors reveal that when an item is misremembered, it tends to be misremembered to a nearby list position with a forward bias. Errors also appear to be clustered around the position following that of the previously recalled item. These twin phenomena of positional and temporal clustering can be distinguished by conditioning the analysis of recall errors on whether the prior response was also an error.

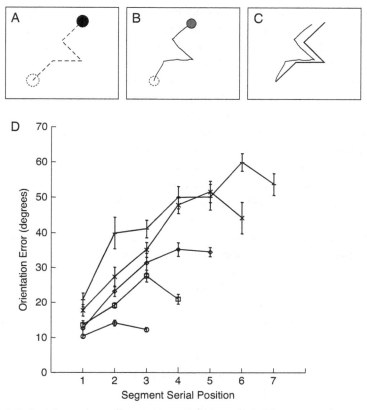

Figure 8.9 Serial-position effects in an imitation task. A. Illustration of a stimulus disc traversing a series of four segments. Open circle represents the starting point of the trajectory. **B.** An example of a participant's attempt to imitate the trajectory shown in A using a stylus on a computer tablet. **C.** Illustration of participant's imitation attempt and the presented stimulus trajectory. This was shown to participants after each trial to provide feedback on the accuracy of their reproduction. **D.** Orientation error for each reproduced segment as a function of serial position and the number of segments in the disc trajectory.

This conditional analysis reveals that errors primarily reflect the type of temporal-clustering phenomena revealed by the lag-CRP analysis of free recall. Prior-list intrusions are rare, but when they happen, they have a greater likelihood of coming from the same position in the prior list as the correct response in the current list. This result points to a role for positional coding in serial recall.

Coding of phonological attributes appears to be particularly important in immediate serial recall, as evidenced by the strong modality and suffix effects.

Recency is enhanced for auditorily presented lists and is easily disrupted by a one-item end-of-list suffix. In addition, recall accuracy depends on the time taken to articulate the words in a list. Lists with items that are phonologically confusable are harder to recall, mainly because of an increase in transposition errors among the acoustically confusable items.

Whereas people can recall meaningful pairs of items equally well in the forward and backward order, recalling longer lists of items reveals a significant forward asymmetry in free-recall, serial-recall and probed-recall tasks. The asymmetry effect in serial recall is particularly strong for auditorily presented lists when the recall direction is known prior to list presentation or when a list has been studied many times in the forward order, as in the alphabet.

A major question that we have not yet addressed concerns the nature of the information being stored in serial-order memory tasks and the way that information is used during recall. The findings discussed above suggest that, to some degree, participants use the just-recalled item as a retrieval cue. Probed-recall studies even suggest that participants may use multiple prior recalls as a cue for recalling the next item. In addition, it seems that positional information may also be used as a retrieval cue. The evidence supporting each of these different types of information will be a major focus of the next chapter.

Whereas early work on serial recall focused on the nature of the associative representations formed during serial learning (see Young, 1968 for a review), most modern research has concentrated on analyzing immediate serial recall of short lists. The analysis of immediate serial recall has highlighted the significant role that phonological coding appears to play in this task. Some researchers see these phonological representations as reflecting the operation of a specialized phonologically based short-term store (referred to here as pSTS, but in the literature this is often referred to as "working memory" or the "phonological loop").

Anyone who has ever administered or participated in a serial-order memory task knows that participants do not recall items as a uniform stream of responses. Rather, participants emit their responses in groups or chunks of items. In the previous section we illustrated this in the IRT serial-position curves from a large study of consonant recall. Although most students of memory recognize that grouping processes are an important characteristic of serial recall, the difficulty in coming up with an objective behavioral measure of grouping makes grouping difficult to study in the laboratory.

In the next chapter we will present the major theories of serial recall and discuss how they fare in explaining the data summarized above. We will also present several additional findings that provide critical tests of those theories.

8.8 STUDY QUESTIONS

1. Describe the major sources of evidence for phonological coding in serial-order memory.
2. Compare the serial-position curve and contiguity effects observed in serial recall and free recall. To what extent are the differences in the data a result of encoding vs. retrieval differences between the two tasks?

9

Theories of Sequence Memory

... The associative threads, which hold together a remembered series, are spun not merely between each member and its immediate successor, but beyond intervening members to every member which stands to it in any close temporal relation. The strength of the threads varies with the distance of the members, but even the weaker of them must be considered as relatively of considerable significance.

Ebbinghaus, *On Memory* (1885) p. 94

Even when the items are exposed successively, a "visually minded" [participant] may assign each item to its place in an imaginary row or column .... Remembering the list consists largely in finding the items in their places.

Woodworth, *Experimental Psychology* (1938) p. 32

The above quotations from Ebbinghaus and Woodworth illustrate the two oldest and still reigning theoretical accounts of how people learn and recall ordered sequences of items: *associative chaining* and *positional coding*. We thus begin our discussion of theories of sequence memory by describing these two classical models. In evaluating the models' ability to explain data on serial-order memory, we present eight major findings that provide critical tests of those two theories. We conclude the chapter with a discussion of *hierarchical associative theory* (also known as *chunking theory*).

9.1 ASSOCIATIVE CHAINING

Associative-chaining theory states that each item in a list is linked to its neighbors, with stronger associations going in the forward direction than in the backward direction (Figure 9.1). In this way, retrieval of the first item in the list facilitates retrieval of the second, and the second facilitates retrieval of the third, and so forth. One can use these associations to chain either forward or backward through the sequence.

The hypothesis that the mental representation of an item becomes directly associated with the immediately preceding and following items is central to many models of sequence memory (Lewandowsky and Murdock, 1989; Wickelgren, 1966; Sompolinsky and Kanter, 1986; Kleinfeld, 1986; Riedel, Kühn, and van Hemmen, 1988). As discussed in chapter 1, the notion of chained associations in which recall of an item in a sequential list facilitates recall of the next item formed the cornerstone of Ebbinghaus' (1885) classic work on memory for sequences.

According to early views of associative chaining, each association was seen as a forward-going link between neighboring items that was strengthened by repetition. Recall proceeds by cuing with the first list item and chaining forward through the list. (Later we will discuss the question of how one might get the chain started when the first item is not explicitly given as the cue to recall.)

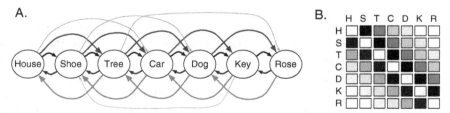

Figure 9.1 Associative chaining. A. Traditional depiction of the associative structures formed according to chaining theory, where darker and thicker arrows indicate stronger associations formed between neighboring list items. Forward associations are often assumed to be stronger than backward associations. **B.** Matrix representation of the associative structures formed during encoding. Darker boxes indicate stronger associations. Lower diagonal cells represent forward associations; upper diagonal cells represent backward associations. Items are indicated by the first letter of each word in the list (cf. Figure 7.1).

One can formalize the idea of chaining either in a SAM-type strength model or in a vector-based neural-network model. In a strength-based chaining model, a single value would characterize the strength of the association between items in list positions j and k. In a network model, the associative strength between neighboring items would be represented in a matrix of weights. Here we will focus first on the SAM-type strength formalism because it serves to illustrate the basic principles and because it allows us to draw on what we have learned in chapter 7. We will later show how one can implement the same ideas in a vector or neural-network model.

9.1.1 Strength Model of Associative Chaining

Let us define the strength of an association between items studied in positions j and k as $S(j, k)$. A pure nearest-neighbor chaining model predicts that studying item k increases both the forward association strength $S(k - 1, k)$ and the backward association strength $S(k, k - 1)$. A more general version of chaining would allow for remote associations, with nearest-neighbor associations being strongest, but with associations becoming progressively weaker as the lag between items increases. That is, $S(k, k + 1) > S(k, k + 2) > S(k, k + 3)$, where the strengths of the associations are often assumed to fall off exponentially with increasing lag. We refer to this generalized model as the *strength model of associative chaining (SMAC)* (Addis, 2004). A similar assumption of remote associations is embodied in the search of associative memory (SAM) model discussed in chapter 7. SAM predicts an exponential fall off in the strength of interitem associations with increasing lag because nearby items spend more time together in STS. The temporal context model (TCM) also implies exponentially graded remote associations, but for very different reasons (see chapter 7).

To use chained associations to recall a list in forward order one must first initiate the recall process by recalling the first list item. It's not clear how to do this in SMAC or any of the other recall models discussed so far. In SAM, recall begins by reporting the contents of STS, but these primarily consist of end-of-list items. In TCM, recall begins by cuing memory with time-of-test context, which will also tend to activate end-of-list items. One could hypothesize that in serial recall, participants pay a great deal of attention to the first list item and then use an attentional gain mechanism (as in TCM) to account for recall initiation. Another approach is to assume that the first item is maintained in an active state until the time of recall. Although neither of these approaches is entirely satisfactory, we can at least separate the recall problem into two components: initiation and transition. SMAC is then a model of recall transitions rather than recall initiation.

Once we have recalled the first list item, we can go to the next stage of the memory search process using the just-recalled item as a cue for the next item. Cuing with the first list item will tend to retrieve the second list item. This is because the associative strength between the first and second list items is greater than the associative strength between the first list item and any other item. As in SAM, it makes sense to strengthen the associations during recall as well as during encoding. This means that when learning a list over multiple study-test trials, both the correct responses and the errors made on the previous trials will be further reinforced in memory.

In a probed-recall task, given item k as a cue, participants are better at recalling item $k + 1$ than item $k - 1$ (Kahana and Caplan, 2002). This effect is even larger when participants are cued with two adjacent items, as in the pair, k, $k + 1$, as a cue for either item $k + 2$ (forward probe) or item $k - 1$ (backward probe). One also sees this forward-recall asymmetry in the free-recall task, where recall of item k is more likely to be followed by recall of item $k + 1$ than by recall of item $k - 1$.[1] In SMAC one can define separate learning rates for forward and backward associations to simulate the forward-recall advantage normally seen in recall tasks.

9.1.2 Network Models of Associative Chaining

It is straightforward to construct a chaining model based on the neural-network theory presented in chapter 5. Assuming that items are represented as vectors of attribute values, we can denote the kth list item as $\mathbf{m}_k$. If the representation of $\mathbf{m}_k$ can be maintained until the presentation of $\mathbf{m}_{k+1}$, then we could store the association between them by forming bidirectional Hebbian weight matrices according to the equation:

$$W(i, j) = \mathbf{m}_k(i)\mathbf{m}_{k+1}(j) + \mathbf{m}_{k+1}(i)\mathbf{m}_k(j).$$

In matrix notation, we can write this more simply as:

$$W = \mathbf{m}_k\mathbf{m}_{k+1}^\top + \mathbf{m}_{k+1}\mathbf{m}_k^\top.$$

Suppose that we can somehow set the state vector of the network to $\mathbf{m}_1$, the vector representation of the first list item. In that case, applying the dynamical rule (see section 5.2.1) would cause the network activation to evolve toward $\mathbf{m}_2$. Assuming that $\mathbf{m}_2$ is successfully recovered, the network would then tend to

1. Individual word pairs do not exhibit this forward asymmetry. Rather, they are equally well recalled in the forward and backward directions (Kahana, 2002).

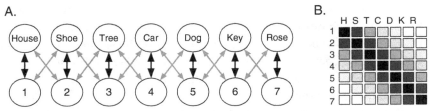

Figure 9.2 Positional coding. A. Traditional depiction of the associative structures formed according to positional coding theory. Numbers indicate positional representations in memory, with 1 indicating the position of the first item and 7 indicating the position of the last item. **B.** Matrix representation of the associative structures formed during encoding. Darker boxes indicate stronger associations between positional codes (indexed across rows) and items in memory (indexed across columns). Items are indicated by the first letter of each word in the list (cf. Figure 7.1).

evolve either back to m_1 or forward to m_3. This is known as the target-ambiguity problem (see Kahana and Caplan, 2002). One can resolve this ambiguity by introducing a temporary suppression (or inhibition) mechanism for recalled items. By biasing the network away from retrieving already-recalled patterns, one can prevent the network from repeatedly cycling between already recalled items. On the other hand, such a mechanism will make it more difficult to recall lists with repeated items, an issue that we will return to in section 9.3.5.

9.2 POSITIONAL CODING

According to *positional-coding* theory, participants associate each list item with a representation of the item's position in the input sequence. The first item is linked most strongly to the Position 1 marker, the second to the Position 2 marker, and so forth (Figure 9.2). The term *positional coding* implies a spatial representation of a temporal series, as described in Woodworth's quote at the start of this chapter. One can imagine that when faced with the challenge of learning a list in order, participants might use a spatial strategy, imagining the items arrayed before them on a table or perhaps imagining themselves learning each item at a different sequential location along a familiar route.[2] But the idea of positional coding here implies an automatic (nonstrategic) process whereby each item is learned by associating it with its relative position within the list.

During recall, items do not cue each other. Rather, cuing with an item's position will tend to retrieve the item, and cuing with an item will tend to

2. The latter strategy is a well-known mnemonic technique called the *method of loci.*

retrieve its position. By sequentially cuing memory with each of the position markers, one can recall the items in either forward or backward order. Unlike chaining, which uses the items and the associations between them to support learning and recall, positional coding assumes that participants represent the ordinal position of each item and that they can use these positional codes to cue item recall.

Positional-coding theory was articulated by Ladd and Woodworth (1911) wherein it was assumed that positional coding worked in conjunction with associative chaining (see Crowder, 1976, for a review of this early work). The major early evidence in favor of this view came from Melton and Irwin's (1940) observation that intrusions of items presented on prior lists tend to have been from positions near that of the correct response on the current list (see also Conrad, 1960; Henson, 1998).

9.2.1 Strength Model of Positional Coding

Let us consider a simple strength-based model of positional coding. In such a model, we may denote the strength of the association between the ith item and the jth position as $S(i, p_j)$. As the list is presented, we then increment $S(i, p_i)$ for each item i. We also allow for the possibility of weaker associations between items and neighboring positions. Thus, we might increment $S(i, p_{i-k})$ and $S(i, p_{i+k})$ by an amount that decreases sharply as k increases. One common assumption is that the strength of associations decreases exponentially with k.

At test, we would cue with position p_j and retrieve one of the list items in proportion to the strength of its association with position p_j. A key difference between chaining and positional-coding models is that in the positional model, you can easily continue cuing memory after a retrieval failure because you can always increment the positional cue. Whereas in the chaining model, a failure to make a transition means that you must rely on the weak remote associations rather than the strong nearest-neighbor association for the next recall.

9.2.2 Network Model of Positional Coding

To construct a neural-network implementation of positional coding, we first need to specify a vector representation for positional codes. This could be accomplished in a manner analogous to the way we modeled temporal context, where temporal context is a vector that gradually drifts over the course of list presentation. Alternatively, we could simply define two vectors of random elements—one vector representing the beginning of the list $\mathbf{p}_1$ and one representing the end of the list $\mathbf{p}_L$. Each interior position $\mathbf{p}_j$ would be defined as the weighted average of these two vectors, with interior positions close to the start of the list weighted more heavily toward $\mathbf{p}_1$ and interior positions close to the end of the list weighted more heavily toward $\mathbf{p}_L$.

To implement a positional-coding neural-network model, we would simply modify the neural-network model of paired-associate memory (see chapter 5, Cued Recall in a Hopfield Network) to learn the associations between position vectors, $\mathbf{p}_j$, and item vectors, $\mathbf{m}_i$. As long as one could somehow cue memory with each successive position, the network would recall the series of items in the studied list.

At the end of this chapter we will discuss a third major class of models called *hierarchical associative models* or *chunking models*. Chunking models are based on the idea that participants learn sequences of items by creating strong associative links among small groups of neighboring items, called chunks, where the size of a chunk is typically around three or four items. For example, in learning an American telephone number, people typically group the digits into subsequences of three and four numbers. Chunking models say that the associative processes that govern recall within a chunk are different from those that govern the transitions between chunks. Before turning to chunking models, we present eight critical experimental findings that have been used to argue for and against chaining and positional-coding theories.

9.3 EIGHT CRITICAL FINDINGS

9.3.1 Transfer and Probe Studies

Early efforts to distinguish chaining and positional-coding accounts of serial recall relied on the classic transfer-of-training method introduced by Ebbinghaus. In these studies, participants first learned List 1 to a criterion level of performance, and then they learned List 2. To the extent that Lists 1 and 2 possess the same item and order information, List 2 learning should be enhanced. For example, if List 2 is the same as List 1, it will be learned very quickly. Alternatively, if List 2 is a scrambled version of List 1, it will be learned slowly. The term *transfer* is used to describe the degree to which knowledge acquired in learning List 1 facilitates learning of List 2. If List 1 learning facilitates List 2 learning relative to some control, it is said that there is significant positive transfer. If List 1 learning impairs List 2 learning, it is said that there is negative transfer.

Suppose that List 1 consists of the items $A_1, A_2, \ldots, A_L$ and that these items are learned to a perfect serial-recall criterion. According to chaining theory, we should find substantial positive transfer if List 2 is composed of paired associates taken from adjacent items in List 1, as in the list of pairs $A_5-A_6, A_1-A_2,$ A_7-A_8, etc. Indeed, if chaining relied solely on nearest-neighbor associations, one would expect participants to be able to recall these pairs perfectly unless they had forgotten the List 1 sequence by the time of the List 2 paired-associate test. Although positive transfer is significant under these conditions, especially on the first few trials of List 2 learning, it is far less than would be expected according to a chaining account. These data suggest that in serial recall, the cue for a given item is not simply the prior item (Young, 1968).

Researchers have also used the transfer method to test positional-coding theory. In this case, List 2 would comprise position-item pairs rather than adjacent-item pairs. For example, after learning the sequence $A_1, A_2, \ldots, A_L$ to a criterion of perfect recall, participants would be asked to learn the list $2-A_2$, $1-A_1$, $4-A_4$, $3-A_3$, etc., where the positional index may either be presented as a numeral or as a spatial position (Ebenholtz, 1963b). According to positional-coding theory, participants should have little problem recalling these pairs, even after a single exposure. This is because positional-coding theory envisions participants learning the mapping between the positions $1, \ldots, L$ and the items $A_1, \ldots, A_L$ during study of List 1. Here again, the data show significant positive transfer but far less than would be expected on the basis of pure positional theory (Young, 1968).

Woodward and Murdock (1968) used the probe-recall method to help distinguish between chaining and positional-coding theories. They gave participants a fixed number of presentations of a serial list and then tested their memory for a single item, either by probing with the preceding item (termed a sequential probe) or by probing with the position of the target item (termed a positional probe). Although participants were well above chance at recalling items using either sequential or positional probes, Woodward and Murdock failed to find any difference between the effectiveness of these two probe types. Overall, these data suggest that sequence learning involves more than either simple chaining or positional coding (see also Giurintano, 1973; Jensen and Rohwer, 1965).

The strength of the conclusions drawn from these transfer and probe studies depends crucially on the degree to which hypothesized internal positional codes can be mapped onto the numerical or positional cues used in these studies. In the case of associative chaining, if the internal associative cue includes multiple preceding items (rather than just one), the degree of transfer obtained in these experiments would be significantly reduced.

9.3.2 Serial-position Effects

According to chaining theory, recall of a given item, A_k, depends on the successful recall of A_{k-1}, which in turn depends on the successful recall of A_{k-2}, etc. If each transition succeeds with probability p, the probability of recalling the kth item will be p^k. Thus, the chaining model predicts that the probability of recalling an item will decrease geometrically from the beginning to the end of the list in forward recall and from the end to the beginning of the list in backward recall. The model does not predict any recency in forward recall or any primacy in backward recall.

In contrast, positional-coding theory predicts a symmetric serial-position curve with small primacy and recency effects. Because positional codes of nearby items are similar to one another, probing with an item in the middle of the list will retrieve mostly the target item and, to a lesser extent, its neighbors. The probability of recalling an item is thus reduced by competition from items in neighboring positions. This interference effect operates less for terminal list items because these items suffer less competition by having neighbors on only one side.

Some positional-coding models assume that participants pay more attention to early list items and thereby increase the primacy effect predicted by the model (an assumption shared with TCM; see section 7.4). Because participants know that they need to start with the beginning of the list, it may seem reasonable to assume that they adopt such a strategy. The problem with this assumption is that backward recall exhibits strong recency and forward recall exhibits strong primacy, even when participants do not know whether they will get a forward- or backward-recall task (Hinrichs, 1968).

9.3.3 Positional Clustering

Both chaining and positional-coding models can account for the tendency of misplaced items to be recalled close to their correct position (this is the positional-clustering effect shown in Figure 8.5). Positional-coding models predict positional-clustering effects because a given item will be more strongly associated with nearby positional codes than with distant positional codes. Chaining models produce positional clustering because of remote associations. For example, the fifth list item will be most strongly associated with the sixth item, but its association with the seventh item will be stronger than its association with the eighth item. If recall is probabilistic, as in the SAM model, the stronger the association, the more likely the transition. Thus, if the sixth item is not recalled, errors are likely to be items studied in neighboring positions.

Traditionally, positional clustering has been taken as one of the major sources of evidence for positional-coding models. However, as we have shown in section 8.4.3, positional-clustering effects are barely detectable when you consider responses that follow errors. This implies that the clustering effect is largely dependent on the accuracy of the prior response, which is exactly what you would predict on the basis of chaining theory.

9.3.4 Temporal Clustering

Temporal clustering is another term for the contiguity effect—the tendency to make recall transitions among neighboring items. In the free-recall task, successive recalled items are most likely to be from neighboring serial positions and they tend to be recalled in the forward order (e.g., recall of item from serial position k followed by recall of item from serial position $k + 1$). The same is true in the serial-recall task.

Chaining models naturally predict this result and further predict a tendency for (transposition) errors in serial recall to be items studied in nearby serial positions. That is, these models predict a higher conditional probability of transitions between items k and $k + 2$ than between items k and $k + 3$ or k and $k + 4$, etc. As discussed in chapter 8, this pattern is consistently observed in free-recall, serial-recall, and serial-learning experiments. The same predictions are made by the SAM and TCM models of free recall.

Most positional-coding models only predict temporal clustering if the first of the two successively recalled items was recalled in the correct output position. Otherwise, these models predict that responses should not specifically depend on the nature of the prior response, except insofar as the previously recalled items tend not to be repeated during recall (due to *response suppression*, as discussed later in this chapter). Contrary to these positional-coding models, temporal clustering in serial recall appears strongly even when the first of the two successively recalled items was recalled in the wrong output position (see Figure 8.6). One possible way of modifying positional coding theory to account for this effect is to allow for the prior response to influence the positional code used to cue the next item. Such a modification might follow the lines of the retrieved context models of free recall discussed in chapter 7.

9.3.5 The Ranschburg Effect

Ranschburg (1902)[3] reported that sequences of items containing a repeated element are harder to reproduce than sequences consisting of all unique elements. For example, the sequence *house, shoe, tree, car, dog, tree, rose* would be harder to recall in order than the sequence *house, shoe, tree, car, dog, key, rose.*

Crowder and Melton (1965) noted the importance of this finding for testing the predictions of associative-chaining models. According to chaining theory, the presence of repeated elements should impair successful recall of a series

---

3. Paul Ranschburg (1870–1945) was a noted Hungarian psychologist and neurologist who made major contributions to a wide range of problems in perception, memory, and neuropsychology. He died during the German occupation of Budapest in January 1945.

because recall of an item would cue not only its successor but the successor of all of the repetitions of that list item. More specifically, chaining theory predicts that recall should be impaired for the items *following* the repeated items but not for the repeated items themselves. For the list *house, shoe, tree, car, dog, tree, rose*, recall of *house* would cue *shoe*, which in turn would cue *tree*. Because *tree* is associated with both *car* and *rose*, cuing with *tree* will prompt a competition between recall of *rose* and *car*. We would thus expect to observe impaired recall of the items following *tree*.

Crowder, and later Jahnke, examined this prediction by looking at error rates for individual list elements (Crowder, 1968; Jahnke, 1969b, 1969a, 1970, 1972). They found that spaced repetition of list items resulted in impaired recall only for the second instance of the repeated item (as compared with a control list that has all unique items).[4] Contrary to the predictions of chaining theory, recall of the items following the repeated items was not impaired. The failure to find associative interference in the Ranschburg paradigm has been a source of embarrassment for the associative-chaining theory of serial recall.

Positional-coding theory also fails to predict the Ranschburg effect. If each list item is associated with a positional code, p_j, as described above, then the list given above would be represented by the associative strength matrix $S(i, p_j)$. In the example given above, p_3 and p_6 would be associated with the first and second presentations of *tree*, respectively. Because the positional cues are distinct, the effectiveness of p_3 as a cue for the first presentation of *tree* is not affected by the association between p_6 and the second presentation of *tree* any more than it would be affected by the association between p_6 and some unrelated item. The same argument applies to p_6 cuing *tree*. In essence, the similarity among the positional cues is the same regardless of whether they are associated with identical or distinct target items. For this reason, positional coding cannot, by itself, explain the Ranschburg effect. This is not only true for the simple positional model described here; even sophisticated modern variants of positional-coding theory (e.g., Burgess and Hitch, 1999) have difficulties explaining the Ranschburg effect.

How then might we explain the Ranschburg effect? According to one prominent account, recalled items are temporarily inhibited, making them difficult to recall for a period of time. This *response-inhibition account* (Jahnke, 1969a) fits naturally within the framework of neural-network models, which need this type of inhibition to prevent the network from reactivating

---

4. For items repeated successively, participants were actually better at recalling both repeated items, with recall of the remaining list being unaffected.

already-recalled items (e.g., Burgess and Hitch, 1999).[5] Still, more research is needed to determine whether this account is correct.

Associative chaining theory counterfactually predicts that recall errors will be most frequent following the recall of a repeated item. One can potentially eliminate this prediction, however, by allowing for compound cuing in recall (Kahana and Caplan, 2002; Kahana et al., 2007). Specifically, in the case of the list *house, shoe, tree, car, dog, tree, rose*, one could easily imagine that the entire sequence *house, shoe, tree* acts as a cue for *car* (rather than the repeated *tree* serving as the sole cue for *car*). In this case, including *house* and *shoe* in the cue should allow the model to bridge over a short segment of associative ambiguity.

9.3.6 Phonological Similarity Effects

It is well established that sequences of phonologically similar items, such as *rough, tough,* and *muff,* are more difficult to serially recall than sequences whose items are phonologically dissimilar (Conrad and Hull, 1964; M. J. Watkins, Watkins, and Crowder, 1974). Sequences of semantically related items (e.g., *diamond, ruby,* and *emerald*) are also harder to recall serially. Yet, these sequences are not as difficult to recall as phonologically similar sequences (Shulman, 1971). Free recall exhibits the opposite pattern, with high-similarity lists resulting in higher levels of recall, at least for the prerecency positions (Crowder, 1979). As noted by Murdock and Saal (1967), similarity results in better access to the items in a list but worse memory for the order in which the words were presented.

Similarity effects can be explained by either chaining or positional-coding theory. According to chaining theory, lists with similar items (phonological or otherwise) pose difficulties for two reasons. First, a cue item can be confused with another list item and thereby evoke the wrong response. Second, even if

5. Greene (1991) suggested that a guessing strategy might account for the Ranschburg impairment. Many Ranschburg experiments use lists consisting of 8–10 digits. With a list of 10 digits, the participant knows exactly which elements are on the list. The task, then, is to learn the positions of those elements. For lists of eight or nine digits, there is very little uncertainty over the set of items in the list—the main uncertainty is over the assignment of items to serial positions. (In some studies employing consonants as list items, all of the items were sampled from a fixed set of 12 consonants. See for example, Crowder [1968]). Kahana and Jacobs (2000) tested this guessing account by having participants learn lists of consonants to a criterion of one perfect recall. They were able to show the classic Ranschburg pattern of results in participants' IRTs (as well as in their error rates). Specifically, participants' IRTs to recall the repeated item were faster when the repeats were massed but slower when the repeats were spaced. Given that participants were not making any errors and the Ranschburg pattern was still observed, this rules out Greene's guessing account.

there is no confusion among the cues, there can be confusion among the targets they evoke. In the presence of noise, a partially retrieved target can be confused with a similar list item. Positional models would not suffer from the interference among the cues because the cues are distinct positions rather than items. These models would predict interference among the targets and could explain the phenomenon on that basis.

Baddeley (1968) examined serial recall of *alternating-similarity* lists; that is, the even (or odd) items were phonologically similar to one another, with the remaining items being phonologically dissimilar. For example, the alternating-similarity lists might be composed of the consonants *TJBMVQD* or *QDMVYTJ*. As a control condition, participants also studied a list consisting of phonologically dissimilar items such as *HJMRYQV*.

Both chaining and positional-coding theories predict superior performance for the nonconfusable (control) lists and inferior performance for the confusable ones, as was observed experimentally (Baddeley, 1968; Henson, Norris, Page, and Baddeley, 1996). Chaining theory, however, makes a specific prediction about the kinds of errors that should be observed in the alternating-list condition. Recall of the confusable item, *T*, in the list *TJBMVQD* should lead to a competition among the nonconfusable items *J*, *M*, and *Q*, thus leading to transposition errors in recall. The logic here is the same as in the studies of the Ranschburg effect, where one expects to see errors following the repeated items because of associative competition. In contrast, recall of the nonconfusable item, *J*, should provide a much less ambiguous cue for *B*. However, in that case, one would expect some competition in the retrieval process because a noisy retrieved representation of *B* may lead to recall of the confusable items *V* or *D*.

Positional-coding theory makes a very different prediction. Because the cue to recall an item is not the preceding item but rather the position in the list, the confusability of the just-recalled item is irrelevant. Instead, all that matters is the confusability of the targets. Thus, one should expect to find that most errors result from transpositions of the confusable items; relatively few transpositions should be observed for the nonconfusable items.

Contrary to chaining theory, Baddeley (1968) found impaired recall only for the confusable items. Recall of the nonconfusable items was relatively unaffected by the presence of confusable items in the list.[6] These findings were replicated in a more thorough analysis of the phenomenon reported by Henson et al. (1996). Serial-position curves from one of Henson's experiments are shown in Figure 9.3.

---

6. In some studies, these items were actually better remembered than control items (Farrell and Lewandowsky, 2003; Farrell, 2006).

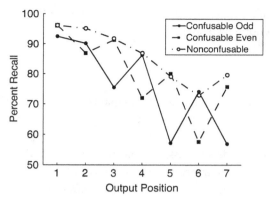

Figure 9.3 Impaired recall for confusable items. Serial-position curves for nonconfusable items (open circles) and for alternating sequences of confusable and nonconfusable, with confusable items in positions 1, 3, 5, and 7 (filled circles) or in positions 2, 4, and 6 (squares). Data from Experiment 2 of Henson et al. (1996).

Some have used the findings shown in Figure 9.3 to argue that chaining is untenable. For example, in a widely cited paper, Botvinick and Plaut (2006) wrote that "... although it was long considered a possibility that short-term memory for serial order might be based on chaining, subsequent empirical work has succeeded in conclusively ruling out this hypothesis. The critical observation was made by Baddeley" (1968; see also Bjork and Healy, 1974; Henson et al., 1996). Before subscribing to their extreme view, one should consider several limitations to the Baddeley-Henson analysis. First, chaining theories can rely on remote associations to overcome the associative interference (McGeoch, 1936; Young, 1962; Horowitz and Izawa, 1963). Second, Baddeley and Henson's methods likely encouraged a positional-coding strategy. The lists were short (six or seven, depending on the group of participants tested) and always consisted of the same number of items. In the studies that showed the strongest results, participants were instructed to write one letter in each box of a row of six (or seven) provided on a response sheet. In the one experiment that used spoken recall, participants were told to use a filler response (the word *blank*) when they could not recall one of the target items. A more diagnostic test of the chaining theory would involve testing memory for longer sequences of items in which segments of multiple confusable items precede a nonconfusable item. Such a test has not been conducted at the time of this writing.

Whereas the Ranschburg effect and the sandwich experiments are particu-larly problematic for chaining theory, there are other phenomena that are more readily explained by chaining than by positional-coding models. We consider two such phenomena below.

9.3.7 Part-Set Cuing

Serra and Nairne (2000) asked participants to study a series of eight items. Then, following a brief distractor period, participants were shown the eight studied items in a scrambled order alongside an eight-position response array. In a standard reordering task, people would be asked to place each of the studied items into their proper positions as indicated by the placeholders in the response array. In the part-set cuing version of this task, people were only asked to fill in four of the placeholders in the response array. Three different conditions determined what information would be given in the remaining four positions in the response array. In a first (*control*) condition, these positions were demarcated by a plus sign, providing no information about what items belonged in those positions. In a second (*congruent*) condition, these positions were filled with the correct ordering of items from the study list. In a third (*incongruent*) condition, these positions were filled with the remaining items but in a random order.

According to a strict positional-coding account, the positions of the items serve as cues for the correct responses, and the presence of the other items should not have any effect. According to an associative chaining account, the presence of the other items in the congruent condition would help cue the recall of the items in the remaining positions. In the incongruent condition, the inclusion of these other items would hurt performance. Serra and Nairne found that performance in the congruent condition was consistently better than in the control condition. Conversely, performance in the incongruent condition was significantly worse. This finding suggests that participants do use information about the sequential dependency between items in reordering tasks, and it is likely that the same information is also used to some extent in serial recall.

9.3.8 Spin Lists

Evidence against pure positional-coding theory comes from the analysis of *spin lists*. Consider the task of learning a list of ~15 words over multiple study-test trials. The usual method used in studies of serial learning is to present a list for study, then ask for immediate serial recall, and then repeat this study-test process until the participant attains a criterion of one perfect recitation.

Now, consider a variant of this procedure in which a single list is presented on each trial starting at a randomly chosen position (Ebenholtz, 1963a). To see how this works, imagine that the list is arranged along a circle, such that the last item is followed by the first item. In this case, you can really start anywhere; there is no beginning or end of the sequence. To make things concrete, the participant might study the sequence *house, shoe, tree, car, dog, key, rose* on Trial 1, the sequence *dog, key, rose, house, shoe, tree* on Trial 2, and the sequence *shoe, tree, car, dog, key, rose, house* on Trial 3.

If one accepts at face value the strong claim that chained associations are not operative in serial recall, and if one further accepts the view that most of serial learning reflects the storage and retrieval of position-to-item associations, then one must wonder how people could ever learn a sequence of items when the starting position varies randomly from trial to trial, as in the spin-list paradigm. Unless participants master such lists on their first study trial, it is hard to imagine how such spin lists could be learned. If, however, associations are formed among neighboring items, as posited by chaining theory, then participants should find spin lists only slightly more difficult to learn than standard (linear) lists, which start at the same point on each trial.

Comparing performance on spin lists with performance on constant starting-position (linear) control lists would indicate the *degree* to which non-positional cues contribute to serial learning. In the extreme case where learning is equivalent under the two conditions, one might reasonably conclude that positional cues do not play a role in serial learning (at least under these conditions).

The data show that participants are able to learn spin lists without great difficulty. Although spin lists are somewhat harder to learn than linear ones, the difference in learning rates is not dramatic (Ebenholtz, 1963a; Bowman and Thurlow, 1963) and can be minimal when participants are aware of the spin structure of the lists (Winnick and Dornbush, 1963). This can be seen in Figure 9.4, which shows serial-position curves from a study by Kahana et al. (2010). The differences in learning rates are much smaller than would be predicted by a strict positional theory but larger than predicted by a strict chaining theory. Furthermore, the modest impairment in learning spin lists stems largely from participants' tendency to commit errors in recall initiation, as would be expected if there is interference between the remembered starting positions on different trials. One could interpret these data as supporting the view that participants make use of both interitem associations and position-to-item associations in serial learning.

9.4 CHAINING VS. POSITIONAL CODING

The chaining hypothesis of serial-order memory has been called into question primarily because of findings obtained with lists that contain repeated or similar items (e.g., Figure 9.3). Because repetitions are inherent in most situations

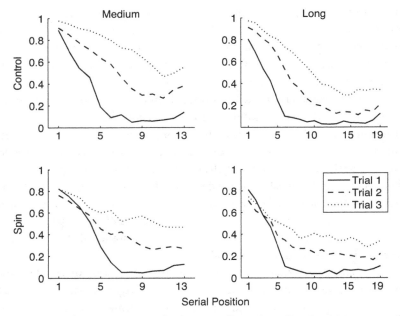

Figure 9.4 Serial-position curves for linear and spin lists. Serial-position curves for learning trials 1–3 of lists presented with constant starting positions (linear lists, top row), or with varied starting positions (spin lists, bottom row). Left panels: list length = 13; right panels: list length = 19. Data from Kahana et al. (2010).

where order memory is required (music, language, motor skills), it has been argued that nearest-neighbor chaining is an inadequate model for serial-order phenomena (Lashley, 1951).

Transfer studies give no conclusive answers but suggest that neither a pure positional-coding nor a pure chaining account is sufficient to explain the data. The Nairne and Serra study points to some role for associative chaining, but their use of a reordering task raises questions about whether the results would also apply to more standard measures of serial recall and serial learning. The spin-list studies reveal the limitations of both pure chaining and pure positional-coding models. These studies suggest that when positional cues are not informative, participants can make use of interitem associative cues (e.g., chaining) to master serial lists.

Chaining models provide a natural account of the primacy effect seen in forward recall and the recency effect seen in backward recall. But chaining models cannot explain the small recency effect seen in forward recall or the small primacy effect seen in backward recall. Positional models can explain both primacy and recency, but they have trouble explaining why primacy is so much larger in forward recall and why recency is so much larger in backward recall. These results are obtained even when participants do not know whether they are to recall the list in forward or backward order until after list presentation (Hinrichs, 1968).

From this evidence it is unlikely that either a pure chaining or a pure positional-coding model can account for the major data on serial recall. This point was recognized long ago by Robert K. Young, an influential scholar of serial-order memory. In a review of the state of research at that time, Young (1968) wrote, "The serial list, following learning, is a highly organized group of items which are related to one another through a chain of associations, through associations between ordinal positions and items or through something else entirely." These observations raise the question of whether a hybrid chaining-positional-coding model is sufficient or whether a completely different model is necessary. So far, there has not been a serious effort to develop such a hybrid model of serial recall. Many details would need to be worked out in developing such a model, but I think it is a promising direction to pursue.

9.5 HIERARCHICAL ASSOCIATIVE THEORY

Hierarchical associative models, or chunking models, are based on the idea that sequences have natural breakpoints dividing the list into smaller parts, or *chunks*. Chunking models envision a hierarchy of associations, with lower levels of the hierarchy representing more elementary attributes and higher levels representing more abstract structures (Anderson and Matessa, 1997; Anderson, Bothell, Lebiere, and Matessa, 1998; Johnson, 1972; Lee and Estes, 1977; Martin and Noreen, 1974; Murdock, 1995, 1997).

Rather than directly associating neighboring items, as envisioned by chaining or buffer models (e.g., SAM), chunking models assert that multiple items can become unitized into a new abstract representation that is distinct from any of the constituent items. Retrieving this abstract, or *superordinate*, representation then provides access to the items within the chunk. An item, in turn, can be used to retrieve the superordinate representation that, in turn, can retrieve the other items associated with it. This kind of hierarchical associative structure is illustrated in Figure 9.5.

As appealing as the idea of chunking is, it is actually difficult to prove that participants form chunks because the idea of a chunk is largely based on participants' behavior and not on the structure of the list itself. Nonetheless, there is considerable evidence for grouping effects in serial recall (see section 8.6) and these effects can be neatly described within the framework

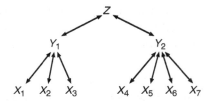

Figure 9.5 Illustration of the hierarchical association theory. Conjunctions of items are used to create higher-level representations, which are associated to the original items.

of chunking models.[7] Another attractive feature of chunking models is that they can create representations that bridge time. If the model is able to make a higher-level "bridging" representation associating successively presented items, then it can capture the contiguity effect. It is less clear whether a model like this can capture the asymmetry effect (Murdock, 1995).

9.6 SUMMARY AND CURRENT DIRECTIONS

The preceding analysis of theory and data on serial recall suggests that participants can use multiple cues in serial learning and that when one cue is rendered ineffective, participants can modify their strategy to make use of the more effective cues. There is considerable evidence that recall of an item does depend on the preceding series of recalls and not just the immediately prior item. Such dependencies can be neatly explained by chaining of direct interitem associations. However, it is also possible that such dependencies arise indirectly through a mediating representation, such as list position, temporal context, or an abstract chunk-type representation. Thus, recall of item j (and $j - 1$, etc.) may facilitate the retrieval of the cue that in turn prompts retrieval of item $j + 1$, but that cue does not have to be identical with the representation of item j. Indeed, one could imagine that the mediating representation includes item, positional, and temporal features. Such elaborated notions of context, and its role in serial-order memory, have emerged in several recent models (e.g., Brown et al., 2000; Burgess and Hitch, 1999, 2006; Botvinick and Plaut, 2006).

Beyond the cues that facilitate retrieval of neighboring items, one needs some mechanism of preventing the model from cycling back and forth between already-recalled items. Such a mechanism could either take the form of an inhibitory process that makes just-recalled items temporarily inaccessible or it

---

7. Grouping effects can also be accounted for by chaining and positional-coding models by assuming that interitem associations vary in strength or by allowing for more similar positional codes within chunks (see Caplan, 2005).

could result from an output encoding process that associated recalled items with a "recalled" context that is very different from the context of the target list. Retrieval could then be focused on those items that are associated with the study context but not the recalled context. The importance of response suppression has been highlighted by numerous investigators (e.g., Page and Norris, 1998; Becker and Lim, 2003; Farrell and Lewandowsky, 2002). As discussed in section 9.3.5, such a mechanism may also help to explain the Ranschburg effect.

A successful model of serial recall must also be able to explain grouping effects and the scalloped pattern of interresponse times observed in serial recall. Although such effects have been argued to reflect hierarchical associative structures, it may be possible to implement grouping effects within standard chaining and positional-coding models. For example, if the strength of the encoded associations varies across item presentations, there will be a tendency for some items to be linked more strongly with their neighbors or with their positional codes than are other items, thus giving rise to apparent grouping effects. These groupings may then be reinforced during recall and, on successive encoding trials, give rise to the strong grouping phenomena observed in serial learning (Martin and Noreen, 1974). At the time of this writing, I am not aware of any models of serial recall that fully incorporate the idea of encoding variability.

Finally, any successful model of serial recall will need to make some specific assumptions about the differences in representations of auditorily and visually presented lists and the ways in which these differences result in the serial-recall task's sensitivity to phonological similarity.

It is puzzling that models of serial and free recall have developed largely in isolation of one another, especially in view of the striking similarities of the two tasks. Both tasks require participants to recall a series of studied items. Also, in both tasks, recall is a dynamic process in which previously recalled items serve as retrieval cues. The behavioral data reveal a number of important commonalities, such as the contiguity effect and forward recall asymmetry (Bhatarah et al., 2006, 2008; Klein et al., 2005; Ward, Tan, and Grenfell-Essam, 2010). There are also a number of critical differences, such as the effect of increasing similarity, which boosts free recall and impairs serial recall. More generally, only serial recall depends critically on participants' memory for the order of the list items, and many of the effects are driven by order errors rather than item errors. Conversely, many of the most interesting findings in free recall arise from the free nature of responding, where the order of recall reveals much about the recall process.

Despite these differences between free and serial recall, I believe that much can be gained by attempting a theoretical unification of the two tasks, as has recently been suggested by Ward and colleagues (Ward et al., 2010). Such a unification may be achieved if we can understand more about the relation between temporal context and positional context and whether, in fact, they reflect a common process. Here the key issue may be the effect of the start of the list on the contextual drift process. Somehow, the beginning of the list must be a salient anchor for memory retrieval given that participants can so easily initiate serial recall, even in the spin list condition. Alternatively, it may be that hierarchical models can be expanded to address some of the key findings in free recall. Those models have great promise, but their theoretical development has lagged behind the more classic associative chaining and positional-coding theories.

9.7 STUDY QUESTIONS

1. Briefly describe the chaining and positional-coding models of serial recall. Describe at least one finding that each model can explain, one finding that is challenging to chaining theory, and one finding that is challenging to positional-coding theory. Finally, which of these two models is more like the SAM model and why?

2. Describe the Ranschburg effect and discuss its implications for associative chaining and positional-coding theories of sequence memory. What role do remote associations and compound cuing play in the predictions of chaining theory? Assuming that neither theory can explain the Ranschburg effect, how would you modify these theories to explain it?

3. Consider the following experiment. Participants first learn the sequence ABCDEFGHIJ, where each letter stands for a word and there are no repeated items in the sequence. Later, the same participants are asked to learn the sequence LMNODEFPQR, the sequence LMNOFPQRST, or the sequence LMNOPQRSTU. What does chaining theory predict about the way people will recall these lists? Include in your explanation a description of which parts of the list should be particularly hard to learn.

4. What aspects of the data on serial recall can be explained by the concepts of remote associations and compound cuing?

REFERENCES

Adams, J. A., and Montague, W. E. (1967). Retroactive inhibition and natural language mediation. *Journal of Verbal Learning and Verbal Behavior, 6,* 525–535.

Addis, K. M. (2004). *Constraining models of serial learning.* Unpublished doctoral dissertation, Brandeis University, Waltham, MA.

Addis, K. M., and Kahana, M. J. (2004). Decomposing serial learning: what is missing from the learning curve? *Psychonomic Bulletin & Review, 11,* 118–124.

Agam, Y., Bullock, D., and Sekuler, R. (2005). Imitating unfamiliar sequences of connected linear motions. *Journal of Neurophysiology, 94(4),* 2832–2843.

Allen, G. A., Mahler, W. A., and Estes, W. K. (1969). Effects of recall tests on long-term retention of paired associate. *Journal of Verbal Learning and Verbal Behavior, 8,* 463–470.

Anderson, J. A. (1970). Two models for memory organization using interacting traces. *Mathematical Biosciences, 8,* 137–160.

———— (1973). A theory for the recognition of items from short memorized lists. *Psychological Review, 80,* 417–438.

Anderson, J. R. (1974). Retrieval of propositional information from long-term memory. *Cognitive Psychology, 6(4),* 451–474.

———— (1981). Interference: The relationship between response latency and response accuracy. *Journal of Experimental Psychology: Human Learning and Memory, 7,* 326–343.

Anderson, J. R., Bothell, D., Lebiere, C., and Matessa, M. (1998). An integrated theory of list memory. *Journal of Memory and Language, 38,* 341–380.

Anderson, J. R., and Matessa, M. (1997). A production system theory of serial memory. *Psychological Review, 104,* 728–748.

Anderson, M. C. (2003). Rethinking interference theory: Executive control and the mechanisms of forgetting. *Journal of Memory and Language, 49(4),* 415–445.

Anderson, M. C., and Spellman, B. A. (1995). On the status of inhibitory mechanisms in cognition: Memory retrieval as a model case. *Psychological Review, 102,* 68–100.

Anderson, R. C., and Watts, G. H. (1969). Bidirectional associations in multi-trial free recall. *Psychonomic Science, 15(6),* 288–289.

Anisfeld, M., and Knapp, M. (1968). Association, synonymity, and directionality in false recognition. *Journal of Experimental Psychology, 77,* 171–179.

Aristotle. (n.d.). De memoria et reminiscentia. 451b10.

Arndt, J., and Reder, L. M. (2002). Word frequency and receiver operating characteristic curves in recognition memory: Evidence for a dual-process interpretation. *Journal of Experimental Psychology: Learning, Memory, and Cognition, 28*(5), 830–842.

Asch, S. E., and Ebenholtz, S. M. (1962). The principle of associative symmetry. *Proceedings of the American Philosophical Society, 106,* 135–163.

Ashby, F. G., Alfonso-Reese, L. A., Turken, U., and Waldron, E. M. (1998). A neuropsychological theory of multiple systems in category learning. *Psychological Review, 105*(3), 442–481.

Ashby, F. G., and Maddox, W. T. (1993). Relations between prototype, exemplar, and decision bound models of categorization. *Journal of Mathematical Psychology, 37,* 372–400.

Ashby, F. G., and Maddox, W. T. (2005). Human category learning. *Annual Review of Psychology, 56,* 149–178.

Ashby, F. G., Queller, S., and Berretty, P. M. (1999). On the dominance of unidimensional rules in unsupervised categorization. *Perception and Pychophysics, 61*(6), 1178–1199.

Ashby, F. G., Tein, J. Y., and Balakrishan, J. D. (1993). Response time distributions in memory scanning. *Journal of Mathematical Psychology, 37,* 526–555.

Atkinson, R. C., and Juola, J. F. (1974). Search and decision processes in recognition memory. In D. H. Krantz, R. C. Atkinson, and P. Suppes (Eds.), *Contemporary developments in mathematical psychology.* San Francisco: Freeman.

Atkinson, R. C., and Shiffrin, R. M. (1968). Human memory: A proposed system and its control processes. In K. W. Spence and J. T. Spence (Eds.), *The psychology of learning and motivation* (Vol. 2, pp. 89–105). New York: Academic Press.

Averbach, E., and Coriell, A. S. (1961). Short-term memory in vision. *Bell System Technical Journal, 40,* 309–328.

Baddeley, A. D. (1968). Prior recall of newly learned items and the recency effect in free recall. *Canadian Journal of Psychology, 22,* 157–163.

——— (1978). The trouble with levels: A reexamination of Craik and Lockhart's framework for memory research. *Psychological Review, 85*(3), 139–152.

——— (1986). *Working memory.* Oxford, England: Clarendon Press.

Baddeley, A. D., and Ecob, J. R. (1973). Reaction time and short-term memory: Implications of repetition effects for the high-speed exhaustive scan hypothesis. *Quarterly Journal of Experimental Psychology, 25,* 229–240.

Baddeley, A. D., and Hitch, G. J. (1977). Recency reexamined. In S. Dornic (Ed.), *Attention and performance VI* (pp. 647–667). Hillsdale, NJ: Lawrence Erlbaum and Associates.

Baddeley, A. D., and Longman, D. J. (1978). The influence of length and frequency of training session on the rate of learning to type. *Ergonomics, 21*(8), 627–635.

Baddeley, A. D., Thomson, N., and Buchanan, M. (1975). Word length and the structure of short-term memory. *Journal of Verbal Learning and Verbal Behavior, 14,* 575–589.

Baddeley, A. D., and Warrington, E. K. (1970). Amnesia and the distinction between long- and short-term memory. *Journal of Verbal Learning and Verbal Behavior, 9*(2), 176–189.

Bahrick, H. P. (1970). Two-phase model for prompted recall. *Psychological Review*, 77(3), 215–222.

Bahrick, H. P., and Phelps, E. (1987). Retention of spanish vocabulary over 8 years. *Journal of Experimental Pyschology: Learning, Memory, and Cognition*, 13(2), 344–349.

Banks, W. P. (2000). Recognition and source memory as multivariate decision processes. *Psychological Science*, 11(4), 267–273.

Barnes, J. M., and Underwood, B. J. (1959). Fate of first-list associations in transfer theory. *Journal of Experimental Psychology*, 58, 97–105.

Bartlett, F. C. (1932). *Remembering: A study in experimental and social psychology*. New York: Cambridge University Press.

Becker, S., and Lim, J. (2003). A computational model of prefrontal control in free recall: Strategic memory use in the California verbal learning task. *Journal of Cognitive Neuroscience*, 15, 821–832.

Bhatarah, P., Ward, G., and Tan, L. (2006). Examining the relationship between free recall and immediate serial recall: The effect of concurrent task performance. *Journal of Experimental Psychology: Learning, Memory, and Cognition*, 32(2), 215–229.

——— (2008). Examining the relationship between free recall and immediate serial recall: The serial nature of recall and the effect of test expectancy. *Memory & Cognition*, 36(1), 20–34.

Bishop, Y. M. M., Fienberg, S. E., and Holland, P. W. (1975). *Discrete multivariate analysis: theory and practice*. Cambridge, MA: MIT Press.

Bjork, E., and Healy, A. (1974). Short-term order and item retention. *Journal of Verbal Learning and Verbal Behavior*, 13(1), 80–97.

Bjork, R. A. (1970). Positive forgetting: The noninterference of items intentionally forgotten. *Journal of Verbal Learning and Verbal Behavior*, 9, 255–268.

Bjork, R. A., and Bjork, E. L. (1992). A new theory of disuse and an old theory of stimulus fluctuation. In S. M. Healy and A. F. Kosslyn (Eds.), *Essays in honor of William K. Estes, vol. 1: From learning theory to connectionist theory; vol. 2: From learning processes to cognitive processes* (pp. 35–67). Hillsdale, NJ: Lawrence Erlbaum and Associates.

Bjork, R. A., and Whitten, W. B. (1974). Recency-sensitive retrieval processes in long-term free recall. *Cognitive Psychology*, 6, 173–189.

Blake, M. J. (1967). Time of day effects on performance in a range of tasks. *Psychonomic Science*, 9(6), 349–350.

Block, R. A. (1971). Effects of instructions to forget in short-term memory. *Journal of Experimental Psychology*, 89, 1–9.

Bloom, L., and Watkins, M. (1999). Two-component theory of the suffix effect: Contrary findings. *Journal of Experimental Psychology Learning Memory and Cognition*, 25, 1452–1474.

Bogacz, R. (2007). Optimal decision-making theories: Linking neurobiology with behaviour. *Trends in Cognitive Sciences*, 11(3), 118–125.

Bogacz, R., Brown, M. W., and Giraud-Carrier, C. (2001). Model of familiarity discrimination in the perirhinal cortex. *Journal of Computational Neuroscience*, 10(1), 5–23.

Botvinick, M. M., and Plaut, D. C. (2006). Short-term memory for serial order: A recurrent neural network model. *Psychological Review, 113*(2), 201–233.

Bousfield, W. A. (1953). The occurrence of clustering in the recall of randomly arranged associates. *Journal of General Psychology, 49*, 229–240.

Bousfield, W. A., Sedgewick, C. H., and Cohen, B. H. (1954). Certain temporal characteristics of the recall of verbal associates. *American Journal of Psychology, 67*, 111–118.

Bower, G. H. (1967). A multicomponent theory of the memory trace. In K. W. Spence and J. T. Spence (Eds.), *The psychology of learning and motivation: Advances in research and theory* (Vol. 1, pp. 229–325). New York: Academic Press.

——— (1972). Stimulus-sampling theory of encoding variability. In A. W. Melton and E. Martin (Eds.), *Coding processes in human memory* (pp. 85–121). New York: John Wiley and Sons.

Bowman, R. E., and Thurlow, W. R. (1963). Determinants of the effect of position in serial learning. *Americal Journal of Psychology, 76*, 436–445.

Brainerd, C. J., Payne, D. G., Wright, R., and Reyna, V. F. (2003). Phantom recall. *Journal of Memory and Language, 48*, 445–467.

Brainerd, C. J., and Reyna, V. F. (2005). *The science of false memory.* New York: Oxford University Press.

Briggs, G. E. (1954). Acquisition, extinction, and recovery functions in retroactive inhibition. *Journal of Experimental Psychology, 47*, 285–293.

Broadbent, D. E. (1958). *Perception and communication.* New York: Pergamon Press.

Brodie, D. A., and Murdock, B. B. (1977). Effects of presentation time on nominal and functional serial position curves in free recall. *Journal of Verbal Learning and Verbal Behavior, 16*, 185–200.

Brown, A. S. (1976). Spontaneous recovery in human learning. *Psychological Bulletin, 83*, 321–328.

Brown, G. D. A., Neath, I., and Chater, N. (2007). A temporal ratio model of memory. *Psychological Review, 114*(3), 539–576.

Brown, G. D. A., Preece, T., and Hulme, C. (2000). Oscillator-based memory for serial order. *Psychological Review, 107*(1), 127–181.

Brown, J. (1958). Some tests of the decay theory of immediate memory. *Quarterly Journal of Experimental Psychology, 10*, 12–21.

Brown, J., Lewis, V. J., and Monk, A. F. (1977). Memorability, word frequency and negative recognition. *Quarterly Journal of Experimental Psychology, 29*, 461–473.

Brown, T. (1824). *Lectures on the philosophy of the human mind.* Philadelphia John Grigg and William P. Bason.

Buhmann, J., Divko, R., and Schulten, K. (1989). Associative memory with high information content. *Physical Review A, 39*, 2689–2692.

Burgess, N., and Hitch, G. J. (1999). Memory for serial order: A network model of the phonological loop and its timing. *Psychological Review, 106*(3), 551–581.

Burgess, N., and Hitch, G. J. (2006). A revised model of short-term memory and long-term learning of verbal sequences. *Journal of Memory and Language, 55*, 627–652.

Burrows, D., and Okada, R. (1975). Memory retrieval from long and short lists. *Science, 188*, 1031–1033.

Buzsáki, G. (2006). *Rhythms of the brain.* New York: Oxford University Press.

Calkins, M. W. (1896). Association: An essay analytic and experimental. *Psychological Review Monographs Supplement, 1*(2).

Caplan, J. B. (2005). Associative isolation: Unifying associative and list memory. *Journal of Mathematical Psychology, 49*, 383–402.

Caplan, J. B., Glaholt, M., and McIntosh, A. R. (2006). Linking associative and list memory: pairs versus triples. *Journal of Experimental Psychology: Learning, Memory & Cognition, 32*(6), 1244–1265.

Carr, H. A. (1931). The laws of association. *Psychological Review, 38*, 212–228.

Carrier, M., and Pashler, H. (1992). The influence of retrieval on retention. *Memory & Cognition, 20*(6), 633–642.

Clark, L. L., Lansford, T. G., and Dallenbach, K. M. (1960). Repetition and associative learning. *American Journal of Psychology, 73*, 22–40.

Clark, S. E., and Tunnicliff, J. L. (2001). Selecting lineup foils in eyewitness identification experiments: Experimental control and real-world simulation. *Law and Human Behavior, 25*, 199–216.

Conrad, R. (1960). Serial order intrusions in immediate memory. *British Journal of Psychology, 51*, 45–48.

Conrad, R., and Hull, A. J. (1964). Information, acoustic confusion and memory span. *British Journal of Psychology, 55*, 429–432.

Cowan, N. (1992). The role of verbal output time in the effects of word length on immediate memory. *Journal of Memory and Language, 31*, 1–17.

Craik, F. I. M. (1970). The fate of primary memory items in free recall. *Journal of Verbal Learning and Verbal Behavior, 9*, 658–664.

Craik, F. I. M., and Levy, B. A. (1970). Semantic and acoustic information in primary memory. *Journal of Experimental Psychology, 86*, 77–82.

Craik, F. I. M., and Lockhart, R. S. (1972). Levels of processing: A framework for memory research. *Journal of Verbal Learning and Verbal Behavior, 11*, 671–684.

Crannell, C. W., and Parish, J. M. (1957). A comparison of immediate memory span for digits, letters, and words. *Journal of Psychology, 44*, 319–327.

Criss, A. H., and Shiffrin, R. M. (2004). Interactions between study task, study time, and the low-frequency hit rate advantage in recognition memory. *Journal of Experimental Psychology: Learning, Memory, and Cognition, 30*, 778–786.

Crowder, R. G. (1968). Intraserial repetition effects in immediate memory. *Journal of Verbal Learning and Verbal Behavior, 7*, 446–451.

Crowder, R. G. (1976). *Principles of learning and memory.* Hillsdale, NJ: Lawrence Erlbaum and Associates.

Crowder, R. G. (1979). Similarity and order in memory. In G. H. Bower (Ed.), *The psychology of learning and motivation: Advances in research and theory: Vol. 13* (pp. 319–353). New York: Academic Press.

Crowder, R. G., and Melton, A. W. (1965). The Ranschburg phenomenon: Failures of immediate recall correlated with repetition of elements within a stimulus. *Psychonomic Science, 2*, 295–296.

Crowder, R. G., and Morton, J. (1969). Precategorical acoustic storage (PAS). *Perception & Psychophysics, 5*, 365–373.

Crowder, R. G., Serafine, M. L., and Repp, B. (1990). Physical interaction and association by contiguity in memory for the words and melodies of songs. *Memory & Cognition, 18*(5), 469–476.

Dallett, K. M. (1965). Primary memory: The effects of redundancy upon digit repetition. *Psychonomic Science, 3*(6), 237–238.

DaPolito, F. J. (1967). Proactive effects with independent retrieval of competing responses. *Dissertation Abstracts International, 27*, 2522–2523.

Darwin, C. J., Turvey, M. T., and Crowder, R. C. (1972). An auditory analogue of the sperling partial report procedure: Evidence for brief auditory storage. *Cognitive Psychology, 3*(2), 255–267.

Davelaar, E. J., Goshen-Gottstein, Y., Ashkenazi, A., Haarmann, H. J., and Usher, M. (2005). The demise of short-term memory revisited: Empirical and computational investigations of recency effects. *Psychological Review, 112*, 3–42.

Davelaar, E. J., Haarmann, H. J., Goshen-Gottstein, Y., and Usher, M. (2006). Semantic similarity dissociates short-term from long-term recency effects: Testing a neurocomputational model of list memory. *Memory & Cognition, 34*(2), 323–334.

Davis, O. C., Geller, A. S., Rizzuto, D. S., and Kahana, M. J. (2008). Temporal associative processes revealed by intrusions in paired-associate recall. *Psychonomic Bulletin & Review, 15*(1), 64–69.

Deese, J. (1959). On the prediction of occurrence of particular verbal intrusions in immediate recall. *Journal of Experimental Psychology, 58*, 17–22.

Deese, J., and Kaufman, R. A. (1957). Serial effects in recall of unorganized and sequentially organized verbal material. *Journal of Experimental Psychology, 54*, 180–187.

Dennis, S., and Humphreys, M. S. (2001). A context noise model of episodic word recognition. *Psychological Review, 108*, 452–478.

Diana, R. A., and Reder, L. M. (2005). The list strength effect: A contextual competition account. *Memory & Cognition, 33*(7), 1289–1302.

Donaldson, W. (1996). The role of decision processes in remembering and knowing. *Memory & Cognition, 24*(4), 523–533.

Dougherty, M., and Harbison, J. (2007). Motivated to retrieve: How often are you willing to go back to the well when the well is dry? *Journal of Experimental Psychology: Learning, Memory, and Cognition, 33*(6), 1108.

Drewnowski, A., and Murdock, B. B. (1980). The role of auditory features in memory span for words. *Journal of Experimental Psychology: Human Learning and Memory, 6*, 319–332.

Dunn, J. C. (2004). Remember-know: A matter of confidence. *Psychological Review, 111*, 524–542.

Ebbinghaus, H. (1885/1913). *On memory: A contribution to experimental psychology.* New York: Teachers College, Columbia University.

Ebenholtz, S. M. (1963a). Position mediated transfer between serial learning and a spatial discrimination task. *Journal of Experimental Psychology, 65*(6), 603–608.

———— (1963b). Serial learning: position learning and sequential associations. *Journal of Experimental Psychology, 66*(4), 353–362.

Eichenbaum, H., Yonelinas, A., and Ranganath, C. (2007). The medial temporal lobe and recognition memory. *Annual Review of Neuroscience, 30*, 123–152.

Ekstrand, B. R. (1966). Backward associations. *Psychological Bulletin, 65,* 50–64.

Ekstrom, A. D., Kahana, M. J., Caplan, J. B., Fields, T. A., Isham, E. A., Newman, E. L., et al. (2003). Cellular networks underlying human spatial navigation. *Nature, 425,* 184–187.

Ellenbogen, J. M., Hulbert, J. C., Stickgold, R., Dinges, D. F., and Thompson-Schill, S. L. (2006). Interfering with theories of sleep and memory: sleep, declarative memory, and associative interference. *Current Biology, 16*(13), 1290–1294.

Ellis, N. C., and Hennelly, R. A. (1980). A bilingual word-length effect: Implications for intelligence testing and the relative ease of mental calculation in welsh and english. *British Journal of Psychology, 71*(1), 43–51.

Epstein, W. (1972). Mechanisms of directed forgetting. In G. H. Bower (Ed.), *The psychology of learning and motivation* (Vol. 6, p. 147–191). New York: Academic Press.

Estes, W. K. (1950). Toward a statistical theory of learning. *Psychological Review, 57,* 94–107.

Estes, W. K. (1955). Statistical theory of spontaneous recovery and regression. *Psychological Review, 62,* 145–154.

Estes, W. K. (1959). *Component and pattern models with Markovian interpretations: Studies in mathematical learning theory.* Stanford, CA: Stanford University Press.

Estes, W. K. (1960). Learning theory and the new "mental chemistry." *Psychological Review, 67,* 207–223.

Estes, W. K. (1972). An associative basis for coding and organization in memory. In A. W. Melton and E. Martin (Eds.), *Coding processes in human memory* (pp. 161–190). Washington, D.C.: Winston.

Estes, W. K. (1976). The structure of human memory. In C. N. Cofer (Ed.), (chap. Structural aspects of associative models for memory). Freeman.

Estes, W. K. (1986). Array models for category learning. *Cognitive Psychology, 18*(4), 500–549.

Estes, W. K. (1994). *Classification and cognition.* Oxford, U. K.: Oxford University Press.

Fagan, J. F. (1970). Memory in the infant. *Journal of Experimental Child Psychology, 9*(2), 217–226.

Fantz, R. L. (1964). Visual experience in infants: Decreased attention familar patterns relative to novel ones. *Science, 146*(*Whole No. 3644*), 668–670.

Farrell, S. (2006). Mixed-list phonological similarity effects in delayed serial recall. *Journal of Memory and Language, 55*(4), 587–600.

Farrell, S., and Lewandowsky, S. (2002). An endogenous distributed model of ordering in serial recall. *Psychonomic Bulletin & Review, 9,* 59–85.

Farrell, S., and Lewandowsky, S. (2003). Dissimilar items benefit from phonological similarity in serial recall. *Journal of Experimental Psychology: Learning, Memory, and Cognition, 29*(5), 838–849.

Farrell, S., and Lewandowsky, S. (2004). Modelling transposition latencies: Constraints for theories of serial order memory. *Journal of Memory and Language, 51,* 115–135.

Farrell, S., and Lewandowsky, S. (2008). Empirical and theoretical limits on lag recency in free recall. *Psychonomic Bulletin and Review, 15,* 1236–1250.

Forrin, B., and Cunningham, K. (1973). Recognition time and serial position of probed item in short-term memory. *Journal of Experimental Pyschology, 99*(2), 272–279.

Gallistel, C. R., and King, A. P. (2009). *Memory and the computational brain: Why cognitive science will transform neuroscience.* New York, NY: Wiley-Blackwell.

Gallo, D. (2006). *Associative illusions of memory: False memory research in DRM and related tasks.* New York: Psychology Press.

Galton, F. (1883). *Inquiries into human faculty and its development.* London: Macmillan and Co.

Gardiner, J. M., and Java, R. I. (1991). Forgetting in recognition memory with and without recollective experience. *Memory & Cognition, 19,* 617–623.

Gardiner, J. M., Ramponi, C., and Richardson-Klavehn, A. (2002). Recognition memory and decision processes: A meta-analysis of remember, know, and guess responses. *Memory, 10,* 83–98.

Gates, A. (1917). Recitation as a factor in memorizing. *Archives of Psychology* (40), 104.

Gelbard-Sagiv, H., Mukamel, R., Harel, M., Malach, R., and Fried, I. (2008). Internally generated reactivation of single neurons in human hippocampus during free recall. *Science, 3,* 96–101.

Gilbert, P. E., and Kesner, R. P. (2003). Localization of function within the dorsal hippocampus: The role of the ca3 subregion in paired-associate learning. *Behavioral Neuroscience, 117*(6), 1385–1394.

Gillund, G., and Shiffrin, R. M. (1984). A retrieval model for both recognition and recall. *Psychological Review, 91,* 1–67.

Giurintano, S. L. (1973). Serial learning process: test of chaining, position, and dual process hypotheses. *Journal of Experimental Psychology, 97*(2), 154–157.

Glanzer, M., Adams, J. K., Iverson, G., and Kim, K. (1993). The regularities of recognition memory. *Psychological Review, 100*(3), 546–567.

Glanzer, M., and Bowles, N. (1976). Analysis of the word-frequency effect in recognition memory. *Journal of Experimental Psychology: Human Learning and Memory, 2,* 21–31.

Glanzer, M., and Cunitz, A. R. (1966). Two storage mechanisms in free recall. *Journal of Verbal Learning and Verbal Behavior, 5,* 351–360.

Glanzer, M., Kim, K., Hilford, A., and Adams, J. K. (1999). Slope of the receiver-operating characteristic in recognition memory. *Journal of Experimental Psychology: Learning, Memory, and Cognition, 25*(2), 500–513.

Glaze, J. A. (1928). The association value of non-sense syllables. *Journal of Genetic Psychology, 35,* 255–267.

Glenberg, A. M. (1976). Monotonic and nonmonotonic lag effects in paired-associate and recognition memory paradigms. *Journal of Verbal Learning and Verbal Behavior, 15,* 1–16.

Glenberg, A. M., and Bradley, M. M. (1979). Mental contiguity. *Journal of Experimental Psychology: Human Learning and Memory, 5,* 88–97.

Glenberg, A. M., Bradley, M. M., Kraus, T. A., and Renzaglia, G. J. (1983). Studies of the long-term recency effect: Support for a contextually guided retrieval theory. *Journal of Experimental Psychology: Learning, Memory & Cognition, 12,* 413–418.

Glenberg, A. M., Bradley, M. M., Stevenson, J. A., Kraus, T. A., Tkachuk, M. J., and Gretz, A. L. (1980). A two-process account of long-term serial position effects. *Journal of Experimental Psychology: Human Learning and Memory, 6,* 355–369.

Godden, D. R., and Baddeley, A. D. (1975). Context-dependent memory in two natural environments: On land and under water. *British Journal of Psychology, 66,* 325–331.

Godden, D. R., and Baddeley, A. D. (1980). When does context influence recognition memory? *British Journal of Psychology, 71*, 99–104.

Golomb, J. D., Peelle, J. E., Addis, K. M., Kahana, M. J., and Wingfield, A. (2008). Effects of adult aging on utilization of temporal and semantic associations during free and serial recall. *Memory & Cognition, 36*(5), 947–956.

Gomulicki, B. R. (1953). The development and present status of the trace theory of memory. *British Journal of Psychology Monograph Supplements, 29*, 1–91.

Gorfein, D. S., and Hoffman, R. R. (1987). *Memory and learning: The Ebbinghaus centennial conference.* Hillsdale, NJ: Lawrence Erlbaum and Associates.

Gorman, A. M. (1961). Recognition memory for nouns as a function of abstractedness and frequency. *Journal of Experimental Psychology, 61*, 23–39.

Goshen-Gottstein, Y., and Steinberg, A. G. (2005). The list-length effect in recognition memory is not as strong (1912) as previously thought. *Unpublished.*

Green, D. M., and Swets, J. A. (1966). *Signal detection theory and psychophysics.* Oxford, England: Wiley.

Greenberg, R., and Underwood, B. J. (1950). Retention as a function of stage of practice. *Journal of Experimental Psychology, 40*(4), 452–457.

Greene, R. L. (1986). Sources of recency effects in free recall. *Psychological Bulletin, 99*, 221–228.

Greene, R. L. (1987). Stimulus suffixes and visual presentation. *Memory & Cognition, 15*(6), 497–503.

Greene, R. L. (1991). The Ranschburg effect: The role of guessing strategies. *Memory & Cognition, 19*, 313–317.

Greene, R. L. (1992). *Human memory: Paradigms and paradoxes.* Hillsdale, NJ: Lawrence Erlbaum and Associates.

Greene, R. L., and Crowder, R. G. (1984). Effects of semantic similarity on long-term recency. *American Journal of Psychology, 97*, 441–449.

Gregg, V. (1976). Word frequency, recognition and recall. In J. Brown (Ed.), *Recall and recognition.* Oxford, England: John Wiley and Sons.

Gregg, V., and Gardiner, J. (1994). Recognition memory and awareness: A large effect of study-test modalities on "know" responses following a highly perceptual orienting task. *European Journal of Cognitive Psychology, 6*, 131–147.

Grossberg, S., and Pearson, L. (2008). Laminar cortical dynamics of cognitive and motor working memory, sequence learning and performance: Toward a unified theory of how the cerebral cortex works. *Psychological Review, 115*(3), 677–732.

Guthrie, E. R. (1935). *The psychology of learning.* Gloucester, MA: Harper.

Hall, J., Sekuler, R., and Cushman, W. (1969). Effects of IAR occurrence during learning on response time during subsequent recognition. *Journal of Experimental Psychology, 79*, 39–42.

Han, S., and Dobbins, I. G. (2008). Examining recognition criterion rigidity during testing using a biased-feedback technique: Evidence for adaptive criterion learning. *Memory & Cognition, 36*(4), 703–715.

Heathcote, A. (2003). Item recognition memory and the receiver operating characteristic. *Journal Experimental Psychology: Learning, Memory and Cogntion, 29*(6), 1210–1230.

Hebb, D. O. (1949). *Organization of behavior.* New York: Wiley.

Hellyer, S. (1962). Frequency of stimulus presentation and short-term decrement in recall. *Journal of Experimental Psychology, 64,* 650.

Henson, R. N. A. (1998). Item repetition in short-term memory: Ranschburg repeated. *Journal of Experimental Psychology: Learning, Memory, and Cognition, 24,* 1162–1181.

Henson, R. N. A., Norris, D. G., Page, M. P. A., and Baddeley, A. D. (1996). Unchained memory: Error patterns rule out chaining models of immediate serial recall. *The Quarterly Journal of Experimental Psychology, 49A,* 80–115.

Herbart, J. F. (1834). Lehrbuch zur Psychologie. In K. Kehrbach (Ed.), *Sämtliche Werke* (2nd ed., Vol. 4, p. 376–377). Königsberg: August Wilhelm Unzer.

Hertz, J., Krogh, A., and Palmer, R. G. (1991). *Introduction to the theory of neural computation.* Redwood City, CA: Addison-Wesley.

Hilford, A., Glanzer, M., Kim, K., and DeCarlo, L. (2002). Regularities of source recognition: Roc analysis. *Journal of Experimental Psychology: General, 131(4),* 494–510.

Hinrichs, J. V. (1968). Prestimulus and poststimulus cuing of recall order in the memory span. *Psychonomic Science, 12,* 261–262.

Hintzman, D. L. (1976). Repetition and memory. In G. H. Bower (Ed.), *The psychology of learning and memory* (pp. 47–91). New York: Academic Press.

Hintzman, D. L. (1981). Simpson's paradox and the analysis of memory retrieval. *Psychological Review, 87,* 398–410.

Hintzman, D. L. (1988). Judgments of frequency and recognition memory in multiple-trace memory model. *Psychological Review, 95,* 528–551.

Hintzman, D. L. (2003). Robert Hooke's model of memory. *Psychonomic Bulletin & Review, 10(1),* 3–14.

Hintzman, D. L., and Block, R. A. (1971). Repetition and memory: Evidence for a multiple-trace hypothesis. *Journal of Experimental Psychology, 88,* 297–306.

Hintzman, D. L., Block, R. A., and Inskeep, N. R. (1972). Memory for mode of input. *Journal of Verbal Learning and Verbal Behavior, 11,* 741–749.

Hintzman, D. L., Caulton, D. A., and Levitin, D. J. (1998). Retrieval dynamics in recognition and list discrimination: Further evidence of separate processes of familiarity and recall. *Memory & Cognition, 26,* 449–462.

Hirshman, E. (1995). Decision processes in recognition memory: Criterion shifts and the list-strength paradigm. *Journal of Experimental Psychology: Learning, Memory, & Cognition, 21,* 302–313.

Hirshman, E., and Arndt, J. (1997). Discriminating alternative conceptions of false recognition: The cases of word concreteness and word frequency. *Journal of Experimental Psychology: Learning, Memory, and Cognition, 23(6),* 1306–1323.

Hirst, W. (1986). Recognition and recall in amnesics. *Journal of Experimental Psychology: Learning, Memory, and Cognition, 12,* 445–451.

Hockley, W. E. (1992). Item versus associative information: Further comparisons of forgetting rates. *Journal of Experimental Psychology: Learning, Memory, and Cognition, 18,* 1321–1330.

Hockley, W. E. (1996). Reflections of the mirror effect for item and associative recognition. *Memory & Cognition, 22(6),* 713–722.

Hockley, W. E. (2008). Memory search: A matter of time. In J. H. Byrne (Ed.), *Learning and memory: A comprehensive reference.* Elsevier.

Hockley, W. E., and Murdock, B. B. (1987). A decision model for accuracy and response latency in recognition memory. *Psychological Review, 94,* 341–358.

Hogan, R. M. (1975). Interitem encoding and directed search in free recall. *Memory & Cognition, 3,* 197–209.

Hogan, R. M., and Kintsch, W. (1971). Differential effects of study and test trials on long-term recognition and recall. *Journal of Verbal Learning & Verbal Behavior, 10*(5), 562–567.

Holdstock, J. S., Mayes, A. R., Roberts, N., Cezayirli, E., Isaac, C. L., O'Reilly, R. C., et al. (2002). Under what conditions is recognition spared relative to recall after selective hippocampal damage in humans. *Hippocampus, 12,* 341–351.

Hollingsworth, H. L. (1928). *Psychology: Its facts and principles.* New York: D. Appleton and Company.

Hooke, R. (1969). *The posthumous works of Robert Hooke: With a new introduction by Richard S. Westfall.* Johnson Reprint Corp.

Hopfield, J. J. (1982). Neural networks and physical systems with emergent collective computational abilities. *Proceedings of the National Academy of Sciences, USA, 79,* 2554–2558.

Horowitz, L. M., and Izawa, C. (1963). Comparison of serial and paired-associate learning. *Journal of Experimental Psychology, 65,* 352–361.

Howard, M. W., Bessette-Symons, B., Zhang, Y., and Hoyer, W. J. (2006). Aging selectively impairs recollection in recognition memory for pictures: Evidence from modeling and receiver operating characteristic curves. *Psychology and Aging, 21*(1), 96–106.

Howard, M. W., and Kahana, M. J. (1999). Contextual variability and serial position effects in free recall. *Journal of Experimental Psychology: Learning, Memory, and Cognition, 25,* 923–941.

Howard, M. W., and Kahana, M. J. (2002a). A distributed representation of temporal context. *Journal of Mathematical Psychology, 46,* 269–299.

Howard, M. W., and Kahana, M. J. (2002b). When does semantic similarity help episodic retrieval? *Journal of Memory and Language, 46,* 85–98.

Howard, M. W., Sederberg, P. B., and Kahana, M. J. (2009). Reply to Farrell & Lewandowsky: Recency-contiguity interactions predicted by the temporal context model. *Psychonomic Bulletin & Review, 16,* 973–984.

Howard, M. W., Youker, T. E., and Venkatadass, V. (2008). The persistence of memory: Contiguity effects across several minutes. *Psychonomic Bulletin & Review, 15,* 58–63.

Huber, D. E. (2008). Immediate priming and cognitive aftereffects. *Journal of Experimental Psychology: General, 137*(2), 324–347.

Hull, C. L. (1943). *Principles of behavior: An introduction to behavior theory.* Oxford, England: Appleton-Century.

Hume, D. (1739). *A treatise of human nature,* D. F. Norton & M. Norton Eds. Clarendon Press.

Humphreys, M. S. (1978). Item and relational information: A case for context independent retrieval. *Journal of Verbal Learning and Verbal Behavior, 17,* 175–187.

Humphreys, M. S., Pike, R., Bain, J. D., and Tehan, G. (1989). Global matching: A comparison of the SAM, Minerva II, Matrix, and TODAM models. *Journal of Mathematical Psychology, 33,* 36–67.

Hunt, R. R., and McDaniel, M. A. (1993). The enigma of organization and distinctiveness. *Journal of Memory and Language, 32*(4), 421–445.

Hyde, T. S., and Jenkins, J. J. (1973). Recall for words as a function of semantic, graphic, and syntactic orienting tasks. *Journal of Verbal Learning and Verbal Behavior, 12*(5), 471–480.

Intraub, H., and Nicklos, S. (1985). Levels of processing and picture memory: The physical superiority effect. *Journal of Experimental Psychology: Learning, Memory, and Cognition, 11*, 284–298.

Izawa, C. (1966). Reinforcement-test sequences in paired-associate learning. *Psychological Reports, 18*(3), 879–919.

Jahnke, J. C. (1969a). Output interference and the Ranschburg effect. *Journal of Verbal Learning and Verbal Behavior, 8*, 614–621.

Jahnke, J. C. (1969b). The Ranschburg effect. *Psychological Review, 76*, 592–605.

Jahnke, J. C. (1970). Probed recall of strings that contain repeated elements. *Journal of Verbal Learning and Verbal Behavior, 9*, 450–455.

Jahnke, J. C. (1972). The effects of intraserial and interserial repetition on recall. *Journal of Verbal Learning and Verbal Behavior, 11*, 706–716.

James, W. (1890). *The principles of psychology.* New York: Henry Holt and Co, Inc.

Jenkins, J. G., and Dallenbach, K. M. (1924). Oblivescence during sleep and waking. *Americal Journal of Psychology, 35*, 605–612.

Jenkins, J. J., and Russell, W. A. (1952). Associative clustering during recall. *Journal of Abnormal and Social Psychology, 47*, 818–821.

Jensen, A. R., and Rohwer, W. D. (1965). What is learned in serial learning? *Journal of Verbal Learning and Verbal Behavior, 4*, 62–72.

Johnson, N. F. (1972). Organization and the concept of a memory code. In A. W. Melton and E. Martin (Eds.), *Coding processes in human memory* (pp. 125–159). Washington, DC: Winston.

Jost, A. (1897). De assoziationsfestigkeit in ihrer abhangigkeit von der verteilung der weilderholungen. *Zeitschrift für Psychologie und Physiologie der Sinnesorgane, 16*, 436–472.

Kahana, M. J. (1993). *Interactions between item, associative, and serial order information.* Unpublished doctoral dissertation, University of Toronto, Toronto, Canada.

Kahana, M. J. (1996). Associative retrieval processes in free recall. *Memory & Cognition, 24*, 103–109.

Kahana, M. J. (2000). Contingency analyses of memory. In E. Tulving and F. I. M. Craik (Eds.), *Oxford handbook of human memory* (pp. 323–384). England: Oxford Press.

Kahana, M. J. (2002). Associative symmetry and memory theory. *Memory & Cognition, 30*, 823–840.

Kahana, M. J., and Bennett, P. J. (1994). Classification and perceived similarity of compound gratings that differ in relative spatial phase. *Perception & Psychophysics, 55*, 642–656.

Kahana, M. J., and Caplan, J. B. (2002). Associative asymmetry in probed recall of serial lists. *Memory & Cognition, 30*, 841–849.

Kahana, M. J., Dolan, E. D., Sauder, C. L., and Wingfield, A. (2005a). Intrusions in episodic recall: Age differences in editing of overt responses. *Journal of Gerontology: Psychological Sciences, 60*, 92–97.

Kahana, M. J., Howard, M. W., and Polyn, S. M. (2008). Associative retrieval processes in episodic memory. In H. L. Roediger III (Ed.), *Cognitive psychology of memory. Vol. 2 of Learning and memory: A comprehensive reference, 4 vols. (J. Byrne, Editor)*. Oxford: Elsevier.

Kahana, M. J., Howard, M. W., Zaromb, F., and Wingfield, A. (2002). Age dissociates recency and lag recency effects in free recall. *Journal of Experimental Psychology: Learning, Memory, and Cognition, 28*, 530–540.

Kahana, M. J., and Jacobs, J. (2000). Inter-response times in serial recall: Effects of intraserial repetition. *Journal of Experimental Psychology: Learning, Memory and Cognition, 26*, 1188–1197.

Kahana, M. J., and Loftus, G. (1999). Response time versus accuracy in human memory. In R. J. Sternberg (Ed.), *The nature of cognition* (pp. 322–384). Cambridge, MA: MIT Press.

Kahana, M. J., and Miller, J. F. (2013). Memory, recall dynamics. In *Encyclopedia of the mind*. H. Pashler (Ed.). Thousand Oaks, CA: SAGE Publications.

Kahana, M. J., Mollison, M. V., and Addis, K. M. (2010). Positional cues in serial learning: The spin list technique. *Memory & Cognition, 38*(1), 92–101.

Kahana, M. J., Rizzuto, D. S., and Schneider, A. (2005b). Theoretical correlations and measured correlations: Relating recognition and recall in four distributed memory models. *Journal of Experimental Psychology: Learning, Memory, and Cognition, 31*, 933–953.

Kahana, M. J., Sederberg, P. B., and Howard, M. W. (2008). Putting short-term memory into context: Reply to Usher and colleagues. *Psycholgical Review, 115*(4), 1119–1126.

Kahana, M. J., and Sekuler, R. (2002). Recognizing spatial patterns: A noisy exemplar approach. *Vision Research, 42*, 2177–2192.

Kahana, M. J., and Wingfield, A. (2000). A functional relation between learning and organization in free recall. *Psychonomic Bulletin & Review, 7*, 516–521.

Kahana, M. J., Zhou, F., Geller, A. S., and Sekuler, R. (2007). Lure-similarity affects visual episodic recognition: Detailed tests of a noisy examplar model. *Memory & Cognition, 35*, 1222–1232.

Karpicke, J. D., and Roediger, H. L. (2007). Repeated retrieval during learning is the key to long-term retention. *Journal of Memory and Language, 57*, 151–162.

Karpicke, J. D., and Roediger, H. L., III. (2008). The critical importance of retrieval for learning. *Science, 319*, 966–968.

Katz, D. (1936). Georg Elias Müller. *Acta Psychologica, 1*, 234–240.

Kausler, D. H. (1994). *Learning and memory in normal aging*. San Diego, CA: Academic Press.

Kelley, R., and Wixted, J. (2001). On the nature of associative information in recognition memory. *Journal of Experimental Psychology: Learning, Memory and Cognition, 27*(3), 701–722.

Kimball, D. R., Smith, T. A., and Kahana, M. J. (2007). The fSAM model of false recall. *Psychological Review, 114*(4), 954–993.

Kinsbourne, M., and George, J. (1974). The mechanism of the word-frequency effect on recognition memory. *Journal of Verbal Learning and Verbal Behavior, 13*, 63–69.

Kintsch, W. (1970). *Learning, memory, and conceptual processes*. New York: John Wiley & Sons.

Kirkpatrick, E. A. (1894). An experimental study of memory. *Psychological Review, 1*(6), 602–609.

Klahr, D., Chase, W. G., and Lovelace, E. A. (1983). Structure and process in alphabetic retrieval. *Journal of Experimental Psychology: Learning, Memory, and Cognition, 9,* 462–477.

Klein, K. A., Addis, K. M., and Kahana, M. J. (2005). A comparative analysis of serial and free recall. *Memory & Cognition, 33,* 833–839.

Kleinfeld, D. (1986). Sequential state generation by model neural networks. *Proceedings of the National Academy of Sciences of the United States of America, 83,* 9469–9473.

Köhler, W. (1947). *Gestalt psychology.* New York: Liveright.

Kolers, P. A., and Ostry, D. J. (1974). Time course of loss of information regarding pattern analyzing operations. *Journal of Verbal Learning and Verbal Behavior, 13,* 599–612.

Koppell, S. (1977). Decision latencies in recognition memory: A signal detection theory analysis. *Journal of Experimental Psychology: Human Learning and Memory, 3,* 445–457.

Koppenaal, L., and Glanzer, M. (1990). An examination of the continuous distractor task and the long-term recency effect. *Memory & Cognition, 18,* 183–195.

Kroh, O. (1935). Georg Elias Müller, ein nachruf. *Zeitschrift für Psychologie, 134,* 150–190.

Lacroix, J. P. W., Murre, J. M. J., Postma, E. O., and Jaap van den Herik, H. (2006). Modeling recognition memory using the similarity structure of natural input. *Cognitive Science, 30,* 121–145.

Ladd, G. T., and Woodworth, R. S. (1911). *Elements of physiological psychology: A treatise of the activities and nature of the mind from the physical and experimental point of view.* New York: Charles Scribner's Sons.

Laks, J. (2001, June 7). *Lecture on behalf of the Organization of Mengele Twins.* Berlin, Germany.

Lamberts, K. (2000). Information-accumulation theory of speeded categorization. *Psychological Review, 107,* 227–260.

Lamberts, K., Brockdorff, N., and Heit, E. (2003). Feature-sampling and random-walk models of individual-stimulus recognition. *Journal of Experimental Psychology: General, 132,* 351–378.

Laming, D. (1999). Testing the idea of distinct storage mechanisms in memory. *International Journal of Psychology, 34,* 419–426.

Laming, D. (2006). Predicting free recalls. *Journal of Experimental Psychology: Learning, Memory, and Cognition, 32*(5), 1146–1163.

Laming, D. (2008). An improved algorithm for predicting free recalls. *Cognitive Psychology, 57,* 179–219.

Landauer, T. K., and Dumais, S. T. (1997). Solution to Plato's problem: The latent semantic analysis theory of acquisition, induction, and representation of knowledge. *Psychological Review, 104,* 211–240.

Landauer, T. K., Foltz, P. W., and Laham, D. (1998). Introduction to latent semantic analysis. *Discourse Processes, 25,* 259–284.

Lashley, K. S. (1951). The problem of serial order in behavior. In L. A. Jeffress (Ed.), *Cerebral mechanisms in behavior.* New York: John Wiley & Sons.

Lee, C. L., and Estes, W. K. (1977). Order and position in primary memory for letter strings. *Journal of Verbal Learning and Verbal Behavior, 16,* 395–418.

Lenné, M. G., Triggs, T. J., and Redman, J. R. (1997). Time of day variations in driving performance. *Accident Analysis and Prevention, 29(4),* 431–437.

Lewandowsky, S., and Murdock, B. B. (1989). Memory for serial order. *Psychological Review, 96,* 25–57.

Loftus, G. R., and Masson, M. E. J. (1994). Using confidence intervals in within-subject designs. *Psychonomic Bulletin & Review, 1,* 476–490.

Lucas, R. E. (1983). *Studies in business-cycle theory.* MIT Press.

Luce, R. D. (1959). Detection and recognition. In R. D. Luce, R. R. Bush, and E. Galanter (Eds.), *Handbook of mathematical psychology* (p. 103–189). New York: Wiley.

Luce, R. D. (1986). *Response times.* Oxford: Oxford University Press.

MacLeod, C. M., and Kampe, K. (1996). Word frequency effects on recall, recognition, and word fragment completion tests. *Journal of Experimental Psychology, 22(1),* 132–142.

Madan, C., Glaholt, M., and Caplan, J. (2010). The influence of item properties on association-memory. *Journal of Memory and Language, 63,* 46–63.

Madigan, S. A. (1969). Intraserial repetition and coding processes in free recall. *Journal of Verbal Learning and Verbal Behavior, 8,* 828–835.

Madigan, S. A. (1971). Modality and recall order interactions in short-term memory for serial order. *Journal of Experimental Psychology, 87,* 294–296.

Madigan, S. A., and McCabe, L. (1971). Perfect recall and total forgetting: A problem for models of short-term memory. *Journal of Verbal Learning and Verbal Behavior, 10,* 101–106.

Malmberg, K. J., and Nelson, T. O. (2003). The word frequency effect for recognition memory and the elevated-attention hypothesis. *Memory & Cognition, 31,* 35–43.

Mandler, G. (1980). Recognizing: The judgment of previous occurrence. *Psychological Review, 87,* 252–271.

Mandler, G., Rabinowitz, J. C., and Simon, R. A. (1981). Coordinate organization: The holistic representation of word pairs. *American Journal of Psychology, 92,* 209–222.

Manning, J. R., Polyn, S. M., Baltuch, G., Litt, B., and Kahana, M. J. (2011). Oscillatory patterns in temporal lobe reveal context reinstatement during memory search. *Proc Natl Acad Sci U S A, 108(31),* 12893–12897.

Marmurek, H. H. (1983). Negative recency in final free recall: Encoding or retrieval. *American Journal of Psychology, 96(1),* 17–35.

Marshall, P. H., and Werder, P. R. (1972). The effects of the elimination of rehearsal on primacy and recency. *Journal of Verbal Learning and Verbal Behavior, 11,* 649–653.

Martin, E. (1965). Transfer and verbal paired associates. *Psychological Review, 72(5),* 327–343.

Martin, E., and Greeno, J. G. (1972). Independence of associations tested. *Psychological Review, 79,* 265–267.

Martin, E., and Noreen, D. L. (1974). Serial learning: Identification of subjective subsequences. *Cognitive Psychology, 6,* 421–435.

Mather, M., Henkel, L. A., and Johnson, M. K. (1997). Evaluating characteristics of false memories: Remember/know judgments and memory characteristics questionnaire compared. *Memory & Cognition, 25(6)*, 826–837.

Maybery, M. T., Parmentier, F. B. R., and Jones, D. M. (2002). Grouping of list items reflected in the timing of recall: implications for models of serial verbal memory. *Journal of Memory and Language, 47*, 360–385.

McCullough, W. S., and Pitts, W. H. (1943). A logical calculus of the ideas immanent in nervous activity. *Bulletin of Mathematical Biophysics, 5*, 115–133.

McDaniel, M. A., and Fisher, R. P. (1991). Tests and test feedback as learning sources. *Contemporary Educational Psychology, 16(2)*, 192–201.

McDaniel, M. A., Kowitz, M. D., and Dunay, P. K. (1989). Altering memory through recall: The effects of cue-guided retrieval processing. *Memory & Cognition, 17(4)*, 423–434.

McElree, B., and Dosher, B. A. (1989). Serial position and set size in short-term memory: The time course of recognition. *Journal of Experimental Psychology: General, 118*, 346–373.

McGeoch, J. A. (1932). Forgetting and the law of disuse. *Psychological Review, 39*, 352–370.

McGeoch, J. A. (1936). The direction and extent of intraserial associations at recall. *Americal Journal of Psychology, 48*, 221–245.

McGeoch, J. A. (1942). *The psychology of human learning: An introduction.* New York: Longmans.

McGeoch, J. A., and Irion, A. L. (1952). *The psychology of human learning, 2nd edition.* New York: Longmans, Green and Co.

McGovern, J. B. (1964). Extinction of associations in four transfer paradigms. *Psychological Monographs: General & Applied, 78(16)*, 1–21.

Melton, A. W., and Irwin, J. M. (1940). The influence of degree of interpolated learning on retroactive inhibition and the overt transfer of specific responses. *American Journal of Psychology, 53*, 173–203.

Melton, A. W., and von Lackum, W. J. (1941). Retroactive and proactive inhibition in retention: evidence for a two-factor theory of retroactive inhibition. *American Journal of Psychology, 54*, 157–173.

Memon, A., Hope, L., Bartlett, J., and Bull, R. (2002). Eyewitness recognition errors: The effects of mugshot viewing and choosing in young and old adults. *Memory & Cognition, 30(8)*, 1219–1227.

Mensink, G.-J. M., and Raaijmakers, J. G. W. (1988). A model for interference and forgetting. *Psychological Review, 95*, 434–455.

Metcalfe, J. (1985). Levels of processing, encoding specificity, elaboration, and CHARM. *Psychological Review, 92*, 1–38.

Meyer, D. E., and Schvaneveldt, R. W. (1971). Facilitation in recognizing pairs of words: Evidence of a dependence between retrieval operations. *Journal of Experimental Psychology, 90*, 227–234.

Miller, J. F., Kahana, M. J., and Weidemann, C. T. (2012). Recall termination in free recall. *Memory & Cognition, 40(4)*, 540–550.

Miller, J. F., Lazarus, E., and Kahana, M. J. (in press). Spatial clustering during memory search. *Journal of Experimental Psychology: Learning, Memory, and Cognition.*

Monaco, J. D., Abbott, L. F., and Kahana, M. J. (2007). Lexico-semantic structure and the word-frequency effect in recognition memory. *Learning and Memory, 14*(2), 204–213.

Monsell, S. (1978). Recency, immediate recognition memory, and reaction time. *Cognitive Psychology, 10,* 465–501.

Moreton, B. J., and Ward, G. (2010). Time scale similarity and long-term memory for autobiographical events. *Psychonomic Bulletin & Review, 17*(4), 510–515.

Moscovitch, M., Nadel, L., Winocur, G., Gilboa, A., and Rosenbaum, R. S. (2006). The cognitive neuroscience of remote episodic, semantic and spatial memory. *Current Opinion in Neurobiology. Special Issue: Cognitive neuroscience, 16,* 179–190.

Mozer, M., Howe, M., and Pashler, H. (2004). Using testing to enhance learning: A comparison of two different hypotheses. In *Proceedings of the Twenty-Sixth Annual Cognitive Science Society* (p. 975–980). Hillsdale, NJ: Erlbaum.

Müller, G. E., and Pilzecker, A. (1900). Experimental contributions to memory theory. *Zeitschrift für Psychologie Eganzungsband, 1,* 1–300.

Müller, G. E., and Schumann, F. (1894). Experimentelle beitrage zur untersuchungen des gedachtnisses. *Zeitschrift für Psychologie und Physiologie der Sinnesorgane,* 6(80–191), 257–339.

Murdock, B. B. (1960). The immediate retention of unrelated words. *Journal of Experimental Psychology, 60,* 222–234.

Murdock, B. B. (1961). The retention of individual items. *Journal of Experimental Psychology, 62,* 618–25.

Murdock, B. B. (1962). The serial position effect of free recall. *Journal of Experimental Psychology, 64,* 482–488.

Murdock, B. B. (1963a). Short-term memory and paired-associate learning. *Journal of Verbal Learning and Verbal Behavior, 2,* 320–328.

Murdock, B. B. (1963b). Short-term retention of single paired associates. *Journal of Experimental Psychology, 65,* 433–443.

Murdock, B. B. (1965). Associative symmetry and dichotic presentation. *Journal of Verbal Learning and Verbal Behavior, 4,* 222–226.

Murdock, B. B. (1966). Forward and backward associations in paired associates. *Journal of Experimental Psychology, 71,* 732–737.

Murdock, B. B. (1967). Recent developments in short-term memory. *British Journal of Psychology, 58,* 421–433.

Murdock, B. B. (1968). Serial order effects in short-term memory. *Journal of Experimental Psychology Monograph Supplement, 76,* 1–15.

Murdock, B. B. (1971). A parallel-processing model for scanning. *Perception & Psychophysics, 10*(4-B), 289–291.

Murdock, B. B. (1972). Short-term memory. In G. H. Bower (Ed.), *The psychology of learning and motivation: advances in reasearch and theory.* (Vol. 5, pp. 67–127). New York: Academic Press.

Murdock, B. B. (1974). *Human memory: Theory and data.* Potomac, MD: Lawrence Erlbaum and Associates.

Murdock, B. B. (1982). A theory for the storage and retrieval of item and associative information. *Psychological Review, 89,* 609–626.

Murdock, B. B. (1985). Convolution and matrix systems: A reply to Pike. *Psychological Review, 92*, 130–132.

Murdock, B. B. (1989). Learning in a distributed memory model. In C. Izawa (Ed.), *Current issues in cognitive processes: The Floweree symposium on cognition* (pp. 69–106). Hillsdale, NJ: Lawrence Erlbaum and Associates.

Murdock, B. B. (1993). TODAM2: A model for the storage and retrieval of item, associative, and serial-order information. *Psychological Review, 100*, 183–203.

Murdock, B. B. (1995). Similarity in a distributed memory model. *Journal of Mathematical Psychology, 39*, 251–264.

Murdock, B. B. (1997). Context and mediators in a theory of distributed associative memory (TODAM2). *Psychological Review, 104*, 839–862.

Murdock, B. B. (2006). Decision-making models of remember-know judgments: Comment on Rotello, Macmillan, and Reeder (2004). *Psychological Review, 113*(3), 648–656.

Murdock, B. B., and Anderson, R. E. (1975). Encoding, storage and retrieval of item information. In R. L. Solso (Ed.), *Information processing and cognition: The Loyola symposium* (pp. 145–194). Hillsdale, NJ: Lawrence Erlbaum and Associates.

Murdock, B. B., and Dufty, P. O. (1972). Strength theory and recognition memory. *Journal of Experimental Psychology, 94*, 284–290.

Murdock, B. B., and Kahana, M. J. (1993a). Analysis of the list strength effect. *Journal of Experimental Psychology: Learning, Memory and Cognition, 19*, 689–697.

Murdock, B. B., and Kahana, M. J. (1993b). List-strength and list-length effects: Reply to Shiffrin, Ratcliff, Murnane, and Nobel. *Journal of Experimental Psychology: Learning, Memory and Cognition, 19*, 1450–1453.

Murdock, B. B., and Metcalfe, J. (1978). Controlled rehearsal in single- trial free recall. *Journal of Verbal Learning and Verbal Behavior, 17*, 309–324.

Murdock, B. B., and Okada, R. (1970). Interresponse times in single-trial free recall. *Journal of Verbal Learning and Verbal Behavior, 86*, 263–267.

Murdock, B. B., and vom Saal, W. (1967). Transpositions in short-term memory. *Journal of Experimental Psychology, 74*, 137–143.

Murdock, B. B., and Walker, K. D. (1969). Modality effects in free recall. *Journal of Verbal Learning and Verbal Behavior, 8*, 665–676.

Muther, W. S. (1965). Erasure or partitioning in short-term memory. *Psychonomic Science, 3*(429), 430.

Nairne, J. S. (1990a). A feature model of immediate memory. *Memory & Cognition, 18*, 251–269.

Nairne, J. S. (1990b). Similarity and long-term memory for order. *Journal of Memory and Language, 29*, 733–746.

Nairne, J. S. (1992). *Position-based search of associate memory.* (Unpublished manuscript).

Nairne, J. S., Neath, I., Serra, M., and Byun, E. (1997). Positional distinctiveness and the ratio rule in free recall. *Journal of Memory and Language, 37*, 155–166.

Neath, I. (1993a). Contextual and distinctive processes and the serial position function. *Journal of Memory and Language, 32*, 820–840.

Neath, I. (1993b). Distinctiveness and serial position effects in recognition. *Memory & Cognition, 21*, 689–698.

Neath, I., and Crowder, R. G. (1996). Distinctiveness and very short-term serial position effects. *Memory, 4*, 225–242.

Nelson, D. L., Bennett, D. J., and Leibert, T. W. (1997). One step is not enough: Making better use of association norms to predict cued recall. *Memory & Cognition, 25*, 785–796.

Nelson, D. L., McEvoy, C. L., and Schreiber, T. A. (2004). The University of South Florida free association, rhyme, and word fragment norms. *Behavior Research Methods, Instruments and Computers, 36(3)*, 402–407.

Nelson, D. L., McKinney, V. M., Gee, N. R., and Janczura, G. A. (1998). Interpreting the influence of implicitly activated memories on recall and recognition. *Psychological Review, 105*, 299–324.

Nelson, D. L., and Zhang, N. (2000). The ties that bind what is known to the recall of what is new. *Psychonomic Bulletin and Review, 7(4)*, 604–617.

Nelson, D. L., Zhang, N., and McKinney, V. M. (2001). The ties that bind what is known to the recognition of what is new. *Journal of Experimental Psychology: Learning, Memory, and Cognition, 27(5)*, 1147–1159.

Newman, S. E. (1987). Ebbinghaus' "on memory": Some effects on early American research. In D. S. Gorfein and R. R. Hoffman (Eds.), *Memory and learning: The Ebbinghaus centennial conference* (pp. 77–87). Hillsdale, NJ: Lawrence Erlbaum and Associates.

Nilsson, L. G., and Gardiner, J. M. (1991). Memory theory and the boundary conditions of the Tulving-Wiseman law. In W. E. Hockley and S. Lewandowsky (Eds.), *Relating theory and data: Essays on human memory in honor of Bennet B. Murdock* (pp. 57–74). Hillsdale, NJ: Lawrence Erlbaum and Associates.

Nobel, P. A., and Shiffrin, R. M. (2001). Retrieval processes in recognition and cued recall. *Journal of Experimental Psychology: Learning Memory, and Cognition, 27*, 384–413.

Norman, K. A. (2002). Differential effects of list strength on recollection and familiarity. *Journal of Experimental Psychology: Learning, Memory, and Cognition, 28*, 1083–1094.

Norman, K. A., Newman, E. L., and Detre, G. (2007). A neural network model of retrieval-induced forgetting. *Psychological Review, 114(4)*, 887–953.

Norman, K. A., and O'Reilly, R. C. (2003). Modeling hippocampal and neocortical contributions to recognition memory: A complementary learning systems approach. *Psychological Review, 110*, 611–646.

Nosofsky, R. M. (1986). Attention, similarity, and the identification-categorization relationship. *Journal of Experimental Psychology: General, 115*, 39–57.

Nosofsky, R. M. (1987). Attention and learning processes in the identification and categorization of integral stimuli. *Journal of Experimental Psychology: Learning, Memory and Cognition, 13*, 87–108.

Nosofsky, R. M. (1992). Exemplar-based approach to relating categorization, identification, and recognition. In F. G. Ashby (Ed.), *Multidimensional models of perception and cognition* (pp. 363–394). Hillsdale, NJ: Lawrence Erlbaum and Associates.

Nosofsky, R. M., and Kantner, J. (2006). Exemplar similarity, study list homogeneity, and short-term perceptual recognition. *Memory and Cognition, 34(1)*, 112–124.

Nosofsky, R. M., Little, D. R., Donkin, C., and Fific, M. (2011). Short-term memory scanning viewed as exemplar-based categorization. *Psychological Review, 118*(2), 280–315.

Nosofsky, R. M., and Palmeri, T. J. (1997). An exemplar-based random walk model of speeded classification. *Psychological Review, 104,* 266–300.

Nosofsky, R. M., and Palmeri, T. J. (1998). A rule-plus-exception model for classifying objects in continuous-dimension spaces. *Psychonomic Bulletin & Review, 5*(3), 345–369.

Novinski, L. (1969). Part-whole and whole-part free recall learning. *Journal of Verbal Learning and Verbal Behavior, 8*(1), 152–154.

Oberly, S. H. (1927). A comparison of the spans of "attention" and memory. *American Journal of Psychology,* 295–302.

Ohrt, D. D., and Gronlund, S. D. (1999). List-length effects and continuous memory: Confounds and solutions. In C. Izawa (Ed.), *On human memory: Evolution, progress, and reflections on the 30th anniversary of the Atkinson-Shiffrin model* (pp. 105–125). Mahwah, NJ.: Lawrence Erlbaum and Associates.

O'Keefe, J., and Dostrovsky, J. (1971). The hippocampus as a spatial map. Preliminary evidence from unit activity in the freely-moving rat. *Brain Research, 34,* 171–175.

Onyper, S. V., Zhang, Y., and Howard, M. W. (2010). Some-or-none recollection: Evidence from item and source memory. *Journal of Experimental Psychology: General, 139*(2), 341–364.

Page, M. P. A., and Norris, D. (1998). The primacy model: A new model of immediate serial recall. *Psychological Review, 105,* 761–781.

Paivio, A. (1986). *Mental representations: A dual coding approach.* Oxford University Press.

Parkinson, S. R. (1978). An alternative interpretation of the stimulus effect. *Journal of Experimental Psychology: Human Learning and Memory, 4*(4), 362–369.

Parks, C. M., and Yonelinas, A. P. (2007). Moving beyond pure signal-detection models: comment on Wixted (2007). *Psychological Review, 114*(1), 188–202.

Patterson, K. E., Meltzer, R. H., and Mandler, G. (1971). Inter-response times in categorized free recall. *Journal of Verbal Learning and Verbal Behavior, 10,* 417–426.

Pavlov, I. (1927). *Conditioned reflexes.* New York: Oxford University Press.

Penney, C. G. (1975). Modality effects in short-term verbal memory. *Psychological Bulletin, 82*(1), 68–84.

Penney, C. G. (1989). Modality effects and the structure of short-term verbal memory. *Memory & Cognition, 17*(4), 398–422.

Peterson, L. R., Hillner, K., and Saltzman, D. (1962). Supplementary report: Time between pairings and short-term retention. *Journal of Experimental Psychology, 64*(5), 550–551.

Peterson, L. R., and Peterson, M. J. (1959). Short-term retention of individual verbal items. *Journal of Experimental Psychology, 58,* 193–198.

Philiastides, M. G., Ratcliff, R., and Sajda, P. (2006). Neural representation of task difficulty and decision making during perceptual categorization: A timing diagram. *Journal of Neuroscience, 26,* 8965–8975.

Phillips, J. L., Shiffrin, R. J., and Atkinson, R. C. (1967). The effects of list length on short-term memory. *Journal of Verbal Learning and Verbal Behavior, 6*, 303–311.

Plaut, D. C. (1995). Semantic and associative priming in a distributed attractor network. In *Proceedings of the Seventeenth Annual Conference of the Cognitive Science Society, Pittsburgh, PA*. London: Psychology Press.

Pollio, H. R., Richards, S., and Lucas, R. (1969). Temporal properties of category recall. *Journal of Verbal Learning and Verbal Behavior, 8*, 529–536.

Polyn, S. M., Burke, J. F., and Kahana, M. J. (submitted). Oscillating distraction intervals in free recall: A test of contextual retrieval theory.

Polyn, S. M., and Kahana, M. J. (2008). Memory search and the neural representation of context. *Trends in Cognitive Sciences, 12*, 24–30.

Polyn, S. M., and Kahana, M. J. (submitted). Temporal isolation of studied items impairs memorability in free recall.

Polyn, S. M., Natu, V. S., Cohen, J. D., and Norman, K. A. (2005). Category-specific cortical activity precedes retrieval during memory search. *Science, 310*, 1963–1966.

Polyn, S. M., Norman, K. A., and Kahana, M. J. (2009). A context maintenance and retrieval model of organizational processes in free recall. *Psychological Review, 116*(1), 129–156.

Posnansky, C. J. (1972). Probing for the functional stimuli in serial learning. *Journal of Experimental Psychology, 96*, 184–193.

Postman, L. (1961). The present status of interference theory. In C. N. Cofer (Ed.), *Verbal learning and verbal behavior.* (pp. 109–118). New York: McGraw-Hill.

Postman, L. (1962). Repetition and paired-associate learning. *American Journal of Psychology, 75*(3), 372–389.

Postman, L. (1969). *Experimental analysis of learning to learn.* Oxford, England: Academic Press.

Postman, L., and Gray, W. (1977). Maintenance of prior associations and proactive inhibiting. *Journal of Experimental Psychology: Human Learning and Memory, 3*, 255–263.

Postman, L., and Keppel, G. (1977). Conditions of cumulative proactive-inhibition. *Journal of Experimental Psychology: General, 106*(4), 376–403.

Postman, L., and Phillips, L. W. (1965). Short-term temporal changes in free recall. *Quarterly Journal of Experimental Psychology, 17*, 132–138.

Postman, L., Stark, K., and Fraser, J. (1968). Temporal changes in interference. *Journal of Verbal Learning & Verbal Behavior, 7*(3), 672–694.

Postman, L., and Underwood, B. J. (1973). Critical issues in interference theory. *Memory & Cognition, 1*, 19–40.

Pratte, M. S., Rouder, J. N., and Morey, R. D. (2010). Separating mnemonic process from participant and item effects in the assessment of roc asymmetries. *Journal Experimental Psychology: Learning, Memory and Cognition, 36*(1), 224–232.

Primoff, E. (1938). Backward and forward associations as an organizing act in serial and in paired-associate learning. *Journal of Psychology, 5*, 375–395.

Proctor, R. W. (1981). A unified theory for matching-task phenomena. *Psychological Review, 88*(4), 291–326.

Raaijmakers, J. G. W. (2003). Spacing and repetition effects in human memory: application of the sam model. *Cognitive Science, 27*(3), 431–452.

Raaijmakers, J. G. W., and Shiffrin, R. M. (1980). SAM: A theory of probabilistic search of associative memory. In G. H. Bower (Ed.), *The psychology of learning and motivation: Advances in research and theory* (Vol. 14, pp. 207–262). New York: Academic Press.

Raaijmakers, J. G. W., and Shiffrin, R. M. (1981). Search of associative memory. *Psychological Review, 88,* 93–134.

Ranschburg, P. (1902). Uber hemmung gleichzeitiger reizwirkungen. *Zeitschrift für Psychologie und Physiologie der Sinnesorgane, 30,* 39–86.

Rao, K. V., and Proctor, R. W. (1984). Study-phase processing and the word frequency effect in recognition memory. *Journal of Experimental Psychology: Learning, Memory, and Cognition, 10,* 386–394.

Rao, V. A., and Howard, M. W. (2008). Advances in neural information processing systems. In J. C. Platt, D. Koller, Y. Singer, and S. Roweis (Eds.), (chap. Retrieved context and the discovery of semantic structure). MIT Press: Cambridge, MA.

Ratcliff, R. (1978). A theory of memory retrieval. *Psychological Review, 85,* 59–108.

Ratcliff, R. (2006). Modeling response signal and response time data. *Cognitive Psychology, 53(3),* 195–237.

Ratcliff, R., Clark, S. E., and Shiffrin, R. M. (1990). List-strength effect: I. Data and discussion. *Journal of Experimental Psychology: Learning, Memory, and Cognition, 16,* 163–178.

Ratcliff, R., Gomez, P., and McKoon, G. (2004). A diffusion model account of the lexical decision task. *Psychological Review, 111,* 159–182.

Ratcliff, R., McKoon, G., and Tindall, M. (1994). Empirical generality of data from recognition memory ROC functions and implications for GMMs. *Journal of Experimental Psychology: Learning, Memory, and Cognition, 20,* 763–785.

Ratcliff, R., Van Zandt, T., and McKoon, G. (1999). Connectionist and diffusion models of reaction time. *Psychological Review, 106(2),* 261–300.

Rawson, K. A., and Kintsch, W. (2005). Rereading effects depend on time of test. *Journal of Educational Psychology, 97(1),* 70–80.

Raymond, B. J. (1969). Short-term storage and long-term storage in free recall. *Journal of Verbal Learning and Verbal Behavior, 8,* 567–574.

Rescorla, R. A. (2004). Spontaneous recovery. *Learning and Memory, 11(5),* 501–509.

Restle, F. (1965). Significance of all-or-none learning. *Psychological Bulletin, 64,* 313–325.

Reynolds, G. D., and Richards, J. E. (2005). Familiarization, attention, and recognition memory in infancy; an event-related potential and cortical source localization study. *Developmental Psychology, 41(4),* 598–615.

Rickard, T. C., Cai, D. J., Rieth, C. A., and Jones, J. (2008). Sleep does not enhance motor sequence learning. *Journal Experimental Psychology: Learning, Memory and Cogntion, 34(4),* 834–842.

Riedel, U., Kühn, R., and van Hemmen, J. L. (1988). Temporal sequences and chaos in neural nets. *Physical Review A, 38,* 1105–1108.

Rizzuto, D. S., and Kahana, M. J. (2001). An autoassociative neural network model of paired-associate learning. *Neural Computation, 13,* 2075–2092.

Roberts, W. A. (1972). Free recall of word lists varying in length and rate of presentation: A test of total-time hypotheses. *Journal of Experimental Psychology, 92,* 365–372.

Robinson, E. S. (1932). *Association theory to-day; an essay in systematic psychology.* New York: The Century Co.

Rock, I. (1957). The role of repetition in associative learning. *American Journal of Psychology, 70,* 186–193.

Rock, I., and Ceraso, J. (1964). Toward a cognitive theory of associative learning. In C. Scheerer (Ed.), *Cognition: Theory, research and promise* (pp. 110–146). New York: Harper and Row.

Rock, I., and Heimer, W. (1959). Further evidence of one-trial associative learning. *American Journal of Psychology, 72,* 1–16.

Rock, I., and Steinfeld, G. (1963). Methodological questions in the study of one-trial learning. *Science, 140(Whole No. 3568),* 822–824.

Roediger, H. L., Balota, D. A., and Watson, J. M. (2001). Spreading activation and arousal of false memories. In H. L. Roediger, J. S. Nairne, I. Neath, and A. M. Surprenant (Eds.), *The nature of remembering: Essays in honor of Robert G. Crowder* (pp. 95–115). Washington, DC: American Psychological Association.

Roediger, H. L., and Karpicke, J. D. (2006). The power of testing memory: Basic research and implications for educational practice. *Perspectives on Psychological Science, 1(3),* 181–210.

Roediger, H. L., and McDermott, K. B. (1995). Creating false memories: Remembering words not presented in lists. *Journal of Experimental Psychology: Learning, Memory and Cognition, 21,* 803–814.

Roediger, H. L., and Payne, D. G. (1985). Recall criterion does not affect recall level or hypermnesia: A puzzle for generate/recognize theories. *Memory & Cognition, 13(1),* 1–7.

Romney, A. K., Brewer, D. D., and Batchelder, W. H. (1993). Predicting clustering from semantic structure. *Psychological Science, 4,* 28–34.

Rotello, C. M., Macmillan, N. A., and Reeder, J. A. (2004). Sum-difference theory of remembering and knowing: A two-dimensional signal-detection model. *Psychological Review, 111,* 588–616.

Rubin, D. C., Hinton, S., and Wenzel, A. (1999). The precise time course of retention. *Journal of Experimental Pyschology: Learning, Memory, and Cognition, 25(5),* 1161–1176.

Rugg, M. D., and Curran, T. (2007). Event-related potentials and recognition memory. *Trends in Cognitive Science, 11(6),* 251–257.

Rundus, D. (1971). An analysis of rehearsal processes in free recall. *Journal of Experimental Psychology, 89,* 63–77.

Rundus, D. (1980). Maintenance rehearsal and long-term recency. *Memory & Cognition, 8(3),* 226–230.

Ryan, J. (1969). Grouping and short-term memory: Different means and patterns of grouping. *Quarterly Journal of Experimental Psychology, 21,* 137–147.

Sahakyan, L., and Kelley, C. M. (2002). A contextual change account of the directed forgetting effect. *Journal of Experimental Psychology: Learning, Memory, and Cognition, 28(6),* 1064–1072.

Sakai, K., and Miyashita, Y. (1991). Neural organization for the long-term memory of paired associates. *Nature, 354,* 152–155.

Salthouse, T. A. (1991). *Theoretical perspectives on cognitive aging.* Hillsdale, NJ: Lawrence Erlbaum and Associates.

Schacter, D. (2001). *Forgotten ideas, neglected pioneers: Richard Semon and the story of memory.* New York: US: Psychology Press.

Scharroo, J., Leeuwenberg, E., Stalmeier, P. F. M., and Vos, P. G. (1994). Alphabetic search: Comment on Klahr, Chase, and Lovelace (1983). *Journal of Experimental Psychology: Learning, Memory, and Cognition, 20,* 234–244.

Schoutten, J. F., and Bekker, J. A. M. (1967). Reaction time and accuracy. *Acta Psychologica, 27,* 143–153.

Schwartz, G., Howard, M. W., Jing, B., and Kahana, M. J. (2005). Shadows of the past: Temporal retrieval effects in recognition memory. *Psychological Science, 16,* 898–904.

Schwartz, G. W., Howard, M. W., and Kahana, M. J. (2004). *Evidence for associative retrieval in item recognition.* (Unpublished undergraduate honors thesis. Brandeis University, Waltham, MA.)

Schwartz, R. M., and Humphreys, M. S. (1973). Similarity judgements and free recall of unrelated words. *Journal of Experimental Psychology, 101,* 10–13.

Schwartz, R. M., and Humphreys, M. S. (1974). Recognition and recall as a function of instructional manipulations of organization. *Journal of Experimental Psychology, 102,* 517–519.

Sederberg, P. B., Gauthier, L. V., Terushkin, V., Miller, J. F., Barnathan, J. A., and Kahana, M. J. (2006). Oscillatory correlates of the primacy effect in episodic memory. *NeuroImage, 32*(3), 1422–1431.

Sederberg, P. B., Howard, M. W., and Kahana, M. J. (2008). A context-based theory of recency and contiguity in free recall. *Psychological Review, 115,* 893–912.

Sederberg, P. B., Miller, J. F., Howard, W. H., and Kahana, M. J. (2010). The temporal contiguity effect predicts episodic memory performance. *Memory & Cognition, 38*(6), 689–699.

Sederberg, P. B., Schulze-Bonhage, A., Madsen, J. R., Bromfield, E. B., Litt, B., Brandt, A., et al. (2007). Gamma oscillations distinguish true from false memories. *Psychological Science, 18*(11), 927–932.

Semon, R. W. (1923). *Mnemic psychology (B. Duffy, trans.).* London: George Allen & Unwin (Original work published 1909).

Serra, M., and Nairne, J. S. (2000). Part-set cuing of order information: Implications for associative theories of serial order memory. *Memory & Cognition, 28*(5), 847–855.

Serruya, M. D., Sederberg, P. B., and Kahana, M. J. (in press). Power shifts track serial position and modulate encoding in human episodic memory. *Cerebral Cortex.*

Shiffrin, R. M., and Raaijmakers, J. G. W. (1992). The SAM retrieval model: A retrospective and prospective. In A. F. Healy, S. M. Kosslyn, and R. M. Shiffrin (Eds.), *From learning processes to cognitive processes: Essays in honor of William K. Estes* (Vol. 1, pp. 69–86). Potomac, MD: Lawrence Erlbaum and Associates.

Shiffrin, R. M., Ratcliff, R., and Clark, S. E. (1990). List-strength effect: II. theoretical mechanisms. *Journal of Experimental Psychology: Learning, Memory, & Cognition, 16*(2), 179–195.

Shiffrin, R. M., Ratcliff, R., Murnane, K., and Nobel, P. A. (1993). TODAM and the list-strength and list-length effects: A reply to Murdock and Kahana. *Journal of Experimental Psychology: Learning, Memory, and Cognition, 19*, 1445–1449.

Shiffrin, R. M., and Steyvers, M. (1997). A model for recognition memory: REM—retrieving effectively from memory. *Psychonomic Bulletin and Review, 4*, 145.

Shulman, H. G. (1971). Similarity effects in short-term memory. *Psychological Bulletin, 75*(6), 399–415.

Siegel, J. M. (2001). The rem sleep-memory consolidation hypothesis. *Science, 294*(5544), 1058–1063.

Singh, S. N., Mishra, S., Bendapudi, N., and Linville, D. (1994). Enhancing memory of television commercials through message spacing. *Journal of Marketing Research, 31*, 384–392.

Sirotin, Y. B., Kimball, D. R., and Kahana, M. J. (2005). Going beyond a single list: Modeling the effects of prior experience on episodic free recall. *Psychonomic Bulletin & Review, 12*(5), 787–805.

Slamecka, N. J. (1968). An examination of trace storage in free recall. *Journal of Experimental Psychology, 76*(4), 504–513.

Slamecka, N. J. (1987). The law of frequency. In D. S. Gorfein and R. R. Hoffman (Eds.), *Memory and learning: The Ebbinghaus centennial conference* (pp. 105–128). Hillsdale, N J: Lawrence Erlbaum and Associates.

Slamecka, N. J., Moore, T., and Carey, S. (1972). Part-to-whole transfer and its relation to organization theory. *Journal of Verbal Learning and Verbal Behavior, 11*, 73–82.

Smith, J. D. (2002). Exemplar theory's predicted typicality gradient can be tested and disconfirmed. *Psychological Science, 13*(5), 437–442.

Smith, P. L., and Ratcliff, R. (2004). Psychology and neurobiology of simple decisions. *Trends in Neurosciences, 27*(3), 161–168.

Smith, S. M. (1988). Environmental context-dependent memory. In G. M. Davies and D. M. Thomson (Eds.), *Memory in context: Context in memory.* (pp. 13–34). Oxford, England: John Wiley & Sons.

Smith, S. M., and Vela, E. (2001). Environmental context-dependent memory: a review and meta-analysis. *Psychonomic Bulletin and Review, 8*(2), 203–220.

Solway, A. Murdock, B. B., and Kahana, M. J. (2012). Positional and temporal clustering in serial order memory. *Memory & Cognition, 40*(2), 177–190.

Sommer, T., Rose, M., and Büchel, C. (2007). Associative symmetry versus independent associations in the memory for object-location associations. *Journal of Experimental Psychology: Learning, Memory, and Cognition, 33*(1), 90–106.

Sompolinsky, H., and Kanter, I. (1986). Temporal association in asymmetric neural networks. *Physical Review Letters, 57*, 2861–2864.

Sperling, G. (1960). The information available in brief visual presentation. *Pyschological Monographs, 74*(11), 22.

Spiers, H. J., Maguire, E. A., and Burgess, N. (2001). Hippocampal amnesia. *Neurocase, 7*, 357–382.

Squire, L. R., Clark, R. E., and Bayley, P. J. (2004). *The cognitive neurosciences* (M. S. Gazzaniga, Ed.). Cambridge, MA: MIT Press.

Squire, L. R., Wixted, J. T., and Clark, R. E. (2007). Recognition memory and the medial temporal lobe: A new perspective. *Nature Reviews Neuroscience, 8*(11), 872–883.

Sternberg, R. J., and Tulving, E. (1977). The measurement of subjective organization in free recall. *Psychological Bulletin, 84*(3), 539–556.

Sternberg, S. (1966). High-speed scanning in human memory. *Science, 153,* 652–654.

Sternberg, S. (1967). Retrieval of contextual information from memory. *Psychological Science, 8,* 55–56.

Sternberg, S. (1969). Memory-scanning: Mental processes revealed by reaction-time experiments. *American Scientist, 57,* 421–457.

Sternberg, S. (1975). Memory scanning: New findings and current controversies. *Quarterly Journal of Experimental Psychology, 27,* 1–32.

Sternberg, S. (2001). Separate modifiability, mental modules, and the use of pure and composite measures to reveal them. *Acta Psychologica, 106*(1–2), 147–246.

Steyvers, M., and Malmberg, K. J. (2003). The effect of normative context variability on recognition memory. *Journal of Experimental Psychology: Learning, Memory, and Cognition, 29*(5), 760–766.

Steyvers, M., Shiffrin, R. M., and Nelson, D. L.(2004). Word association spaces for predicting semantic similarity effects in episodic memory. In A. F. Healy (Ed.), *Cognitive psychology and its applications: Festschrift in honor of Lyle Bourne, Walter Kintsch, and Thomas Landauer.* Washington, DC: American Psychological Association.

Strand, B. Z. (1970). Change of context and retroactive inhibition. *Journal of Verbal Learning & Verbal Behavior, 9*(2), 202–206.

Stretch, V., and Wixted, J. T. (1998). Decision rules for recognition memory confidence jugments. *Journal of Experimental Psychology: Learning. Memory, and Cognition, 24(6),* 1397–1410.

Strong, E. K., Jr. (1912). The effect of length of series upon recognition memory. *Psychological Review, 19,* 447–462.

Sumby, W. H. (1963). Word frequency and serial position effects. *Journal of Verbal Learning and Verbal Behavior, 1,* 443–450.

Suzuki, W. A. (2007). Making new memories: the role of the hippocampus in new associative learning. *Annals of the New York Academy of Science, 1097,* 1–11.

Swets, J. A. (1998). Separating discrimination and decision in detection, recognition and matters of life and death. In D. Osherson, D. Scarborough, and S. Sternberg (Eds.), *An invitation to cognitive science* (Vol. 4: Methods, Models, and Conceptual Issues, pp. 635–702). Cambridge, MA: MIT Press.

Tan, L., and Ward, G. (2000). A recency-based account of the primacy effect in free recall. *Journal of Experimental Psychology: Learning, Memory, and Cognition, 26,* 1589–1626.

Terrace, H. S. (2010). The comparative psychology of serially organized behavior. In S. Fountain, J. H. Danks, and M. K. McBath (Eds.), *Biomedical implications of model systems of complex cognitive capacities.* New York: Sage.

Thapar, A., and Greene, R. L. (1993). Evidence against a short-term store account of long-term recency effects. *Memory & Cognition, 21,* 329–337.

Thorndike, E. L. (1932). *The fundamentals of learning.* New York: Bureau of Publications, Teachers College.

Thune, L. E. (1951). Warm-up effect as a function of level of practice in verbal learning. *Journal of Experimental Psychology, 42*(4), 250–256.

Titchener, E. B. (1916). *A beginner's psychology.* Macmillan and Co.

Townsend, J. T. (1976). A stochastic theory of matching processes. *Journal of Mathematical Psychology, 14*, 1–52.

Townsend, J. T. (1984). Uncovering mental processes with factorial experiments. *Journal of Mathematical Psychology, 28*(4), 363–400.

Townsend, J. T., and Fific, M. (2004). Parallel versus serial processing and individual differences in high-speed search in human memory. *Perception and Pychophysics, 66*(6), 953–962.

Tulving, E. (1962). Subjective organization in free recall of "unrelated" words. *Psychological Review, 69*(4), 344–354.

Tulving, E. (1966). Subjective organization and effects of repetition in multi-trial free-recall learning. *Journal of Verbal Learning and Verbal Behavior, 5* (2), 193–197.

Tulving, E. (1968). Theoretical issues in free recall. In T. R. Dixon and D. L. Horton (Eds.), *Verbal behavior and general behavior theory* (pp. 2–36). Englewood Cliffs, NJ: Prentice-Hall.

Tulving, E. (1972). Episodic and semantic memory. In E. Tulving and W. Donaldson (Eds.), *Organization of memory* (pp. 381–403). New York: Adademic Press.

Tulving, E. (1974). Cue-dependent forgetting. *American Scientist, 62*(1), 74–82.

Tulving, E. (1985). Memory and consciousness. *Canadian Psychology, 26*, 1–12.

Tulving, E., and Arbuckle, T. Y. (1963). Sources of intratrial interference in immediate recall of paired associates. *Journal of Verbal Learning and Verbal Behavior, 1*, 321–334.

Tulving, E., and Hastie, R. (1972). Inhibition effects of intralist repetition in free recall. *Journal of Experimental Psychology, 92*, 297–304.

Tulving, E., and Madigan, S. A. (1970). Memory and verbal learning. *Annual Review of Psychology, 21*, 437–484.

Tulving, E., and Osler, S. (1968). Effectiveness of retrieval cues in memory for words. *Journal of Experimental Psychology, 77*(4), 593–601.

Tulving, E., and Psotka, J. (1971). Retroactive inhibition in free recall: Inaccessibility of information available in the memory store. *Journal of Experimental Psychology, 87*, 1–8.

Tulving, E., and Thompson, D. M. (1973). Encoding specificity and retrieval processes in episodic memory. *Psychological Review, 80*, 352–373.

Tulving, E., and Watkins, M. J. (1974). On negative transfer: Effects of testing one list on the recall of another. *Journal of Verbal Learning and Verbal Behavior, 13*, 181–193.

Tulving, E., and Wiseman, S. (1975). Relation between recognition and recognition failure of recallable words. *Bulletin of the Psychonomic Society, 6*, 79–82.

Tzeng, O. J. L. (1973). Positive recency in delayed free recall. *Journal of Verbal Learning and Verbal Behavior, 12*, 436–439.

Underwood, B. J. (1945). The effect of successive interpolations and proactive inhibition. *Psychological Monographs, 59*, v + 33.

Underwood, B. J. (1948). 'Spontaneous recovery' of verbal associations. *Journal of Experimental Psychology, 38*, 429–439.

Underwood, B. J. (1957). Interference and forgetting. *Psychological Review, 64*, 49–60.

Underwood, B. J. (1969). Some correlates of item repetition in free-recall learning. *Journal of Verbal Learning and Verbal Behavior, 8*, 83–94.

Underwood, B. J. (1970). A breakdown of the total-time law in free-recall learning. *Journal of Verbal Learning and Verbal Behavior, 9*(5), 573–580.

Underwood, B. J. (1972). Are we overloading memory? In W. Melton and E. Martin (Eds.), *Coding processes in human memory.* Washington, DC: Winston.

Underwood, B. J. (1983). *Attributes of memory.* Glenview, IL: Scott, Foresman.

Underwood, B. J., Rehula, R., and Keppel, G. (1962). Item-selection in paired-associate learning. *American Journal of Psychology, 75*(3), 353–371.

Unsworth, N., Heitz, R., and Parks, N. (2008). The importance of temporal distinctiveness for forgetting over the short term. *Psychological Science, 19*(11), 1078.

Usher, M., Davelaar, E. J., Haarmann, H. J., and Goshen-Gottstein, Y. (2008). Short-term memory after all: Comment on Sederberg, Howard and Kahana (2008). *Psychological Review, 115*, 1108–1118.

Vargha-Khadem, F., Gadian, D. G., Watkins, K. E., Connely, A., Van Paesschen, W., and Mishkin, M. (1997). Differential effects of early hippocampal pathology on episodic and semantic memory. *Science, 277*, 376–380.

Verde, M. F., and Rotello, C. M. (2004). Strong memories obscure weak memories in associative recognition. *Psychonomic Bulletin & Review, 11*, 1062–1066.

Walker, I., and Hulme, C. (1999). Concrete words are easier to recall than abstract words: Evidence for a semantic contribution to short term serial recall. *Journal of Experimental Psychology: Learning, Memory, and Cognition, 25*(5), 1256–1271.

Walker, M. P., and Stickgold, R. (2006). Sleep, memory, and plasticity. *Annual Review of Psychology, 57*, 139–166.

Wallace, W. H., Turner, S. H., and Perkins, C. (1957). *Preliminary studies of human information storage.* Philadelphia, PA: Institute for Cooperative Research, University of Pennsylvania.

Ward, G. (2002). A recency-based account of the list length effect in free recall. *Memory & Cognition, 30*, 885–892.

Ward, G., Tan, L., and Grenfell-Essam, R. (2010). Examining the relationship between free recall and immediate serial recall: the effects of list length and output order. *Journal of Experimental Psychology: Learning, Memory, and Cognition, 36*(5), 1207–1241.

Watkins, M. J., LeCompte, D. C., and Kim, K. (2000). Role of study strategy in recall of mixed lists of common and rare words. *Journal of Experimental Psychology: Learning, Memory, and Cognition, 26*, 239–245.

Watkins, M. J., Neath, I., and Sechler, E. S. (1989). Recency effect in recall of a word list when an immediate memory task is performed after each word presentation. *American Journal of Psychology, 102*, 265–270.

Watkins, M. J., and Todres, A. K. (1980). Suffix effects manifest and concealed: Further evidence for a 20-second echo. *Journal of Verbal Learning and Verbal Behavior, 19*, 46–53.

Watkins, M. J., Watkins, O. C., and Crowder, R. G. (1974). The modality effect in free and serial recall as a function of phonological similarity. *Journal of Verbal Learning and Verbal Behavior, 13*, 430–447.

Watkins, O. C., and Watkins, M. J. (1980). The modality effect and echoic persistence. *Journal of Experimental Psychology: General, 109,* 251–278.

Waugh, N. C. (1961). Free versus serial recall. *Journal of Experimental Psychology, 62,* 496–502.

Waugh, N. C. (1963). Immediate memory as a function of repetition. *Journal of Verbal Learning and Verbal Behavior, 2,* 107–112.

Waugh, N. C. (1970). Associative symmetry and recall latencies: A distinction between learning and performance. *Acta Psychologica, 33,* 326–337.

Webb, L. W. (1917). Transfer of training and retroaction: A comparative study. *Psychological Monographs, 24(3),* 1–90.

Wernicke, C. (1900). *Grundriss der psychiatrie.* Leipzig: G. Thieme.

Wheeler, M. A. (1995). Improvement in recall over time without repeated testing: Spontaneous recovery revisited. *Journal of Experimental Psychology: Learning, Memory, and Cognition, 21(1),* 173–184.

Whitely, P. L. (1927). The dependence of learning and recall upon prior intellectual activities. *Journal of Experimental Psychology, 10,* 489–508.

Wickelgren, W. A. (1966). Associative intrusions in short-term recall. *Journal of Experimental Psychology, 72,* 853–858.

Wickelgren, W. A. (1967). Rehearsal grouping and hierarchical organization of serial position cues in short-term memory. *Quarterly Journal of Experimental Psychology, 19,* 97–102.

Wickelgren, W. A., and Norman, D. A. (1966). Strength models and serial position in short-term recognition memory. *Journal of Mathematical Psychobiology, 3,* 316–347.

Wickens, T. D. (2002). *Elementary signal detection theory.* Oxford: Oxford University Press.

Williams, J. P. (1961). Supplementary report: A selection artifact in Rock's study of the role of repepitition. *Journal of Experimental Psychology, 62(6),* 627–628.

Winnick, W. A., and Dornbush, R. L. (1963). Role of positional cues in serial rote learning. *Journal of Experimental Psychology, 66(4),* 419–421.

Wixted, J. T. (2007a). Dual-process theory and signal-detection theory of recognition memory. *Psychological Review, 114(1),* 152–176.

Wixted, J. T. (2007b). Spotlighting the probative findings: Reply to Parks and Yonelinas. *Psychology Review, 114,* 203–209.

Wixted, J. T., and Stretch, V. (2004). In defense of the signal detection interpretation of remember/know judgments. *Psychonomic Bulletin & Review, 11(4),* 616–641.

Wolford, G. (1971). Function of distinct associations for paired-associate performance. *Psychological Review, 78,* 303–313.

Woodward, A., and Murdock, B. B. (1968). Positional and sequential probes in serial learning. *Canadian Journal of Psychology, 22,* 131–138.

Woodworth, R. S. (1938). *Experimental psychology.* New York: H. Holt and Company.

Wright, A. A., Santiago, H. C., Sands, S. F., Kendrick, D. F., and Cook, R. G. (1985). Memory processing of serial lists by pigeons, monkeys, and people. *Science, 229(4710),* 287–289.

Yates, F. A. (1966). *The art of memory.* London, England: Routledge and Kegan Paul.

Yntema, D. B., and Trask, F. P. (1963). Recall as a search process. *Journal of Verbal Learning and Verbal Behavior, 2,* 65–74.

Yonelinas, A. P. (1994). Receiver-operating characteristics in recognition memory: evidence for a dual-process model. *Journal of Experimental Psychology: Learning, Memory, and Cognition, 20*(6), 1341–54.

Yonelinas, A. P. (1997). Recognition memory ROCs for item and associative information: The contribution of recollection and familiarity. *Memory & Cognition, 25*, 747–763.

Yonelinas, A. P. (2001). Components of episodic memory: the contribution of recollection and familiarity. *Philosophical Transactions of the Royal Society, Series B, 356*(1413), 1363–1374.

Yonelinas, A. P. (2002). The nature of recollection and familiarity: A review of 30 years of research. *Journal of Memory and Language, 46*, 441–517.

Yonelinas, A. P., Kroll, N. E. A., Dobbins, I. G., Lazzara, M., and Knight, R. T. (1998). Recollection and familiarity deficits in amnesia: Convergence of remember-know, process dissociation, and receiver operating characteristic data. *Neuropsychology, 12*, 323–339.

Yonelinas, A. P., Otten, L. J., Shaw, K. N., and Rugg, M. D. (2005). Separating the brain regions involved in recollection and familiarity in recognition memory. *Journal of Neuroscience, 25*(11), 3002–3008.

Yonelinas, A. P., and Parks, C. M. (2007). Receiver operating characteristics (ROCs) in recognition memory: a review. *Psychological Bulletin, 133*(5), 800–832.

Yotsumoto, Y., Kahana, M. J., Wilson, H. R., and Sekuler, R. (2007). Recognition memory for realistic synthetic faces. *Memory & Cognition, 35*(6), 1233–1244.

Young, D. (1979). The effect of repetition on search through active memory. *Acta Psychologica, 43*, 491–506.

Young, R. K. (1962). Tests of three hypotheses about the effective stimulus in serial learning. *Journal of Experimental Psychology, 63*, 307–313.

Young, R. K. (1968). Serial learning. In T. R. Dixon and D. L. Horton (Eds.), *Verbal behavior and general behavior theory* (pp. 122–148). Englewood Cliffs, NJ: Prentice-Hall.

Zaromb, F. M., Howard, M. W., Dolan, E. D., Sirotin, Y. B., Tully, M., Wingfield, A., et al. (2006). Temporal associations and prior-list intrusions in free recall. *Journal of Experimental Psychology: Learning, Memory, and Cognition, 32*(4), 792–804.

Zhang, J., and Mueller, S. T. (2005). A note on ROC analysis and non-parametric estimate of sensitivity. *Psychometrika, 70*, 203–212.

AUTHOR INDEX